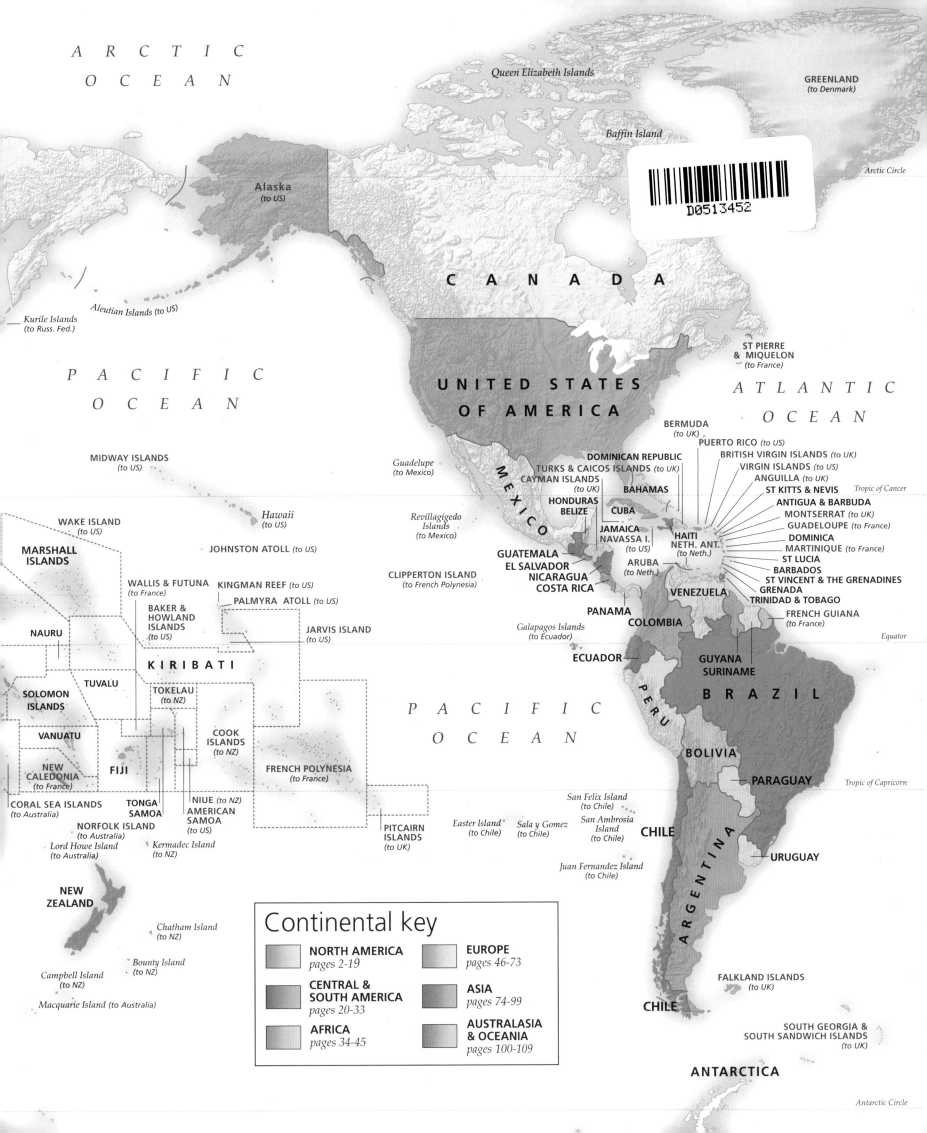

ARCTIC
OCEAN

Queen Elizabeth Islands

GREENLAND
(to Denmark)

Baffin Island

Arctic Circle

Alaska
(to US)

Kurile Islands
(to Russ. Fed.)

Aleutian Islands (to US)

PACIFIC
OCEAN

C A N A D A

ST PIERRE
& MIQUELON
(to France)

ATLANTIC
OCEAN

UNITED STATES
OF AMERICA

BERMUDA
(to UK)

PUERTO RICO (to US)
BRITISH VIRGIN ISLANDS (to UK)
VIRGIN ISLANDS (to US)
ANGUILLA (to UK)
ST KITTS & NEVIS
ANTIGUA & BARBUDA
MONTSERRAT (to UK)
GUADELOUPE (to France)
DOMINICA
MARTINIQUE (to France)
ST LUCIA
BARBADOS
ST VINCENT & THE GRENADINES
GRENADA
TRINIDAD & TOBAGO
FRENCH GUIANA
(to France)

MIDWAY ISLANDS
(to US)

Guadelupe
(to Mexico)

DOMINICAN REPUBLIC
TURKS & CAICOS ISLANDS (to UK)
CAYMAN ISLANDS
(to UK)   BAHAMAS
HONDURAS   CUBA
BELIZE
JAMAICA
NAVASSA I.
(to US)
HAITI
NETH. ANT.
(to Neth.)

Tropic of Cancer

Hawaii
(to US)

Revillagigedo
Islands
(to Mexico)

WAKE ISLAND
(to US)

JOHNSTON ATOLL (to US)

MARSHALL
ISLANDS

WALLIS & FUTUNA
(to France)

KINGMAN REEF (to US)

PALMYRA ATOLL (to US)

CLIPPERTON ISLAND
(to French Polynesia)

GUATEMALA
EL SALVADOR
NICARAGUA
COSTA RICA

ARUBA
(to Neth.)

VENEZUELA

NAURU

BAKER &
HOWLAND
ISLANDS
(to US)

JARVIS ISLAND
(to US)

PANAMA

COLOMBIA

Galapagos Islands
(to Ecuador)

GUYANA
SURINAME

Equator

K I R I B A T I

ECUADOR

B R A Z I L

TUVALU

TOKELAU
(to NZ)

PACIFIC

OCEAN

PERU

SOLOMON
ISLANDS

VANUATU

COOK
ISLANDS
(to NZ)

BOLIVIA

PARAGUAY

Tropic of Capricorn

NEW
CALEDONIA
(to France)

FIJI

FRENCH POLYNESIA
(to France)

San Felix Island
(to Chile)

CORAL SEA ISLANDS
(to Australia)

TONGA
SAMOA

NIUE (to NZ)
AMERICAN
SAMOA
(to US)

Easter Island
(to Chile)

Sala y Gomez
(to Chile)

San Ambrosia
Island
(to Chile)

CHILE

NORFOLK ISLAND
(to Australia)

Lord Howe Island
(to Australia)

Kermadec Island
(to NZ)

PITCAIRN
ISLANDS
(to UK)

Juan Fernandez Island
(to Chile)

URUGUAY

NEW
ZEALAND

Chatham Island
(to NZ)

Bounty Island
(to NZ)

Campbell Island
(to NZ)

Macquarie Island (to Australia)

Continental key

NORTH AMERICA
pages 2-19

EUROPE
pages 46-73

CENTRAL &
SOUTH AMERICA
pages 20-33

ASIA
pages 74-99

AFRICA
pages 34-45

AUSTRALASIA
& OCEANIA
pages 100-109

FALKLAND ISLANDS
(to UK)

SOUTH GEORGIA &
SOUTH SANDWICH ISLANDS
(to UK)

CHILE

ANTARCTICA

Antarctic Circle

CHILDREN'S WORLD ATLAS

Consultant
Dr David Green

Written by
Simon Adams • Mary Atkinson • Sarah Phillips

A Dorling Kindersley Book

Dorling Kindersley

LONDON, NEW YORK, MUNICH,
MELBOURNE, and DELHI

Project editors Lucy Hurst, Sadie Smith,
Shaila Awan, Amber Tokeley
Art editors Joe Conneally, Sheila Collins,
Rebecca Johns, Simon Oon, Andrew Nash
Senior editor Fran Jones
Senior art editor Floyd Sayers
Managing editor Andrew Macintyre
Managing art editor Jane Thomas
Picture research Carolyn Clerkin, Brenda Clynch
DK Pictures Sarah Mills
Production Jenny Jacoby
DTP designer Siu Yin Ho

Cartography Department
Senior Cartographic Editor Simon Mumford
Cartographer Ed Merritt
Digital Cartography Encompass Graphics Limited
Satellite images Rob Stokes
3D Globes Planetary Visions Ltd., London

This *Children's World Atlas* has been conceived by Dorling Kindersley Limited

First published in Great Britain in 2003 by
Dorling Kindersley Limited,
80 Strand, London WC2R 0RL

A Penguin Company

2 4 6 8 10 9 7 5 3

Copyright © 2003 Dorling Kindersley Limited

All rights reserved. No part of this publication may be
reproduced, stored in a retrieval system, or transmitted
in any form or by any means, electronic, mechanical,
photocopying, recording or otherwise, without the
prior written permission of the copyright owner.

A CIP catalogue record for this book is
available from the British Library.

ISBN 0 -7513-6817-2

Colour reproduction by Colourscan, Singapore
Printed and bound by L.E.G.O., Italy

See our complete catalogue at
www.dk.com

Contents

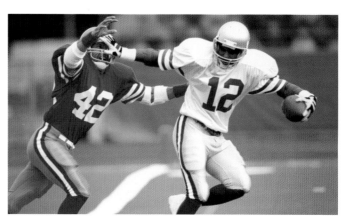

NORTH AMERICA 2

CENTRAL AND SOUTH AMERICA 20

Introducing Earth

TO US, THE EARTH SEEMS HUGE. Vast oceans stretch further than the eye can see and separate the giant landmasses that are home to billions of people, animals, and plants. However, Earth is just one of the nine planets that orbit the Sun – a huge, burning-hot star in the centre of our Solar System. The Solar System and all the stars in the night sky are part of our galaxy – the Milky Way, which contains as many as 200 billion stars. Beyond our galaxy are millions more galaxies. They all add together to make up the Universe.

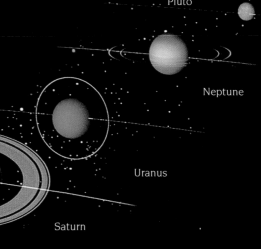

Pluto

Neptune

Uranus

Saturn

Jupiter

Earth

Mars

Venus

Moon

Mercury

Sun

THE SOLAR SYSTEM

Planet Earth is part of a system of planets and their moons, as well as numerous asteroids and comets, which orbit around a huge star we call the Sun. The Sun itself consists of gas. Nuclear reactions inside its core produce the heat and light that make life on Earth possible. The Earth is the third of four small terrestrial (Earth-like) planets that orbit close to the Sun. Further out in our Solar System are four huge gas planets, while distant Pluto, the smallest planet, is made of rock and ice.

A PLANET'S "year" is the time it takes to orbit the Sun. Earth's year is 365.25 days, but distant Pluto takes as long as 90,588 days to complete its orbit.

Crust

Mantle of silicate

Iron and nickel outer core

Inner core

THE EARTH

Earth's distance from the Sun allows just the right amount of heat and light to support life. It is warm enough for water to exist in liquid form – in fact, two-thirds of the Earth's surface is covered with water. As well as water, the planet consists of seven landmasses, or continents, which include Antarctica.

THE EARTH'S STRUCTURE

The Earth is not a solid ball. It is made up of different layers, much like an onion. The outer layer, or crust, is a thin sheet of rock that forms the continents and the ocean floor. Beneath it is the mantle, a layer of hot and, in places, molten (liquid) rock about 3,000 km (1,900 miles) thick. At the centre of the Earth is a core of hot metal, which is liquid on the outside and solid on the inside.

OUR MOON

Unlike some other planets in the Solar System, the Earth has only one moon. The Moon is our nearest neighbour in space and circles the Earth once every 29.53 days. It is about a quarter of the size of Earth and is made of rock. Despite having no light of its own, it is clearly visible from Earth because it reflects sunlight.

MOVING EARTH

The continents that make up the Earth's surface are always on the move. Eight large and several smaller plates, which form the landmasses of the Earth – called tectonic plates – float on top of the mantle. Because the Earth's interior is extremely hot, magma wells up to the cooler surface and forces these plates to move and crack. This happens very slowly, but when it does, it releases huge forces that can create new land, form mountains, and cause earthquakes.

THE HIMALAYAS are a range of mountains that contain the world's highest peak, Mount Everest.

MOUNTAIN BUILDING

Mountains form in three main ways. In the case of the Himalayas, Alps, and Rockies, two tectonic plates collided, causing the Earth's crust to buckle, crumple, and be forced upwards to create high mountains and deep valleys. But mountains can also be the result of volcanic eruption, or caused by the edges of two plates fracturing into cracks called faults, pushing a chunk of land upwards to create a block mountain.

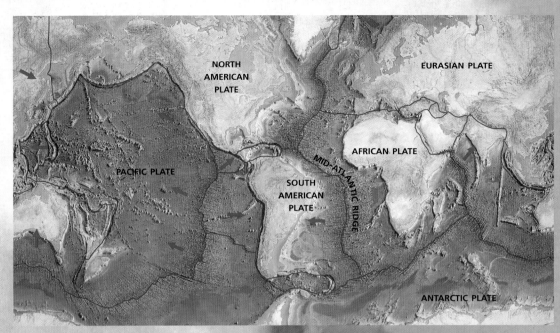

NORTH AMERICAN PLATE

EURASIAN PLATE

AFRICAN PLATE

PACIFIC PLATE

SOUTH AMERICAN PLATE

MID-ATLANTIC RIDGE

ANTARCTIC PLATE

VOLCANOES

When two continental plates collide, one of them can be subducted, or pushed down, under the other into the Earth's hot mantle. The rocks of the subsiding plate melt, and may be forced up through the cracks to erupt onto the Earth's surface as a volcano. In addition, volcanoes may form when plates pull apart. Molten rock from the Earth's mantle rises up to fill the gap as the plates spread. Volcanoes can be separated into three different categories: active (continuously erupting), dormant (sleeping), or extinct.

THE HAWAIIAN volcano Kilauea is constantly erupting. Its name means "spewing" in Hawaiian.

Moving plates

The Earth's continental plates move in three ways: pulling apart, moving together, or sliding past one another. Where two plates pull apart, magma (molten rock) from the Earth's mantle wells up and fills the gap. If this happens on the ocean floor, it creates an underwater spreading ridge. If two plates collide, either they fuse to form a mountain range or one subsides under the other, causing volcanoes to appear. Where two plates slide past each other, a transform fault appears, and earthquakes can occur. Often a long crack or fault line appears on the Earth's surface.

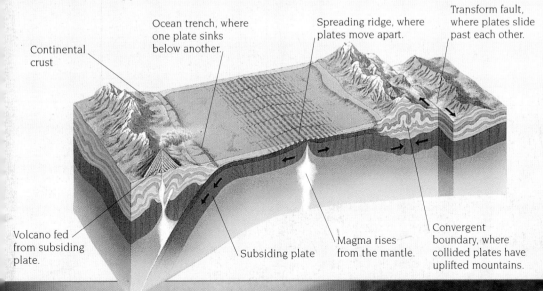

Continental crust

Ocean trench, where one plate sinks below another.

Spreading ridge, where plates move apart.

Transform fault, where plates slide past each other.

Volcano fed from subsiding plate.

Subsiding plate

Magma rises from the mantle.

Convergent boundary, where collided plates have uplifted mountains.

Climate and Vegetation

ON EARTH, A REGION'S WEATHER CAN CHANGE from day to day and even from hour to hour. But its climate – the average pattern of weather and temperature over a long period of time – remains fairly constant. Climate is affected by latitude (how far north or south of the Equator a region is), height above sea level, prevailing winds, and the circulation of ocean currents. An area's climate, as well as its landscape, affects the type of plant life, or vegetation, found there. Climate and vegetation also affect the lives of the animals, birds, and people that make the area their home.

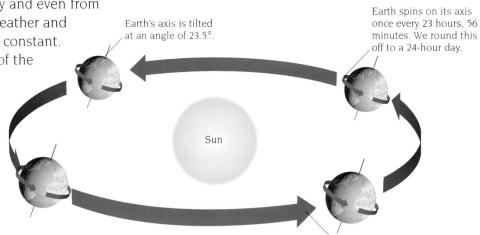

Earth's axis is tilted at an angle of 23.5°.

Earth spins on its axis once every 23 hours, 56 minutes. We round this off to a 24-hour day.

Sun

Earth circles, or orbits, the Sun once every 365.25 days, a length of time known as a year.

SPRING

SUMMER

AUTUMN

WINTER

THE FOUR SEASONS

As the Earth orbits the Sun, its tilted axis gradually leans each hemisphere towards the Sun and then away from it. This causes the seasons. For example, summer occurs when a hemisphere leans towards the Sun and gets more sunlight, more heat, and longer days. Most regions of the world have four seasons, but some areas near the Equator are always hot and have only wet and dry seasons.

EARTH'S ORBIT

The Earth does not sit upright on its axis but tilts at an angle of 23.5°. It maintains this same tilt as it travels around the Sun on its 950 million-km (590 million-mile) journey – a journey that lasts for one year. The Earth also spins on its axis, turning once every 24 hours to give us night and day.

ASIA

EUROPE

NORTH AMERICA

ATLANTIC

OCEAN

PACIFIC

OCEAN

TROPIC OF CANCER

AFRICA

EQUATOR PACIFIC

CENTRAL & SOUTH AMERICA

OCEAN

TROPIC OF CAPRICORN

INDIAN

OCEAN

AUSTRALASIA & OCEANIA

ANNUAL RAINFALL

■ More than 2,000 mm (79 in)

□ 500–2,000 mm (20–79 in)

□ Less than 500 mm (20 in)

RAINFALL

This map of the world shows the amount of rain that falls in a year. The light brown areas receive so little rain that they tend to be either hot desert or cold polar regions. They are difficult places in which to live, and have little vegetation. The blue areas receive a moderate amount of rainfall each year. The purple areas are mainly areas of rainforest, where high rainfall allows vegetation to flourish.

PEOPLE AND CLIMATE

Some climates are easier to live in than others, but people can still adapt to a variety of different environments. These Moroccan girls (left) live in the Sahara desert. They are members of a nomadic tribe that travel from place to place in search of food and water. Other tribes have made their homes in humid rainforests, and others inhabit the icy polar regions.

SATELLITE MAP of the world's average surface temperature in January.

WORLD TEMPERATURES

This map compares temperatures during January. The values range from –38°C (–36°F) in the purple regions, through blue, green, yellow, and red, to black, which is 40°C (104°F). As expected, temperatures are hotter near the Equator and cooler near the poles. Australia is tilted closer to the Sun during January, giving it a scorching summer.

VEGETATION ZONES

Several factors influence the vegetation (plant life) and animal life of a particular region – the climate, latitude, and physical landscape. After studying the different types of plant life, scientists have divided the Earth into nine main vegetation zones, or biomes. Over millions of years, plants and animals, as well as people, have adapted to life in these different zones, often developing special features that enable them to survive.

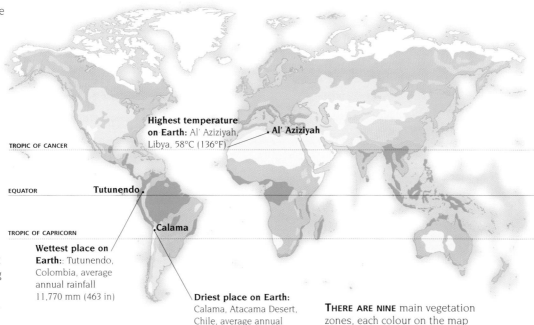

TROPIC OF CANCER

Highest temperature on Earth: Al' Aziziyah, Libya, 58°C (136°F)

• Al' Aziziyah

EQUATOR   Tutunendo .

TROPIC OF CAPRICORN

.Calama

Wettest place on Earth:: Tutunendo, Colombia, average annual rainfall 11,770 mm (463 in)

Driest place on Earth: Calama, Atacama Desert, Chile, average annual rainfall 0 mm (0 in)

THERE ARE NINE main vegetation zones, each colour on the map corresponds to the boxes below.

☐ POLAR AND TUNDRA

The freezing areas around the North and South Poles are covered with ice. South of the North Pole lies the tundra, where lower layers of soil stay frozen. Only hardy mosses, lichens, and shrubs can survive.

☐ TAIGA

The word taiga is Russian for "cold forest". It refers to the regions of northern Canada, Scandinavia, and Russia. These areas are home to forests of evergreens such as fir, spruce, and pine, all of which are able to withstand the cold, long, snow-filled winters.

☐ MOUNTAIN REGIONS

In mountain ranges, the higher the altitude, the colder it gets. Though vegetation can survive on the lower parts of the mountains, there is a point, called the tree line, above which it is too cold for trees to grow. Snow can be found on high peaks all year round.

☐ TEMPERATE FOREST

Temperate climates – not too hot or too cold – occur in northern Europe, eastern North America, and eastern Asia. These areas often contain forests of deciduous trees, which lose their leaves in winter. Though many have been cut down, large woodland areas still survive.

☐ MEDITERRANEAN

This vegetation zone refers not just to areas around the Mediterranean Sea in Europe, but also to places such as California, USA. With hot, dry summers and cool winters, vegetation such as olive and citrus trees are able to grow.

☐ DRY GRASSLAND

Hot, dry summers and very cold winters, as well as sparse rainfall, give rise to areas too dry for trees to grow. These vast, dry grasslands are often found in the centre of continents, such as the prairies of North America. They are sometimes ploughed and used to grow wheat or raise cattle.

☐ TROPICAL RAINFOREST

The regions of tropical rainforest lie either side of the Equator, where the climate is hot and wet all year round. Up to 50,000 different species of trees, as well as millions of species of plants, animals, birds, and insects – 50 per cent of all animal and plant life – flourish in these humid conditions.

☐ HOT DESERT

The hottest places on Earth are deserts, though at night temperatures may plummet to below freezing. These dry regions get no rain for years at a time, so very little vegetation is found here. Cacti, evolved to cope without water for long periods, are usually the only plants that can survive here.

☐ TROPICAL GRASSLAND

Between tropical rainforests and hot deserts lie tropical grasslands, such as the pampas of South America and the African savannah. Tall grasses, low trees, and shrubs grow in these hot climates, which have only two seasons: wet and dry.

Population

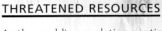

EVERY SECOND, AROUND THE WORLD, four people are born and two people die. This means that over a year, the world's population increases by about 70 million people. In some of the richest countries of the world, population growth is slow. Elsewhere – especially in the poorer countries of Asia, Africa, and South America – the population is growing rapidly. Cities in such regions are growing fastest, and several now have populations of over 10 million people. When it comes to providing employment, housing, education and health care, such rapid growth rates can strain resources to the limit.

IN BURKINO FASO, less than 30 per cent of the population has access to a clean water supply, such as the water pump shown here.

THREATENED RESOURCES

As the world's population continues to rise, more people are chasing fewer natural resources. Only a small proportion of the Earth's land is suitable for growing food, while in some areas fresh water for drinking, cooking, and irrigating crops is scarce. Fossil fuels, such as oil and natural gas, will soon be in short supply, unless people begin to conserve energy or develop alternatives, such as solar power.

LIFE EXPECTANCY

A person's life expectancy is a measure of how long they are likely to live. This can vary dramatically from country to country, and depends on many factors including health care, nutrition, and access to fresh water. At present, the world's average life expectancy is 63 years.

Moscow
8.6 million

London
7 million

EUROPE

ASIA

Paris
9.3 million

NORTH
AMERICA

Tehran
6.8 million

Lahore
5 million

Tianjin
8.8 million

New York
7.4 million

Beijing
10.9 million

Seoul
10.2 million

Istanbul
6.4 million

Dhaka
6.1 million

Tokyo
7.8 million

Cairo
6.8 million

Karachi
9.3 million

Shanghai
13.5 million

AFRICA

Delhi
8.4 million

Hong Kong
6.8 million

Mexico City
16.7 million

Bombay
(Mumbai)
12.6 million

Calcutta
11 million

Bangkok
5.6 million

Bogotá
6 million

Madras
(Chennai)
5.4 million

Jakarta
8.3 million

AUSTRALASIA
& OCEANIA

SOUTH
AMERICA

Lima
6.5 million

KEY:
- ■ Over 5 million people
- ◦ 1–5 million people
- · 50,000–1 million people

Rio de Janeiro
10.2 million

Santiago
5.1 million

São Paulo
16.6 million

Buenos Aires
11.7 million

FAMILY PLANNING

To help slow population growth, many countries now provide people with better health education and information, allowing them to plan the size of their families. Some governments even actively promote smaller families, as shown in this Chinese poster (above). But in many poorer parts of the world, a large family is often still necessary, so that the workload can be shared.

DISTRIBUTION OF PEOPLE

This map (above) shows the current populations of the major cities of the world. At the start of the 20th century, only one in ten people lived in a city. But over time people have been forced into the cities to find work, as factors such as poverty and loss of land have pushed them out of the countryside. Today, half the world's population lives in cities.

POPULATION GROWTH

In the past, the world's population grew slowly, but from about 1800, the pace began to quicken. Better diet, clean water, and improved health care helped to reduce the death rate. In advanced countries, children began to survive longer, so people started to have smaller families. However, because many people in the poorer countries still have large families, the rate of population growth has exploded.

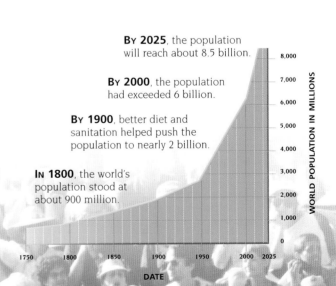

BY 2025, the population will reach about 8.5 billion.

BY 2000, the population had exceeded 6 billion.

BY 1900, better diet and sanitation helped push the population to nearly 2 billion.

IN 1800, the world's population stood at about 900 million.

WORLD POPULATION IN MILLIONS

8,000
7,000
6,000
5,000
4,000
3,000
2,000
1,000
0

1750 1800 1850 1900 1950 2000 2025

DATE

Mapping the World

ABOUT THE ATLAS

This atlas is divided into six continental sections – North America, Central and South America, Africa, Europe, Asia, and Australasia and Oceania. Each country, or group of countries, then has its own map that shows cities, towns, and main geographical features, such as rivers, lakes, and mountain ranges. Photographs and text provide detailed information about life in that country – its people, traditions, politics, and economy. Each continental section has a different colour border to help you locate that section. There is also a gazetteer and an index to help you access information.

MAP LOCATOR
This map shows, in red, the location of each country, part of a country, or group of countries in relation to the continent in which it belongs. There is a locator for each map in the book.

PAGE CONTINUATION
The numbers that appear in a triangle at the top and side borders tell the reader the page of the neighbouring country, or region. For example, on USA: Midwest, the area that lies directly north of the Great Lakes is Eastern Canada – page 6 in the book.

USA: Midwest

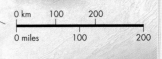

LONGITUDE AND LATITUDE
Lines of longitude are vertical lines that run through the Poles. Lines of latitude are horizontal lines that run parallel to the Equator. These imaginary lines help locate places on a map.

FOREIGN NAMES

Features on the maps are generally labelled in the language of that country. For example, it would be:
Lake on English-speaking countries
Lago on Spanish-speaking countries
Lac on French-speaking countries
However, if a feature is well-known, or mentioned in the main text on the page, it will appear there in English so that readers can find it easily.

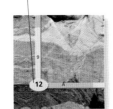

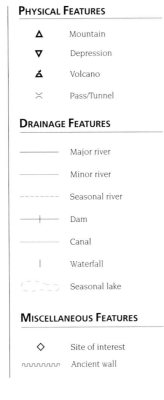

USING THE GRID REFERENCES
The letters and numbers around the outside of the page form a grid to help you find places on the map. For example, to find Wichita, look up its name in the gazetteer (pp 112–133), and you'll find the reference 12 G8. The first number is the page, the letter and number refer to the square made by following up or down from G and across from 8 to form G8.

SCALE
Each map features a scale that shows how distances on the map relate to kilometres and miles. The scale guide can be used to see how big a country is. Not all maps in the book are drawn to the same scale.

KEY TO MAP SYMBOLS

BORDERS

▬▬▬	International border: Border between countries which is mutually recognized.
────	State border: Border used in some large countries to show internal divisions.
▬▬ ▬▬	Disputed border: Border used in practice, but not mutually agreed between two countries.
• • • •	Claimed border: Border which is not mutually recognized – where territory belonging to one country is claimed by another.
✕ ✕ ✕	Ceasefire line
▪ ▪ ▪ I	Undefined boundary

PHYSICAL FEATURES

△	Mountain
▽	Depression
▲	Volcano
✕	Pass/Tunnel

DRAINAGE FEATURES

────	Major river
────	Minor river
- - - -	Seasonal river
─┼─	Dam
────	Canal
I	Waterfall
⌒⌒⌒	Seasonal lake

MISCELLANEOUS FEATURES

◇	Site of interest
⁓⁓⁓	Ancient wall

COMMUNICATIONS

════	Highway
────	Major road
────	Minor road
────	Railway
✈	Airport

TOWNS & CITIES

▣	More than 500,000
◉	100,000 – 500,000
○	50,000 – 100,000
○	Less than 50,000
●	National capital
◉	Internal administrative capital
◉	Polar research station

LATITUDE & LONGITUDE

────	Lines of Latitude/ Longitude
────	Equator
- - - -	Tropics
25°	Degrees of Latitude/ Longitude

NAMES

REGIONS

FRANCE	Country
JERSEY (to UK)	Dependent territory
KANSAS	Administrative region
Dordogne	Cultural region

TOWNS & CITIES

PARIS	National capital
SAN JUAN	Dependent territory capital city

NAMES *continued*

Seattle **Limón** Comayagua San José	Other towns & cities

PHYSICAL

Andes *Ardennes*	Landscape features
Balearic Islands	Island group
Majorca	Island
Lake Baikal	Lake/River /Canal
PACIFIC OCEAN	
Gulf of Mexico *Bay of Campeche*	Sea features
Chile Rise	Undersea feature

OTHER FEATURES

Tropic of Cancer	Graticule text

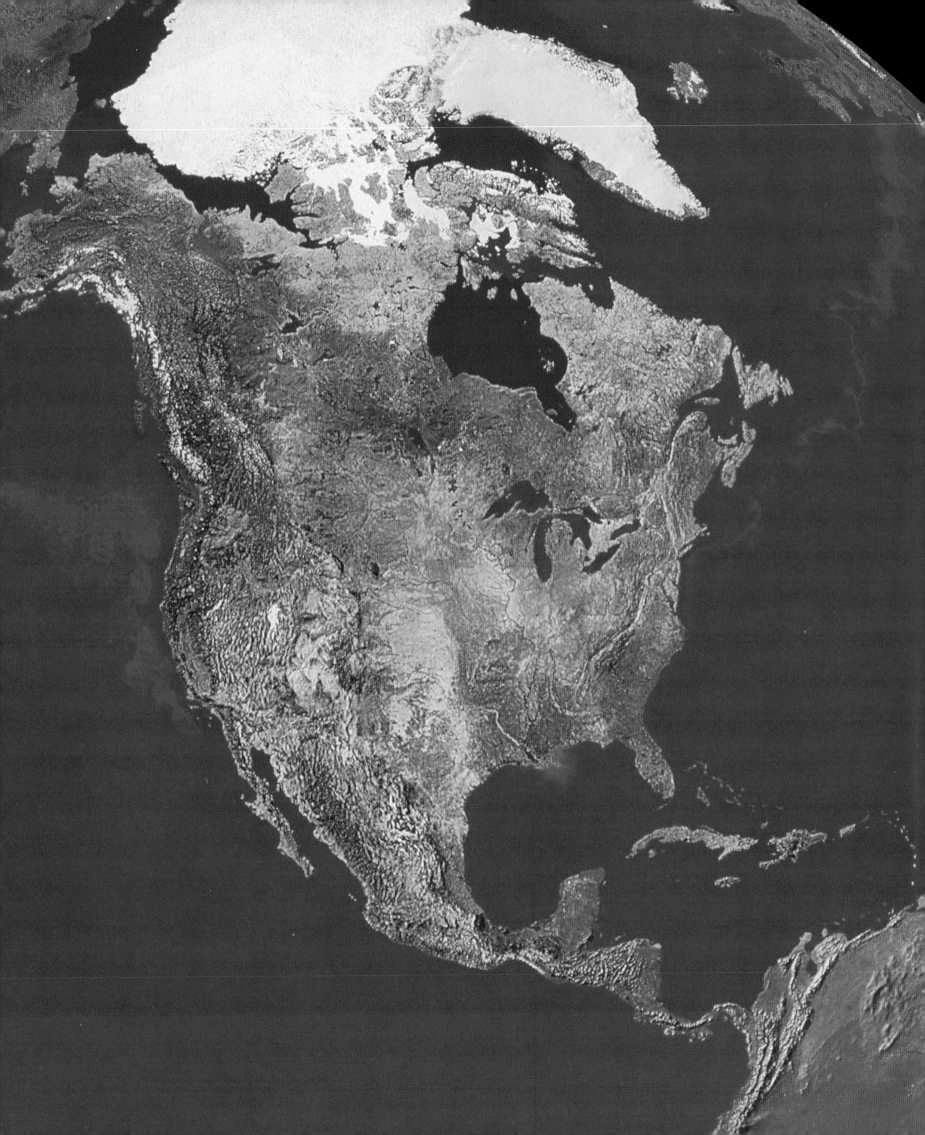

NORTH AMERICA

NORTH AMERICA INCLUDES the United States of America,

Canada, and Mexico. Its population of 413 million is largely

based on immigrants, who arrived here from the 1500s onwards. North

America's varied landscape ranges from frozen tundra in the

north to hot desert and lush rain forest in the south.

Mexico is Spanish speaking and, despite vast oil and gas reserves, is relatively

poor. In contrast, the USA and Canada enjoy high standards of living and most

people speak English – except for the French-speakers in

Québec. They also have other features in common – they are

roughly the same size and share the longest undefended

land border in the world. However, the USA has a far larger

population and is the wealthiest nation on Earth. American technology, such

as computer software, has a global influence – as does its film and music.

Western Canada and Alaska

CANADA IS A HUGE COUNTRY and its western half stretches from the flat prairies in the east to the towering Rocky Mountains in the west, and from the relatively mild south to the permanently frozen area north of the Arctic Circle. Harsh conditions over much of the region mean that most of the population is concentrated in cities in the south, such as Vancouver, Calgary, and Winnipeg. The prairies – once a vast expanse of grassland – are now used mainly for growing wheat on huge mechanized farms. Oil and natural gas are found there as well. These natural resources are also important in Alaska, a part of the United States. The majority of Alaska's people moved there to work in these lucrative industries.

FORESTRY

Large parts of western Canada are covered in forests and lumbering is a major part of the local economy. The trees are used to make buildings, furniture, and paper. In the past, whole areas of trees were cleared but now sustainable methods such as selective cutting and replanting are practised.

FELLED trees are transported down a river near Vancouver.

TOTEM POLES

The native peoples of British Columbia use totem poles to record their clan history. Each carved and painted totem describes a real or mythical event and often features animals that the clan has a connection with, such as the eagle (left).

DOGSLED RACING

The state sport of Alaska is dogsled racing. Here, competitors take part in the annual Iditarod Trail Sled Dog Race, a gruelling run across the rugged landscape for drivers and their teams of dogs.

VANCOUVER

This city's vibrant cultural mix is typical of Canada's diversity. Many Chinese, as well as other ethnic groups, live here and reflect Vancouver's historic role as a destination for migrants. Its bustling economy, mild climate, and cultural links make it an attractive place to live.

Map labels

Chukchi Sea

ARCTIC OCEAN

Prince Patrick Island
Mould Bay

Beaufort Sea

Banks Island

Near Islands

Bering Strait

Wevok
Point Lay
Barrow

Rat Islands

Gambell
Wales
Kivalina

Saint Lawrence Island

Deering

Coville River

Prudhoe Bay
Umiat
Kaktovik

Sachs Harbour

Norton Sound

Arctic Circle

Brooks Range

Bering Sea

Nunivak Island

Alakanuk

Grayling
Yukon River
Kokrines

ALASKA
(to US)

Fort Yukon

Tuktoyaktuk
Amundsen Gulf
Holman

Aklavik
Inuvik
Fort McPherson
Paulatuk

Pribilof Islands

Kwigillingok

Fairbanks

Yukon River

Aleutian Islands

Andreanof Islands

Atka

Platinum

Kuskokwim Mts

Alaska Range

Mount McKinley 6194m
McKinley Park

Fort Good Hope

Great Bear Lake
Echo Bay

Kugluktuk

Umnak Island
Unalaska Island
Unimak Island

Dutch Harbor

Bristol Bay

Iliamna Lake
Susitna
Anchorage

Hope
Gulkana
Valdez
Chitina

YUKON TERRITORY

Mackenzie

Mackenzie

NORTHWEST TERRITORIES

Belkofski

Alaska Peninsula

Shumagin Islands

Kodiak
Cordova
Katalla
Kodiak Island

Mount Logan 5959m

Whitehorse

Tungsten
Fort Simpson

Edzo
Yellowknife

Great Slave Lake

PACIFIC OCEAN

Gulf of Alaska

Yakutat

Haines
Gustavus
Atlin

Fort Providence
Fort Liard

Hay River
Fort Smith

Juneau

Fort Nelson

Fort Vermilion

Alexander Archipelago

Kake

BRITISH COLUMBIA

Fort St. John

Fort McMurray

Port Alexander
Ketchikan

Ware

Prince Rupert
Queen Charlotte Islands

Kitimat

Prince George

ALBERTA
Grande Prairie
Athabasca
Athabasca

Ocean Falls
Queen Charlotte Sound

Mount Waddington

Port Hardy

Mount Robson

Edmonton
North

Leduc
Red Deer
Calgary

Campbell River
Vancouver Island
Nanaimo

Kamloops
Vancouver

Kelowna
Lethbridge

Victoria

Cranbrook
Milk River

UNITED

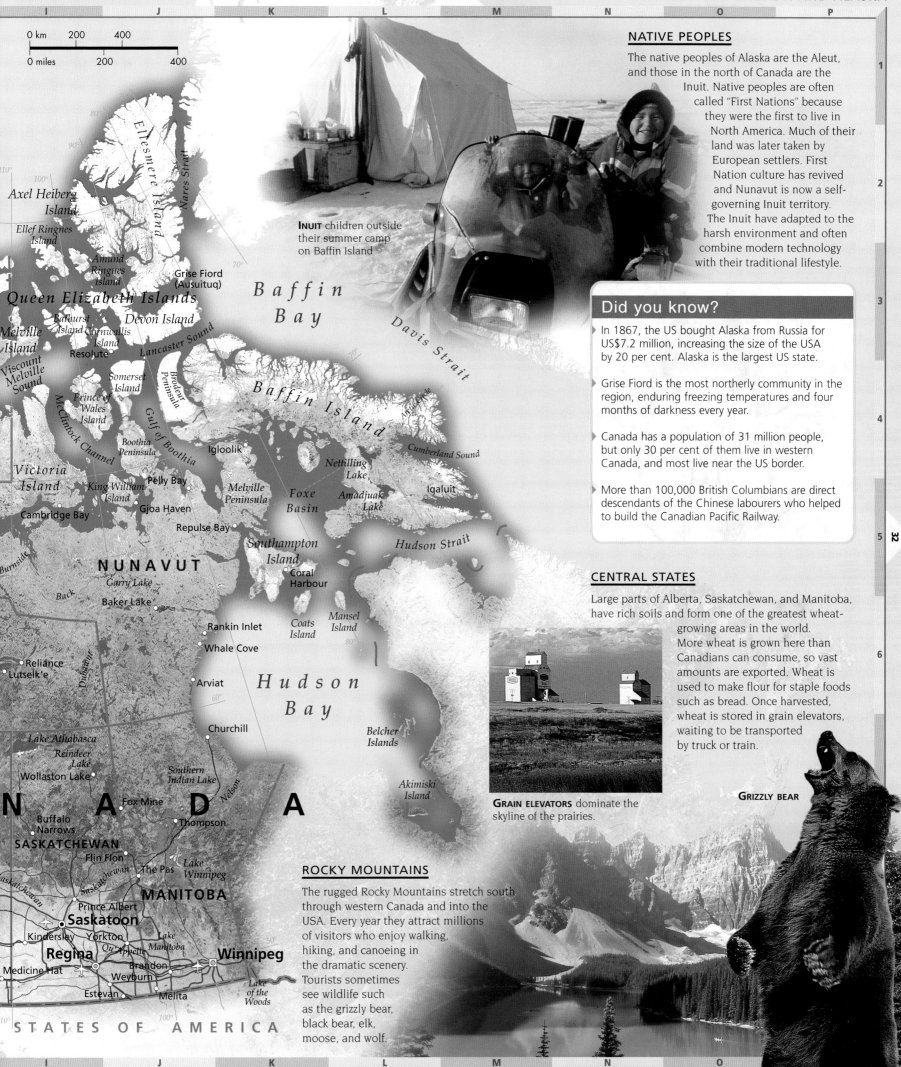

0 km   200   400

0 miles   200   400

Axel Heiberg
Island

Ellef Ringnes
Island

Ellesmere Island

Nares Strait

Amund
Ringnes
Island

Grise Fiord
(Ausuituq)

Queen Elizabeth Islands

Melville
Island

Bathurst
Island
Cornwallis
Island

Devon Island

Resolute

Lancaster Sound

Viscount
Melville
Sound

Prince of
Wales
Island

Somerset
Island

Brodeur
Peninsula

Gulf of Boothia

**Baffin
Bay**

Davis Strait

McClintock Channel

Boothia
Peninsula

Baffin Island

Victoria
Island

King William
Island

Pelly Bay

Igloolik

Nettilling
Lake

Cumberland Sound

Cambridge Bay

Gjoa Haven

Melville
Peninsula

Foxe
Basin

Amadjuak
Lake

Iqaluit

Repulse Bay

Burnside

Back

NUNAVUT

Garry Lake

Southampton
Island

Coral
Harbour

Hudson Strait

Baker Lake

Rankin Inlet

Coats
Island

Mansel
Island

Reliance
Lutselk'e

Whale Cove

Dubawnt

Arviat

**Hudson
Bay**

Lake Athabasca

Reindeer
Lake

Churchill

Belcher
Islands

Wollaston Lake

Southern
Indian Lake

Nelson

Akimiski
Island

N   **A**   **D**   **A**

Fox Mine

Buffalo
Narrows

Thompson

SASKATCHEWAN

Flin Flon

Saskatchewan

The Pas

Lake
Winnipeg

Prince Albert

MANITOBA

Saskatoon

Kindersley

Yorkton

Lake
Manitoba

Regina

Qu'Apelle

Winnipeg

Medicine Hat

Brandon

Weyburn

Lake
of the
Woods

Estevan

Melita

STATES OF AMERICA

NATIVE PEOPLES

The native peoples of Alaska are the Aleut, and those in the north of Canada are the Inuit. Native peoples are often called "First Nations" because they were the first to live in North America. Much of their land was later taken by European settlers. First Nation culture has revived and Nunavut is now a self-governing Inuit territory. The Inuit have adapted to the harsh environment and often combine modern technology with their traditional lifestyle.

INUIT children outside their summer camp on Baffin Island

Did you know?

▶ In 1867, the US bought Alaska from Russia for US$7.2 million, increasing the size of the USA by 20 per cent. Alaska is the largest US state.

▶ Grise Fiord is the most northerly community in the region, enduring freezing temperatures and four months of darkness every year.

▶ Canada has a population of 31 million people, but only 30 per cent of them live in western Canada, and most live near the US border.

▶ More than 100,000 British Columbians are direct descendants of the Chinese labourers who helped to build the Canadian Pacific Railway.

32

CENTRAL STATES

Large parts of Alberta, Saskatchewan, and Manitoba, have rich soils and form one of the greatest wheat-growing areas in the world. More wheat is grown here than Canadians can consume, so vast amounts are exported. Wheat is used to make flour for staple foods such as bread. Once harvested, wheat is stored in grain elevators, waiting to be transported by truck or train.

GRAIN ELEVATORS dominate the skyline of the prairies.

GRIZZLY BEAR

ROCKY MOUNTAINS

The rugged Rocky Mountains stretch south through western Canada and into the USA. Every year they attract millions of visitors who enjoy walking, hiking, and canoeing in the dramatic scenery. Tourists sometimes see wildlife such as the grizzly bear, black bear, elk, moose, and wolf.

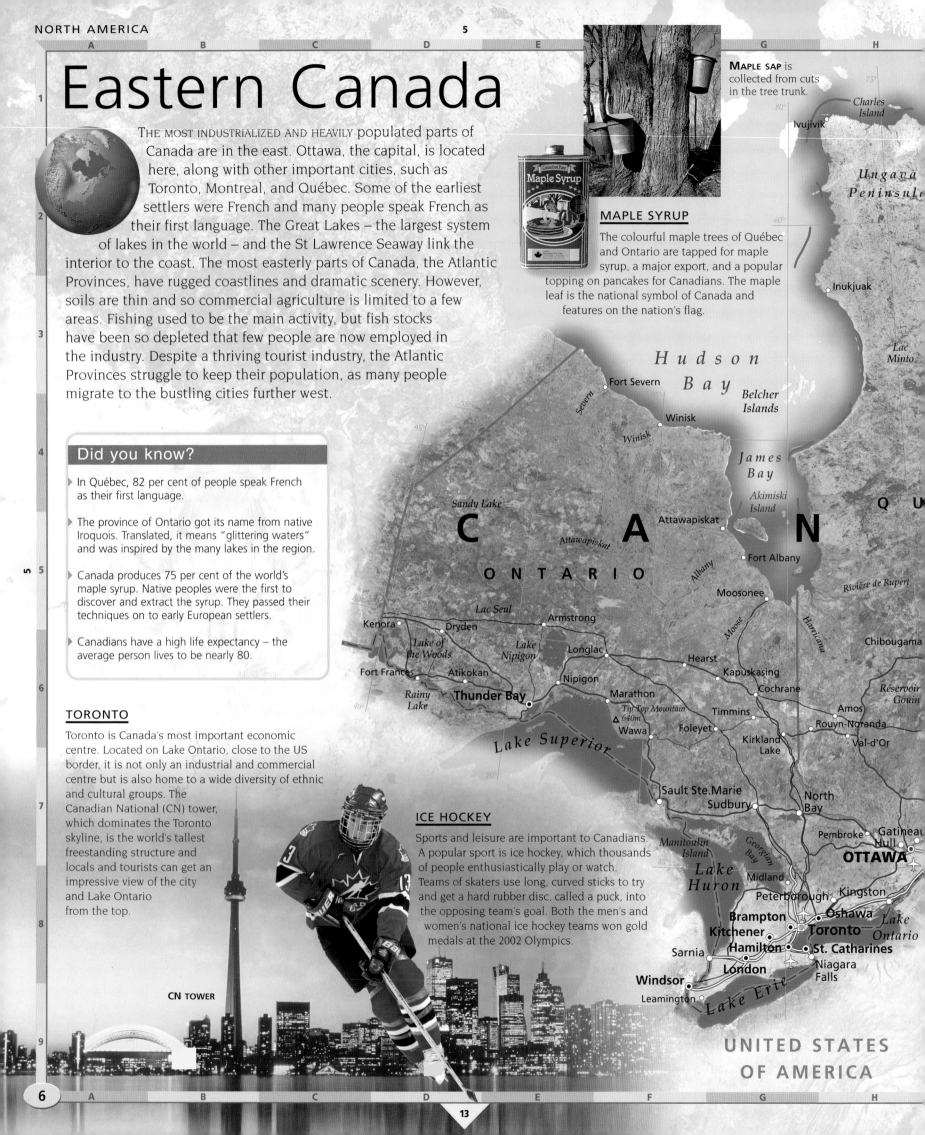

Eastern Canada

THE MOST INDUSTRIALIZED AND HEAVILY populated parts of Canada are in the east. Ottawa, the capital, is located here, along with other important cities, such as Toronto, Montreal, and Québec. Some of the earliest settlers were French and many people speak French as their first language. The Great Lakes – the largest system of lakes in the world – and the St Lawrence Seaway link the interior to the coast. The most easterly parts of Canada, the Atlantic Provinces, have rugged coastlines and dramatic scenery. However, soils are thin and so commercial agriculture is limited to a few areas. Fishing used to be the main activity, but fish stocks have been so depleted that few people are now employed in the industry. Despite a thriving tourist industry, the Atlantic Provinces struggle to keep their population, as many people migrate to the bustling cities further west.

MAPLE SAP is collected from cuts in the tree trunk.

MAPLE SYRUP

The colourful maple trees of Québec and Ontario are tapped for maple syrup, a major export, and a popular topping on pancakes for Canadians. The maple leaf is the national symbol of Canada and features on the nation's flag.

Did you know?

▸ In Québec, 82 per cent of people speak French as their first language.

▸ The province of Ontario got its name from native Iroquois. Translated, it means "glittering waters" and was inspired by the many lakes in the region.

▸ Canada produces 75 per cent of the world's maple syrup. Native peoples were the first to discover and extract the syrup. They passed their techniques on to early European settlers.

▸ Canadians have a high life expectancy – the average person lives to be nearly 80.

TORONTO

Toronto is Canada's most important economic centre. Located on Lake Ontario, close to the US border, it is not only an industrial and commercial centre but is also home to a wide diversity of ethnic and cultural groups. The Canadian National (CN) tower, which dominates the Toronto skyline, is the world's tallest freestanding structure and locals and tourists can get an impressive view of the city and Lake Ontario from the top.

CN TOWER

ICE HOCKEY

Sports and leisure are important to Canadians. A popular sport is ice hockey, which thousands of people enthusiastically play or watch. Teams of skaters use long, curved sticks to try and get a hard rubber disc, called a puck, into the opposing team's goal. Both the men's and women's national ice hockey teams won gold medals at the 2002 Olympics.

UNITED STATES OF AMERICA

Charles Island

Ungava Peninsula

Ivujivik

Inukjuak

Lac Minto

Hudson Bay

Fort Severn

Belcher Islands

Winisk

Severn

Winisk

James Bay

Akimiski Island

Sandy Lake

Attawapiskat

Attawapiskat

C   A   N   Q

O N T A R I O

Fort Albany

Albany

Moosonee

Rivière de Rupert

Lac Seul

Armstrong

Moose

Chibougamau

Kenora   Dryden

Lake of the Woods

Lake Nipigon

Longlac

Hearst

Kapuskasing

Cochrane

Réservoir Gouin

Fort Frances   Atikokan

Nipigon

Marathon

Timmins

Amos

Rouyn-Noranda

Rainy Lake

Thunder Bay

Tip Top Mountain △ 640m

Wawa

Foleyet

Kirkland Lake

Val-d'Or

Lake Superior

Sault Ste.Marie

Sudbury

North Bay

Pembroke

Gatineau
Hull

Manitoulin Island

Georgian Bay

Lake Huron

Midland

OTTAWA

Peterborough

Kingston

Brampton

Oshawa

Kitchener

Toronto

Hamilton

St. Catharines

Sarnia

Lake Ontario

London

Niagara Falls

Windsor

Leamington

Lake Erie

Atlantic Provinces

Nova Scotia, New Brunswick, Prince Edward Island, and Newfoundland and Labrador attract tourists for their landscape, wildlife, and quaint sea-side villages. Icebergs are a regular sight off the coast of Newfoundland and Labrador as they drift south from the Arctic.

FISHERIES

The Grand Banks, off the coast of Newfoundland, are shallow waters that once contained huge stocks of fish. Stocks have declined, however, due to overfishing and now catches are severely restricted. This has resulted in hardship for those who relied on fishing for their livelihood.

FRENCH signs in Québec city

FRENCH CANADA

Québec Province is the main French-speaking part of Canada. With a different language and cultural traditions from other parts of the country, there have been calls in the past for Québec to become independent from the rest of Canada.

ST LAWRENCE SEAWAY

Stretching far inland, the St Lawrence Seaway provides a link from the Great Lakes to the Atlantic. A series of huge locks descends from Lake Ontario to sea level, allowing ocean-going ships to transport their cargo as far inland as Lake Superior. Large amounts of iron ore, for example, are transported inland from Labrador to Ontario for processing. Corn, soy, and other agricultural products move in the opposite direction, from the prairies east to the markets of the world.

Map labels:

Baffin Island
Hudson Strait
Resolution Island
80°
Akpatok Island
Button Islands
60°
Ungava Bay
Koksoak
Kuujjuaq
Rivière à la Baleine
Caniapiscau
Lac Bienville
Schefferville
Nain
Hopedale
Makkovik
Cape Harrison
Cartwright
NEWFOUNDLAND & LABRADOR
Labrador Sea
Smallwood Reservoir
Lake Melville
Churchill
55°
55°
Réservoir de Caniapiscau
St.Anthony
50°
Eastmain
Réservoir Manicouagan
Laurentian Mountains
Havre-St-Pierre
Île d'Anticosti
Strait of Belle Isle
Lac Mistassini
Sept-Îles
Corner Brook
Newfoundland
Gander
Grand Falls
St.John's
E B E C
A
D
A
Baie-Comeau
Gaspé
Gulf of St. Lawrence
St.Lawrence
Lac St-Jean
Matane
Péninsule de Gaspé
Chicoutimi
Rimouski
Îles de la Madeleine
Channel-Port aux Basques
Cape Race
Jonquière
Rivière-du-Loup
Bathurst
Cabot Strait
ST PIERRE & MIQUELON
(to France)
La Tuque
Edmundston
PRINCE EDWARD ISLAND
55°
Charlesbourg
NEW BRUNSWICK
Charlottetown
Glace Bay
Québec
St-Georges
Amherst
Sydney
Trois-Rivières
Moncton
New Glasgow
Cape Breton Island
45°
Laval
Oromocto
Truro
Drummondville
Fredericton
NOVA SCOTIA
Montréal
Sherbrooke
Saint John
Dartmouth
Sable Island
60°
Halifax
Bay of Fundy
Liverpool
Yarmouth
ATLANTIC OCEAN

0 km   100   200
0 miles   100   200

Map grid letters: I J K L M N O P (top and bottom)
Map grid numbers: 1 2 3 4 5 6 7 8 9 (right side)

USA: Northeast

THE NORTHEASTERN UNITED STATES is a heavily populated area that is steeped in history. This is traditionally the main immigration point into the States, with the Statue of Liberty lighting the way for those arriving into New York by boat. People from all over the world have settled in this region to live and work, creating a "melting pot" of cultures and ethnic groups. Important historical events, such as the signing of the Declaration of Independence and the Constitution, took place in Philadelphia. These documents set the foundations for American life today. It is also here that the capital and centre of government was established. Today, while industry and agriculture are still important, finance and commerce are the driving forces of the economy.

Did you know?

▶ There are more than 100 universities and colleges in Boston.

▶ Every minute, about 180 million litres (40 million gallons) of water plunges over Niagara Falls, located on the border between the USA and Canada.

▶ The White House in Washington, DC, has been home to every president except George Washington, whom the city is named after.

▶ The stock exchange on Wall Street, New York City, is the world's largest. The street's name came from a wall built by Dutch settlers to keep the British out.

CENTRE OF GOVERNMENT

All three branches of the federal government, the executive, legislative, and judicial, reside in Washington, DC. The United States Congress (the legislative branch) meets here in the Capitol building. Many of the city's residents work for the government.

THE SEAT of government is here at the Capitol building.

THRIVING CITY

New York is the largest city in the USA. Historically it grew because it has a good harbour and sits at the mouth of the Hudson River. Immigrants from overseas flooded into the city in the 19th and 20th centuries, boosting its population and economy. Today, it is the main financial centre, not just of the USA, but of the world.

Lake Ontario
Hudson River
Appalachian Mountains
New York City

PITTSBURGH

Once a major steel-manufacturing centre with a polluted environment, Pittsburgh is now a thriving financial centre with a large number of corporate headquarters. Bridges span the three rivers that run through the city, connecting the core downtown area (above) to the suburbs.

CANADA
ONTARIO

St. Lawrence
Ogdensburg
Adirondack Mountains
Watertown
Oswego
Boonville
Lake Ontario
Rochester Syracuse
Niagara Falls
Lockport Newark Utica
Mohawk River
NEW YORK
Niagara Falls
Buffalo Avon Oneonta
Hamburg Dansville
Catskill Mountains
Lake Erie
Dunkirk Ithaca
Binghamton
Erie Jamestown Elmira
Sayre
Warren Mansfield
Middletow
Scranton
Meadville Wilcox Wilkes Barre Milford
Allegheny Plateau
PENNSYLVANIA
Mercer Lock Haven Stroudsberg
Allegheny River
Du Bois Milton
Allentown
OHIO Butler State College
Indiana Reading Trenton
Aliquippa Pittsburgh Altoona Philadelphia
Harrisburg
Washington Carlisle Lancaster
Bedford York Wilmington
Uniontown Cherry Hill
Hagerstown Aberdeen Vineland
Cumberland Towson
WEST Oakland Baltimore Dover
VIRGINIA Columbia DELAWAR
Annapolis
WASHINGTON D.C.
VIRGINIA Cambridge
MARYLAND Ocean City
Salisbury
Chesapeake Bay

CRANBERRIES

The northeast USA is a major cranberry-growing region. Cranberries grow in flooded bogs, and once harvested – often with high-tech equipment (above) – they can be eaten in pies and sauces.

MAINE

Although Maine is a large state, it is relatively sparsely populated. Early settlers were attracted to its coastline, and fishing communities gradually sprang up. To this day, fishing remains an important activity, while colourful foliage attracts tourists in the autumn.

MAINE is famous for its clam chowder and lobsters.

THANKSGIVING

The first Thanksgiving was held in 1621 as a gesture of friendship between Pilgrims and American Indians after the Pilgrims' first successful harvest. Americans honour that tradition every November by gathering with family and friends to give thanks for life's blessings and to share a meal.

HIGHER EDUCATION

A large number of universities are located in this region, including two of the most famous – Harvard (above) and Yale. As well as studying, students enjoy a full campus life, including taking part in sport. Links between industry and education are strong so many high-tech companies have been established here.

TOURISTS can take a lift to the top of the Statue of Liberty.

NEW YORK CITY

The centre of US commerce and business is New York City. People living here have a fast-paced lifestyle, and many travel by train or ferry from the suburbs to work in the towering high-rise office blocks of Manhattan. People travelling by boat across the harbour pass the Statue of Liberty, a huge monument that represents freedom and opportunity to Americans.

Map labels

NEW BRUNSWICK
Madawaska
Presque Isle
Mars Hill
Houlton
△ Mount Katahdin 1605m
Moosehead Lake
Jackman
Milo
Lincoln
Calais
Machias
MAINE
Bangor
Millbridge
Searsport
Bar Harbor
Bay of FunDy
QUEBEC
Newport
VERMONT
Waterville
Mount Desert Island
Attsburgh
Lake Champlain
Burlington
Berlin
Augusta
Camden
Montpelier
Mount Washington 1917m
Lewiston
Bath
Chelsea
NEW HAMPSHIRE
Rutland
Lebanon
Laconia
Portland
Gulf of Maine
Hillsboro
Rochester
Biddeford
Glens Falls
Concord
Portsmouth
Green Mountains
Connecticut River
Manchester
Nashua
Lawrence
OCEAN
Schenectady
Lowell
Troy
Greenfield
Albany
Pittsfield
Worcester
Boston
Hudson River
MASSACHUSETTS
Provincetown
Cape Cod
Springfield
Pawtucket
Orleans
Kingston
Windsor
Providence
New Bedford
Bristol
Hartford
Warwick
Martha's Vineyard
Torrington
CONNECTICUT
RHODE ISLAND
Nantucket
Nantucket Island
Waterbury
New Haven
Groton
Yonkers
Bridgeport
Stamford
ATLANTIC
Paterson
New York
Long Island
Newark
Middletown
NEW JERSEY
Atlantic City

0 km 50 100 150
0 miles 50 100 150

USA: South

THE SOUTHERN STATES OF THE USA have a varied landscape and an interesting mix of people, both culturally and economically. Some areas of the region are poor, especially the Appalachian Mountain communities, while other parts, such as the Florida coast, are wealthy and attract many people from other states and countries. The cultural mix includes people of Latin American origin, African Americans, Cajuns (French-Canadians), and European Americans, giving rise to diverse music styles, dialects, pastimes, and food. While coal mining in the Appalachian Mountains has declined in recent years, agriculture is still important, as are tourism and industry. Tourism is particularly important in Florida and in New Orleans near the mouth of the mighty Mississippi River.

0 km 50 100 150 200
0 miles 50 100 150 200

COTTON CROPS

Cotton was once the mainstay crop of the south and was grown by African-American slaves. Today, cotton is still important for the economy of the region and is grown in large fields and harvested with huge machinery. Cotton has many uses, primarily as the raw material for textiles.

COTTON POD, OR BOLL

Did you know?

▶ The Mississippi is the largest river in North America, and the third largest in the world. It stretches 3,770 km (2,340 miles) from Lake Itasca in Minnesota to its mouth near New Orleans.

▶ Memphis, Tennessee, is named after the ancient Egyptian capital situated south of the Nile Delta.

▶ Half the nation's peanuts are grown in Georgia. Most of them are made into peanut butter.

MUSIC ORIGINS

The southern USA is famous for its music, much of which reflects the cultural mix of the region. New Orleans and other parts of Louisiana are the birthplaces of jazz and Cajun music, while bluegrass and country have origins in Nashville and Memphis. These music styles started here, but quickly spread throughout the country and developed even further in the cities.

JAZZ musician on Bourbon Street in New Orleans.

A CHEF holds a skillet of jambalaya, a Cajun dish.

CAJUN CULTURE

The Cajuns in this region are French-speaking people who were expelled from Canada in the 18th century. They mixed with other cultures in Louisiana, but their French influence can be seen in the music, food, and place names, such as Lafayette.

FLORIDA EVERGLADES

The increasing population of Florida means that the Everglades, swampy plains inhabited by alligators and other wildlife, are under threat as land is needed for houses and farms. However, the Everglades National Park protects part of this important ecosystem.

Map labels

INDIANA
MISSOURI
OKLAHOMA
ARKANSAS
TENNESSEE
KENTUCKY
TEXAS
LOUISIANA
MISSISSIPPI
ALABAMA

Cincinnati, Newport, Louisville, Frankfort, Evansville, Lexington, Henderson, Owensboro, Richmond, Elizabethtown, Paducah, Hopkinsville, Bowling Green, Somerset, Clarksville, Cookeville, Rogers, Bull Shoals Lake, Mountain Home, Pocahontas, Union City, Nashville, Fayetteville, Walnut Ridge, Blytheville, Dyersburg, Franklin, Murfreesboro, Maryvill, Boston Mountains, Fort Smith, Jonesboro, Jackson, Lawrenceburg, Columbia, Watts B Lake, Russellville, Searcy, West Memphis, Memphis, Chattanooga, Cleveland, North Little Rock, Forrest City, Corinth, Huntsville, Dalton, Ouachita Mountains, Little Rock, Holly Springs, Florence, Decatur, Scottsboro, Rome, Hot Springs, Benton, Clarksdale, Tupelo, Hamilton, Cullman, Marietta, Atlanta, Pine Bluff, Grenada, Anniston, Gadsden, Red River, Texarkana, Greenwood, Columbus, Tuscaloosa, Birmingham, Camden, Greenville, Shreveport, El Dorado, Bastrop, Yazoo City, Alexander City, Griffin, Ruston, Monroe, Canton, ALABAMA, Bossier City, Tallulah, Clinton, Meridian, Demopolis, Opelika, Columbus, Natchitoches, Vicksburg, Jackson, Prattville, Montgomery, Phenix City, Alexandria, Natchez, Laurel, Troy, De Ridder, Brookhaven, Hattiesburg, Andalusia, Ozark, Albany, McComb, Brewton, Dothan, Bainbridge, Opelousas, Bogalusa, Prichard, Mobile, Crestview, Lake Seminole, Baton Rouge, Lake Charles, Lafayette, Gulfport, Biloxi, Pensacola, Fort Walton Beach, Tallahassee, New Iberia, Metairie, Panama City, Morgan City, New Orleans, Houma, Chandeleur Islands, Cape San Blas, Venice, Mississippi River Delta, Gulf of Mexico, Apalachee Bay

Rivers: Arkansas River, Mississippi River, Tennessee River, Cumberland Plateau, Red River, Ouachita River, Sabine River, Pearl River, Tombigbee River, Alabama River, Chattahoochee River, Kentucky Lake, Green River

PENNSYLVANIA 40°

OHIO

WEST VIRGINIA
Spruce Knob 1482m △

Parkersburg
Clarksburg
Winchester
Dale City
Arlington
WASHINGTON D.C.
Harrisonburg
Fredericksburg
MARYLAND
Staunton
Charlottesville
Portsmouth
Huntington
Charleston
Saint Albans
Beckley
Bluefield
VIRGINIA
Richmond
Lynchburg
Petersburg
Chesapeake Bay
Pikeville
Pulaski
Roanoke
Newport News
Cape Charles
Norfolk
Portsmouth
Virginia Beach
London
Middlesboro
Kingsport
Danville
James River
Potomac River
Roanoke River
Bristol
Greeneville
Elizabeth City
Winston Salem
Greensboro
Durham
Rocky Mount
Knoxville
Mount Mitchell 2037m △
High Point
Cary
Raleigh
Greenville
Cape Hatteras 35°
Asheville
NORTH CAROLINA
Goldsboro
New Bern
Pamlico Sound
Gastonia
Fayetteville
Havelock
Spartanburg
Rock Hill
Charlotte
Laurinburg
Jacksonville
Greenville
Union
Onslow Bay
Gainesville
SOUTH CAROLINA
Florence
Wilmington
Greenwood
Cape Fear
Athens
Clark Hill Lake
Columbia
Myrtle Beach
Long Bay
Aiken
Lake Marion
Augusta
Orangeburg
Georgetown
GEORGIA
North Charleston
Savannah River
Milledgeville
Macon
Charleston
Dublin
Statesboro
Vidalia
Hilton Head Island
Cordele
Altamaha River
Savannah
Hinesville
Tifton
Waycross
Brunswick
Valdosta
Thomasville
Okefenokee Swamp

ATLANTIC OCEAN

Jacksonville
Lake City
Saint Augustine
Gainesville
Lake George
30°
Ocala
Daytona Beach
De Land
Deltona
Spring Hill
Orlando
Cape Canaveral
Clearwater
Lakeland
Melbourne
Largo
Lake Kissimmee
Tampa
Saint Petersburg
FLORIDA
Fort Pierce
Tampa Bay
Sarasota
Hutchinson Island
Port Charlotte
Lake Okeechobee
West Palm Beach
Charlotte Harbor
Fort Myers
Boca Raton
Pompano Beach
Naples
Big Cypress Swamp
Fort Lauderdale
The Everglades
Miami Beach
Miami
Cape Sable
Key Largo
Florida Bay
Florida Keys
25°
Straits of Florida
Key West
80°

KENTUCKY DERBY

Every year on the first Saturday of May, the Kentucky Derby takes place in Louisville. This horse race, and the festivities based around it, mark the beginning of spring for people in the area. The best horses and jockeys, as well as massive crowds of spectators from around the country, travel here for the event .

TOURISM

Tourism is an important industry in the south, especially for Florida. As well as warm weather and appealing scenery, tourists are attracted to the theme parks around Orlando. Jobs and income are generated by tourism, with many people working in retail outlets, restaurants, hotels, and theme parks.

KUMBA roller coaster at Busch Gardens is the fastest in Florida.

MARTIN LUTHER KING, JR.

Martin Luther King, Jr. (left) was born in Atlanta in 1929. In the 1960s, he led many peaceful protests to end the laws that discriminated against black Americans. King was assassinated in 1969 and has since been seen as a symbol of the struggle for racial equality. Many African Americans live in the southern USA where, before the Civil War (1861–65), their ancestors were forced to work on cotton plantations and farms.

MARTIN LUTHER KING, JR. speaking at the final rally of the March Against Fear, Mississippi, 1966

FLORIDA'S SUNSHINE COAST

Florida's sunny weather and sandy beaches have traditionally attracted many retired people, many of whom live in apartments along the coast in resorts such as Miami Beach (right). Florida also attracts young people, particularly to the vibrant city of Miami, where many immigrants from Central America, Cuba, and other Caribbean islands live, and Spanish is spoken by half the population. The Florida Keys, an island chain in the south of the peninsula, is also popular with tourists, and contains one of the largest living coral formations in North America.

USA: Midwest

THE AMERICAN MIDWEST is dominated by the Great Plains, once the home of cattle ranches, cowboys, and tribes of American Indian people. However, the discovery of gold in South Dakota brought a rush of settlers to the area. This, combined with a decline in buffalo numbers, led to the eventual displacement of the American Indians from the Plains. The area is prone to dramatic weather – with tornadoes, freezing blizzards, and blazing hot summers. To the west, vast areas of farmland generate more wheat and maize than anywhere else in the world. East of the Mississippi the landscape varies and, although farming is still important, this is the industrial centre of the country. Big cities, such as Chicago, Detroit, and Cleveland form the major manufacturing centres.

BUFFALO ON THE PLAINS

Up to 100 million buffalo once grazed on the Great Plains. They provided local American Indians with food for the family, and skin for clothes and teepees. But over-hunting and the destruction of their habitat by early European settlers drastically reduced the number of animals. Buffalo are now a protected species that live in reserves. This herd is from a reserve in South Dakota.

THE DAKOTA people used buffalo bones to make shields and tools. The animal's bladder made a bag for carrying water.

MOUNT RUSHMORE NATIONAL MEMORIAL

Mount Rushmore was created as a tribute to the American presidency. Four of the United States' greatest presidents – Lincoln, Roosevelt, Jefferson, and Washington – were carved into the granite cliff between 1927 and 1941. Teams of workers hung from saddles anchored to the mountain to complete the work, often enduring harsh winds or blazing sun. Today, it is a popular tourist attraction.

Each carved face is about 18 m (60 ft) high.

TORNADO ALLEY

Dramatic tornadoes, or "twisters", regularly tear through the states of Kansas and Missouri, along a path known as Tornado Alley. Tornadoes occur when warm and cold air masses meet. As the warm air rises, it cools, and under the right conditions, it can suck in more and more air until a whirling twister develops. The more air that is drawn in, the greater the power of the tornado.

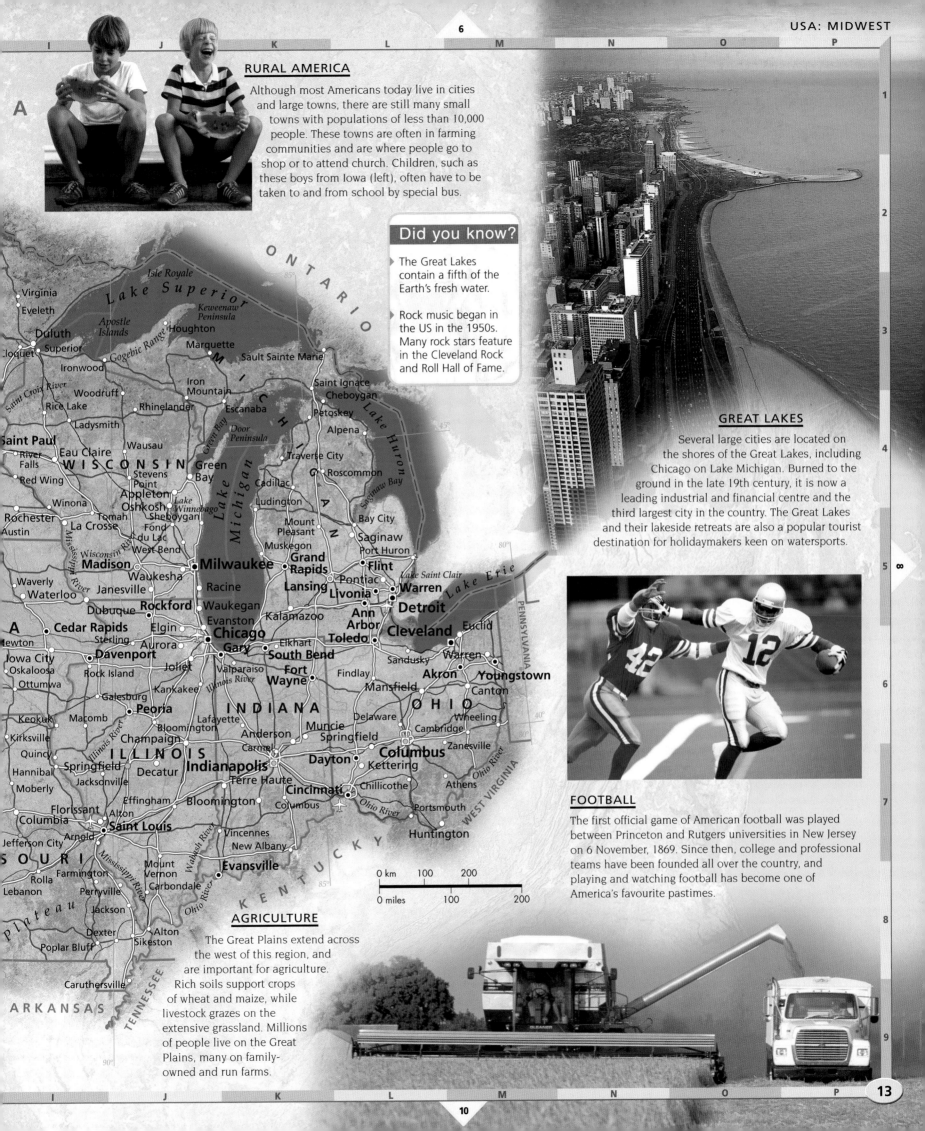

RURAL AMERICA

Although most Americans today live in cities and large towns, there are still many small towns with populations of less than 10,000 people. These towns are often in farming communities and are where people go to shop or to attend church. Children, such as these boys from Iowa (left), often have to be taken to and from school by special bus.

Did you know?

- The Great Lakes contain a fifth of the Earth's fresh water.

- Rock music began in the US in the 1950s. Many rock stars feature in the Cleveland Rock and Roll Hall of Fame.

GREAT LAKES

Several large cities are located on the shores of the Great Lakes, including Chicago on Lake Michigan. Burned to the ground in the late 19th century, it is now a leading industrial and financial centre and the third largest city in the country. The Great Lakes and their lakeside retreats are also a popular tourist destination for holidaymakers keen on watersports.

FOOTBALL

The first official game of American football was played between Princeton and Rutgers universities in New Jersey on 6 November, 1869. Since then, college and professional teams have been founded all over the country, and playing and watching football has become one of America's favourite pastimes.

AGRICULTURE

The Great Plains extend across the west of this region, and are important for agriculture. Rich soils support crops of wheat and maize, while livestock grazes on the extensive grassland. Millions of people live on the Great Plains, many on family-owned and run farms.

0 km   100   200

0 miles   100   200

USA: West

THE ROCKY MOUNTAINS separate the coastal region from the drier inland states. Large and fast-growing cities, such as San Francisco, Los Angeles, and San Diego, hug the Pacific Coast, and have attracted many migrants because of good job opportunities. Inland, blazing desert and towering mountains provide some of the most dramatic landscapes in the country. National parks, such as Yellowstone in northwestern Wyoming and Montana, and Yosemite in central California, protect some of these wilderness areas. Further east, the foothills of the Rockies give way to vast plains grazed by large herds of cattle.

NORTHERN FORESTS

The coastal areas of Oregon and Washington contain large forests. These produce economically important timber, but much land is also left in its natural state and is popular with hikers. Most people here live in large cities like Seattle, and in the fertile inland valleys.

CALIFORNIA AGRICULTURE

California is warm, fertile, and, with irrigation, ideal for agriculture. Grapes are an important crop north of San Francisco in the Napa Valley. Further south, citrus crops, such as oranges also flourish. Premium farming land is under threat, however, as the population expands.

Did you know?

- The American Indian name for Death Valley is *Tomesha*, which means "land where the ground is on fire."

- The majority of the world's geysers and hot springs are in Yellowstone National Park.

LOS ANGELES

This sprawling city – the second largest in the USA – is home to migrants from all over the world, as well as from other states in the country. Sandwiched between the coast and the mountains, the city has massive air pollution problems. This mostly arises from the exhaust fumes from the high number of cars used by commuters on the city's highways.

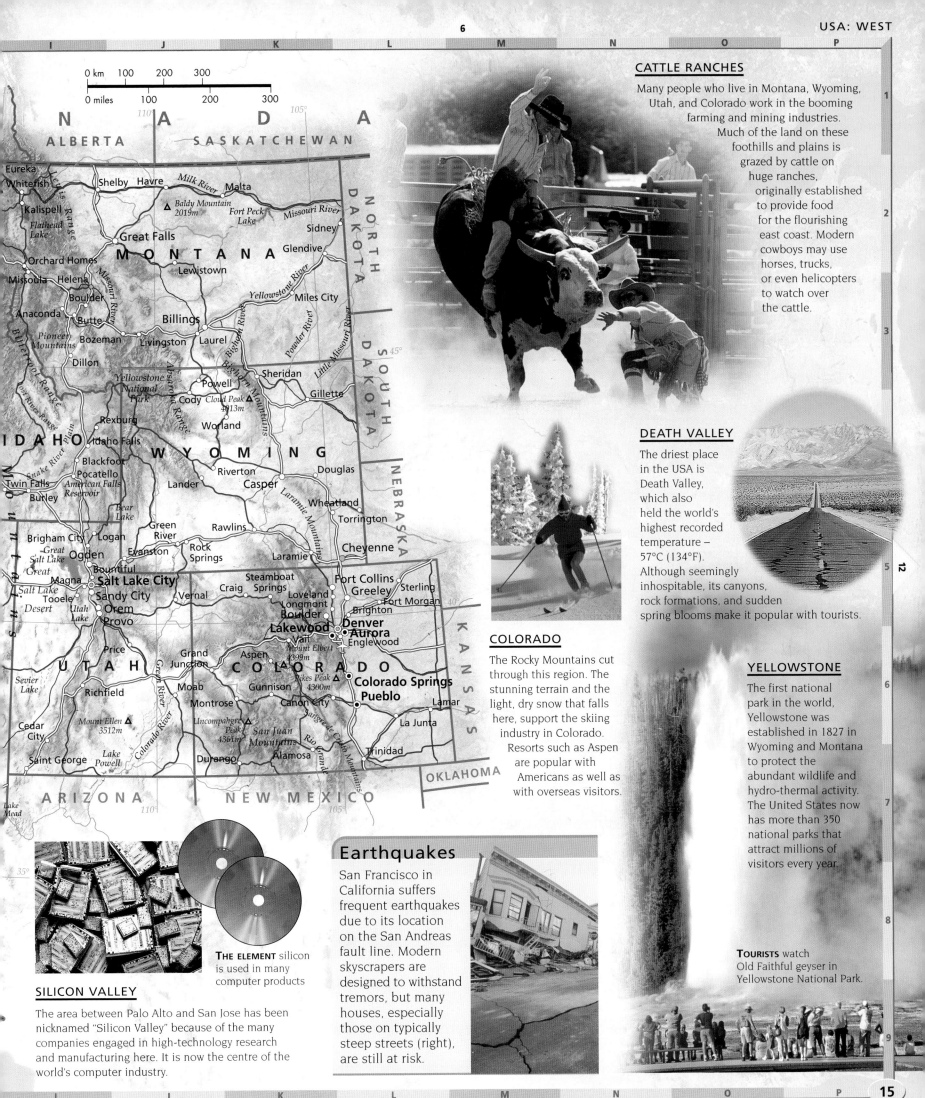

0 km 100 200 300

0 miles 100 200 300

CANADA

ALBERTA   SASKATCHEWAN

Eureka
Whitefish
Shelby Havre   Milk River   Malta
Kalispell
Flathead Lake
Baldy Mountain 2019m   Fort Peck Lake
Missouri River
Sidney
Great Falls
Orchard Homes
Glendive
MONTANA
Missoula Helena
Lewistown
Boulder
Anaconda
Butte Billings
Yellowstone River
Miles City
Pioneer Mountains
Bozeman
Livingston Laurel
Powder River
Little Missouri River
Dillon
Yellowstone National Park
Powell
Sheridan
Gillette
Cody   Cloud Peak 4013m
Rexburg
Worland
IDAHO
Idaho Falls
WYOMING
Blackfoot
Pocatello
Riverton
Douglas
Twin Falls
Lander Casper
Burley
American Falls Reservoir
Wheatland
Bear Lake
Torrington
Green River
Rawlins
Brigham City Logan
Cheyenne
Ogden Evanston Rock Springs
Laramie
Great Salt Lake
Bountiful
Salt Lake City
Steamboat Springs
Fort Collins
Greeley
Sterling
Magna
Sandy City
Craig
Loveland
Longmont
Fort Morgan
Salt Lake Desert
Orem
Vernal
Boulder
Brighton
Tooele
Provo
Lakewood
Denver
Utah Lake
Aurora
Englewood
Price
Vail
Mount Elbert 4399m
UTAH
Grand Junction
Aspen
Sevier Lake
Moab
Gunnison
COLORADO
Pikes Peak 4300m
Colorado Springs
Richfield
Montrose
Canon City
Pueblo
Mount Ellen 3512m
Uncompahgre Peak 4361m
San Juan Mountains
Lamar
Cedar City
La Junta
Colorado River
Durango
Alamosa
Rio Grande
Trinidad
Saint George
Lake Powell
OKLAHOMA
Lake Mead
ARIZONA   **NEW MEXICO**

NORTH DAKOTA
SOUTH DAKOTA
NEBRASKA
KANSAS

CATTLE RANCHES

Many people who live in Montana, Wyoming, Utah, and Colorado work in the booming farming and mining industries. Much of the land on these foothills and plains is grazed by cattle on huge ranches, originally established to provide food for the flourishing east coast. Modern cowboys may use horses, trucks, or even helicopters to watch over the cattle.

DEATH VALLEY

The driest place in the USA is Death Valley, which also held the world's highest recorded temperature – 57°C (134°F). Although seemingly inhospitable, its canyons, rock formations, and sudden spring blooms make it popular with tourists.

COLORADO

The Rocky Mountains cut through this region. The stunning terrain and the light, dry snow that falls here, support the skiing industry in Colorado. Resorts such as Aspen are popular with Americans as well as with overseas visitors.

YELLOWSTONE

The first national park in the world, Yellowstone was established in 1827 in Wyoming and Montana to protect the abundant wildlife and hydro-thermal activity. The United States now has more than 350 national parks that attract millions of visitors every year.

TOURISTS watch Old Faithful geyser in Yellowstone National Park.

THE ELEMENT silicon is used in many computer products

SILICON VALLEY

The area between Palo Alto and San Jose has been nicknamed "Silicon Valley" because of the many companies engaged in high-technology research and manufacturing here. It is now the centre of the world's computer industry.

Earthquakes

San Francisco in California suffers frequent earthquakes due to its location on the San Andreas fault line. Modern skyscrapers are designed to withstand tremors, but many houses, especially those on typically steep streets (right), are still at risk.

USA: Southwest

THE SOUTHWEST IS AN AREA of great contrasts. Much of Oklahoma and Texas consists of flat, rolling grasslands and huge farms, while both Arizona and New Mexico are hot, arid, and mountainous, with vast canyons and river valleys carving their way through the land. Since the discovery of oil in 1901, Texas has become the country's top oil producer after Alaska, with Houston as the centre of the billion-dollar industry. Tourism is also important to the southwest, as visitors flock to see the Grand Canyon, the Painted Desert, and other natural wonders. Buildings here reflect the mix of American Indians, Hispanic, European American, and modern American cultures.

SUBURBS OF PHOENIX, ARIZONA

HOT PLACE TO LIVE

The climate across much of the southwest is hot and dry, with summer temperatures often reaching 38°C (100°F). Although water can be scarce, many people have a swimming pool in their garden so they can cool off.

DESERT LIFE

The Saguaro cactus (left) can reach up to 15 m (50 ft) tall, grow as many as 40 branches, and live for 200 years. Cacti, yucca, and other plants have all adapted to the hot, dry desert conditions found in the southwest. So, too, have many animals, including the deadly rattlesnake.

SAGUARO CACTI in the Sonoran Desert

0 km 50 100 150 200

0 miles 50 100 150 200

THE GRAND CANYON

The Grand Canyon in northern Arizona is one of the natural wonders of the world. This incredibly deep gorge was slowly cut out of the rock by the Colorado River, beginning six million years ago. People can hike around its edge or venture down into the canyon to camp for the night.

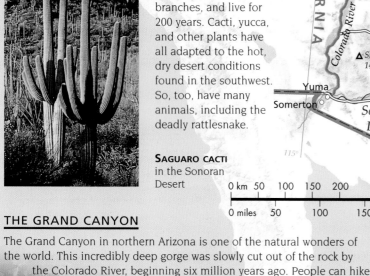

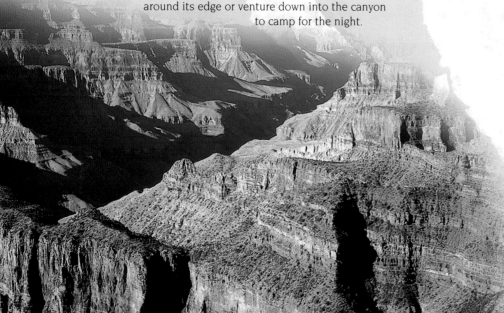

AMERICAN-INDIAN CULTURES

American Indians, including Navajo, Hopi, and Apache, used to live across the southwest but are now concentrated in reservations set up by the US government. The largest of these is in Arizona and New Mexico, and is home to the Navajo people. The Navajo farm the land and produce crafts, like the woven blanket wrapped around these Navajo children (below).

KACHINA dolls are made by the Hopi.

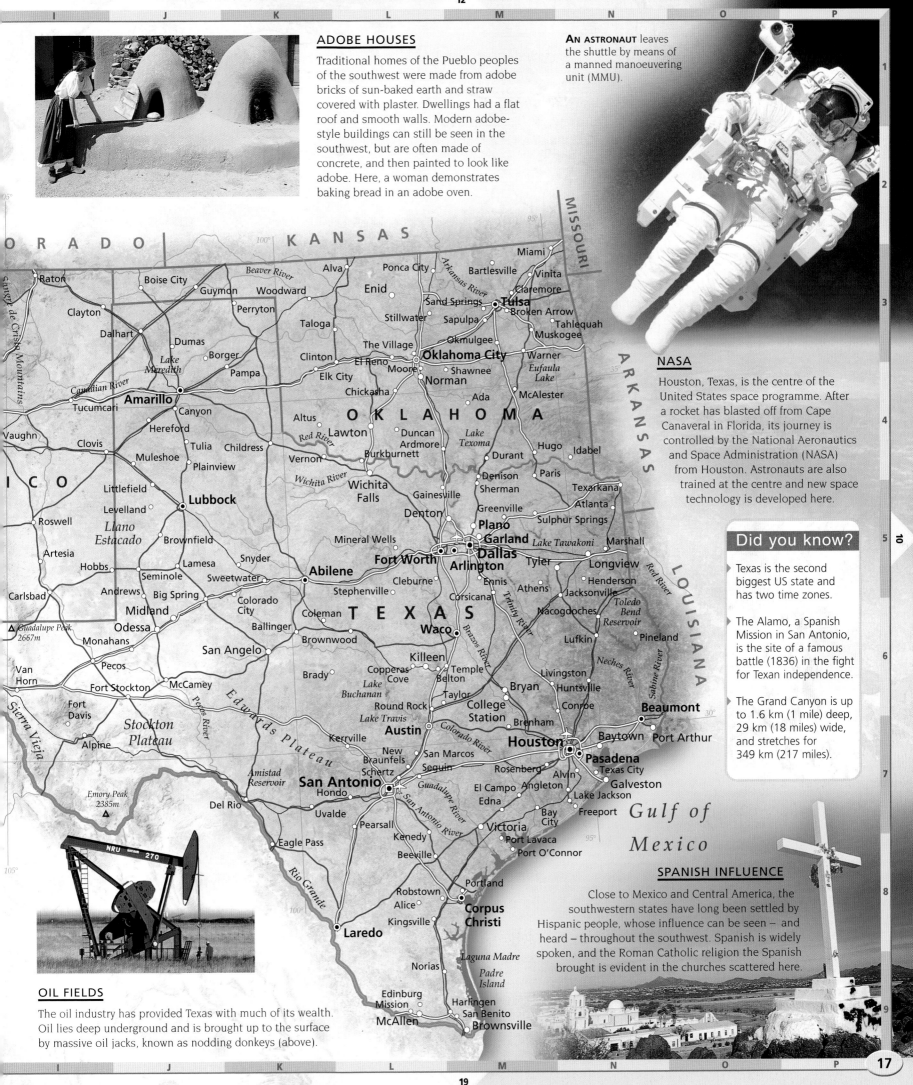

ADOBE HOUSES

Traditional homes of the Pueblo peoples of the southwest were made from adobe bricks of sun-baked earth and straw covered with plaster. Dwellings had a flat roof and smooth walls. Modern adobe-style buildings can still be seen in the southwest, but are often made of concrete, and then painted to look like adobe. Here, a woman demonstrates baking bread in an adobe oven.

AN ASTRONAUT leaves the shuttle by means of a manned manoeuvering unit (MMU).

NASA

Houston, Texas, is the centre of the United States space programme. After a rocket has blasted off from Cape Canaveral in Florida, its journey is controlled by the National Aeronautics and Space Administration (NASA) from Houston. Astronauts are also trained at the centre and new space technology is developed here.

Did you know?

▶ Texas is the second biggest US state and has two time zones.

▶ The Alamo, a Spanish Mission in San Antonio, is the site of a famous battle (1836) in the fight for Texan independence.

▶ The Grand Canyon is up to 1.6 km (1 mile) deep, 29 km (18 miles) wide, and stretches for 349 km (217 miles).

SPANISH INFLUENCE

Close to Mexico and Central America, the southwestern states have long been settled by Hispanic people, whose influence can be seen – and heard – throughout the southwest. Spanish is widely spoken, and the Roman Catholic religion the Spanish brought is evident in the churches scattered here.

OIL FIELDS

The oil industry has provided Texas with much of its wealth. Oil lies deep underground and is brought up to the surface by massive oil jacks, known as nodding donkeys (above).

Mexico

ONCE HOME TO THE great Aztec and Mayan civilizations, then the focus of Spanish conquistadors who came in search of wealth, the culture and architecture of Mexico today reflects its colourful past. The majority of Mexicans are *mestizo* (mixed race), of Spanish and native Indian descent. Mexico City, site of the ancient Aztec capital, is today one of the largest cities in the world, with a population of over 16 million. Despite oil and natural gas reserves, and a plentiful supply of labour, large numbers of Mexicans are still poor, especially in the rural areas and the urban slums.

ALONG THE BORDER

In 1994, Mexico signed the North American Free Trade Agreement (NAFTA), which effectively bound its economy to that of the USA. A large industrial area has developed along the Mexican border with the USA, and many American companies have relocated south of the border to benefit from the lower labour costs.

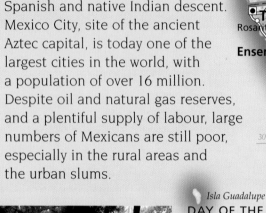

DAY OF THE DEAD

One of the biggest festivals in Mexico is the Day of the Dead. It is believed that once a year the souls of the dead can come back and visit their loved ones. In celebration of this, special food is prepared to welcome the souls, and offerings of flowers, candles, and incense are made at the gravesides.

LIFE IN THE CITY

Mexico City is the political, economic, and cultural hub of the country, and is home to some 16 million people. Its site, in a basin surrounded by a mountain, means that expansion is difficult. Air pollution from factories and cars cannot escape, so that on most days a thick layer of smog builds up over the city. Attempts to deal with the pollution, including banning cars from some parts, have had limited success.

THE VOLCANO
Popocatépetl is the highest peak around the city.

MEXICO CITY is contained within a ring of mountains.

WORKING ON THE LAND

Agriculture employs seven million people – about one-quarter of Mexico's work force. However, only 12 per cent of the land is suitable for farming because it is so mountainous and dry. The peasant communities of the south rely on farming for their food, while communities in the north are more industrialized. Here, the agave plant is being harvested near the town of Tequila.

UNITED STATES OF

Mexicali
Tijuana
Rosarito
Ensenada
San Luis
Ciudad Juárez
Nogales
Agua Prieta
Samalayuca
Cananea
Caborca
Magdalena
Cumpas
Nuevo
Casas Grandes
El Sueco
Ojinaga
El Sáuz
San Pedro
de la Cueva
Chihuahua
Delicias
Hermosillo
Cuauhtémoc
Ciudad Camargo
Empalme
Guaymas
Esperanza
Ciudad
Obregón
Navojoa
San Francisco
del Oro
Hidalgo
del Parral
Santa Barbara
Huatabampo
San Blas
Gómez Palacio
Los Mochis
Guasave
Guamúchil
Navolato
Culiacán
Durango
El Dorado
La Paz
Miraflores
Mazatlán
Escuinapa
Acaponeta
Tuxpan
Tepic
Puerto Vallarta
Manzanillo

Isla Guadalupe
Isla Ángel de la Guarda
Isla Tiburón
Isla Cedros
Guerrero Negro
San Ignacio
Isla Magdalena
Isla Santa Margarita
Bahía Sebastián Vizcaíno
Bahía de La Paz
Islas Marías
Loreto

Colorado River
Desierto de Altar
Sierra San Pedro Mártir
Río Bavispe
Río Yaqui
Río Grande
Río Bravo del Norte
Río Conchos
Santa Genoveva 2406m
Jiménez

Sierra Madre Occidental
Sierra de la Giganta

Baja California
Gulf of California

PACIFIC OCEAN

Tropic of Cancer

M E
M E X

TOURIST INDUSTRY

One of Mexico's largest employment sectors is tourism. The tourists are attracted by the numerous beautiful beaches on both the Pacific and Caribbean coasts, as well as Mexico's rich blend of history and culture. Popular tourist sites include the archaeological remains of the Aztec and Mayan civilizations, such as the Mayan ruins of the city of Palenque.

A MEXICAN sells baskets at Puerto Escondido

CHEWING GUM

Chicle is a latex produced by the sapodilla tree, native to the Yucatan Peninsula. In 1867, American inventor Thomas Adams added sugar to chicle pellets and invented an early form of chewing gum. This worker (right) is stretching heated chicle with a stick, preparing it to be made into chewing gum.

FAMILY TIES

Mexico has a large population, half of which are aged 21 or under. Very often extended families live together in one house, with the mother at the centre of the family. Mother's Day remains one of the most important dates in the Mexican calendar.

ANCIENT RULERS

The Aztecs ruled a large part of this region from about 1428 until 1521, when they were conquered by the Spanish. Their capital, Tenochtitlán, was located on the site that is now Mexico City. The influence of this great civilization has left its mark on Mexico – more than a million Mexicans speak Nahuatl, the native Aztec language. This feather headdress (left) is thought to have belonged to Moctezuma, the last Aztec ruler.

AZTEC HEADDRESS

Did you know?

▶ Mexico has the most Spanish-speaking people in the world, but there are also 62 native languages in use.

▶ Mexico is the world's main producer of silver, which is mined in the centre of the country.

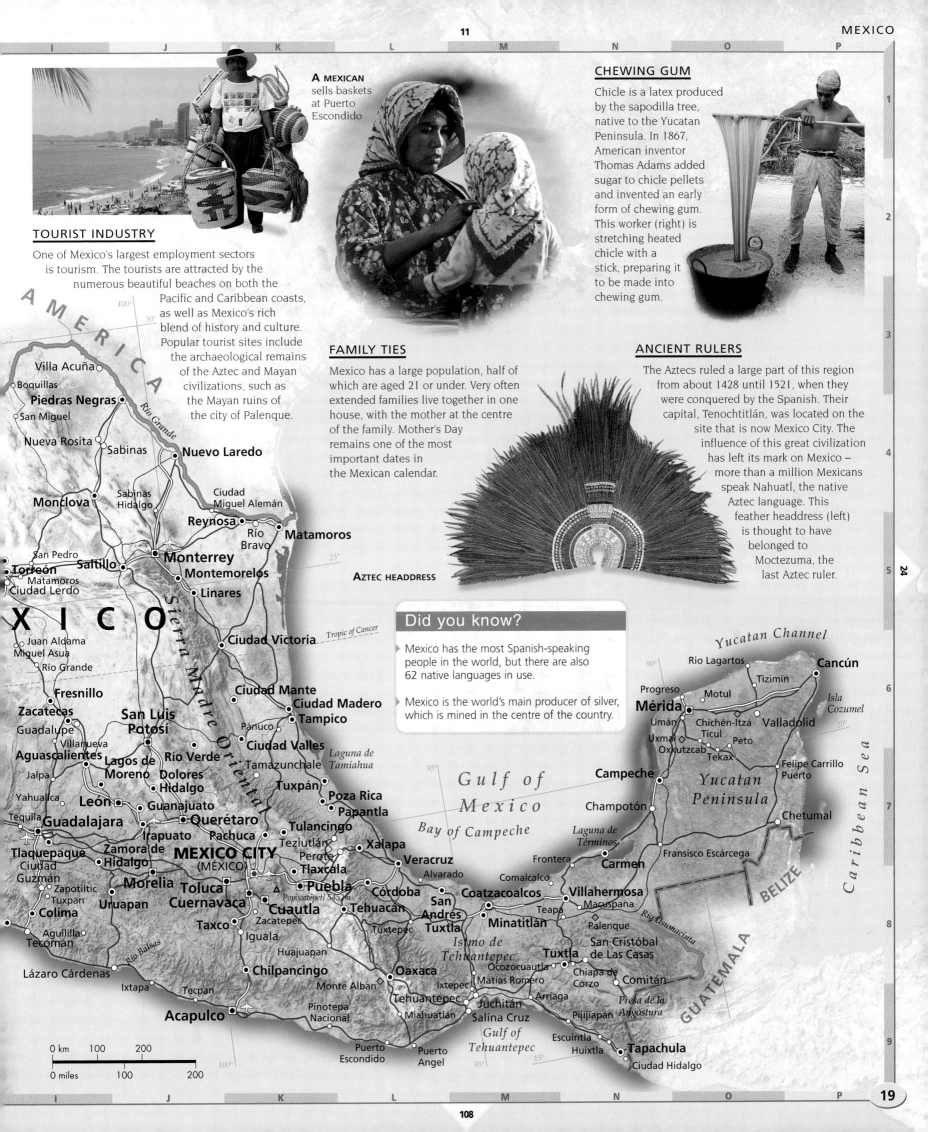

AMERICA

Villa Acuña
Boquillas
Piedras Negras
San Miguel
Nueva Rosita
Sabinas
Nuevo Laredo
Monclova
Sabinas Hidalgo
Ciudad Miguel Alemán
Reynosa
Río Bravo
Matamoros
San Pedro
Torreón **Saltillo**
Monterrey
Matamoros
Ciudad Lerdo
Montemorelos
Linares
M E X I C O
Juan Aldama
Miguel Asua
Río Grande
Fresnillo
Ciudad Victoria
Tropic of Cancer
Zacatecas
Guadalupe
Ciudad Mante
San Luis Potosí
Ciudad Madero
Tampico
Villanueva
Pánuco
Aguascalientes
Lagos de Moreno
Río Verde
Ciudad Valles
Jalpa
Tamazunchale
Laguna de Tamiahua
Yahualica
Dolores Hidalgo
León **Guanajuato**
Tequila
Guadalajara
Querétaro
Tulancingo
Poza Rica
Papantla
Gulf of Mexico
Irapuato
Pachuca
Teziutlán
Xalapa
Bay of Campeche
Tlaquepaque
Zamora de Hidalgo
MEXICO CITY (MÉXICO)
Perote
Tlaxcala
Veracruz
Ciudad Guzmán
Zapotiltic
Morelia **Toluca**
Puebla
Alvarado
Comalcalco
Tuxpan
Cuernavaca
Cuautla
Córdoba
San **Tehuacán**
Coatzacoalcos
Frontera
Carmen
Laguna de Términos
Colima
Uruapan
Taxco
Zacatepec
San Andrés
Villahermosa
Macuspana
Aguililla
Tuxtla
Popocatépetl 5452 m
Iguala
Tuxtepec
Minatitlán
Teapa
Palenque
Tecomán
Huajuapan
Istmo de Tehuantepec
San Cristóbal de Las Casas
Lázaro Cárdenas
Chilpancingo
Río Balsas
Oaxaca
Ocozocuautla
Chiapa de Corzo
Comitán
Ixtapa
Monte Alban
Ixtepec
Matías Romero
Presa de la Angostura
Tecpan
Tehuantepec
Tuxtla
Acapulco
Pinotepa Nacional
Miahuatlán
Juchitán
Arriaga
Salina Cruz
Pijijiapán
Gulf of Tehuantepec
Escuintla
Huixtla
Tapachula
Puerto Escondido
Puerto Angel
Ciudad Hidalgo

Yucatan Channel
Río Lagartos
Cancún
Progreso
Tizimín
Motul
Mérida
Chichén-Itzá
Valladolid
Isla Cozumel
Umán
Ticul
Peto
Uxmal
Oxkutzcab
Tekax
Felipe Carrillo Puerto
Campeche
Yucatan Peninsula
Champotón
Chetumal
Fransisco Escárcega
BELIZE
Caribbean Sea
GUATEMALA
Río Usumacinta

0 km   100   200
0 miles   100   200

CENTRAL & SOUTH
AMERICA

FROM THE VOLCANOES of Central America to the towering

Andes Mountains and vast grassy plains of South America,

this region offers a vast range of landscapes. South America is triangle-

shaped, tapering down from the warm Caribbean Sea

to the icy tip of Cape Horn. In the north lies the Amazon

rainforest, the largest tropical rainforest in the world. Some 420 million

people live in Central and South America, in 32 countries that vary in size

from small islands to the vast expanse of Brazil. The

languages, history, and cultures of this continent have

been shaped by colonization. The main influence has

been Spanish, which is still widely spoken. Portugal has

left its stamp on Brazil, while English, French, and Dutch influences remain

evident in several countries on the mainland and in the Caribbean.

Central America

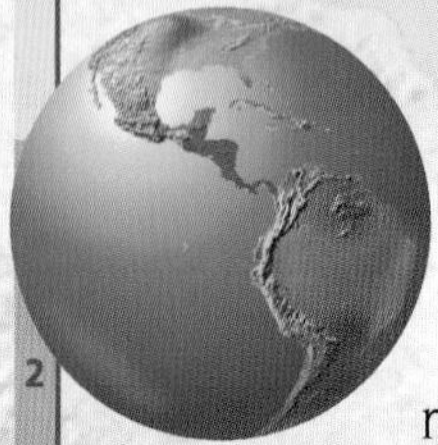

VOLCANOES, EARTHQUAKES, and hurricanes threaten the livelihoods of people in the seven countries of Central America. People have also struggled with poverty and civil war. In more recent years, however, peace and economic recovery have offered hope, and education is now free in all countries. Remains of the ancient Mayan civilization that flourished until the 16th century when the Spanish invaded, can be seen throughout the region. Large numbers of the native population died after the invasion, mostly from disease. Today, Spanish is the main language of the region.

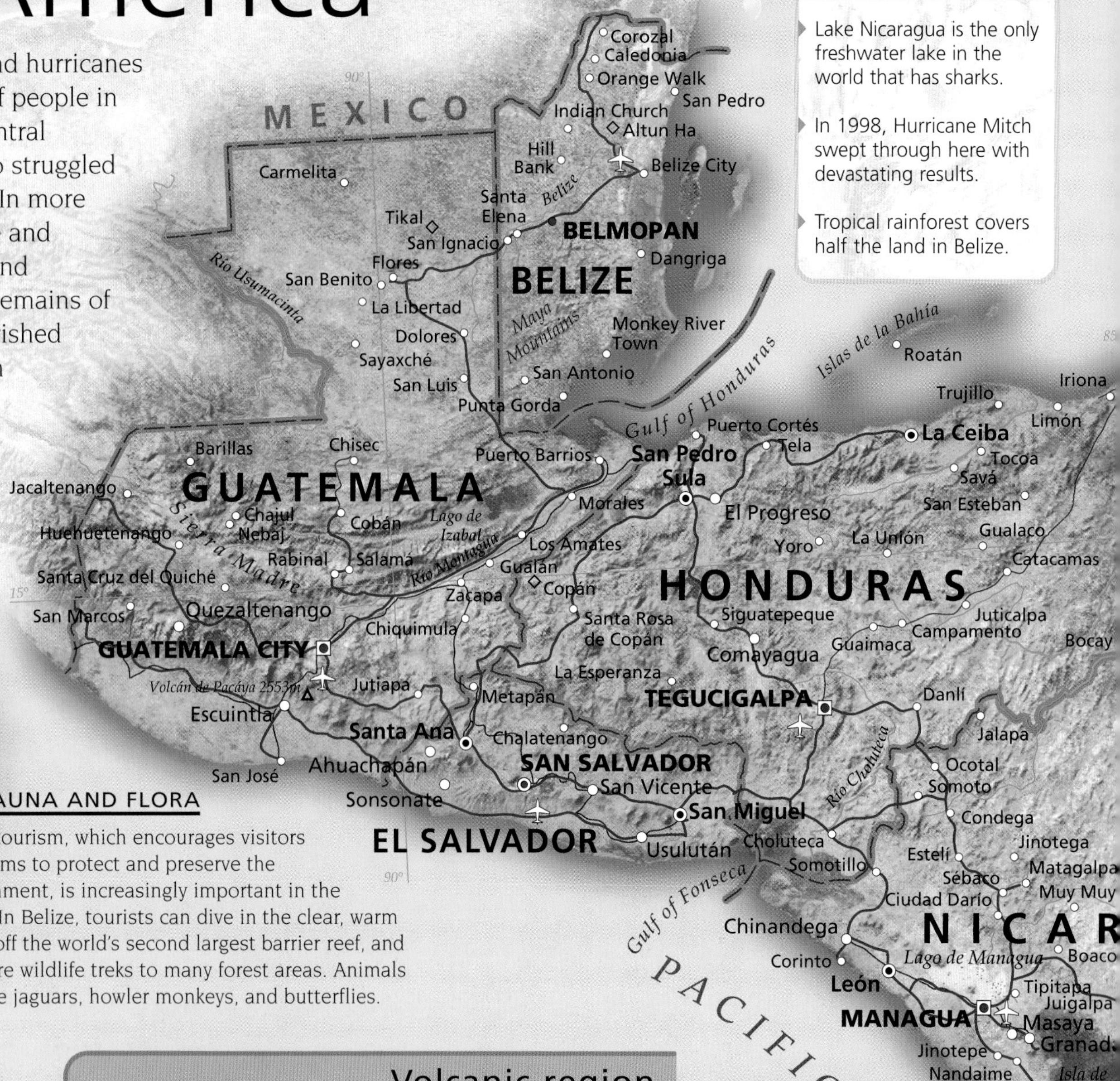

Did you know?

- Lake Nicaragua is the only freshwater lake in the world that has sharks.

- In 1998, Hurricane Mitch swept through here with devastating results.

- Tropical rainforest covers half the land in Belize.

FAUNA AND FLORA

Ecotourism, which encourages visitors but aims to protect and preserve the environment, is increasingly important in the region. In Belize, tourists can dive in the clear, warm waters off the world's second largest barrier reef, and there are wildlife treks to many forest areas. Animals include jaguars, howler monkeys, and butterflies.

TEMPLE PYRAMIDS

Between AD 250–900, the Maya designed ceremonial centres filled with temples, courts, and plazas. Without metal, they shaped tools from the solid lava of volcanoes to carve the limestone buildings. The largest site is at Tikal (left), in Guatemala, where temple remains lie in a huge area of tropical rainforest.

Pyramid has nine sloping terraces.

Steps lead up to the temple at the top.

Volcanic region

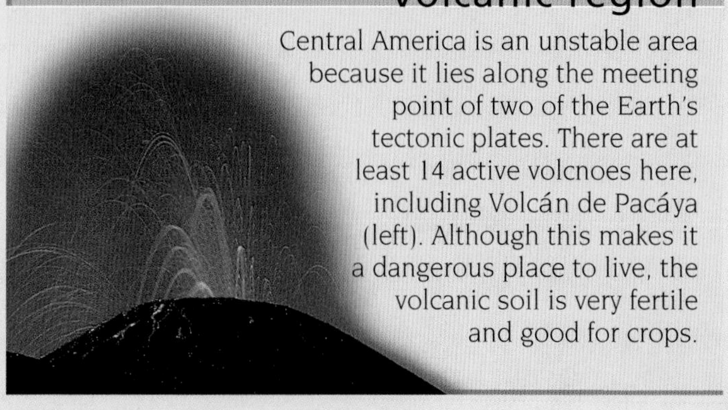

Central America is an unstable area because it lies along the meeting point of two of the Earth's tectonic plates. There are at least 14 active volcnoes here, including Volcán de Pacáya (left). Although this makes it a dangerous place to live, the volcanic soil is very fertile and good for crops.

DECORATED CHURCHES

The Spanish colonizers of the 1500s, and the missionaries who came with them, converted the native population and established Roman Catholicism throughout Central America. They also built many fabulously decorated churches. The one shown here, El Merced, is built in a low, "squat" style to resist the ever-present threat of earthquakes. The majority of people still follow the Roman Catholic faith.

Map labels

MEXICO

Corozal
Caledonia
Orange Walk
Indian Church
San Pedro
Altun Ha
Hill Bank
Belize City
Carmelita
Santa Elena
Tikal
BELMOPAN
San Ignacio
Flores
BELIZE
Dangriga
San Benito
Río Usumacinta
La Libertad
Dolores
Maya Mountains
Monkey River Town
Sayaxché
San Antonio
San Luis
Punta Gorda
Islas de la Bahía
Roatán
Barillas
Chisec
Gulf of Honduras
Puerto Cortés
Trujillo
Iriona
Limón
Puerto Barrios
San Pedro Sula
Tela
La Ceiba
Jacaltenango
GUATEMALA
Morales
El Progreso
Tocoa
Savá
San Esteban
Gualaco
Catacamas
Chajul
Nebaj
Cobán
Lago de Izabal
Los Amates
Yoro
La Unión
Huehuetenango
Rabinal
Salamá
Gualán
HONDURAS
Santa Cruz del Quiché
Sierra Madre
Zacapa
Río Motagua
Copán
Juticalpa
Campamento
San Marcos
Chiquimula
Santa Rosa de Copán
Siguatepeque
Guaimaca
Bocay
Quezaltenango
Comayagua
Danlí
GUATEMALA CITY
La Esperanza
TEGUCIGALPA
Jalapa
Volcán de Pacáya 2553m
Jutiapa
Metapán
Ocotal
Somoto
Escuintla
Santa Ana
Chalatenango
SAN SALVADOR
Condega
Jinotega
San José
Ahuachapán
San Vicente
Estelí
San Miguel
Coluteca
Sébaco
Matagalpa
Sonsonate
EL SALVADOR
Usulután
Somotillo
Ciudad Darío
Muy Muy
Gulf of Fonseca
Chinandega
NICAR
Corinto
Lago de Managua
Boaco
León
MANAGUA
Tipitapa
Juigalpa
Masaya
Granada
Jinotepe
Nandaime
Isla de Ometepe
Belén
Rivas
PACIFIC OCEAN
La Cruz
Golfo de Papagayo
Liberia
Filadelfia
Nicoya
Península de Nicoya

FOOD MARKETS

Coffee, bananas, and sugar cane are all key exports from here to the food markets of the world. Most are cultivated on large plantations. However, food for the local population, such as potatoes, avocados, rice, and maize, is grown on small farms and sold at local markets.

NATIVE PEOPLES

These Cuna Indians of Panama wear traditional embroidered clothes. Native Indians and mestizos (people of mixed heritage) form a small minority in the region, although the ethnic mix varies from country to country. In Guatemala, more than half the people are direct descendants of the Maya Indians.

MARKETS, such as this one in Guatemala City, sell fresh fruit and vegetables.

BANANA INDUSTRY

The hot, wet climate of Honduras is perfect for cultivating fruit, such as bananas. These are often grown on huge plantations, which employ local people who may work long hours for very little pay. Once cut down, the bananas are washed, inspected, and packed into boxes to be sent abroad. Bananas are a major export for Honduras.

As bananas grow, they begin to point upwards.

COFFEE BEANS

Costa Rica was the first country in Central America to grow coffee and, today, produces more than 160,000 tonnes each year. Coffee is harvested from the fruit of the coffee bush. Once picked, the beans are left to dry in the sun. This worker is raking the beans as they dry.

PANAMA CANAL

Forming a vital link between the Atlantic and Pacific Oceans, the Panama Canal is one of the world's busiest waterways. After sharing the canal with the US, Panama took full control in 1999. Over the years, trade has made Panama City a major financial centre.

Brus Laguna
Laguna de Caratasca
Puerto Lempira
Río Patuca
Río Coco
Cayos Miskitos
Waspam
Tuapi
Yablis
Bonanza
Puerto Cabezas
Siuna
Mosquito Coast
Prinzapolka
Barra de Río Grande
La Sirena
Laguna de Perlas
AGUA
El Rama
Bluefields
Lago de Nicaragua
Punta Gorda
San Carlos
San Juan del Norte
Upala
Río San Juan
Bagaces
Puerto Viejo
Cañas
Quesada
COSTA RICA
Alajuela
Heredia
Siquirres
SAN JOSÉ
Limón
Puntarenas
Cartago
Guabito
Caribbean Sea
Portobelo
Istmo de Panamá
El Porvenir
Colón
Cristóbal
Ailigandí
Cordillera de San Blas
Gulf of Darien
Cerro Chirripó Grande 3819m
Cordillera de Talamanca
Almirante
Panama Canal
Lago Gatún
San Miguelito
Lago Bayano
Puerto Obaldía
Quepos
Mosquito Gulf
Balboa
PANAMA CITY
Chimán
Buenos Aires
Laguna de Chiriquí
Capira
La Palma
Bahía de Coronado
Cortés
Palmar Sur
Volcán Barú 3475m
Penonomé
Archipiélago de las Perlas
Isla del Rey
El Real
Garaché
Yaviza
Boquete
Cordillera Central
Aguadulce
P A N A M A
Serranía del Darién
La Concepción
David
Santiago
Chitré
Jaqué
Península de Osa
Golfo Dulce
Ocú
Gulf of Panama
COLOMBIA
Golfo de Nicoya
Golfo de Chiriquí
Guarumal
Las Tablas
Peninsula de Azuero
Isla de Coiba
Isla Cébaco

0 km 50 100 150 200
0 miles 50 100 150 200

32

The Caribbean

UNITED STATES OF AMERICA

THIS REGION CONSISTS of thousands of islands stretching from Cuba in the west to Trinidad and Tobago in the east. European colonists wanted control of the islands in the 1500s, but the diseases they brought wiped out most of the local Carib and Arawak peoples. African slaves, imported to work on plantations, replaced local peoples and today most of the population are descended from those Africans. English, Spanish, and French are spoken in different countries, depending on which European power claimed the territory. Tourism and agriculture are major sources of employment.

Grand Bahama Island
Freeport
Marsh Harbour
Great Abaco
Bimini Islands
Berry Islands
Northeast Providence Channel
Nicholls Town
NASSAU
New Providence
Eleuthera Island
Rock Sound
Andros Town
Exuma Cays
Exuma Sound
Cat Island
Andros Island
San Salvador
Anguilla Cays
BAHAMAS
George Town
Great Exuma Island
Rum Cay
Long Island
Clarence Town
Crooked Island Passage
Crooked Island
Acklins Island
Mayaguana Passage

HAVANA (LA HABANA)
Tropic of Cancer
Straits of Florida
Pinar del Río
Artemisa
Guanabacoa
Cárdenas
Matanzas
Consolación del Sur
Sagua la Grande
Santa Clara
Cienfuegos
Placetas
Archipiélago de Camagüey
Nueva Gerona
Cayo Largo
Sancti Spíritus
Morón
Ciego de Ávila
Ragged Island Range
CUBA
Isla de la Juventud
Bahía de Cochino
Nuevitas
Lake Rosa
Archipiélago de los Canarreos
Camagüey
Matthew Town
Yucatan Channel
Archipiélago de los Jardines de la Reina
Las Tunas
Holguín
Manzanillo
Bayamo
Guantánamo
Cayman Brac
Palma Soriano
Santiago de Cuba
Windward Passage
Little Cayman
GEORGE TOWN
Grand Cayman
Guantánamo Bay (to US)
Île de la Gonâve
NAVASSA ISLAND (to US)
Jérémie
CAYMAN ISLANDS (to UK)
Montego Bay
Greater
Jamaica Channel
Cayes
Spanish Town
JAMAICA
KINGSTON
Caribbean Sea

CUBA

Cuba is the largest island and the only communist country in the region. It has a rich mix of people and customs. The Cuban government invested its money in improving social services so the people benefit from a good health service and a high literacy rate. Children who complete pre-university education are awarded the *Bachillerato*.

CUBA specializes in making top-quality cigars.

JAMAICA

The Rastafarian religion began in Kingston, Jamaica, in the 1930s. Followers worship Haile Selassie, the former Emperor of Ethiopia (Ras Tafari), and believe that God will lead black people back to Ethiopia, the Promised Land. Jamaica is also home to reggae music, a rhythmic blend of African, European, and South American styles that can be heard across the island. The lyrics often tell of hardship and political struggle.

THE RASTAFARIAN religion forbids the cutting of hair.

Did you know?

▶ The Bahamas consists of hundreds of coral islands, but only about 40 of them are inhabited.

▶ The most densely populated country is Barbados.

▶ Steel bands, which use old oil drums as instruments, originated in Trinidad and Tobago.

▶ Rastafarians often wear red, green, and yellow because these are the colours of the Ethiopian flag.

| 0 km | 50 | 100 | 150 | 200 |
| 0 miles | 50 | 100 | 150 | 200 |

CARIBBEAN CROPS

The semi-tropical climate here creates ideal conditions for many crops, especially sugar. The growing and processing of sugar is an important industry in Cuba, Jamaica, and many of the Lesser Antilles, providing jobs and income for the region. Fermented cane sugar is used to make rum and is a major export.

Sugar cane
Breadfruit
Sweet potato
Papaya
Okra

Hurricanes

The Caribbean islands can be devastated by hurricanes between May and October each year. These powerful and damaging storms occur when a normal storm builds up energy as it moves across the Atlantic Ocean. Eventually, violent winds and torrential rain are released on the islands.

FAMILY LIFE

Family is very important here, and is usually the centre of everyday life. Some Caribbean people migrated to other countries, such as the UK, but return when they retire – often bringing considerable money back with them.

TROPICAL ISLES

White sands and warm seas attract vast numbers of visitors to these islands. Tourism is important to the economies of many countries including the Bahamas and the Dominican Republic. Many people work in tourism-related jobs, such as in hotels.

HAITI

Haiti was the first Caribbean country to become independent. However, political unrest, combined with poor soils, have made Haiti one of the poorest countries in the world. Health care and sanitation levels are poor and, as a result, life expectancy is low.

HAITIAN MAN selling flowers

A TIME TO CELEBRATE

The celebration of Divali (Hindu), Eid-ul-Fitr (Muslim), and Christmas (Christian) reflect the varied religions of people in Trinidad and Tobago. The woman above is dressed for Carnival in Port of Spain to mark the beginning of the Christian season of Lent.

Tropic of Cancer

Mayaguana

Caicos Passage

TURKS & CAICOS ISLANDS
(to UK)

Little Inagua

Great Inagua

● **COCKBURN TOWN**

DOMINICAN REPUBLIC

Monte Cristi

Cap-Haïtien

Puerto Plata

Santiago

San Francisco de Macorís

● Gonaïves

HAITI

Cordillera Central

La Vega

La Romana

PORT-AU-PRINCE

SANTO DOMINGO

Isla Saona

Jacmel

Isla Beata

Mona Passage

Isla Mona

n t i l l e s

SAN JUAN

Caguas

Ponce

Mayagüez

PUERTO RICO
(to US)

VIRGIN ISLANDS
(to US)

BRITISH VIRGIN ISLANDS
(to UK)

ROAD TOWN

CHARLOTTE AMALIE

St Croix

L e e w a r d

ANGUILLA
(to UK)

THE VALLEY

Sint Maarten
(to Netherlands)

ANTIGUA & BARBUDA

Barbuda

BASSETERRE

Antigua

ST JOHN'S

SAINT KITTS & NEVIS

MONTSERRAT
(to UK)

PLYMOUTH

Grande Terre

Pointe-à-Pitre

GUADELOUPE
(to France)

BASSE-TERRE

Marie-Galante

Basse-Terre

DOMINICA

● **ROSEAU**

Martinique

Pass

MARTINIQUE
(to France)

FORT-DE-FRANCE

St Lucia Channel

ST LUCIA ● **CASTRIES**

Vieux Fort

Saint Vincent Passage

BARBADOS

Saint Vincent

SAINT VINCENT & THE GRENADINES

KINGSTOWN

The Grenadines

BRIDGETOWN

GRENADA **ST GEORGE'S**

A T L A N T I C *O C E A N*

Islands

L e s s e r A n t i l l e s

L e s s e r A n t i l l e s

W i n d w a r d I s l a n d s

ARUBA
(to Netherlands)

NETHERLANDS ANTILLES
(to Netherlands)

ORANJESTAD

Curaço

Bonaire

● **WILLEMSTAD**

COLOMBIA

VENEZUELA

Tobago

PORT-OF-SPAIN

TRINIDAD & TOBAGO

Trinidad

Gulf of Paria

San Fernando

Northwest South America

HIGH MOUNTAINS AND PLATEAUS, dense tropical rainforest, and coastal swamps are found in this region. In the 16th century, promises of untold riches attracted the Spanish to the countries here. They found the vast empire of the Incas, which stretched from what is now Peru into Northern Colombia. To the north and east, other colonizers arrived – Dutch, English, and French. Today, although the countries are independent, with the exception of French Guiana, Spanish remains the main language. The population is mainly a mix of native peoples and Europeans, except along the Caribbean coast where descendants of former African slaves live.

ANDES MOUNTAINS

The Andes, the world's longest mountain chain, extends 7,250 km (4,505 miles) down the western edge of South America. Barley, wheat, and potatoes grow well in highland areas, and are cultivated on the terraced hillsides.

FRENCH GUIANA

French Guiana is the only remaining colony in South America, and is governed by France. Tropical forests cover more than four-fifths of its land. In 1968, the European Space Agency established a launch site on the coast at Kourou, which is still used today.

CARACAS

Venezuela's population is growing rapidly and more than 87 per cent of the people now live in cities. The oil industry brings in considerable wealth, but many people are still poor. Although Caracas (left), Venezuela's capital city, is an important financial centre, it has many shantytowns.

Map labels

ATLANTIC OCEAN

CAYENNE
Ouanary
St-Georges
Camopi
Sinnamary
Kourou
St-Laurent-du-Maroni
Grand-Santi
FRENCH GUIANA (to France)
Tumuc-Humac Mountains (claimed by Suriname)

PARAMARIBO
New Amsterdam
Totness
Apoera
SURINAME
Courantyne River
(claimed by Suriname)

GEORGETOWN
Charity
Matthews Ridge
Aurora
Linden
Orealla
Lethem
Kurupukari
Kamarang
GUYANA
Essequibo River
Peters Mine
(Venezuela claims all of Guyana west of Essequibo River)

Toba go
TRINIDAD & TOBAGO
Trinidad
Isla Blanquilla
Isla de Margarita
Porlamar
La Asunción
Carúpano
Cumaná
Puerto La Cruz
Barcelona
Maturín
Tucupita
Ciudad Guayana
Upata
El Tigre
Anaco
El Callao
El Dorado
Angel Falls
Kamarang
Pakaraima Mountains
Guiana Highlands
BRAZIL

CARACAS
Maracay
Valencia
Valle de la Pascua
Ciudad Bolívar
San Fernando
VENEZUELA
Rio Orinoco
Río Caroní
Río Caura
Río Paragua

Puerto Ayacucho
Puerto Carreño
Río Meta

Caribbean Sea
Puerto López
Puerto Fijo
Coro
Maracaibo
Cabimas
Ciudad Ojeda
Barquisimeto
Valera
El Vigía
Mérida
San Cristóbal
Acarigua
Guanare
Barinas
Gulf of Darién

Santa Marta
Riohacha
Barranquilla
Soledad
Cartagena
Sincelejo
Montería
Valledupar
Aguachica
Bucaramanga
Barrancabermeja
Cúcuta
PANAMA

Medellín
Dabeiba
Bello
Quibdó
Manizales
Pereira
Armenia
Tuluá
Cali
Buenaventura
Popayán
Pasto
Tumaco
Nuquí
Caucasia
Río Cauca
Central
Yarumal
Tunja
Zipaquira
Ibagué
Palmira
Neiva
Garzón
Pitalito
Mocoa
Florencia
Sogamoso
Yopal
BOGOTÁ
Villavicencio
COLOMBIA
San José del Guaviare
Mitú
Río Vaupés
Río Meta
Río Guaviare
Río Apaporis

Esmeraldas
Santo Domingo de los Colorados
Manta
Portoviejo
Guayaquil
Machala
Tumbes
Ibarra
Tulcán
QUITO
Ambato
Riobamba
Milagro
Cuenca
Loja
ECUADOR
Equator
Iquitos
Río Putumayo
Río Napo
Río Caquetá
Amazon

PACIFIC OCEAN

ANGEL FALLS

Each year thousands of tourists visit the spectacular Angel Falls on the River Churún in eastern Venezuela. They were spotted by an American pilot, Jimmy Angel, in 1935, and later named after him. The water drops for 979 m (3,212 ft), making Angel Falls the highest uninterrupted waterfall in the world.

Did you know?

One-tenth of Suriname is now a nature reserve, established to protect the rainforests.

The railway from Lima climbs 4,818 m (15,806 ft) into the Andes and is the highest in the world.

Potatoes were first grown in the Peruvian Andes by the Incas. Flour was made from the dried potatoes.

THE INCAS

The Incas first lived in the mountainous area near Cusco in Peru. By the time of the Spanish invasion, the Inca Empire extended north into southern Colombia and south through Bolivia and into Argentina and Chile. The Quechua Indians were the most powerful group in the empire, and theirs was the official language. The Quechua and Aymará peoples now live on the high plains in the Andes.

QUECHUA woman from Peru

LIFE ON THE HIGH PLAINS

The Altiplano is a cold plateau at high altitude between two ranges of the Andes Mountains in southwest Bolivia and southern Peru. The native peoples who live here graze sheep and llamas on the windy plains. They have generally retained their own language and customs.

MACHU PICCHU

The conquering Spaniards never found the remains of this important Inca city – it remained a secret until Hiram Bingham, an American archaeologist and explorer, discovered its ruins hidden in the forest in 1911. Situated on a high ridge northwest of Cusco, this magnificent ruined city covers 13 sq km (5 sq miles), and has small houses, temples, and stairways built around a central square.

MINERALS

Many countries in this area have extensive reserves of gold, silver, copper, and gems. Colombia produces more than half the world's emeralds. The Incas made good use of these resources and created many beautiful golden objects, such as this llama (below).

LAKE TITICACA

At 3,812 m (12,503 ft), Lake Titicaca is the highest navigable lake in the world. It is also South America's largest lake. The Uru people live here in houses built on huge, floating reed islands. They grow potatoes, hunt birds, and catch fish, using boats made from tightly bundled reeds (right).

Brazil

THE VIBRANT CULTURE OF BRAZIL – with its fusion of music and dance – reflects the rich mix of its ethnic groups. The country also boasts immense natural resources with well-developed mining and manufacturing industries. Brazil grows all its own food, and exports large quantities of coffee, sugar cane, soya beans, oranges, and cotton. However, the wealth is not evenly distributed, with some people living in luxury, while most struggle with poverty. São Paulo is home to almost 10 million people, but poverty and lack of housing means that many live in shantytowns without running water or sanitation. Brazil was colonized in the 16th century by the Portuguese, who established their language and their Roman Catholic faith. It remains a deeply Catholic country with a strong emphasis on family life.

COFFEE

Brazil produces about one-quarter of the world's coffee, which is grown on large plantations in the states of Parana and São Paulo. However, as world coffee prices go up and down so much, Brazilians are now growing other crops for export as well.

AMAZON RAINFOREST

Covering more than one-third of Brazil, the rainforest is home to a huge variety of animal and plant life. At one time, more than 5 million native Indians also lived here, but now only about 200,000 remain. Over the years, vast areas of forest have been cut down to provide timber for export, to make way for farmland, or to mine minerals such as gold, silver, and iron. The Kaxinawa Indians (left) still cultivate root vegetables as a food crop.

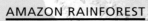

THE BRAZILIAN morpho butterfly has brilliant blue wings and lives in rainforests from Brazil to Venezuela.

BRASÍLIA

Brasília became Brazil's new capital (after Rio de Janeiro) in 1960 as part of a scheme to develop the interior. Situated on land that was once rainforest, the city is laid out in the shape of an aeroplane. Government buildings are in the "cockpit", residential areas are in the "wings".

FOOTBALL ENTHUSIASTS

Brazilians are passionate about football, which is played everywhere from beaches to shantytowns. There is fervent support for the national team, which has won the World Cup more times than any other country, most recently in 2002.

PEOPLE OF BRAZIL

Brazilians come from a variety of different ethnic groups, including descendants of the original native Indians, the Portuguese colonizers, African slaves brought over to work in the sugar plantations, and European migrants.

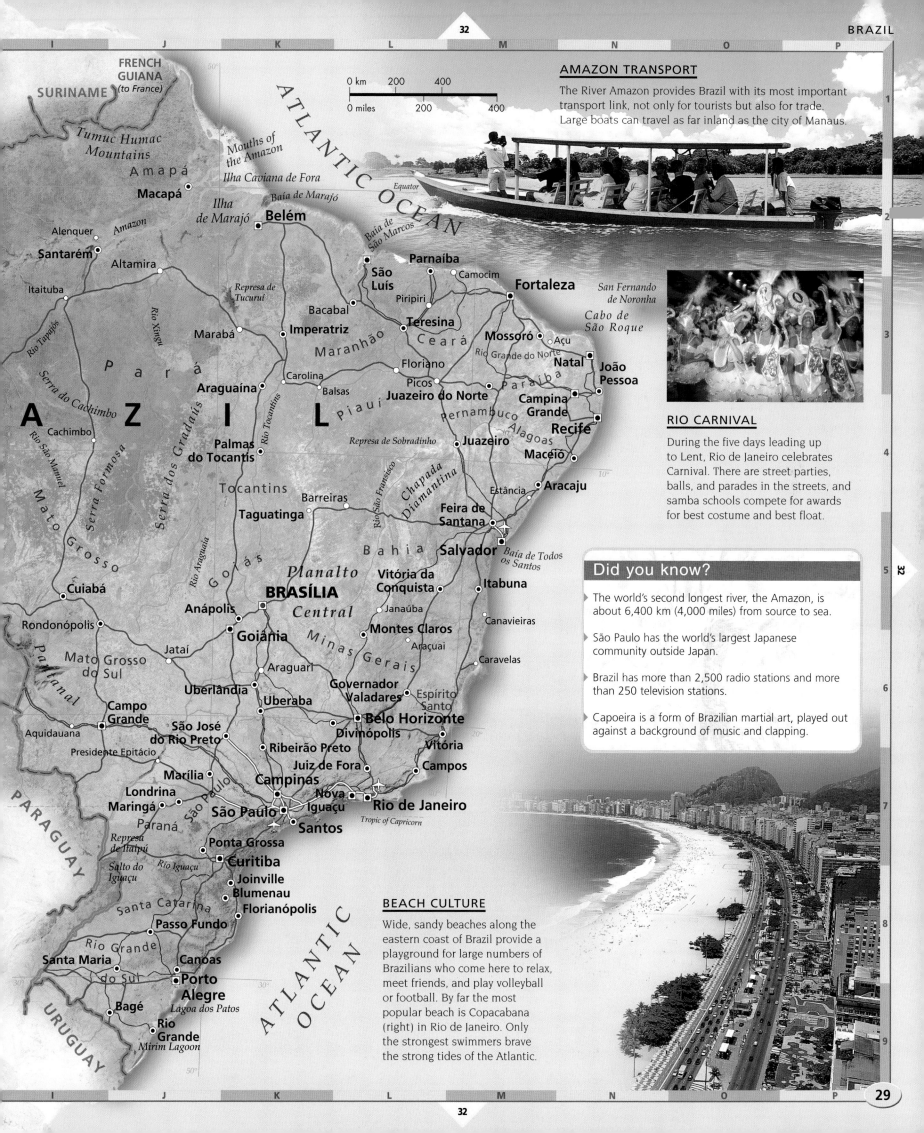

FRENCH GUIANA
(to France)
SURINAME

Tumuc Humac Mountains

Amapá

Macapá

Mouths of the Amazon

Ilha Caviana de Fora

ATLANTIC OCEAN

Alenquer

Amazon

Baía de Marajó

Equator

Belém

Ilha de Marajó

Baía de São Marcos

Santarém

Altamira

Itaituba

Represa de Tucuruí

Parnaíba

São Luís

Camocim

Fortaleza

San Fernando de Noronha

Marabá

Imperatriz

Bacabal

Teresina

Cabo de São Roque

Rio Tapajós

Rio Xingu

P a r á

Maranhão

Ceará

Mossoró

Açu

Rio São Manuel

Serra do Cachimbo

Araguaína

Carolina

Floriano

Picos

Natal

João Pessoa

Rio Grande do Norte

Paraíba

Cachimbo

A Z I L

Serra dos Gradaús

Balsas

Juazeiro do Norte

Piauí

Pernambuco

Campina Grande

Recife

Serra Formosa

Palmas do Tocantis

Rio Tocantins

Represa de Sobradinho

Juazeiro

Alagoas

Maceió

Tocantins

Rio São Francisco

Chapada Diamantina

Estância

Aracaju

Mato Grosso

Barreiras

B a h i a

Feira de Santana

Taguatinga

Planalto

Vitória da Conquista

Salvador

Baía de Todos os Santos

Cuiabá

Goiás

BRASÍLIA

Janaúba

Itabuna

Rio Araguaia

Anápolis

Central

Rondonópolis

Goiânia

Montes Claros

Canavieiras

Jataí

Minas Gerais

Araçuaí

Mato Grosso do Sul

Araguari

Caravelas

Aquidauana

Uberlândia

Uberaba

Governador Valadares

Espírito Santo

Campo Grande

Belo Horizonte

Presidente Epitácio

São José do Rio Preto

Divinópolis

Vitória

Pantanal

Ribeirão Preto

Campos

Marília

Juiz de Fora

Londrina

Campinas

Maringá

São Paulo

Nova Iguaçu

Rio de Janeiro

Paraná

São Paulo

Tropic of Capricorn

Santos

Represa de Itaipú

Ponta Grossa

PARAGUAY

Rio Iguaçu

Curitiba

Salto do Iguaçu

Joinville

Blumenau

Florianópolis

Santa Catarina

Passo Fundo

Rio Grande

Santa Maria

Canoas

do Sul

Porto Alegre

ATLANTIC OCEAN

Bagé

Lagoa dos Patos

URUGUAY

Rio Grande

Mirim Lagoon

AMAZON TRANSPORT

The River Amazon provides Brazil with its most important transport link, not only for tourists but also for trade. Large boats can travel as far inland as the city of Manaus.

RIO CARNIVAL

During the five days leading up to Lent, Rio de Janeiro celebrates Carnival. There are street parties, balls, and parades in the streets, and samba schools compete for awards for best costume and best float.

Did you know?

▶ The world's second longest river, the Amazon, is about 6,400 km (4,000 miles) from source to sea.

▶ São Paulo has the world's largest Japanese community outside Japan.

▶ Brazil has more than 2,500 radio stations and more than 250 television stations.

▶ Capoeira is a form of Brazilian martial art, played out against a background of music and clapping.

BEACH CULTURE

Wide, sandy beaches along the eastern coast of Brazil provide a playground for large numbers of Brazilians who come here to relax, meet friends, and play volleyball or football. By far the most popular beach is Copacabana (right) in Rio de Janeiro. Only the strongest swimmers brave the strong tides of the Atlantic.

Southern South America

TOWERING MOUNTAINS, vast grassy plains, and hot deserts create a very diverse geographical landscape. The four countries in this region – Chile, Paraguay, Uruguay, and Argentina – were once Spanish colonies but gained their independence in the early 1800s. Each country has an elected government but their economies remain fragile. Most of the population speak Spanish and are mestizo – of mixed Spanish and native Indian descent – except for Argentina, where 97 per cent are descended from Europeans.

Atacama Desert

Sandwiched between the high Andes and the sea, the Atacama Desert in northern Chile is one of the hottest and driest areas in the world. Rain hardly ever falls here. This harsh landscape, however, is rich in copper deposits.

ITAIPÚ DAM

The enormous Itaipú dam on the Paraná River in Paraguay is one of the world's largest hydro-electric projects. It can generate all the electricity Paraguay needs as well as large amounts for export.

URUGUAY'S CAPITAL

The capital of Uruguay, Montevideo, is home to nearly half the country's population. It is also the main port and economic centre. This lively capital lies on the east bank of the Río de la Plata, and is a popular holiday resort because of its white sandy beaches.

MONTEVIDEO's rich history shows in the mix of Colonial Spanish, Italian, and art deco styles of architecture.

CHILEAN EDUCATION

Chile has the highest literacy rate (ability to read and write) in all of South America. Between the ages of 6 and 13 schooling is both free and compulsory.

26

28

108

DANCING THE TANGO

Popular around the world today, the tango originated in the slums of Buenos Aires in the late 1800s. This passionate dance with its characteristic rhythm is accompanied by music on a type of concertina known as a *bandoneon*, together with piano and violin.

Did you know?

- The national drink in South America is *mate*. This healthy tea is made from a bitter herb, and drinking it with friends is a daily custom for most people.

- Across the region, four out of every five people live in cities.

- Chile has the largest concentration of astronomical observatories in the world because of its exceptionally clear skies.

BUENOS AIRES

More than one-third of Argentina's population lives in or around the capital Buenos Aires. A thriving port on the River Plate estuary, it is the largest city in Argentina. The colourful La Boca district (above) with its painted walls is home to the descendants of Italian immigrants.

A GAUCHO herds cattle in the Pampas region.

PAMPAS

Vast, treeless plains called the Pampas – which means "flat" in Spanish – cover much of southern and western Argentina. The Pampas are used to grow cereals and raise cattle. Gauchos, Argentinian cowboys, work on large ranches, or *estancias*.

WINES FROM CHILE

About 90 per cent of Chileans live in the central region, where the rich soil is ideal for a wide range of agriculture. Vines were brought to Chile by the Spaniards, and the country now has an important wine-making industry that exports wine all over the world.

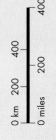

ANDES MOUNTAIN WEATHER

The Andes stretch the entire length of South America, and this has a major effect on the weather. As westerly air from the Pacific Ocean rises over the mountains, its moisture can fall as rain and snow. By the time it reaches the eastern side, the air is much drier and the landscape is more arid.

0 km   200   400

0 miles   200   400

Map labels

ATLANTIC OCEAN

ARGENTINA

CHILE

PACIFIC OCEAN

Santa Rosa
Olavarría
Azul
Tandil
Necochea
Mar del Plata
Dolores
Balcarce
Tres Arroyos
Coronel Dorrego
Bahía Blanca
Bahía Blanca
Punta Alta
Choele Choel
San Antonio Oeste
Viedma
Golfo San Matías
Península Valdés
Golfo Nuevo
Rawson
Trelew
Río Negro
Río Colorado
Cipolletti
Neuquén
Zapala
Maquinchao
Río Chubut
Río Chico
Comodoro Rivadavia
Golfo San Jorge
Caleta Olivia
Puerto Deseado
Río Deseado
Puerto San Julián
Río Chico
Río Santa Cruz
Bahía Grande
Río Gallegos
Strait of Magellan
Isla de los Estados
Beagle Channel
Cape Horn (Cabo de Hornos)
Tierra del Fuego
Porvenir
Ushuaia
Punta Arenas
Puerto Natales
Cochrane
Chile Chico
Cerro San Valentín 4058m
Coihaique
Puerto Aisén
Golfo de Penas
Archipiélago de los Chonos
Golfo Corcovado
Ancud
Castro
Isla de Chiloé
Puerto Montt
Osorno
Puerto Varas
Loncoche
Valdivia
Temuco
Río Bío Bío
Los Ángeles
Concepción
Talcahuano
Chillán
Parral
Linares
Lebu
San Carlos de Bariloche
Nahuel Huapi
Lago Nahuel Huapi
Esquel
Paso de Indios
Lago Musters
Sarmiento
Lago Buenos Aires
Perito Moreno
El Calafate
Cerro Murillo Sur 3050m
Cerro Paine 2670m
Isla Wellington
Penuajó
Lauquen
la Plata
Nahuel Huapi

Atlantic Ocean

THE WORLD'S SECOND LARGEST OCEAN, the Atlantic covers one-fifth of the Earth's surface. It separates the Americas from Europe and Africa. The world's youngest ocean, the Atlantic started to form about 180 million years ago, as the continental plates began to separate. This movement continues today, as the oceanic plates that meet at the Mid-Atlantic Ridge continue to pull apart. The Atlantic is a major source of fish, but due to overfishing, stocks are now low. Many shipping routes cross the Atlantic, and pollution is an international problem as ships dump chemicals and waste. There are substantial reserves of oil and gas in the Gulf of Mexico, off the coast of West Africa, and in the North Atlantic.

GREENLAND

The largest island in the world, Greenland is a self-governing part of Denmark. Most Greenlanders live on the southwest coast. Mainly Inuit, with some Danish-Norwegian influences, they make their living by seal hunting, fishing, and fur trapping.

Fishing for halibut

TOURISM

The volcanic islands and black beaches of the eastern Atlantic, especially the Canaries (left), Madeira, and the Azores, are popular with tourists, who are attracted by the scenery and sub-tropical climate.

Warm currents

The Gulf Stream flows up the east coast of North America and across the Atlantic. It brings warm water and a mild climate to northern Europe, which would otherwise be cooler.

MID-ATLANTIC RIDGE

Tristan da Cunha island

At the centre of the ridge is a valley at least 16 km (10 miles) wide.

UNDERWATER MOUNTAINS

The Mid-Atlantic Ridge is a great underwater mountain chain that runs the entire length of the Atlantic. It was formed by magma that oozed up from the seabed, cooled to create solid rock, and gradually built up to form a ridge. Some peaks are so high that they break the surface to form volcanic islands such as the country of Iceland.

ATLANTIC FISHING INDUSTRY

The Atlantic Ocean contains more than half the world's total stock of fish. Herring, anchovy, sardine, cod, flounder, and tuna are among the most important fish found here. However, overfishing, particularly of cod and tuna, has caused a significant decline in numbers.

WHALES

Many whales live in the Atlantic, migrating from summer feeding grounds in the cold polar regions to warmer waters in the Caribbean for the winter. They give birth and mate again before returning north.

Humpback whale breaching

FALKLANDS

Set in the windy South Atlantic off the coast of Argentina, the Falkland Islands belong to the UK but are also claimed by Argentina. Fishing and sheep farming are important. The land is rocky, mountainous, boggy, and almost treeless.

NORTH AMERICA

BERMUDA (to UK)

Gulf of Mexico

Hatteras Plain

Greater Antilles

Puerto Rico Trench

Caribbean Sea

Colombian Basin

Lesser Antilles

Guatemala Basin

Panama Basin

Galapagos Islands (to Ecuador)

Peru-Chile Trench

Peru Basin

SOUTH

Andes

PACIFIC OCEAN

Chile Basin

Peru-Chile Trench

Chile Rise

GREENLAND
(to Denmark)

Labrador
Sea

Denmark Strait

ICELAND

REYKJAVIK

Reykjanes
Basin

Iceland

Labrador
Basin

Charlie-Gibbs Fracture Zone

Rockall Bank

FAEROE ISLANDS
(to Denmark)

British
Isles

North
Sea

Baltic Sea

EUROPE

Newfoundland

Grand Banks of
Newfoundland

Newfoundland
Basin

Bay of
Biscay

Alps

Azores
(to Portugal)

East Azores Fracture Zone

Mediterranean Sea

Bermuda
Rise

Sohm
Plain

Madeira
(to Portugal)

Great Meteor
Tablemount

Canary Islands
(to Spain)

Atlas Mountains

Sargasso
Sea

Madeira
Plain

Sahara

Nares
Plain

Kane Fracture Zone

Cape Verde
Basin

Cape Verde
Plain

Sahel

ATLANTIC

Doldrums Fracture Zone

PRAIA

**CAPE
VERDE**

AFRICA

Sierra
Leone
Rise

Sierra
Leone
Basin

OCEAN

Demerara
Plain

Amazon
Fan

Ceará Plain

Mid-

Guinea
Basin

Gulf of
Guinea

Ascension Fracture Zone

Fernando de
Noronha
(to Brazil)

Pernambuco
Plain

ASCENSION ISLAND
(to St Helena)

AMERICA

Brazil
Basin

Angola
Basin

ST HELENA
(to UK)

Zubov
Seamount

Vitória
Seamount

Ilha da
Trindade
(to Brazil)

Santos
Plateau

Atlantic Ridge

Walvis Ridge

Orange Fan

Cape
Basin

Rio Grande
Rise

Cape of
Good Hope

Argentine
Basin

TRISTAN DA CUNHA
(to St Helena)

Gulf of San Matías

Zapiola Ridge

Gough Fracture Zone

Gough Island
(to Tristan da Cunha)

Gulf of San Jorge

FALKLAND ISLANDS
(to UK)

Scotia
Sea

**SOUTH SANDWICH
ISLANDS**
(to UK)

**BOUVET
ISLAND**
(to Norway)

Cape
Horn

Drake Passage

SOUTH GEORGIA
(to UK)

SOUTHERN OCEAN

East Scotia
Basin

Mid-Atlantic Ridge

THE MINERAL-RICH
waters of Iceland's
Blue Lagoon are
said to be
beneficial to
people's health.

ICELAND

Iceland is situated in the North Atlantic on
the Mid-Atlantic Ridge. As a result, it has at
least 20 active volcanoes and suffers
frequent earthquakes. There are
numerous thermal springs with boiling
mud lakes and geysers. Water from hot
springs (above) is used to provide hot
water and heating for much of
Iceland's population, most of whom
live on the coast. The warm Gulf
Stream ensures that the country's
ports stay ice-free in winter.

Did you know?

▶ Iceland has fewer people per
square kilometre (mile) than
any other country in Europe.

▶ The Atlantic is the most
polluted ocean in the world.

ICEBERGS

Icebergs in the Atlantic Ocean are
formed when icesheets and glaciers
reach the sea. Parts break off and start
to drift, driven by winds and currents.

AFRICA

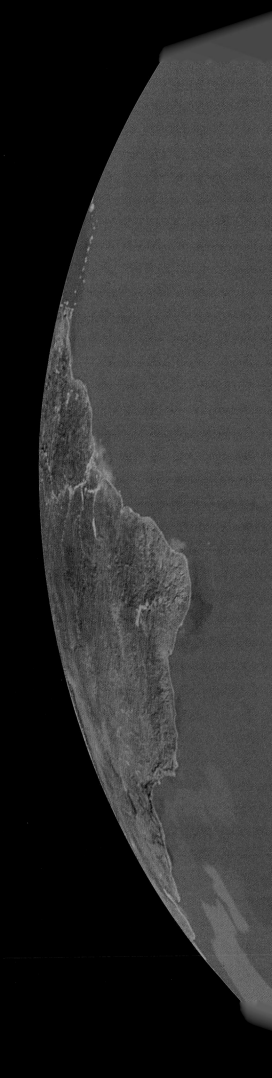

THE SECOND LARGEST CONTINENT after Asia, Africa has plenty of record-breakers.

The Sahara is the world's largest desert, the Nile its longest river, Lake

Victoria its second-largest freshwater lake, and the Congo

river basin its second largest tropical rainforest. The

people of Africa are culturally and religiously diverse – those north of the

Sahara are mainly Muslim, while people in the south follow

a variety of religions, including Christianity. With a rapidly

growing population of 793 million, spread across 52 countries, Africa also

contains some of the world's poorest countries. Many

economies depend heavily on exporting one crop or

product, and if prices fall, the country becomes poorer. Most people live on

the land and are vulnerable to drought, floods, and famine,

with limited access to clean drinking water. However,

a growing number of people are moving to cities in search of a better life.

Northwest Africa

FOUR COUNTRIES, plus the disputed area of Western Sahara, make up this part of Africa. Algeria, Libya, and Tunisia have rich supplies of oil and natural gas that boost their economies. Morocco relies on tourism, phosphates used for chemicals and fertilizer, and agriculture. In the fertile valleys of the Atlas Mountains, farmers grow grapes, citrus fruit, dates, and olives. The area also attracts tourists to its colourful markets, historical sites, and sandy beaches. The Sahara Desert dominates the region, particularly in Algeria and Libya.

SUN AND SEA

Many tourists visit Tunisia and Morocco each year to enjoy the warm climate and sandy beaches. Tourism provides jobs for the local people and brings much-needed income.

ARAB INFLUENCE

Arab invasions during the 7th and 11th centuries have influenced the culture, religion (Islam), architecture, and language of northwest Africa. Today, Arabic is the main language, and more than 95 per cent of the people here are Muslim.

MOROCCAN MARKET

In a *souk*, or market, craftworkers sell handmade products to tourists. Goods are displayed in booths along the bustling streets.

MUSLIMS go to worship at the Hassan II mosque in Casablanca, Morocco.

BERBERS

The Berber people were the original inhabitants of northwest Africa. Most now live in the Atlas Mountains or the desert. Although most Berbers converted to Islam when the Arabs arrived, they kept their own language and way of life. In 2001, Algeria recognized Berber as an official language.

A BERBER WOMAN works on the land in the Atlas Mountains.

Map labels

ATLANTIC OCEAN
Strait of Gibraltar
GIBRALTAR (to UK)
Ceuta (to Spain)
Tangier
Ksar-el-Kebir
Tetouan
Chefchaouen
Melilla (to Spain)
Oran
Tizi Ouzou
ALGIERS (ALGER)
Chlef
Blida
Mostaganem
Sidi Bel Abbès
Salé
Kénitra
Fès
Oujda
Tlemcen
Djelfa
RABAT
Casablanca
Mohammedia
Jerada
Hauts Plateaux
Chott ech Chergui
El-Jadida
Safi
Khouriboga
Beni-Mellal
Atlas Mountains
Atlas Saharien
Laghouat
Essaouira
Marrakech
Ghardaïa
MOROCCO
Er-Rachidia
Figuig
Agadir
Ouarzazate
Béchar
Grand Erg Occidental
El Goléa
Tiznit
Hamada du Dra
Tan-Tan
ALGER
LAÂYOUNE
El Mahbas
Tindouf
Adrar
Plateau du Tademaït
I-n-Salah
Boujdour
Smara
Bou Craa
Erg Iguîdi
Reggane
Galtat-Zemmour
MAURITANIA
WESTERN SAHARA (disputed territory under Moroccan occupation)
Ad Dakhla
Erg Chech
S
Tropic of Cancer
Tanezrouft
MALI
Lagouira

DATE PALMS

Dates are an important crop for Algeria and Tunisia. Date palms are often grown at oases, where water lies close to the surface of the desert. Here the clusters of dates are shown ripening beneath polythene. Leaves from the trees can be used for thatch and the trunk is cut for timber.

ANCIENT RUINS

Phoenicians, Romans, and Greeks from ancient times have all left their mark on this part of Africa. Today, tourists come to admire the historical sites along the coast. These ruins at Carthage, near Tunis, date from the 9th century BC, when the Romans controlled the whole of the north African coast.

RUINS OF A ROMAN BATH AT CARTHAGE

Did you know?

▶ The stones from dates can be roasted and ground to make a traditional date coffee.

▶ Since Spain gave up control of Western Sahara in 1976, Morocco has been fighting a guerrilla group of desert tribesmen for control of the area.

SURVIVAL IN THE SAHARA

The Sahara Desert covers almost one-third of Africa and is an inhospitable place to live with high daytime temperatures and freezing nights. The Tuareg are nomads for whom the desert is home. Traditionally, they keep camels for transport, and to provide meat, milk, and hides. Many Tuareg now live in the cities.

TUAREG NOMADS in the Sahara carry salt to trade in markets.

Mediterranean Sea

Bizerte
Annaba
Carthage
Sétif
TUNIS
Constantine
Sousse
Kairouan
Batna
Kasserine
Mahdia
Biskra
Chott Melghir
Gafsa
Sfax
Tozeur
Golfe de Gabès
Gabès
Chott el Jerid
Médenine
Île de Jerba
El Oued
TUNISIA
Zuwārah
TRIPOLI (ṬARĀBULUS)
Touggourt
Az Zāwiyah
Al Khums
Benghazi (Banghāzī)
Ouargla
Yafran
Misrātah
Al Jabal al Akhḍar
Gharyān
Gulf of Sirte (Khalīj Surt)
Nālūt
Surt
Ajdābiyā
Grand Erg Oriental
Marsā al Burayqah
Wādī al Ḥamīm
Al Bayḍā'
Al Marj
Darnah
Ṭubruq
Al Jaghbūb
Jālū
Marādah
Great Sand Sea
Waddān
EGYPT
LIBYA
Bordj Omar Driss
Tiguentourine
Birāk
Sabhā
Awbārī
Libyan
Zawīlah
Tassili-n-Ajjer
Al 'Uwaynāt
Ramlat Rabyānah
Al Khufrah
Desert
Tropic of Cancer
Ahaggar
Djanet
Idhān Murzuq
Tahat 2918m
Pic Bette 2286m
SUDAN
Tamanrasset
NIGER
CHAD

0 km 100 200
0 miles 100 200

LIBYAN OIL RESOURCES

The discovery of oil and gas in 1959 brought considerable wealth to Libya, and currently makes up 99 per cent of the country's exports. As a result, Libya's cities have grown as people have moved from rural areas to find work in the oil industry. Some of the money from oil is being spent on better healthcare and education for Libyans.

LIBYAN OIL FIELD

Northeast Africa

THIS REGION, KNOWN AS the Horn of Africa, contains the oldest civilizations in the continent, and some of its poorest countries. The borders that divide the countries today were mostly created by colonial rulers in the last hundred years. Pastoral nomads with their herds of animals often cross these borders in search of pasture. Most people still live in the countryside and farm the land, but increasing numbers are moving to cities. Tourism and agriculture are important sources of income for Egypt and Kenya, two of the richest and fastest-growing countries in the region. Elsewhere, tribal rivalries and disputes over land and resources have sometimes erupted into full-scale war and these, together with drought and poverty, have blighted the lives of millions of people in this region.

RIVER NILE

The Nile is the world's longest river. It flows north from Burundi to run along the Tanzania/Rwanda border, then through Uganda, Sudan, and Egypt to the coast. Most of Egypt's population lives around the valley and delta of the Nile, which provides the region's water. The river also provides irrigation for local crops, such as cotton.

SUEZ CANAL

The Suez Canal is one of the world's longest and most important artificial waterways. It links the Mediterranean Sea with the Gulf of Suez and the Red Sea, providing a crucial shortcut from Europe to India and East Asia. The tolls from the canal are a great source of income for Egypt.

LOSING FARMLAND

As the population grows in Ethiopia, more and more people cut down forests for firewood, or to cultivate new areas for food crops. The soil, no longer held firm by the trees, is easily blown or washed away, and valuable farmland is lost.

PLOUGHING fields
in Ethiopia

ABU SIMBEL

Tourists come to Egypt to see the pyramids at Giza and the temples along the Nile, such as these two built at Abu Simbel, south of Aswan. Tourism brings in money to preserve these historical sites.

0 km   100   200   300   400
0 miles   100   200   300   400

Map labels

Mediterranean Sea

Sidi Barâni
El'Alamein
Alexandria
Zagazig
Dumyât
Port Said
Isma'iliya
Suez
Delta   Nile
Suez Canal
Qattara
Depression   -133m
Siwa
Bawiti
Qasr
Faráfra
El Giza
CAIRO
Beni Suef
El Minya
Mallawi
Asyût
Sohâg
El Khârga
Akhmim
Qena
Luxor
Isna
Idfu
Aswân
Lake Nasser
Aswan Dam
Hurghada
Gulf of Suez
Sinai
Gebel Katherîna 2637m
Tropic of Cancer

E G Y P T

Sahara el Gharbiya
(Western Desert)
Gilf Kebir
Plateau
Great Sand Sea
Gulf Kebir

Jabal al
Uwaynât
1907m

L I B Y A

Tropic of Cancer

C H A D

Umm Buru
Kebkabiya
El Geneina
Nyala
Ed Da'ein
El Fasher
Sodiri
El'Atrun
Wadi Howar
D a r f u r

S U D A N

Wadi Halfa
Akasha
Delgo
Argo
Dongola
Ed Debba
Akasha
Merowe
Abu Hamed
Shereik
Atbara
Ed Damer
Nubian Desert
Nile
Nile
Khartoum
Omdurman
KHARTOUM
Wad Medani
Umm Ruwaba
El Obeid
Er
Rahad
Dilling
Sennar
Blue Nile
White Nile
Wadi el Milk

Port
Sudan
Suakin
Tokar
Haiya
Massawa
Zula
Red Sea
(administered
by Sudan)
Wadi Oko
Danakil Desert
ERITREA
ASMARA
Kassala
Khashm
el Girba
Teseney
Gedaref
Mek'elê
Weldiya
Lalibela
Gonder
Tána Hayk'
Bahir Dar
Ed Damazin
Mäychew
Gulf of Aden
Caluula
Boosaaso
Karin   2407m
DJIBOUTI
Aseb
Obock
Dikhil
Weldiya

(administered
by Egypt)

Map labels

INDIAN OCEAN

SOMALIA

ETHIOPIA

KENYA

TANZANIA

UGANDA

RWANDA

BURUNDI

DEM. REP. CONGO

CENTRAL AFRICAN REPUBLIC

MOZAMBIQUE

MALAWI

ZAMBIA

ADDIS ABABA (ĀDĪS ĀBEBA)

MOGADISHU (MUQDISHO)

NAIROBI

DODOMA

DAR ES SALAAM

KAMPALA

KIGALI

BUJUMBURA

Bandarbeyla · Sinujiif · Garoowe · Gaalkacyo · Gaalkacyo · Gellinsoor · Dhuusa Marreeb · Buulobarde · Baraawe · Marka · Jawhar · Beledweyne · Baydhabo · Xuddur · Baardheere · Jamaame · Kismaayo · Buur Gaabo · Garsen · Malindi · Mombasa · Pemba · Tanga · Zanzibar

Berbera · Hargeysa · Harēr · Dirē Dawa · Āwash · Mīeso · Nazrēt · Burē · Gorē · Agaro · Jīma · Negēlē · Yabēlo · Moyale · Marsabit · Meru · Nyeri · Nakuru · Arusha · Moshi · Kilimanjaro · Morogoro

Kadugli · Sumeih · Raga · Wau · Tonj · Rumbek · Tambura · Yambio · Maridi · Juba · Amadi · Bor · Kapoeta · Lira · Gulu · Arua · Masindi · Entebbe · Masaka · Mbarara · Kabale · Biharamulo · Bukoba · Mwanza · Musoma · Shinyanga · Nzega · Tabora · Singida · Iringa · Mbeya · Sumbawanga · Kipili · Kigoma · Kasulu

Great Rift Valley · Ethiopian Highlands · Lake Turkana · Lake Victoria · Lake Tanganyika · Lake Albert · Lake Edward · Lake Kivu · Lake Rukwa · Lake Nyasa · White Nile · Masai Steppe · Equator

---

Did you know?

The Masai tribe lives on the borders of Kenya and Tanzania. Between the ages of 14 and 30, young Masai men live in the bush and learn how to become great warriors.

Water makes up almost one-fifth of the surface area of Uganda.

RELIGIOUS BELIEFS

The Ethiopian Orthodox Union Church has been in existence since the 4th century AD. It is a branch of the Coptic Church, and mixes Christian beliefs, such as Catholic saints, with some traditional African spiritual beliefs.

Coptic cross

TEA IN KENYA

Kenya is an important world producer of tea, which is grown on plantations in the highland areas (such as this one below). High rainfall here ensures a good crop. Coffee is also a valuable export.

KENYAN workers carefully select tea leaves for picking.

CAIRO

The largest city in Africa is Cairo, the capital of Egypt. The city has a population of nearly seven million. Here, Arab, African, and European influences exist alongside more traditional Egyptian customs.

BUSY STREET bazaar in Cairo

SUDANESE DINKA

There are more than 500 different tribes in Sudan, who speak over 100 languages and dialects. Like many tribal people here, the Dinka are nomadic – their cattle graze on the plains east of the Nile. Cattle are central to their lives – young Dinka men officially become adults with an initiation ceremony in which they are given an ox of their own.

YOUNG DINKA MAN

MOUNTAIN GORILLAS

The Volcanoes National Park in Rwanda is one of the few places where you can still see a mountain gorilla (right) in the wild. These animals are threatened with extinction because of poachers and the destruction of their habitat. Tanzania and Kenya also have many important game reserves, which preserve the wildlife of the savannah.

West Africa

0 km 100 200 300 400

0 miles 100 200 300 400

DRAMATICALLY DIFFERENT CLIMATE and landscapes influence life in West Africa. In the hot, dry, northern areas of the Sahara and Sahel, it is extremely difficult to grow crops. To the south, the climate is warm and wet, and crops such as cocoa and coffee are grown on large plantations. The region also has many valuable minerals. Despite these rich resources, most countries are very poor. Since independence from colonial powers, there has been much political unrest, often sparked by poverty and tribal rivalries in the region. West Africa is also divided by religion, with Islam dominant in the north and Christianity in the south.

GAMBIA

In recent years, tourism has become increasingly important to the economy of Gambia. Visitors come to see wildlife along the River Gambia and to visit the Atlantic coast beaches. These safari tourists are admiring a giant termite mound.

PEOPLE OF GHANA

Family ties and a sense of community are important to the people of Ghana, and ceremonies throughout each year mark the events of childbirth, puberty, marriage, and death. About half of Ghanaians are Ashanti people whose ancestors developed one of the richest and most notable civilizations in Africa.

DIAMONDS AND GOLD

West Africa has many valuable minerals, including diamonds, uranium, copper, and gold. In Sierra Leone, where diamonds (left) provide crucial income, the mines were a focus of fighting in the civil war between rebel groups and the government.

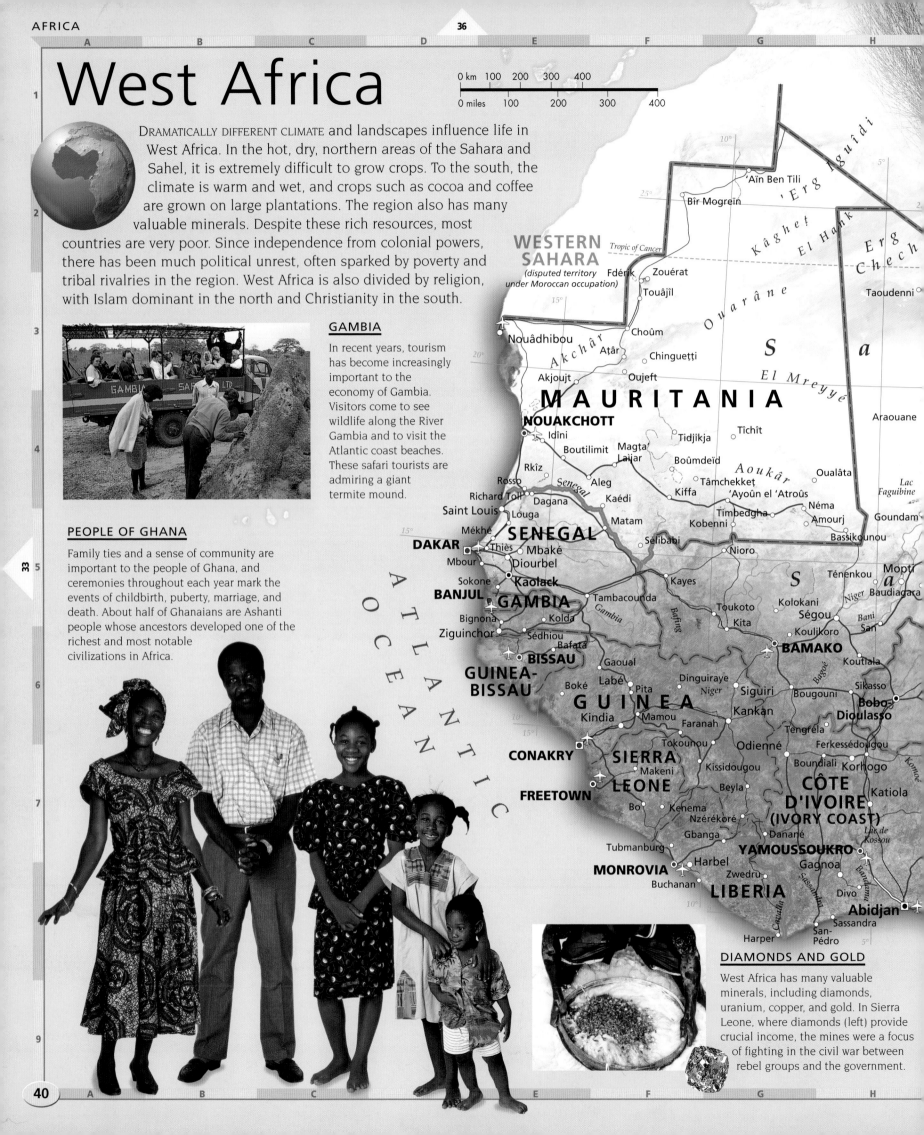

33

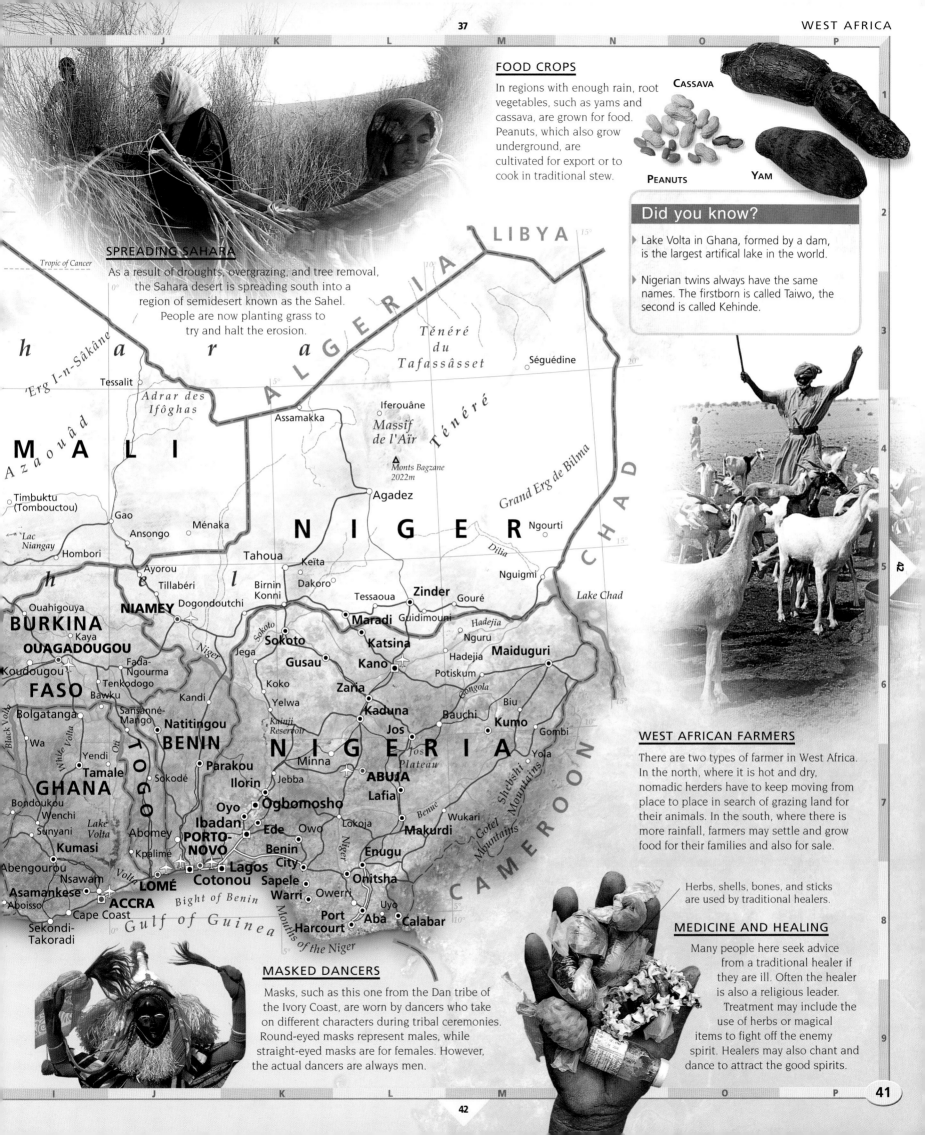

FOOD CROPS

In regions with enough rain, root vegetables, such as yams and cassava, are grown for food. Peanuts, which also grow underground, are cultivated for export or to cook in traditional stew.

CASSAVA

PEANUTS

YAM

Did you know?

▸ Lake Volta in Ghana, formed by a dam, is the largest artifical lake in the world.

▸ Nigerian twins always have the same names. The firstborn is called Taiwo, the second is called Kehinde.

SPREADING SAHARA

As a result of droughts, overgrazing, and tree removal, the Sahara desert is spreading south into a region of semidesert known as the Sahel. People are now planting grass to try and halt the erosion.

Tropic of Cancer

LIBYA

ALGERIA

Ténéré du Tafassâsset

Séguédine

'Erg I-n-Sâkâne

Tessalit

Adrar des Ifôghas

Iferouâne

h a r a

Azaouâd

Assamakka

Massif de l'Aïr

Ténéré

△ Monts Bagzane 2022m

Grand Erg de Bilma

CHAD

MALI

Timbuktu (Tombouctou)

Gao

Agadez

Lac Niangay

Ansongo

Ménaka

NIGER

Ngourti

Hombori

Tahoua

Keïta

Dilia

Nguigmi

Ayorou

Tillabéri

Birnin Konni

Dakoro

Tessaoua

Gouré

Lake Chad

Ouahigouya

Dogondoutchi

NIAMEY

Zinder

Guidimouni

Hadejia

BURKINA

Kaya

Sokoto

Maradi

Katsina

Nguru

OUAGADOUGOU

Jega

Gusau

Kano

Hadejia

Maiduguri

Koudougou

Fada-Ngourma

Niger

Koko

Zaria

Potiskum

FASO

Tenkodogo

Bawku

Kandi

Yelwa

Gongola

Biu

Bolgatanga

Sansanné-Mango

Kaduna

Bauchi

Kumo

Wa

Natitingou

Kainji Reservoir

Jos

Gombi

Yendi

BENIN

Minna

Jos Plateau

Yola

NIGERIA

Tamale

Parakou

Ilorin

Jebba

ABUJA

Shebshi Mountains

GHANA

Sokodé

Ogbomosho

Lafia

Bondoukou

Oyo

Ede

Owo

Lokoja

Makurdi

Wukari

Benue

Gotel Mountains

Wenchi

Lake Volta

Ibadan

PORTO-NOVO

Benin City

Enugu

CAMEROON

Sunyani

Abomey

Kpalimé

Lagos

Niger

Onitsha

Kumasi

LOMÉ

Cotonou

Sapele

Owerri

Abengourou

Nsawam

Warri

Uyo

Asamankese

ACCRA

Bight of Benin

Port Harcourt

Aba

Calabar

Aboisso

Cape Coast

Gulf of Guinea

Sekondi-Takoradi

Mouths of the Niger

TOGO

Abuja

WEST AFRICAN FARMERS

There are two types of farmer in West Africa. In the north, where it is hot and dry, nomadic herders have to keep moving from place to place in search of grazing land for their animals. In the south, where there is more rainfall, farmers may settle and grow food for their families and also for sale.

Herbs, shells, bones, and sticks are used by traditional healers.

MEDICINE AND HEALING

Many people here seek advice from a traditional healer if they are ill. Often the healer is also a religious leader. Treatment may include the use of herbs or magical items to fight off the enemy spirit. Healers may also chant and dance to attract the good spirits.

MASKED DANCERS

Masks, such as this one from the Dan tribe of the Ivory Coast, are worn by dancers who take on different characters during tribal ceremonies. Round-eyed masks represent males, while straight-eyed masks are for females. However, the actual dancers are always men.

Central Africa

ALL EIGHT COUNTRIES IN Central Africa were European colonies with a painful history of slavery. Since the 1960s, independence has brought them mixed success. Rich mineral deposits and the discovery of offshore oil have provided income for Cameroon, Congo, and Gabon, while civil war and repressive governments have damaged other countries in the region. These include Chad and the Central African Republic, two of the world's poorest countries. Although the north is mainly arid, Africa's largest tropical rainforest dominates the south, with the powerful Congo River linking the interior with the coast. The tiny, volcanic country of Sao Tome and Principe lies off the coast of Gabon.

RELIGIOUS BELIEFS

Although Christianity is the main religion here, many people also follow traditional beliefs. These suggest that natural objects, such as mountains and rivers, have a spirit. Masks, like this Bambuku head, are sometimes used to scare off evil spirits.

VILLAGE LIFE

Most people in rural areas live in villages or small towns. Some grow crops, such as cotton or cassava, for sale, but many exist by growing food just for their family.

Mud-brick home

FISHING IN LAKE CHAD

Lake Chad is an important source of food but it is shrinking at an alarming rate. A shallow lake, it is now only about 6 m (20 ft) deep. Its surface area has also reduced, due to droughts and the demand for water to irrigate the land.

PEOPLE OF CHAD

With almost half the country lying in the arid Sahara Desert, about 80 per cent of Chadians work on farmland near the River Chari in the south. Across Chad there are large numbers of ethnic groups, speaking over 100 languages. Women here live an average of just 53 years and have 6.5 children.

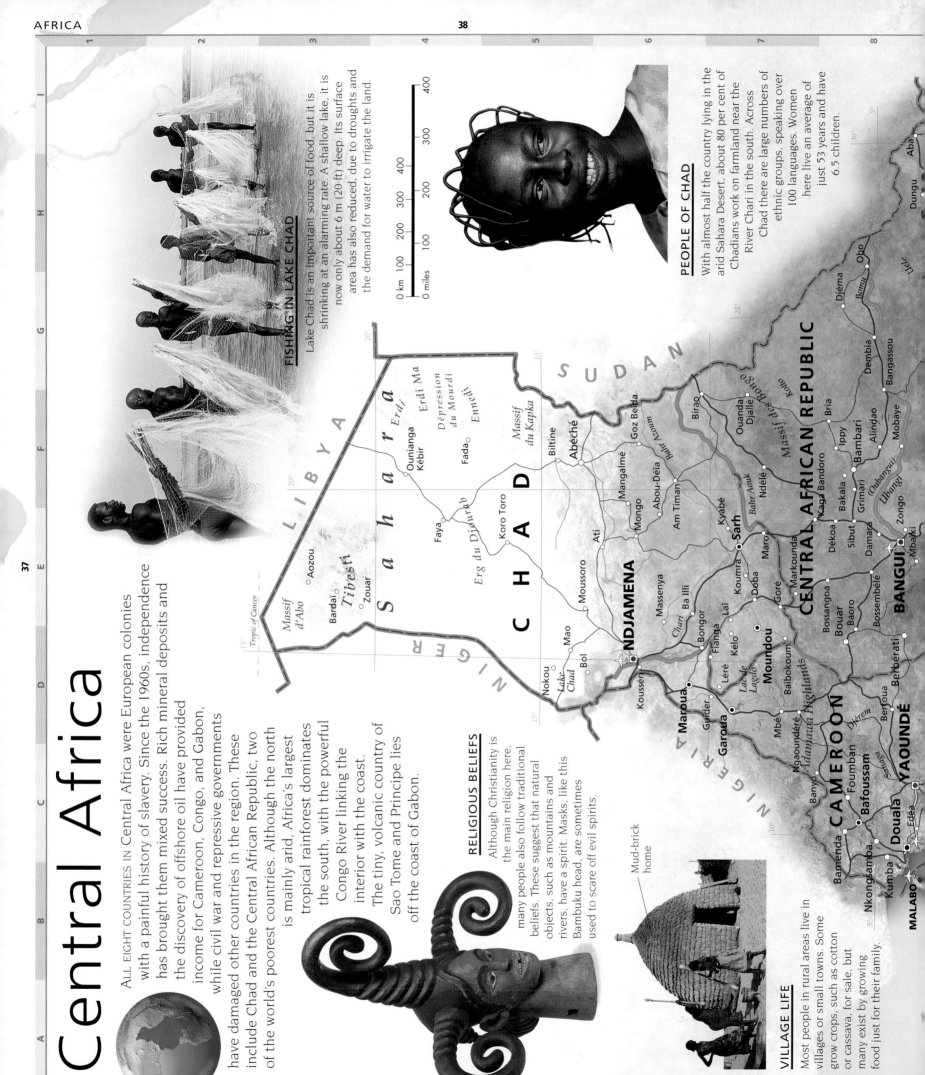

0 km 100   200   300   400
0 miles   100   200   300   400

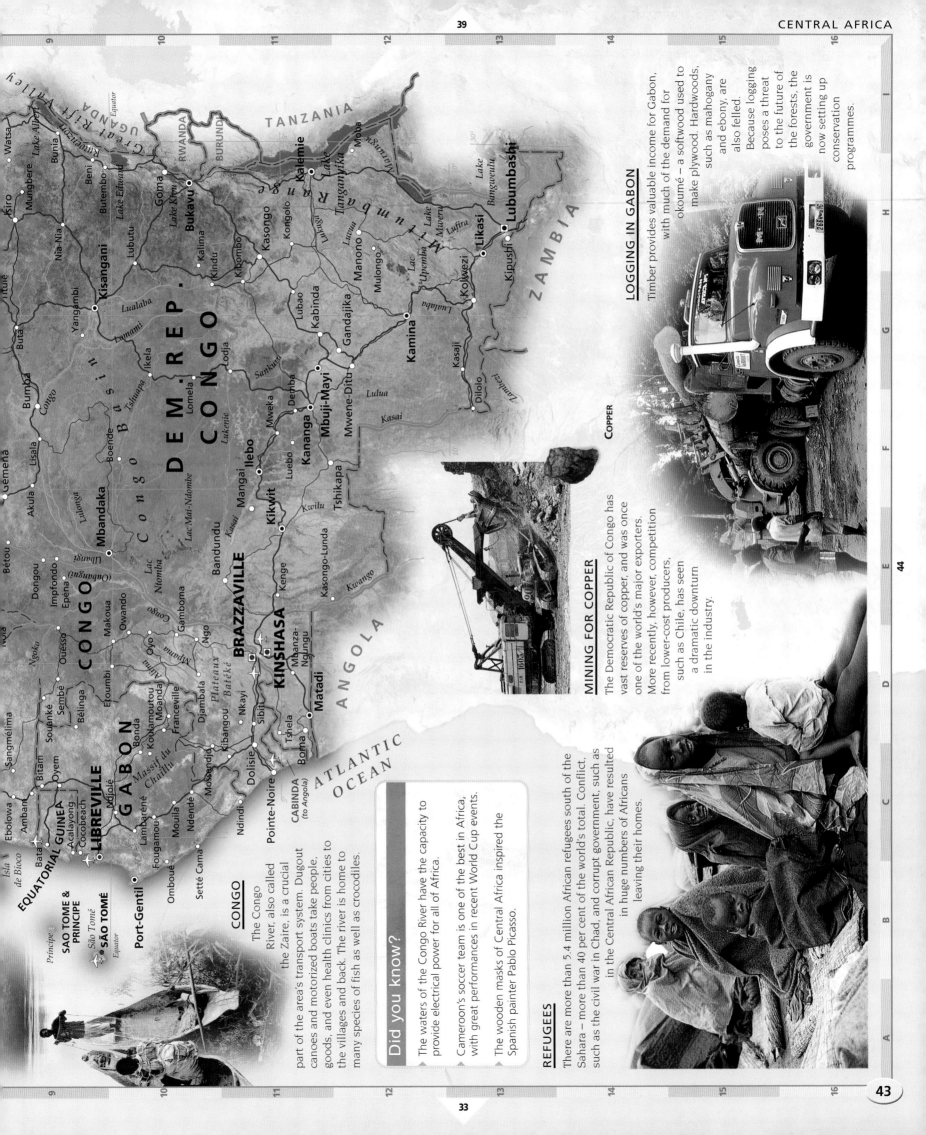

Map labels

Great Rift Valley
Ruwenzori

TANZANIA
UGANDA
RWANDA
BURUNDI
ZAMBIA
ANGOLA

DEM. REP. CONGO
CONGO
GABON
EQUATORIAL GUINEA
SAO TOME & PRINCIPE

Congo Basin
Mitumba Range

Isiro
Watsa
Mungbere
Lake Albert
Bunia
Beni
Butembo
Nia-Nia
Lake Edward
Goma
Bukavu
Lake Kivu
Kalima
Kindu
Kasongo
Kongolo
Kibombo
Kalemie
Lake Tanganyika
Moba
Lake Rukwa
Mont Nkungu
Lake Mweru
Lufira
Kalemie
Likasi
Lubumbashi
Kipushi
Kolwezi
Kasaji
Dilolo
Zambezi
Lake Bangweulu

Kisangani
Yangambi
Lualaba
Lomami
Ikela
Lodja
Lubao
Kabinda
Gandajika
Kamina
Mulongo
Manono
Lukuga
Lualaba
Luvua

Buta
Bumba
Congo
Lisala
Akula
Gemena
Boende
Tshuapa
Lomela
Sankuru
Mweka
Demba
Mbuji-Mayi
Mwene-Ditu
Lulua
Kasai
Kananga
Tshikapa
Lubao

Mbandaka
Lulonga
Ubangi (Oubangui)
Lac Mai-Ndombe
Mangai
Ilebo
Kikwit
Kwilu
Luebo
Kasai
Kasongo-Lunda

Bétou
Dongou
Impfondo
Epéna
Ouesso
Makoua
Owando
Oyo
BRAZZAVILLE
Ngo
Gamboma
Plateaux Batéké
KINSHASA
Mbanza-Ngungu
Matadi
Boma
Tshela
ATLANTIC OCEAN
Bandundu
Lac Ntomba
Kenge
Kwango
Congo

Ngoko
Ouésso
Souanké
Sembé
Makoua
Ntoumbi
Etoumbi
Djambala
Mossendjo
Dolisie
Sibiti
Nkayi
Kibangou
Pointe-Noire
CABINDA (to Angola)
Loudima
Mouanda
Franceville
Koulamoutou
Lambaréné
Fougamou
Ndendé
Bonda

GABON
Ntoum
Bitam
Oyem
LIBREVILLE
Cocobeach
Acalayong
Mdjolé
Port-Gentil
Omboué
Settè Cama
Ndindi
Massif du Chaillu

Sangmélima
Ebolowa
Ambam
Bata
EQUATORIAL GUINEA
Isla de Bioco

Principe
SAO TOME & PRINCIPE
SÃO TOMÉ
São Tomé
Equator

CONGO

The Congo River, also called the Zaire, is a crucial part of the area's transport system. Dugout canoes and motorized boats take people, goods, and even health clinics from cities to the villages and back. The river is home to many species of fish as well as crocodiles.

Did you know?

▶ The waters of the Congo River have the capacity to provide electrical power for all of Africa.

▶ Cameroon's soccer team is one of the best in Africa, with great performances in recent World Cup events.

▶ The wooden masks of Central Africa inspired the Spanish painter Pablo Picasso.

REFUGEES

There are more than 5.4 million African refugees south of the Sahara – more than 40 per cent of the world's total. Conflict, such as the civil war in Chad, and corrupt government, such as in the Central African Republic, have resulted in huge numbers of Africans leaving their homes.

COPPER

MINING FOR COPPER

The Democratic Republic of Congo has vast reserves of copper, and was once one of the world's major exporters. More recently, however, competition from lower-cost producers, such as Chile, has seen a dramatic downturn in the industry.

LOGGING IN GABON

Timber provides valuable income for Gabon, with much of the demand for okoumé – a softwood used to make plywood. Hardwoods, such as mahogany and ebony, are also felled. Because logging poses a threat to the future of the forests, the government is now setting up conservation programmes.

Southern Africa

FROM THE DRAMATIC Namib and Kalahari deserts in the west, to the tropical forests in the north, Southern Africa is a region of contrasts. Oil, diamonds, gold, and other precious metals are all mined here. There are huge inland plains that are home to a variety of wildlife, and large areas devoted to agriculture. But flooding and droughts, together with civil unrest, have hampered development so that despite an abundance of natural resources, many countries remain poor.

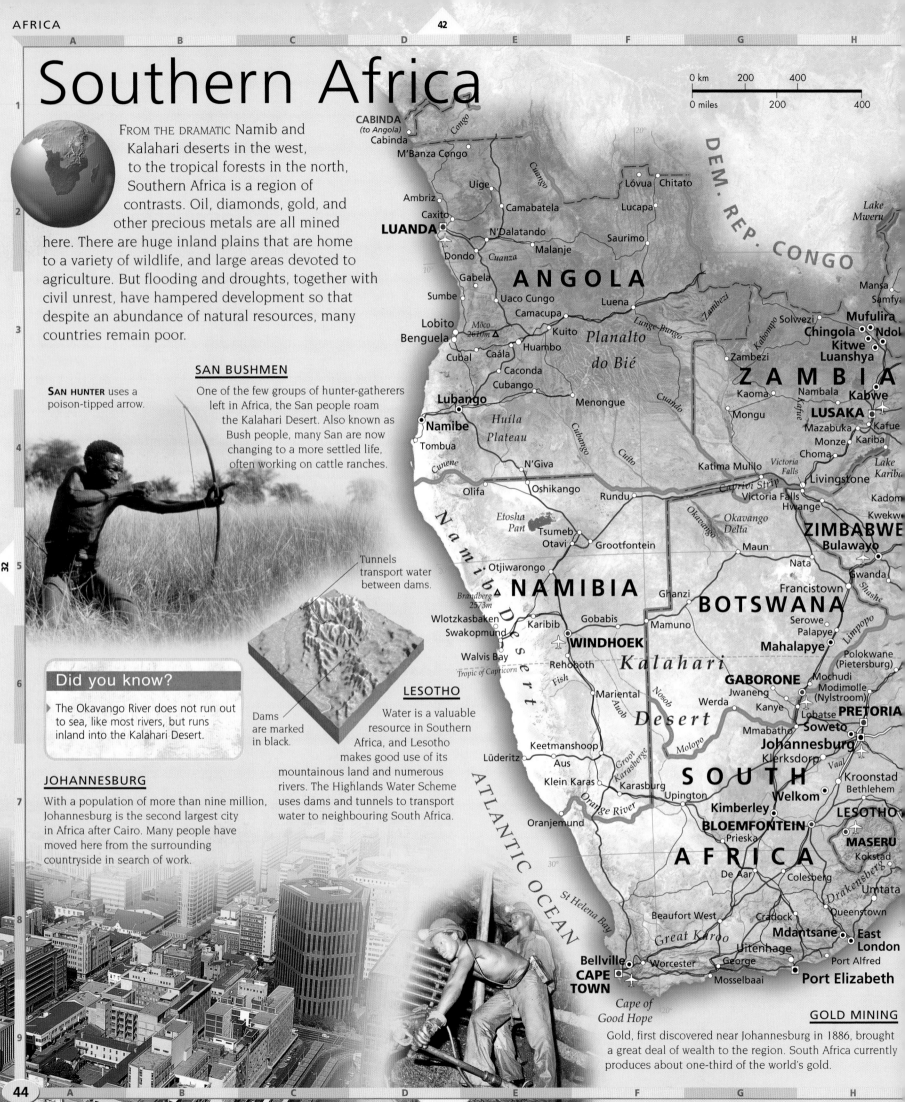

SAN hunter uses a poison-tipped arrow.

SAN BUSHMEN

One of the few groups of hunter-gatherers left in Africa, the San people roam the Kalahari Desert. Also known as Bush people, many San are now changing to a more settled life, often working on cattle ranches.

Tunnels transport water between dams.

Did you know?

▶ The Okavango River does not run out to sea, like most rivers, but runs inland into the Kalahari Desert.

Dams are marked in black.

LESOTHO

Water is a valuable resource in Southern Africa, and Lesotho makes good use of its mountainous land and numerous rivers. The Highlands Water Scheme uses dams and tunnels to transport water to neighbouring South Africa.

JOHANNESBURG

With a population of more than nine million, Johannesburg is the second largest city in Africa after Cairo. Many people have moved here from the surrounding countryside in search of work.

GOLD MINING

Gold, first discovered near Johannesburg in 1886, brought a great deal of wealth to the region. South Africa currently produces about one-third of the world's gold.

0 km 200 400
0 miles 200 400

CABINDA (to Angola)
Cabinda
M'Banza Congo
Congo
Uíge
Ambriz
Camabatela
Lóvua Chitato
Caxito
LUANDA
N'Dalatando
Lucapa
Saurimo
Dondo
Cuanza
Malanje
Gabela
ANGOLA
Sumbe
Uaco Cungo
Luena
Mansa
Samfya
Lobito
Camacupa
Zambezi
Mufulira
Benguela
Môco 2610m
Kuito
Planalto do Bié
Solwezi Chingola Ndol
Cubal Caála Huambo
Zambezi
Kitwe
Caconda
Lunge-Bungo
Luanshya
ZAMBIA
Cubango
Kaoma
Nambala Kabwe
Lubango
Menongue
Cuando
Mongu
LUSAKA
Huíla Plateau
Mazabuka Kafue
Namibe
Cubango
Monze Kariba
Tombua
Cuito
Choma
Cunene
N'Giva
Katima Mulilo
Victoria Falls
Lake Kariba
Olifa
Oshikango
Rundu
Caprivi Strip
Livingstone
Etosha Pan
Victoria Falls
Kadom
Tsumeb
Okavango
Hwange
Kwekw
Otavi Grootfontein
Okavango Delta
ZIMBABWE
Otjiwarongo
Maun
Bulawayo
Brandberg 2573m
Nata
Gwanda
NAMIBIA
Ghanzi
Francistown
Shashe
Wlotzkasbaken Karibib Gobabis
BOTSWANA
Swakopmund
Mamuno
Serowe
Palapye
WINDHOEK
Kalahari
Mahalapye
Limpopo
Walvis Bay
Rehoboth
Polokwane (Pietersburg)
Tropic of Capricorn
Fish
GABORONE
Mochudi
Mariental
Nosob
Modimolle (Nylstroom)
Auob
Jwaneng
Werda
PRETORIA
Kanye
Lobatse
Keetmanshoop
Desert
Mmabatho
Soweto
Lüderitz
Aus
Molopo
Johannesburg
Klerksdorp
Vaal
Klein Karas
Groot Karasberge
Upington
SOUTH
Kroonstad
Karasburg
Welkom
Bethlehem
Oranje River
Kimberley
LESOTHO
Oranjemund
BLOEMFONTEIN
MASERU
Prieska
Kokstad
AFRICA
De Aar
Colesberg
Drakensberg
Umtata
St Helena Bay
Beaufort West
Cradock
Queenstown
Great Karoo
Mdantsane
East London
Bellville
Uitenhage
Worcester
George
Port Alfred
CAPE TOWN
Mosselbaai
Port Elizabeth
Cape of Good Hope
ATLANTIC OCEAN
DEM. REP. CONGO
Lake Mweru
Cuango
Cuanza
Lunge-Bungo

MOZAMBIQUE FLOODS

In Mozambique, floods in 2000 and again in 2001 ruined crops, swept away livestock, and left millions homeless and vulnerable. Many people now rely on foreign aid to stay alive.

TOBACCO PLANTATION

VICTORIA FALLS

At Victoria Falls, situated on the Zambia-Zimbabwe border, the mighty Zambezi River drops 128 m (420 ft) down a narrow chasm. The sound of the crashing water can be heard 40 km (25 miles) away.

WORKING ON THE LAND

In both Malawi and Mozambique, agriculture employs more than four out of every five workers. Important crops include cotton, tea, tobacco, and sugar.

MADAGASCAN MAMMALS

Madagascar has an unusual range of mammals that developed in isolation after the island split from the African mainland. It is the only place where lemurs, members of the primate family, live in the wild.

RING-TAILED LEMUR

APARTHEID

In 1994, Nelson Mandela (below) became the first black president to govern South Africa. This historic event marked the end of white rule and the first fair elections in the new "Rainbow Nation". Apartheid was a policy of racial segregation and restricted the rights of black people.

WILDLIFE

Southern Africa is home to a huge variety of animals. Numerous parks have been created to protect the animals and their habitat. The Gaza-Kruger-Gonarezhou Transfrontier Park joins parks in Mozambique, South Africa, and Zimbabwe to form the largest conservation and ecotourism park in Africa.

Map labels

TANZANIA
Lake Rukwa
Lake Nyasa
MALAWI
Mbala
Kasama
Isoka
Mzuzu
Mpika
Serenje
Chipata
LILONGWE
Salima
Monkey Bay
Rio Rovuma
Negomane
Mocímboa da Praia
Rio Lugenda
Rio Messalo
Mucojo
Pemba
Lúrio
Rio Lúrio
Nacala
Lumbo
Nampula
Albufeira de Cahora Bassa
Vila do Zumbo
Zómba
Blantyre
Tete
Milange
Nyamapanda
Nsanje
Mocuba
HARARE
Inyangani 2591m
Chitungwiza
Mutare
Chimoio
Quelimane
Masvingo
Zvishavane
Beira
Machanga
Rio Save
Musina (Messina)
Changane
Inhambane
Quissico
Xai-Xai
MAPUTO
MBABANE
SWAZILAND
Dundee
Pietermaritzburg
Durban
INDIAN OCEAN
MOZAMBIQUE
Zambezi
Mozambique Channel

MORONI
COMOROS
Grande Comore
Anjouan
Mohéli
MAMOUDZOU
MAYOTTE (to France)

Tanjona Bobaomby
Antsiranana
Ambanja
Analalava
Antsohihy
Maromokotro 2376m
Sambava
Antalaha
Mahajanga
Maroantsetra
Bemaraha
Fenoarivo
Toamasina
ANTANANARIVO
Betafo
Morondava
Ambositra
Mananjary
Makay
Mangoky
MADAGASCAR
Fianarantsoa
Ihosy
Manakara
Toliara
Manakara
Farafangana
Vangaindrano
Tropic of Capricorn
Amboasary
Tanjona Vohimena

ST-DENIS
RÉUNION (to France)
PORT LOUIS
MAURITIUS
Mascarene Islands

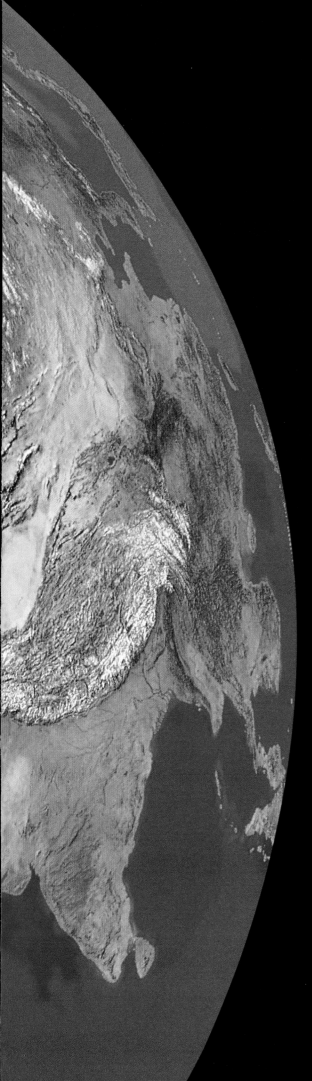

EUROPE

EUROPE IS THE SECOND smallest continent in the world, but it is one of the most densely populated, with more than 727 million people living in its 44 countries. Most Europeans  live in cities. They watch TV, use mobile phones, surf the Internet, drive cars, and in comparison with many other people in the world, are quite prosperous. The European climate is mild, although winters are cold in the north and east and summers are hot in the south. Over the past 500 years,  Europeans have conquered much of the world, setting up huge empires in every continent. These empires are now gone, but  their influences remain. Many people around the world still speak a European language, such as English, French, or Spanish, and European culture has been exported to many parts of the globe. As members of the European Union, many countries are forging closer economic and political links.

Scandinavia and Finland

THE THREE SCANDINAVIAN countries of Norway, Sweden, and Denmark, along with neighbouring Finland, are among the most northerly countries in Europe. Here the winters are long and cold. In the far north above the Arctic Circle, the Sun remains below the horizon for up to two months a year. Because of the harsh winter climate and the geographical isolation, Scandinavia has attracted little immigration, so the population is not very ethnically diverse. Finland is the most densely forested country in Europe, and wood accounts for 30 per cent of its exports. All four countries are highly industrialized and are among the wealthiest in the world.

SKIING

During the winter months, much of Scandinavia is covered with snow, so skiing is one of the easiest forms of transport. It is also a very popular sport.

URBAN POPULATIONS

Scandinavia has a high urban population. Many people live in towns and cities, with less than a fifth living in the countryside. Since it is an area covered in lakes, fjords, and surrounded by sea, many people also live near the water.

COPENHAGEN in Denmark is the largest city in Scandinavia.

LAPLAND

Northern Sweden and Finland are known as Lapland. Here the local Sami people survive the cold and inhospitable climate by herding reindeer, which they breed for their meat, milk, and skins.

SAMI man in traditional costume

RUSSIAN FEDERATION

FINLAND

SWEDEN

NORWAY

Barents Sea

North Cape (Nordkapp)

ARCTIC OCEAN

Norwegian Sea

Gulf of Bothnia

Lapland

Kjolen

0 km   100   200
0 miles   100   200

INDUSTRIAL STRENGTH

Manufacturing is an important source of employment and wealth throughout Scandinavia. Many of the goods produced, such as cars in Sweden, electronic goods in Denmark (above), and mobile phones in Finland, are exported all over the world. In Denmark, many people also work in agriculture, fish processing, and brewing.

Did you know?

Ski is Norwegian for "strip of wood".

Two-thirds of all Danish people have surnames that end in "sen", such as Hansen, meaning "son".

Sweden recycles more aluminium cans than any other country in the world.

THE SAUNA

The sauna, or steam bath, was invented in Finland about 1,000 years ago as a way of cleaning and relaxing the body. After a hot sauna, many Finns cool off by plunging into an icy pool (above) or a snowdrift.

NORWEGIAN FJORDS

The west coast of Norway has thousands of deep inlets, known as fjords, gouged out of the mountains by glaciers during the last Ice Age and then flooded by the sea. The fjords run inland between high mountains and are a favourite destination for cruise ships bringing tourists to admire the stunning scenery.

BUILDING WITH WOOD

Much of Norway and Sweden, and two-thirds of Finland, is covered by dense forests of birch, pine, spruce, and other trees. Many people work in the forestry industry, producing wood for the construction and furniture industries. This great natural resource is also used to build homes and churches, like this medieval stave church (left) in Norway.

SAVING THE ENVIRONMENT

The people of Scandinavia are very environmentally conscious and recycle as many household items as they can. Strict national laws protect the environment from industrial waste and pollution, although there is growing concern about the levels of pollution in the Baltic Sea.

The British Isles

FOR SUCH A SMALL GROUP OF ISLANDS, the British Isles has a very rich history. This is evident from its legacy of ancient ruins, medieval castles, dramatic cathedrals, and grand country houses. Once a leading industrial and colonial power, British monarchs ruled an empire that circled the globe. As a result, English is still widely spoken around the world. Today, many traditional industries, such as shipbuilding, mining, and engineering, have declined, and the emphasis is now on banking and insurance, as well as pharmaceuticals. The British Isles consists of two countries: the United Kingdom of Great Britain and Northern Ireland (the UK), and the Republic of Ireland.

Did you know?

▶ Edinburgh, in Scotland, is built on the core of an extinct volcano.

▶ The Romans founded London in AD 43. They named it Londinium.

▶ Wales has more than 200 castles.

IRELAND

Tourists visit Ireland every year, attracted by its unspoiled countryside and lively cities, such as Dublin (left). Once part of Britain, Ireland gained independence in 1922. It is now one of the fastest-growing economies in Europe.

HORSE BREEDING

Lush pastures and a mild climate have encouraged the breeding of thoroughbred racehorses in Ireland. Stud farms here raise some of the best racehorses in the world.

IRISH HORSE and rider on a training run

SCOTLAND

Scotland and England united as a single country in 1707. Today, however, Scotland is a self-governing part of the UK, with its own parliament and distinct legal and educational systems. Edinburgh, above, is a popular city with a magnificent castle. Each summer, it hosts an international arts festival.

NORTH SEA ENERGY

Beneath the shallow seas around Britain, there are supplies of oil and natural gas. Large oil rigs raise oil and gas to the surface where it is pumped by pipeline to be refined on the mainland. Supplies are now beginning to run low and new, more distant areas are being explored.

MONEY MATTERS

The City of London is the UK's financial centre with more than 500 banks. Lloyd's Insurance Building (right) is one of the city's modern skyscrapers. Built of steel and glass, it has lifts on the outside.

Map labels

ATLANTIC OCEAN

Shetland Islands — Unst, Fetlar, Yell, Mainland, Lerwick, Fair Isle

Orkney Islands — Sanday, Kirkwall, Mainland, Hoy

North Sea

Outer Hebrides — Isle of Lewis, Stornoway, Harris, North Uist, South Uist, Barra, St Kilda

Inner Hebrides — Isle of Skye, Stromeferry, Rhum, Eigg, Coll, Tiree, Isle of Mull, Firth of Lorn, Iona, Islay, Jura, Kintyre

The Minch
The Little Minch

North West Highlands — Ben Hope 927m, Ben Nevis, Ullapool, Inverness, Loch Ness, Fort William, Mallaig, Oban

SCOTLAND — Thurso, John o'Groats, Wick, Elgin, Moray Firth, Spey, Dee, Aviemore, Grampian Mountains, Forfar, Perth, Tay, Stirling, Forth, Glasgow, Hamilton, Clyde, Paisley, Greenock, East Kilbride, Kilmarnock, Prestwick, Ayr, Isle of Arran, Dumfries

Aberdeen, Peterhead, Fraserburgh, Montrose, Arbroath, Dundee, St Andrews, Firth of Forth, Dunfermline, Edinburgh, Galashiels, Hawick, Southern Uplands, Berwick-upon-Tweed

Firth of Clyde, Loch Lomond, Loch Fyne, Stranraer

NORTHERN IRELAND — Londonderry, Coleraine, Strabane, Newtownabbey, Belfast, Bangor, Downpatrick, Strabane, Omagh, Armagh, Portadown, Newry, Dundalk

Lough Neagh, Lower Lough Erne, Upper Lough Erne, Donegal, Donegal Bay, Sligo, Boyle, Cavan, Longford, Castlebar, Colloney, Connaught, Ardee

UNITED KINGDOM

ISLE OF MAN — Douglas

Carlisle, Penrith, Workington, Whitehaven, Lake District, Kendal, Barrow-in-Furness, Lancaster, Blackpool, Preston

Newcastle upon Tyne, South Shields, Sunderland, Durham, Hartlepool, Darlington, Cheviot Hills, Tees, Pennines, Middlesbrough, Whitby, Northallerton, Scarborough, Harrogate, Bridlington, York, Leeds, Castleford, Beverley, Kingston upon Hull, Ribble, Ouse

LONDON

The capital of the UK is London, a sprawling city on the banks of the River Thames. It is the political and financial centre of the country, as well as home to more than 7 million people. One of its most recent attractions is the London Eye – a giant ferris wheel, 135 m (443 ft) high.

When the pods reach the top, you can see all of the city beneath you.

STONEHENGE in southern England, was built from about 3000 BC onward.

CHANNEL ISLANDS (to UK)
ST PETER PORT
Guernsey   Sark
ST HELIER
Jersey
Alderney

WALES

Wales was formally united with England in 1536, but retains its own language and traditions. Welsh is spoken widely in some parts, and public signs appear in both Welsh and English. Coal mining and steel production were important in the south, but have both declined. Rugby is the national game.

MULTICULTURAL SOCIETY

Britain once controlled a world empire with colonies in every continent. Many people – from the Indian subcontinent, Africa, and the Caribbean in particular – came here and brought their cultures with them. Today, about one in 20 British people are from ethnic minorities, but are integrated into British life.

WALES PLAYS IRELAND at rugby in the Millennium Stadium, Cardiff.

BRITISH LANDMARKS

Tourism is a major industry in Britain. Visitors come from all over the world to see the many churches, castles, and ancient monuments, such as Stonehenge (above), and to admire the pretty villages. Many also come for the theatres, galleries, and shops in Britain's vibrant cities.

0 km   50   100
0 miles   50   100

Map labels: North Sea, Irish Sea, Celtic Sea, St George's Channel, English Channel, Channel Tunnel

IRELAND — DUBLIN, Dún Laoghaire, Lucan, Arklow, Wicklow Mts, Wexford, Carlow, Kilkenny, Newbridge, Athlone, Port Laoise, Nenagh, Limerick, Ennis, Galway, Galway Bay, Lough Corrib, Loughrea, Cashel, Clonmel, Waterford, Youghal, Cork, Rathkeale, Abbeyfeale, Tralee, Killarney, Dingle Bay, Bantry, Bantry Bay, Leinster, Munster, Liffey, Barrow, Blackwater, Shannon, Lough Derg

WALES — Cardiff, Swansea, Newport, Llanelli, Carmarthen, Fishguard, Haverfordwest, Milford Haven, Bangor, Holyhead, Anglesey, Aberystwyth, Tywyn, Barmouth, Cardigan Bay, Brecon Beacons, Cambrian Mountains, Snowdonia, Port Talbot, Kidderminster, Wye

ENGLAND — LONDON, Liverpool, Birkenhead, Manchester, Sheffield, Chester, Crewe, Stoke-on-Trent, Derby, Nottingham, Leicester, Birmingham, Wolverhampton, Coventry, Shrewsbury, Stafford, Worcester, Gloucester, Cheltenham, Northampton, Milton Keynes, Oxford, Luton, Bedford, Cambridge, Peterborough, Kettering, Nuneaton, Lincoln, Doncaster, Boston, Skegness, Louth, Grimsby, King's Lynn, Norwich, Great Yarmouth, Lowestoft, Ipswich, Felixstowe, Harwich, Colchester, Southend-on-Sea, Margate, Canterbury, Dover, Folkestone, Maidstone, Hastings, Eastbourne, Brighton, Hove, Crawley, Woking, Guildford, Reading, Swindon, Newbury, Andover, Winchester, Southampton, Portsmouth, Havant, Isle of Wight, Newport, Bournemouth, Poole, Weymouth, Lyme Bay, Bridport, Exeter, Exmouth, Tiverton, Taunton, Bristol, Bath, Weston-super-Mare, Barnstaple, Ilfracombe, Bideford, Dartmoor, Exmoor, Torquay, Plymouth, Saltash, Tamar, Bodmin, Newquay, St Austell, Truro, Falmouth, Penzance, Land's End, Isles of Scilly, Salisbury, Yeovil, Stonehenge, Cotswold Hills, St Albans, Watford, Stevenage, Harlow, Croydon, Newmarket, Mersey, Trent, The Wash, The Fens, Thames, Severn

The Low Countries

THE NETHERLANDS, BELGIUM, AND LUXEMBOURG are known as the Low Countries because the land is so flat and low-lying. In the case of the Netherlands, much of the land is below sea level – Netherlands is Dutch for "under lands". The three countries are among the richest in Europe and, while farming still plays an important part, they all have strong, modern economies based on manufacturing and trade.

Luxembourg in particular is known as a tax haven and is a major centre for international finance. Their location at the mouth of the River Rhine and other major European rivers, places the three countries at the heart of western European trade and politics – all three were founder members of the European Economic Community (now the European Union or EU) established in 1957.

ROTTERDAM

Every year, more than 30,000 sea-going ships and 110,000 barges call at the port of Rotterdam. Lying at the mouth of the River Rhine, this port is the largest in the world, and is where vast container ships from all over the world load or unload their cargoes. The smaller barges help to transport goods further inland. With the port's ultra-modern Vessel Traffic System (VTS) it's possible to track ships on a radar screen up to 60 km (37 miles) off the coast and 40 km (25 miles) inland.

Did you know?

- Tulips were introduced into the Netherlands from Turkey in 1562. Black tulips were the most valuable.

- Belgium combines two cultures: the French-speaking Walloons and the Dutch-speaking Flemings.

- In Belgium, French fries, known as *frites*, are served in a paper cone or dish, with a dollop of mayonnaise. They are generally eaten using a small wooden fork.

RECLAIMING THE LAND

Over the centuries, the Dutch have reclaimed land from the sea. They did this by building huge dykes, or dams, to keep out the sea, and then draining the surface water into canals. Windmills originally pumped out the water, but electric pumps are now used.

Land below sea level on main map

DUTCH PEOPLE

The Dutch once ruled a vast empire in Indonesia, the Caribbean, and South America. As a result, many nationalities now live here. Ethnic minorities make up about 45 per cent of the people and the majority of primary school children have a non-Dutch background.

CROPS

Fertile soil and good irrigation have helped the Netherlands become a major exporter of agricultural products, with vegetables and tomatoes forming important crops. It is also famous for its bulbs and cut flowers, notably tulips.

DUTCH TULIP

GERMANY

NETHERLANDS

West Frisian Islands (Waddeneilanden)

Schiermonnikoog · Ameland · Terschelling · Vlieland · Texel

Waddenzee · IJsselmeer · Flevoland · IJssel

Delfzijl · Appingedam · **Groningen** · Eemshaven · Loppersum · Zuidhorn · Haren · Zuidlaren · Vlagtwedde · Borger · Emmen · Coevorden · Hardenberg · Den Ham · Denekamp · Hengelo · **Enschede**

Dokkum · Winsum · Menaldum · Leek · Leeuwarden · Drachten · Assen · Beilen · Hoogeveen · Staphorst · Almelo · Rijssen · Goor · Haaksbergen

Harlingen · Sneek · Joure · Heerenveen · Wolvega · Steenwijk · Meppel · Zwolle · Tubbergen · Deventer · Zutphen · Dieren · Eibergen

Den Helder · Schagen · Opmeer · Hoorn · Emmeloord · Lelystad · Nunspeet · Zeewolde · Vaassen · Apeldoorn · Ede

Alkmaar · Castricum · Velsen-Noord · Purmerend · Zaanstad · Almere · Baarn · Hilversum · Amersfoort · Zeist

AMSTERDAM · Haarlem · Amstelveen · Sassenheim · Utrecht · Zoetermeer · Leiden · Noordwijk aan Zee

THE HAGUE ('S-GRAVENHAGE)

AMSTERDAM

The old architecture and picturesque canals make Amsterdam one of the most visited cities in Europe. Occasionally the canals freeze over and city officials may decide it's safe for people to go skating. Amsterdam is also home to some of the world's best museums, including the Van Gogh Museum.

CYCLISTS have their own traffic lights – this one is green for "go".

CYCLING

The flatness of the land makes the Netherlands ideal for cycling, and more than half a million people cycle to school or work each day. Most of the roads have special cycle lanes, and bicycles are often the quickest form of transport to get around the crowded towns and cities. The use of bicycles also reduces car use and thus cuts down the amount of air pollution.

TRILINGUAL

The Grand Duchy of Luxembourg lies between Germany, France, and Belgium. As a result, the majority of the people are trilingual – German and French are widely spoken as is Letzebuegesch, the national language. The capital, also known as Luxembourg, has more than 200 banks.

FLAGS of the member states of the European Union

BELGIAN QUALITY

Belgium is renowned for its beautiful historic buildings, and for its excellent food, especially chocolates. Belgians have been making top-quality chocolates for more than 100 years and pralines, a type of filled chocolate, are a speciality. Brussels even boasts a chocolate museum.

France

IN DIRECT CONTRAST TO ITS mainly rural landscape, France is a modern nation with most people now living in towns and cities. It has flourishing industries and is the fifth richest economy in the world, after the USA, Japan, Germany, and the UK. A country of varied scenery, from gently rolling farmland in the north to a stretch of dry, warm Mediterranean coast in the south, France also shares two mountain ranges – the Pyrenees and the Alps. Each of the 22 regions within France, which includes the island of Corsica, has its own distinct identity and culture. The tiny countries of Andorra and Monaco lie next to France.

Did you know?

▶ Some of the world's finest perfumes come from southern France, where fields of lavender, roses, and jasmine are grown. As many as 300 oils may be used to make one perfume.

▶ Boules, the national game of France, is still played in village squares around the country.

▶ *Poisson d'avril*, or April fish, is the name given to anyone who is fooled on April 1st. Confectionery shops sell fish-shaped chocolate, and people send funny cards with fish on them.

HIGH-SPEED TRAVEL

France has the world's fastest train, the TGV – *train à grande vitesse* – which travels at an average speed of 300 kmh (186 mph). The TGV network connects Paris with all the country's major regional cities, which makes it easier to commute or visit relatives. It also extends to Germany, Italy, Belgium, Switzerland, and through the Channel Tunnel to Britain.

NUCLEAR POWER

Three-quarters of France's electricity is produced by nuclear power plants (above), making the country largely self-sufficient in energy and one of the main producers of nuclear power in Europe. Hydro-electric plants are also an important source of power.

STREETS OF PARIS

Tourists flock to Paris to visit its world-famous museums and art galleries, shop in its elegant stores, and soak up its vibrant atmosphere. Montmartre, which overlooks the city, is famous for its artists. Close by, in the Place du Tertre (above), visitors can have their portrait painted.

53

32

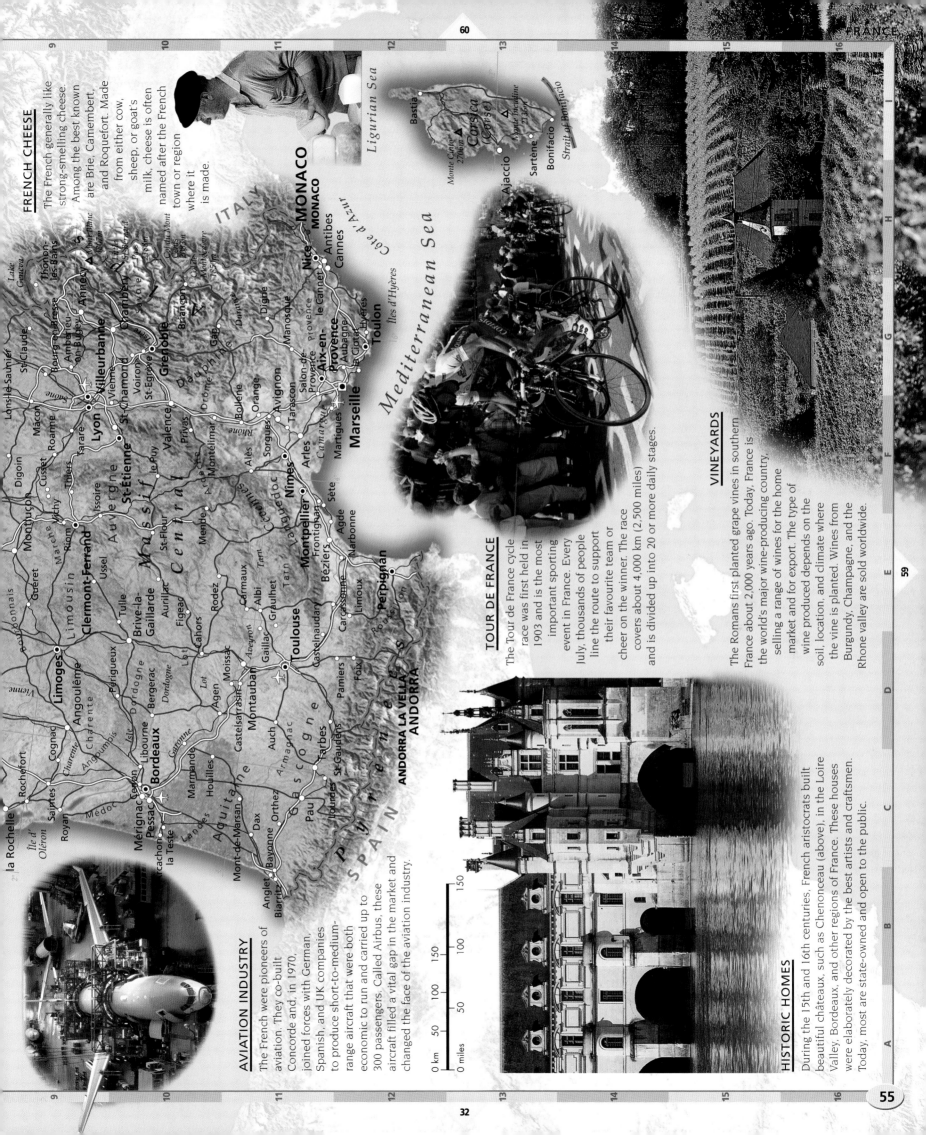

FRENCH CHEESE

The French generally like strong-smelling cheese. Among the best known are Brie, Camembert, and Roquefort. Made from either cow, sheep, or goat's milk, cheese is often named after the French town or region where it is made.

AVIATION INDUSTRY

The French were pioneers of aviation. They co-built Concorde and, in 1970, joined forces with German, Spanish, and UK companies to produce short-to-medium-range aircraft that were both economic to run and carried up to 300 passengers. Called Airbus, these aircraft filled a vital gap in the market and changed the face of the aviation industry.

TOUR DE FRANCE

The Tour de France cycle race was first held in 1903 and is the most important sporting event in France. Every July, thousands of people line the route to support their favourite team or cheer on the winner. The race covers about 4,000 km (2,500 miles) and is divided up into 20 or more daily stages.

VINEYARDS

The Romans first planted grape vines in southern France about 2,000 years ago. Today, France is the world's major wine-producing country, selling a range of wines for the home market and for export. The type of wine produced depends on the soil, location, and climate where the vine is planted. Wines from Burgundy, Champagne, and the Rhone valley are sold worldwide.

HISTORIC HOMES

During the 15th and 16th centuries, French aristocrats built beautiful châteaux, such as Chenonceau (above), in the Loire Valley, Bordeaux, and other regions of France. These houses were elaborately decorated by the best artists and craftsmen. Today, most are state-owned and open to the public.

Germany and the Alpine States

LYING AT THE VERY HEART of Europe, Germany is one of the world's wealthiest nations. It is also Europe's leading industrial power. An extensive network of rivers and canals forms an important waterway for transporting goods around Germany and also to other European countries. To the south lie the Alpine states of Switzerland, Austria, Liechtenstein, and Slovenia. Although German is the main language in all but Slovenia, each of the five countries has its own distinct history, culture, and sense of national identity. The entire region boasts beautiful alpine scenery, forests, mountains, and lakes.

GERMAN INDUSTRY

The Ruhr Valley used to be the powerhouse of the German economy, with vast coal and iron mines and a massive steel industry. Today, its economy is more diverse, ranging from heavy engineering to high-tech goods. It is the world's third largest car producer (above).

FOOD AND DRINK

Traditional German food and drink include smoked sausage, *sauerkraut* (pickled cabbage), and beer. The annual Munich *Oktoberfest* is Germany's biggest beer festival.

THE BERLIN WALL

After World War II, Germany was split, with a US-backed capitalist state in the west and a Russian-backed communist state in the east. The wall was built in 1961 to stop East Germans leaving for a better life in the West. The wall divided Berlin and separated families, friends, and a nation for 28 years. When Germany was reunited in 1990, the Berlin Wall was finally demolished.

THE WALL consisted of 155 km (96 miles) of barbed-wire barricade and a concrete wall with an average height of 3.6 m (11.8 ft).

GENEVA

The Swiss city of Geneva lies on the shores of Lake Geneva, Europe's largest alpine lake. This orderly city is a global centre for banking and finance. It is also a base for many international organizations, such as the Red Cross.

SWISS WATCHES

The Swiss invented the first wristwatch, the first quartz watch, and the first water-resistant watch. With their worldwide reputation for quality and style, timepieces make up the country's third largest export.

ALPINE SCENERY

The Alps run from southeast France and spread eastwards through Switzerland and northern Italy into Austria and Slovenia. A popular tourist destination, the Alps are famous for dramatic scenery and winter sports. Cable cars (below) carry skiers and hill walkers higher up the mountains.

Did you know?

▲ Germany is famous for its Christmas markets, and the one held in Nuremberg is the oldest.

▲ From 1961–89, 171 people died trying to climb the Berlin Wall.

▲ Liechtenstein is so small that it only has 19 km (12 miles) of single-track railway.

SLOVENIA

Independent since 1991, Slovenia has retained a strong national culture and identity, despite centuries of rule by overlords. Colourful embroidery and distinctive headwear (right) are part of their folk culture.

VIENNA

Vienna is a city of music, cafes, and delicious pastries. It has many baroque buildings, palaces, cathedrals, and famous concert halls. These are a reminder of when the city was the centre of the Austro-Hungarian Empire that controlled much of east and central Europe.

St Stephen's Cathedral, generally known as Stephansdom

Spain and Portugal

THE COUNTRIES OF SPAIN AND PORTUGAL share an area of land called the Iberian Peninsula. In the north, this land is cut off from the rest of Europe by the Pyrenees Mountains, while to the south, it is separated from Africa by the Strait of Gibraltar. The region was once ruled by Islamic people from North Africa, known as the Moors. Evidence of their occupation can still be seen from buildings in the cities of Andalucía. The Moors were eventually defeated in 1492, and for a while, Portugal came under Spanish control, as did much of Europe. During the 20th century, both countries were ruled by brutal dictatorships, which were overthrown in the 1970s. They are now modern democracies.

Did you know?

▶ In Spain, it is customary for families to eat dinner late in the evening, usually around 9 p.m. So after school, children eat a snack called *merienda*.

▶ Bullfights, known as *touradas*, are still popular in Portugal, despite opposition from local and international animal welfare groups.

HARVESTING CORK

Cork is made from the outer bark of the evergreen cork oak tree. The bark is carefully stripped off, flattened, laid out in sheets, and then left to dry. The cork is used for many products, such as stoppers for wine bottles, matting, and tiles. Portugal is the world's leading exporter of cork.

LISBON

The capital city of Portugal is Lisbon, which is situated at the mouth of the River Tagus on a series of steep hills and valleys. In 1755, two-thirds of the city was completely destroyed by an earthquake and tidal wave, but was rebuilt with beautiful squares and public buildings. Many explorers set sail from Lisbon in their quest to find new lands.

TRAMS are a feature of Lisbon streets, and a popular form of transport for both the locals and tourists.

FISHING

Spain and Portugal have well-developed fishing industries – with large-scale fleets and many smaller local fleets. However, overfishing along Portugal's coastline and out in the North Atlantic, plus a massive oil spill off the coast of Galicia in 2002, have put many people's livelihoods at risk.

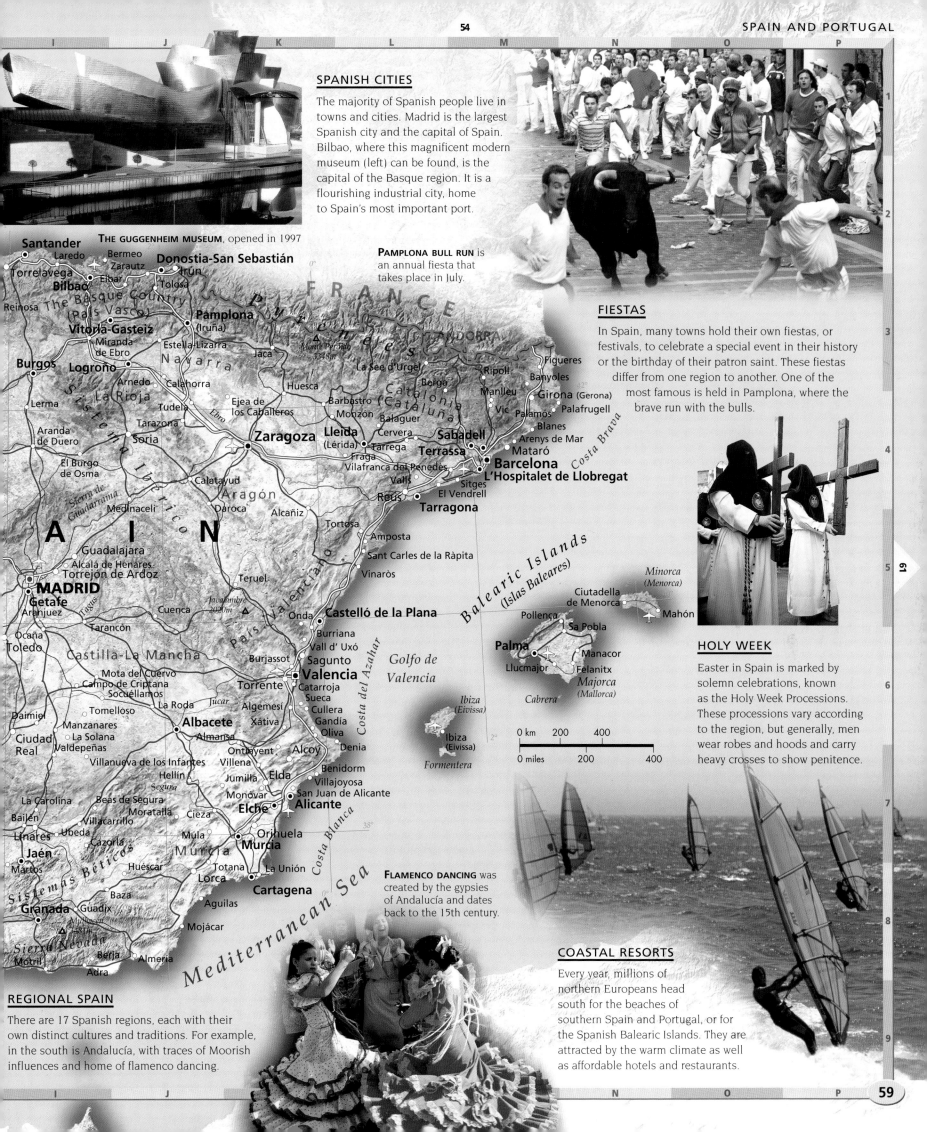

SPANISH CITIES

The majority of Spanish people live in towns and cities. Madrid is the largest Spanish city and the capital of Spain. Bilbao, where this magnificent modern museum (left) can be found, is the capital of the Basque region. It is a flourishing industrial city, home to Spain's most important port.

THE GUGGENHEIM MUSEUM, opened in 1997

PAMPLONA BULL RUN is an annual fiesta that takes place in July.

FIESTAS

In Spain, many towns hold their own fiestas, or festivals, to celebrate a special event in their history or the birthday of their patron saint. These fiestas differ from one region to another. One of the most famous is held in Pamplona, where the brave run with the bulls.

HOLY WEEK

Easter in Spain is marked by solemn celebrations, known as the Holy Week Processions. These processions vary according to the region, but generally, men wear robes and hoods and carry heavy crosses to show penitence.

FLAMENCO DANCING was created by the gypsies of Andalucía and dates back to the 15th century.

COASTAL RESORTS

Every year, millions of northern Europeans head south for the beaches of southern Spain and Portugal, or for the Spanish Balearic Islands. They are attracted by the warm climate as well as affordable hotels and restaurants.

REGIONAL SPAIN

There are 17 Spanish regions, each with their own distinct cultures and traditions. For example, in the south is Andalucía, with traces of Moorish influences and home of flamenco dancing.

Map labels

FRANCE

ANDORRA

Santander, Laredo, Bermeo, Zarautz, Donostia-San Sebastián, Torrelavega, Bilbao, Eibar, Irún, Tolosa, Reinosa, The Basque Country (País Vasco), Pamplona (Iruña), Vitoria-Gasteiz, Miranda de Ebro, Estella-Lizarra, Jaca, Monte Perdido 3348m, Burgos, Logroño, Arnedo, Calahorra, Huesca, La Seo d'Urgel, Berga, Ripoll, Figueres, Banyoles, Girona (Gerona), Manlleu, Lerma, La Rioja, Sistema Ibérico, Aranda de Duero, Soria, Tarazona, Ejea de los Caballeros, Barbastro, Monzón, Balaguer, Cervera, Vic, Palamós, Palafrugell, El Burgo de Osma, Calatayud, Aragón, Lleida (Lérida), Tàrrega, Fraga, Sabadell, Terrassa, Blanes, Arenys de Mar, Costa Brava, Zaragoza, Daroca, Alcañiz, Vilafranca del Penedès, Barcelona, L'Hospitalet de Llobregat, Medinaceli, Sierra de Guadarrama, Guadalajara, Alcalá de Henares, Torrejón de Ardoz, Teruel, Javalambre 2020m, Tortosa, Valls, Reus, Sitges, El Vendrell, Tarragona, Amposta, Sant Carles de la Ràpita, Vinaròs, MADRID, Getafe, Aranjuez, Tagus, Cuenca, Onda, Castelló de la Plana, Burriana, Vall d'Uxó, Sagunto, País Valenciano, Costa del Azahar, Ocaña, Toledo, Tarancón, Castilla-La Mancha, Mota del Cuervo, Campo de Criptana, Socuéllamos, La Roda, Burjassot, Catarroja, Torrente, Valencia, Algemesí, Sueca, Cullera, Gandía, Oliva, Xàtiva, Júcar, Golfo de Valencia, Daimiel, Tomelloso, Manzanares, La Solana, Valdepeñas, Villanueva de los Infantes, Almansa, Ontinyent, Villena, Alcoy, Denia, Albacete, Ciudad Real, Hellín, Jumilla, Elda, Benidorm, Villajoyosa, Monóvar, San Juan de Alicante, La Carolina, Beas de Segura, Moratalla, Cieza, Elche, Alicante, Bailén, Villacarrillo, Segura, Mula, Orihuela, Costa Blanca, Linares, Úbeda, Cazorla, Murcia, Totana, La Unión, Jaén, Martos, Huéscar, Lorca, Cartagena, Sistemas Béticos, Baza, Aguilas, Granada, Guadix, Mojácar, Sierra Nevada, Berja, Almería, Motril, Adra

Balearic Islands (Islas Baleares), Ciutadella de Menorca, Minorca (Menorca), Mahón, Pollença, Sa Pobla, Palma, Manacor, Felanitx, Llucmajor, Majorca (Mallorca), Cabrera, Ibiza (Eivissa), Formentera

Golfo de Valencia, Mediterranean Sea

0 km 200 400
0 miles 200 400

Italy

THE BOOT-SHAPED COUNTRY of Italy stretches from the mountainous north down to the Mediterranean Sea. For much of its history, Italy consisted of city-states – such as Florence and Venice – and was only united in 1870. Regional differences in Italy are huge, as each region has its own cuisine, customs, and dialect, and is geographically quite distinct. As a result, many Italians identify themselves first by region and then by country. The national division, however, is between the rich north and the poorer south, a rugged region with several active volcanoes and the occasional severe earthquake. The mainland of Italy includes two tiny independent states – San Marino and Vatican City.

COLOSSEUM

One of Rome's greatest sights is the Colosseum, which opened in AD 80. Deadly gladiatorial combats and animal fights were staged here before crowds of up to 55,000 people.

The oval-shaped Colosseum stood at 189 m (620 ft) high.

ANDREA BOCELLI

HOME OF OPERA

The idea of setting drama to music originated in Italy during the 16th century. Since then, Italian composers, such as Rossini, Verdi, and Puccini, have made opera the most popular musical form in Italy. Many cities have their own opera houses.

Did you know?

▶ The *Sartiglia* of Oristano is a festival in Sardinia. Before the tournament, masked horsemen must pierce the centre of a silver star with their swords while riding past at high speed.

▶ Vatican City has a permanent population of only about 1,000 people, although a further 3,400 come to work in the city-state each day.

▶ More than 600 different types of pasta are eaten in Italy.

CARNIVAL MASKS

CITY OF CANALS

The beautiful city of Venice is made up of 118 islands, 177 canals, and 400 bridges. The only way to get around is to walk or take a boat: a *vaporetto*, *motoscafo*, or *motonave*. The most familiar boat, however, is the gondola. Each year, in the days before Ash Wednesday, Venice hosts a carnival when the city celebrates with fireworks, and everyone wears spectacular masks.

FOOTBALL FANS

Italians are mad about football and fanatically follow the performance of teams such as Juventus, Milan, Roma, and Lazio. Italian teams have regularly won major European championships, and the national team has won the World Cup three times – in 1934, 1938, and 1982.

Seas and waters

Adriatic Sea

Ionian Sea

Tyrrhenian Sea

Mediterranean Sea

Gulf of Salerno

Golfo di Gaeta

Golfo di Taranto

Strait of Otranto

Strait of Messina

Strait of Sicily

Strait of Bonifacio

Malta Channel

HOME LIFE

Family life is important in Italy, and most people live at home until they marry. This is partly due to lack of cheap housing. Lunch (pranzo) is often the main meal of the day.

Places

Termoli
San Severo
Campobasso
Isernia
Manfredonia
Foggia
Cerignola
Barletta
Andria
Molfetta
Bitonto
Bari
Benevento
Avellino
Altamura
Matera
Potenza
Puglia
Manduria
Taranto
Brindisi
Lecce
Maglie
Gallipoli
Caserta
Torre del Greco
Salerno
Battipaglia
Agropoli
Campania
Sapri
Lauria
Conshina
Sala
Appennino Lucano
Castrovillari
Rossano
La Sila
Ciro Marino
Crotone
Catanzaro
Siderno
Cosenza
Amantea
Lamezia
Palmi
Reggio di Calabria
Strait of Messina
Isola Stromboli
Isola Lipari
Isole Eolie
Isola Vulcano
Cefalù
Palermo
Messina
Catania
Mount Etna 3340m
Simeto
Siracusa
Modica
Pozzallo
Ragusa
Vittoria
Gela
Caltanissetta
Agrigento
Alcamo
Marsala
Castelvetrano
Trapani
Sicily (Sicilia)
MALTA
Gozo
VALLETTA
Malta
Isola di Pantelleria
Isole Pelagie

ROME (ROMA)
VATICAN CITY
Tivoli
Anzio
Latina
Terracina
Gaeta
Isole Ponziane
Isola di Capri
Naples (Napoli)
Vesuvio
Volturno
Avezzano
Tempio Pausania
la Maddalena
Isola Asinara
Porto Torres
Sassari
Alghero
Olbia
Siniscola
Ozieri
Nuoro
Macomer
Oristano
Villacidro
Iglesias
Carbonia
Cagliari
Quartu Sant' Elena
Sardinia (Sardegna)
Punta La Marmora 1834m

OLIVE HARVEST

Italy is the world's largest producer of olive oil, followed by Spain and Greece. The oil is produced by first pressing the fruits of the olive tree between steel or stone rollers, then squeezing oil from the pulp using a press. Olive trees flourish in the fertile soils and the mild, frost-free climate of southern Italy.

Olives are gathered in large nets.

VATICAN CITY

This tiny state in Rome is the centre of the Roman Catholic church and home to the Pope. As well as St Peter's basilica and the surrounding buildings and gardens, the Vatican boasts Michelangelo's Sistine Chapel. The state has its own flag, postage stamps, and coins.

SWISS GUARDS, in their red, yellow, and blue striped costumes, stand at the gates into Vatican City.

RENAISSANCE ITALY

Florence (below) sits either side of the River Arno. During the 14th century, a new movement in art and architecture, known as the Renaissance, or rebirth, began in Italy. Painters and sculptors, such as Leonardo da Vinci, Michelangelo, and Raphael created beautiful works of art often based on religious themes. Many of these can still be seen in the galleries and churches of Florence.

0 km   50   100

0 miles   50   100

Central Europe

FOUR COUNTRIES LIE at the heart of Central Europe – Poland, the Czech Republic, Slovakia, and Hungary. The region is characterized by wide plains, broken by gentle hills and the Carpathian Mountain range in the south. In the late 1980s, these countries broke from years of communist rule. The new democratic governments were faced with the problems of trying to modernize their country. These changes are ongoing, but in some of the countries, such as the Czech Republic, there are signs of improvement and a rise in living standards.

GOLDEN PRAGUE

Prague, capital of the Czech Republic, is one of Europe's most beautiful cities. It contains many old buildings with golden roofs and grand squares. Unlike other Central European cities, Prague escaped serious damage during both world wars, and thus retains much of its charm.

FAMILY FARMS

Poland has one of the largest agricultural sectors in Europe, with more than a quarter of the workforce employed on the land. Most farms are still small, family-run businesses, growing grains, sugar beet, and potatoes. Large numbers of pigs and other animals are also kept.

TRADITIONAL TRADES

The countries of Central Europe, except Slovakia, are heavily industrialized. Vast coal mines, steel works (above), and engineering works dominate the urban landscape. Although some of these sites are old and poorly equipped, these countries are trying to update machinery and introduce measures to improve standards on environmental pollution.

RELIGION

The Roman Catholic Church is very strong throughout Central Europe. Attending mass on Sunday and observing religious holidays, such as Christmas and Easter, are important features of family life.

PART OF PRAGUE'S colourful history is preserved in buildings around the Old Town Square.

BELARUS

KALININGRAD
(to Russian Federation)

Gulf of Danzig
Vistula Lagoon

Baltic Sea

Pomeranian Bay

GERMANY

POLAND

Suwałki
Gołdap
Augustów
Grajewo
Białystok
Kuźnica
Sokółka
Łapy
Bielsk Podlaski
Biała Podlaska
Międzyrzec Podlaski
Radzyń Podlaski
Włodawa
Chełm
Lublin
Krasnystaw
Zamość
Tomaszów Lubelski
Stalowa Wola
Leżajsk
Jarosław
Mielec
Tarnobrzeg
Dębrowa Tarnowska
Miechów
Kraków
Gliwice
Chorzów
Katowice
Rybnik
Opole
Częstochowa
Zawiercie
Będzin
Kozle
Kędzierzyn Koźle
Racibórz
Zabkowice Śląskie
Kłodzko
Wałbrzych
Świdnica
Jelenia Góra
Legnica
Wrocław
Brzeg
Oława
Kluczbork
Namysłów
Wieluń
Bełchatów
Radomsko
Piotrków Trybunalski
Tomaszów Mazowiecki
Skierniewice
Łódź
Zgierz
Pabianice
Sieradz
Kalisz
Ostrów Wielkopolski
Leszno
Rawicz
Głogów
Lubin
Poznań
Gniezno
Września
Konin
Koło
Kutno
Włocławek
Płock
Kujawski
Aleksandrów Kujawski
Inowrocław
Mogilno
Żnin
Bydgoszcz
Chodzież
Piła
Wałcz
Trzcianka
Czarnków
Oborniki
Nowy Tomyśl
Zielona Góra
Nowa Sól
Nowogród
Gorzów Wielkopolski
Świebodzin
Sulęcin
Międzyrzecz
Słubice
Krosno Odrzańskie
Żary
Żagań
Lubsko
Zgorzelec
Gubin
Szprotawa
Bolesławiec
Jawor
Szczecinek
Szczecin
Goleniów
Stargard Szczeciński
Pyrzyce
Choszczno
Białogard
Koszalin
Kołobrzeg
Sławno
Słupsk
Lębork
Wejherowo
Rumia
Gdynia
Gdańsk
Tczew
Malbork
Elbląg
Braniewo
Lidzbark Warmiński
Biskupiec
Dobre Miasto
Olsztyn
Ostróda
Iława
Kwidzyn
Grudziądz
Świecie
Chełmno
Toruń
Lipno
Rypin
Brodnica
Działdowo
Nidzica
Mława
Ciechanów
Płońsk
Sierpc
Pułtusk
Nowy Dwór Mazowiecki
Pruszków
WARSAW (WARSZAWA)
Wyszków
Ostrów Mazowiecka
Ostrołęka
Łomża
Kolno
Szczytno
Pisz
Giżycko
Kętrzyn
Ełk
Bartoszyce
Mazury
Narew
Bug
Wisła
Warta
Odra
Noteć
Sudety
Śnieżka
WARSAW (WARSZAWA)
Radom
Skarżysko-Kamienna
Starachowice
Kielce
Jędrzejów
Sandomierz
Góra Kalwaria
Garwolin
Łuków
Ryki
Puławy
Ponitowa
Świętokrzyski
Góra
Opatów
Małopolska
Wyżyna
Siedlce
Mazowiecki
Mazowiecki

Świnoujście
Świdwin
Drawsko

Decin
Ústí nad Labem
Liberec
Teplice
Most
Chomutov
Kladno
Karlovy Vary
Cheb
PRAGUE (PRAHA)
Hradec Králové
Litoměřice
Lovosice
Turnov
Podebrady
Poděbrady

FOLK CULTURE

Traditional folk culture is still preserved in Slovakia, and is seen as an essential part of regional identity. Throughout the year, especially during the summer months, folk festivals are held in many towns. The people dress up in their colourful regional folk costumes, play traditional instruments, and sing and dance.

LANDSCAPE OF SLOVAKIA

Slovakia is divided between a fertile, lowland south and a more rugged, mountainous north. The country is far more rural than its industrial neighbour, the Czech Republic. Most Slovaks live in small towns and mountain villages. The Tatra Mountains in the north are popular with skiers and hikers, who bring in much-needed tourist income.

Did you know?

▶ In 1993, Czechoslovakia was divided into two countries – the Czech Republic and Slovakia.

▶ Budapest was once two cities – Buda on the right bank of the River Danube, and Pest on the left bank.

▶ Poland has the oldest operating salt mine, now a World Heritage Site, in Wieliczka near Kraków. The layers of salt go down 327 m (1,073 ft).

INDUSTRIAL LIFE

The Czech Republic is Central Europe's most industrialized country. It is renowned for its centuries-old glass industry. The region also produces some of the world's best-known beers. Pilsener lager, for example, originated in the town of Plzeň, while Budweiser beer has been brewed at České Budějovice for over a century.

HOT SPRINGS

A land of fertile plains, Hungary is also famous for its numerous hot springs. In the capital city of Budapest, there are more than 100 hot springs. The warm waters rise naturally from the ground, and the spas and baths are centred on these springs. They are as popular today as they were centuries ago, when the Romans used the hot springs on the Buda side of the city.

SZÉCHENYI BATHS has the hottest spa water in Budapest.

Southeast Europe

UNTIL 1991 CROATIA, Bosnia and Herzegovina, Serbia and Montenegro, and Macedonia were all part of Yugoslavia. Ethnic tensions between the Serbs and other peoples in Yugoslavia caused a series of bloody wars that broke the country up. Peace was eventually restored in 1999, but all four countries have suffered intense economic problems as a result. So, too, has Albania since its communist government collapsed. The five nations do, however, have huge potential, with considerable agricultural and mineral resources. In the north, the River Danube is an important trading route for both Croatia and Serbia, while Croatia has a flourishing tourist industry along its beautiful Adriatic coast.

THE ADRIATIC

The long Adriatic coastline of Croatia is one of the most beautiful in Europe. The wooded hillsides, pretty beaches, such as Markarska (right), islands, and historic towns once attracted tourists from all over Europe. Now that the country is no longer involved in the war, tourists are returning, contributing vital income to the national economy.

GROWING FOOD

The most fertile area in this region lies along the River Danube in northern Serbia and eastern Croatia. Here, vegetables, fruit, maize, and cereals are grown, as well as grapes for wine-making. Most farms are small-scale family businesses, growing a wide range of crops.

FAMILY-RUN ALLOTMENTS

SERBO-CROAT

The people of Croatia, Bosnia and Herzegovina, and Serbia all speak the same language, Serbo-Croat, but write it in different scripts. Croatians are predominantly Roman Catholic and write the language in the Roman script, as do the people of Bosnia. Serbians, however, are mainly Eastern Orthodox, and write using the Russian Cyrillic script.

SPORTING ACHIEVEMENT

Croatia is a great sporting nation. Skier Janica Kostelic became Croatia's first triple Olympic champion, after winning three gold medals at the 2002 Winter Games. In January 2003, Janica and her brother, Ivica, both won World Cup Alpine Races.

JANICA KOSTELIC

Did you know?

- The Dalmatian dog is named after the coastal region of Dalmatia in Croatia, its first known home.

- In the mountains of Albania, announcements of a death, birth, or marriage are passed from one house to another by a gunshot or a shout that echoes through the mountains.

- Bosnia and Herzegovina hosts the Sarajevo annual film festival.

POSTAGE STAMP WITH ROMAN SCRIPT

POSTAGE STAMP WITH CYRILLIC SCRIPT

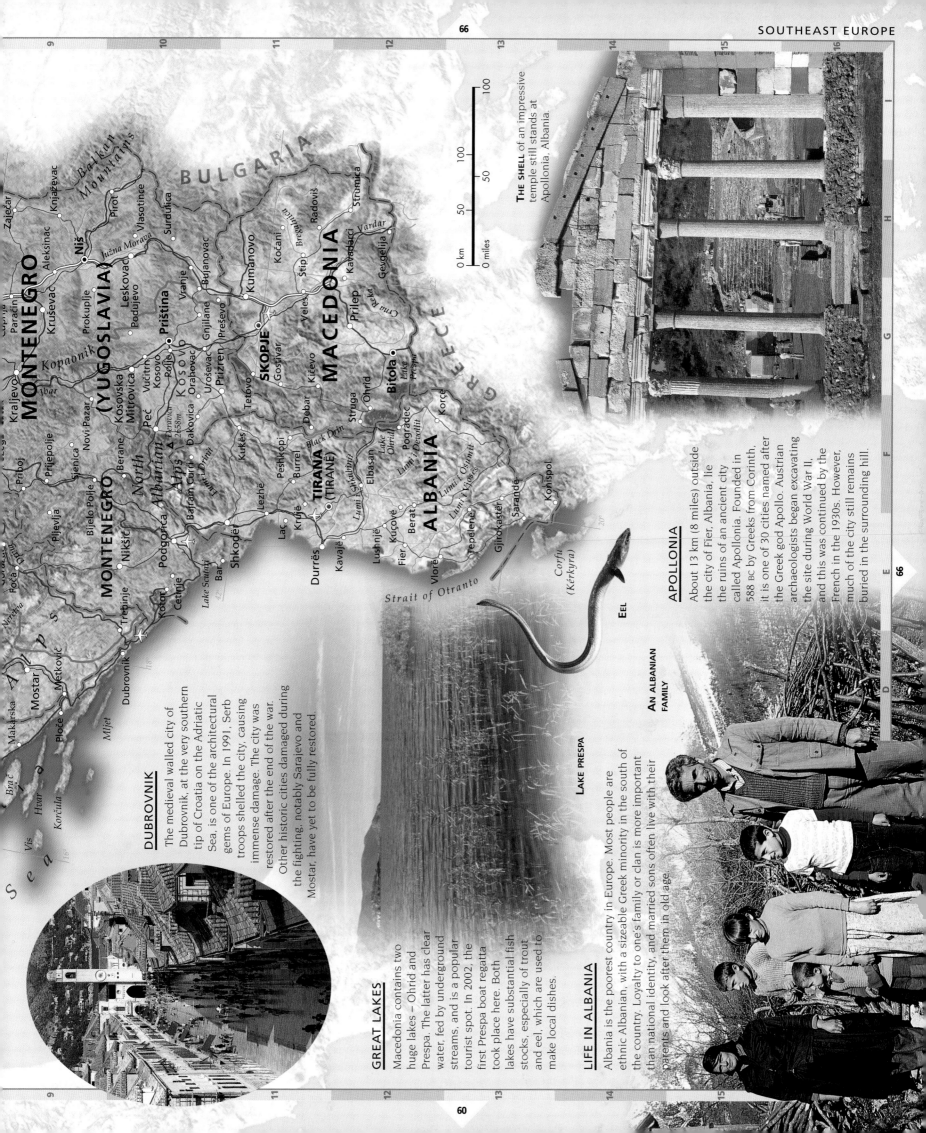

THE SHELL of an impressive temple still stands at Apollonia, Albania.

APOLLONIA

About 13 km (8 miles) outside the city of Fier, Albania, lie the ruins of an ancient city called Apollonia. Founded in 588 BC by Greeks from Corinth, it is one of 30 cities named after the Greek god Apollo. Austrian archaeologists began excavating the site during World War II, and this was continued by the French in the 1930s. However, much of the city still remains buried in the surrounding hill.

EEL

AN ALBANIAN FAMILY

LAKE PRESPA

DUBROVNIK

The medieval walled city of Dubrovnik, at the very southern tip of Croatia on the Adriatic Sea, is one of the architectural gems of Europe. In 1991, Serb troops shelled the city, causing immense damage. The city was restored after the end of the war. Other historic cities damaged during the fighting, notably Sarajevo and Mostar, have yet to be fully restored.

GREAT LAKES

Macedonia contains two huge lakes – Ohrid and Prespa. The latter has clear water, fed by underground streams, and is a popular tourist spot. In 2002, the first Prespa boat regatta took place here. Both lakes have substantial fish stocks, especially of trout and eel, which are used to make local dishes.

LIFE IN ALBANIA

Albania is the poorest country in Europe. Most people are ethnic Albanian, with a sizeable Greek minority in the south of the country. Loyalty to one's family or clan is more important than national identity, and married sons often live with their parents and look after them in old age.

Bulgaria and Greece

FOR MORE THAN FOUR CENTURIES Bulgaria and Greece were ruled by the Ottoman Turks. Bulgaria gained independence in 1908, while southern Greece became independent in 1832, and was joined by northern Greece in 1913. After World War II, Bulgaria became a communist state, and Greece was ruled by the military from 1967 until 1974. Both states are now democracies, although Bulgaria remains relatively poor and underdeveloped in comparison with Greece, which is a member of the European Union. Although they share a common border, the two countries are quite different. The Greek mainland is mountainous with only one-third of the land suitable for cultivation. By contrast, Bulgaria is more fertile with a strong agricultural tradition. Tourism is an important source of income to both countries, with visitors flocking to the Black Sea resorts in Bulgaria, to the Greek mainland to see the ancient ruins, and to the Greek islands in search of sandy beaches.

Did you know?

Every June, Bulgaria holds a Festival of the Roses to celebrate the flowers harvested for their oils.

First held in Athens in 1896, the modern Olympic Games will be staged there again in 2004.

Melbourne in Australia has the second largest number of Greek speakers in the world after Athens.

BULGARIAN AGRICULTURE

Wheat, maize, and other cereals grow in the fertile Danube river valley in the north of the country. Tobacco (right) grows in the Maritsa river valley in the southeast, while grapes for the wine industry flourish on the slopes of the Balkan Mountains. The festival of Kukerov Dan, with traditional processions, celebrates the start of the agricultural year.

ARCHITECTURE

Bulgaria contains many fine old churches, monasteries, and mosques, despite the damage done to the country during World War II. Rila Monastery (above) was founded by a hermit monk who took to the mountains in search of solitude in 927 AD. After a fire in 1833, Rila was rebuilt and the magnificent church now boasts three great domes, a museum, and 1,200 frescoes.

LANGUAGE

The 24 characters in the Greek alphabet date from the 8th century BC, when the first texts were written in classical Greek. Since then, the language has evolved and is now spoken by 11 million people around the world.

CITY LIFE

Bulgarians make up about 85 per cent of the total population of the country. The rest are Turkish, Macedonian, or Roma. Most people live in apartment blocks in the main towns and cities. They are more likely to use public transport as not all households have a car.

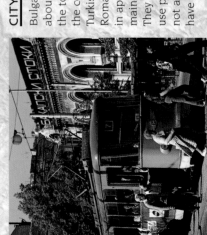

TRAMS provide an efficient way for people to get around the city of Sofia.

GREEK WEDDING

About 94 per cent of Greeks follow the Greek Orthodox religion, and weddings follow the rites of the Orthodox Church. At the ceremony, it is traditional for the best man to place wreaths of orange blossom, linked by a silk ribbon, on the heads of the bride and the groom (above).

ATHENS

The capital city of Greece is dominated by the Parthenon, a temple built in 447–438 BC on a rocky hill known as the Acropolis. Modern-day Athens is a sprawling city where the large number of cars cause serious air pollution.

GREEK ISLANDS

More than 2,000 islands lie off the mainland of Greece. The Cyclades and Dodecanese in the Aegean Sea are often rocky and arid, while the Ionian Islands, such as Zakynthos (below), are more fertile. Tourists often travel from one island to another by ferry or hovercraft.

EARTHQUAKES

The idyllic landscape of the Greek Islands, such as Santorini (left), can be rocked by earthquakes. This is because the islands and mainland of Greece, as well as Bulgaria, sit on a plate boundary. There is now a Greek Seismic Code that outlines regulations on all new buildings.

CORINTH CANAL

The Corinth Canal was built to provide a shortcut for ships between the Aegean and Ionian Seas. Dug through solid limestone, the steep-sided canal was begun in 1882 by the French and completed in 1893 by the Greeks.

100
100
50
50
100

0 km
0 miles

GREECE

ALBANIA

Aegean Sea

Ionian Sea

Ionian Islands
(Iónioi Nísoi)

Mediterranean Sea

Mirtóo Pelagos

Sea of Crete
(Kritikó Pélagos)

Dodecanese (Dodekánisos)

Cyclades (Kykládes)

Northern Sporades
(Vóreioi Sporádes)

Pindus Mountains (Pindos)

Peloponnese
(Pelopónnisos)

Lakonikós Kólpos

ATHENS (ATHINA)
Piraeus (Peiraiás)

Rhodes (Ródos)
Lindos

Crete (Kríti)
Irákleio

Lárisa
Vólos
Pátra

Ukraine, Moldova & Romania

THROUGHOUT MUCH OF THE last century, Ukraine and Moldova formed part of the Soviet Union, while Romania was ruled for 20 years by the dictator Nicolae Ceausescu. In 1989 Ceausescu was overthrown, while Ukraine and Moldova became independent in 1991. Today the three countries are struggling to come to terms with their communist inheritance and transform themselves into modern democracies. All three lack modern technology and face serious economic and environmental problems arising from outdated industry. They also face increasing ethnic tensions with their minority populations – Hungarians in Romania, as well as Russians left behind in Ukraine and Moldova after the collapse of the Soviet Union.

CITY LIFE

Romania has many cities and towns with a mix of old and new buildings. Sibiu (left) was founded in the 12th century and, at one time, had 19 guilds – each representing a different craft – within its city walls. Much remains from this colourful history, especially in the painted buildings of the old town.

FOLK CUSTOMS

Despite years of communist rule, folk customs thrived in the rural areas of Romania and Ukraine. In Ukraine, singers perform *dumas*, historical epics that tell of slavery under the Turks. One of the traditional instruments is a *bandura* (left), a stringed instrument that sounds like a harpsichord.

DRACULA'S CASTLE

Situated in Transylvania – and a favourite tourist destination – lies Bran Castle. This is where author Bram Stoker's fictional blood-drinking Count Dracula lived. The story is probably based on 15th-century Romanian prince Vlad Dracul who reigned for less than 10 years but caused more than 50,000 deaths.

Did you know?

▶ The word Transylvania means "land beyond the forests".

▶ Russia's famous beetroot soup – *borscht* – comes from Ukraine.

▶ Built entirely underground, Crivoca winery north of Chisinau, Moldova, stretches over 60 km (37 miles).

EASTER BREAD

In Romania, Easter is celebrated with a meal of roast lamb served with a bread called *cozonac*. This is made by pounding nuts, raisins, and even cocoa, into the dough.

Map labels:

BELARUS
POLAND
Pripet
Pripet Marshes
Bug
Styr
Sluch
Kovel'
Sarny
Olevs'k
Ovruch
Volodymyr-Volyns'kyy
Kivertsi
Korosten'
Luts'k
Rivne
Novohrad-Volyns'kyy
Malyn
Radomyshl'
Sokal'
Dubno
Shepetivka
Zhytomyr
Chervonohrad
Zhovkva
Kremenets'
Izyaslav
Polonne
Yavoriv
L'viv
Zolochiv
Berdychiv
Horodok
Zbarazh
Starokostyantyniv
Sambir
Khodoriv
Berezhany
Ternopil'
Kozyatyn
Boryslav
Stryy
Chortkiv
Khmel'nyts'kyy
U K R
Kalush
Vinnytsya
Dolyna
Ivano-Frankivs'k
Zhmerynka
Lypovets'
Uzhhorod
Nadvirna
Kam'yanets'-Podil's'kyy
Haysyn
Mukacheve
Kolomyya
Podil's'ka Vysochyna
Tul'chyn
Berehove
Khust
Chernivtsi
Mohyliv-Podil's'kyy
Dniester
Vynohradiv
Hora Hoverla 2061m
Negresti-Oas
Darabani
Soroca
Satu Mare
Baia Mare
Rădăuti
Dorohoi
Balta
Carei
Borsa
Botosani
Bălti
Ribnita
Marghita
Somes
Suceava
Falticeni
Păscani Ungheni
Kotovs'k
Simleu Silvaniei
Zalău
Năsăud
MOLDOVA
Oradea
Dej
Bistrita
Bicaz
Roman
Iasi
Călărasi
Alesd
Cluj-Napoca
Toplita
Dubăsari
Salonta
Beius
Turda
Târgu Mures
Piatra-Neamt
Bacău
Hîncesti
Tighina
Curtici
Transylvania
Cristuru
Miercurea-Ciuc
Vaslui
Tiraspol
Arad
Muntii Apuseni
Alba Iulia
Medias
Secuiesc
Târgu Ocna
Basarabeasca
Mures
Lipova
Deva
R O M A N I A
Bârlad
Jimbolia
Lugoj
Hunedoara
Sibiu
Făgăras
Ciadîr-Lunga
Timisoara
Timis
Otelu Rosu
Hateg
Vârful Moldoveanu
Sfântu Gheorghe
Tecuci
Cahul
Artsyz
Bocsa
Petrosani
Transylvanian Alps
Brasov
Focsani
Bolhrad
Ozero Yalpuh
Oravita
Resita
Câmpulung
Sinaia
Râmnicu Sărat
Galati
Reni
Kiliya
Târgu Jiu
Râmnicu Vâlcea
Câmpina
Brăila
Izmayil
Orsova
Motru
Mizil
Buzău
Măcin
Tulcea
Drobeta-Turnu Severin
Strehaia
Târgoviste
Ploiesti
Urziceni
Babadag
Filiasi
Wallachia
Titu
Buftea
Ialomita
Tăndărei
Hârsova
Lacul Razim
Craiova
Slatina
Caracal
BUCHAREST (BUCURESTI)
Fetesti
Medgidia
Calafat
Băilesti
Roșiori de Vede
Alexandria
Călărasi
Oltenita
Constanta
Danube (Dunărea)
Corabia
Olt
Zimnicea
Giurgiu
Techirghiol
Eforie Sud
Mangalia
B U L G A R I A
SLOVAKIA
HUNGARY
SERBIA & MONTENEGRO (YUGOSLAVIA)
Carpathian Mountains
Siret
Prut

INDUSTRY IN THE UKRAINE

Ukraine is the world's fourth largest producer of steel and has a large coal industry as well as reserves of oil and gas. Today, however, much of its industry is out of date and inefficient. Most of the heavy industry is situated in the central Dnieper river valley.

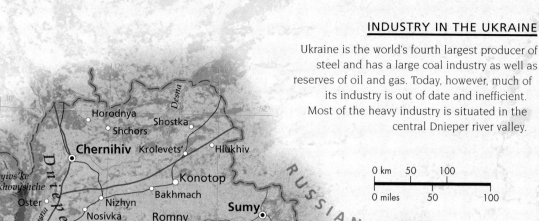

Liquid iron ore

0 km 50 100

0 miles 50 100

HOLIDAYS BY THE SEA

The Black Sea resorts of the Crimea, in southern Ukraine, were once a favourite holiday destination for Russians heading south for the summer sun. Today, resorts here, such as Yalta (below), are still popular, although the facilities are poor when compared with similar places around the Mediterranean Sea.

PEOPLE OF ROMANIA

Romanians speak Romansch – a language closely related to French, Italian, and Spanish. The country also has a sizeable Hungarian and Roma minority, which have both been discriminated against in recent years. Most Hungarian speakers live in the region of Romania known as Transylvania.

CHILDREN from the Maramures region of Transylvania.

RICH SOILS OF MOLDOVA

Moldova consists of partially wooded plains intercut with rivers and streams. About 75 per cent of the land is rich in chernozem (black) soil, which is very fertile. Wine and sunflower production is important here. Fruit and vegetables, such as pumpkins (left), also grow well.

Map labels

RUSSIAN FEDERATION

Horodnya
Shostka
Shchors
Chernihiv   Krolevets'   Hlukhiv
Konotop
Kyyivs'ke Vodoskhovyshche
Oster   Nizhyn   Bakhmach
Romny
Sumy
KIEV (KYYIV)   Brovary
Boyarka   Pryluky   Lebedyn
Vasyl'kiv   Yahotyn   Pyryatyn   Psel
Fastiv   Kaniv's'ke Vodoskhovyshche   Zolochiv
Hrebinka   Lubny   Myrhorod   Derhachi
Bila Tserkva   Lyubotyn
Kharkiv
A I N E   Hlobyne   Poltava   Merefa   Kup"yans'k
Horodyshche   Cherkasy   Donets   Ostil
Tal'ne   Shpola   Chyhyryn   Kremenchuts'ke Vodoskhovyshche   Izyum   Starobil's'k
Uman'   Oleksandrivka   Kremenchuk   Kreminna
Mala Vyska   Znam"yanka   Dniprodzerzhyns'ke Vodoskhovyshche   Slov"yans'k   Rubizhne
Kirovohrad   Oleksandriya   Novomoskovs'k   Kramators'k   Syeverodonets'k
Ulyanivka   Zhovti Vody   Pavlohrad   Kostyantynivka   Lysychans'k
Vil'shanka   Dniprodzerzhyns'k   Dnipropetrovs'k   Zolote
Pervomays'k   P"yatykhatky   Horlivka   Luhans'k
Kryve Ozero   Dolyns'ka   Synel'nykove   Yenakiyeve   Stakhanov
Arbyzynka   Kryvyy Rih   Pokrovs'ke   Makiyivka   Krasnodon
Novyy Buh   Inhulets'   Donets'k   Krasnyy Luch
Voznesens'k   Ordzhonikidze   Nikopol'   Zaporizhzhya   Torez
Pivdennyy Buh   Kam"yanka-Dniprovs'ka   Marhanets'   Orikhiv   Amvrosiyivka
Mykolayiv   Dniprorudne   Volnovakha   Dokuchayevs'k
Zhovtneve   Dnieper (Dnipro)   Kakhovs'ka Vodoskhovyshche   Polohy   Novoazovs'k
Black Sea   Kakhovka   Tokmak   Mariupol'
Ochakiv   Kherson   Molochans'k   Gulf of Taganrog
Odesa   Hola Prystan'   Tsyurupyns'k   Melitopol'
Illichivs'k   Chaplynka   Akinovka   Prymors'k   Berdyans'k
Lowland   Novotroyits'ke
Armyans'k   Heniches'k   Sea of Azov
Kalanchak   Krasnoperekops'k   Karkinits'ka Zatoka
Chornomors'ke   Rozdol'ne   Dzhankoy   Zatoka Syvash
Black Sea   Krasnohvardiys'ke   Kerch
Yevpatoriya   Nyzhn'ohirs'kyy   Lenine
Saky   Crimea (Kryms'kyy Pivostriv)   Feodosiya   Kerch Strait
Simferopol'   Bakhchysaray   Krymski Hory
Sevastopol'   Alushta
Yalta   Alupka

Baltic States & Belarus

THE THREE BALTIC STATES, Estonia, Latvia, and Lithuania, all share a small stretch of coast on the Baltic Sea. Belarus lies between Poland, Ukraine, and the Russian Federation. Following independence from the Soviet Union in 1991, all these countries faced problems such as price rises, food shortages, and pollution. However, the Baltic States have since tried to reform their societies and economies along western lines. Belarus has kept close links with Russia and has been the slowest to reform. This mainly rural country remains isolated from the rest of Europe and, with few natural resources, remains one of its poorest nations.

SINGING REVOLUTION

Estonia is known for its classical music tradition – most notably its choirs. This love of music was most powerful when people raised their voices during the Singing Revolution in 1988 (right), part of their move towards independence.

POLITICAL RALLY IN TALLINN

TALLINN OLD TOWN

With its colourful buildings, turreted walls, and gabled roofs Tallinn is one of the best-preserved capital cities in Europe. All the winding, cobbled streets lead to the Town Hall Square (left).

AMBER

Two-thirds of the world's amber, the fossilized resin of pine trees, is washed up from the seabed along the Baltic coast. Amber is used to make jewellery, among other things.

Did you know?

- Riga, the capital of Latvia, is often ice-bound from December to April.

- Rubbing amber with a cloth will make it electrically charged, attracting bits of paper.

- Belarus used to be known as Belorussia, a name that means "White Russia".

- Lithuania is the only one of the Baltic countries whose respect for animals means that they have no zoos or circuses.

RUSSIAN FEDERATION

Map labels

Gulf of Finland
Baltic Sea
Gulf of Riga
Narva Bay

Estonia: TALLINN, Narva, Narva Reservoir, Sillamäe, Kohtla-Järve, Rakvere, Tapa, Rakke, Tartu, Põlva, Võru, Otepää, Valga, Viljandi, Paide, Rapla, Pärnu, Sindi, Audru, Kundu, Loksa, Aegviidu, Raasiku, Maardu, Keila, Paldiski, Risti, Haapsalu, Lihula, Virtsu, Kärdla, Hiiumaa, Emmaste, Vormsi, Väinameri, Orissaare, Kuressaare, Saaremaa, Sääre, Mõisaküla, Võnnu, Puurmani, Palamuse, Kallaste, Rõngu, Suure-Jaani, Lake Peipus, Lake Pskov, Rapina, Uulu

Latvia: RĪGA, Daugavpils, Rēzekne, Valmiera, Cēsis, Sigulda, Jelgava, Bauska, Tukums, Dobele, Saldus, Ventspils, Liepāja, Kuldīga, Talsi, Kolka, Roja, Mērsrags, Salacgrīva, Ainaži, Alūksne, Balvi, Viļaka, Gulbene, Madona, Jēkabpils, Līvāni, Krāslava, Dagda, Ludza, Kārsava, Malta, Spogi, Krāslava, Jaunjelgava, Aizkraukle, Pļaviņas, Viesīte, Nereta, Ilūkste, Varakļāni, Rokiškis, Limbaži, Valka, Smiltene, Rūjiena, Staicele, Burtnieku Ezers, Alūja, Kolkasrags, Rūhnu, Engure, Jūrmala, Iecava, Birži, Pasvalys, Western Dvina, Lielupe, Gauja, Venta, Usmas Ezers, Engures Ezers, Kandava, Broceni, Mazirbe, Pāvilosta, Grobiņa, Rucava, Kurzeme, Vidzeme, Ape, Rugāji

Lithuania: VILNIUS, Kaunas, Šiauliai, Panevėžys, Klaipėda, Kretinga, Plungė, Telšiai, Mažeikiai, Kelmė, Raseiniai, Jurbarkas, Šilutė, Neman, Tauragė, Šilalė, Skaudvilė, Šakiai, Jonava, Ukmergė, Utena, Zarasai, Anykščiai, Visaginas, Kaišiadorys, Trakai, Rūdiškės, Merkinė, Alytus, Prienai, Kalvarija, Marijampolė, Veisiejai, Druskininkai, Vilkaviškis, Varėna, Eišiškės, Salininkai, Ašmyany, Radviliškis, Pakruojis, Subačius, Kėdainiai, Dotnuva, Naujamiestis, Joniškis, Papilė, Kuršėnai, Gargždai, Skuodas, Salantai, Darbėnai, Neringa, Smarhon, Paberžė, Giedraičiai, Žemaičių Aukštumas, Aukštumas, Neris, Viliya, Vilija

Kaliningrad (to Russian Federation): KALININGRAD, Chernyakhovsk, Gusev, Sovetsk, Gvardeysk, Zelenogradsk, Pionerskiy, Svetlogorsk, Primorsk, Baltiysk, Mamonovo, Bagrationovsk, Zheleznodorozhny, Courland Lagoon

POLAND

Belarus (part): Hrodna, Polatsk, Navapolatsk, Haradok, Vyetryna, Yezyaryshcha, Harany, Shumilina, Obal', Sarochyna, Dryssa, Vyerkhnyadzvinsk, Bihosava, Myadzyel, Hlybokaye, Pastavy, Smarhon, Vidzy, Braslaw, Hrandzichy, Parechcha, Voranava, Hervyaty, Ashmyany

MINSK CITY

The capital of Belarus, Minsk, was destroyed during World War II and then rebuilt in a starkly modern style. Minsk is the country's economic centre.: Cars, trucks and tractors, chemicals, timber products, and a range of high-tech goods are all produced here. Farm produce (above) is also sold in the markets.

FORESTS AND LAKES

All four countries are low-lying with many moors, bogs, unspoiled lakes, and fir and pine forests. Forestry is an important industry, providing wood pulp for paper making, and timber for furniture and houses.

GYMNASTICS

The former Soviet Union worked its young athletes and gymnasts extremely hard in order to win Olympic medals and thus national glory. Many of the most famous gymnasts came from Belarus, notably Olga Korbut and, more recently, Svetlana Boginskya (right), who has won 3 gold, 1 silver, and 1 bronze Olympic medals.

FERNS THRIVE in this Latvian forest.

FARMING

The fertile soils and flat landscapes make this region good for farming. The Baltic States, particularly Latvia (left), have large dairy farms. Belarus is a major producer of flax – used to make linen and other products. Potatoes – used to make vodka – sugar beet and other root crops are also grown here.

LITHUANIAN COSTUME

In some Lithuanian villages people still wear traditional folk costume, especially for festive occasions. Women's clothing is generally colourful (left) and might include a white linen shirt, a skirt, and an apron. The decoration and style of the costume shows which region of Lithuania the wearer comes from.

TEXTILES

Development of the textile industry (above) in these countries is strong, with foreign investment from Sweden (for Latvia) and Indonesia (for Lithuania) helping growth. Clothes, bedlinen, curtains, and towels are just some of the items made for export.

0 km 50 100

0 miles 50 100

RUSSIAN FEDERATION

POLAND

B E L A R U S

U K R A I N E

European Russia

SEPARATED FROM ASIAN RUSSIA by the Ural Mountains, European Russia is so large that it spans four time zones. The climate and landscape range from cold desert and frozen tundra in the north to the warm coast of the Black Sea in the southwest. Forests and grassy steppes cover huge areas of the country. More than 100 million people – two-thirds of the total Russian population – live in European Russia, most of them in cities such as the capital, Moscow. Since the collapse of communism in 1991, many Russians have experienced a fall in their standard of living. There are shortages of food and manufactured goods, crime rates have risen, and so has unemployment. As a result, Russia is the only European country in which life expectancy has fallen in the last decade.

ST PETERSBURG

Once Russia's capital, St Petersburg was built in the 18th century by Csar Peter the Great as a "Window on the West". Today, it is a popular tourist destination, full of grand palaces and extravagant architecture (left). The city spreads over some 40 islands, linked by a network of canals and rivers.

THE CHURCH ON SPILLED BLOOD marks the spot where Tsar Alexander II was murdered in 1881.

EDUCATION

Children have to attend school here from the age of 7 through to 17. Although the state system is free, education has declined since the fall of communism due to chronic underfunding. Private schools are now becoming increasingly popular.

BALLET

Russia is famous for its ballet companies, such as the Bolshoi Ballet of Moscow and the Kirov Ballet of St Petersburg. Most of the ballets performed are classics, such as Swan Lake or Sleeping Beauty. Developed in Europe in the 19th century, ballet became a popular entertainment in the 20th century.

SLEEPING BEAUTY is performed here by dancers from the Kirov Ballet.

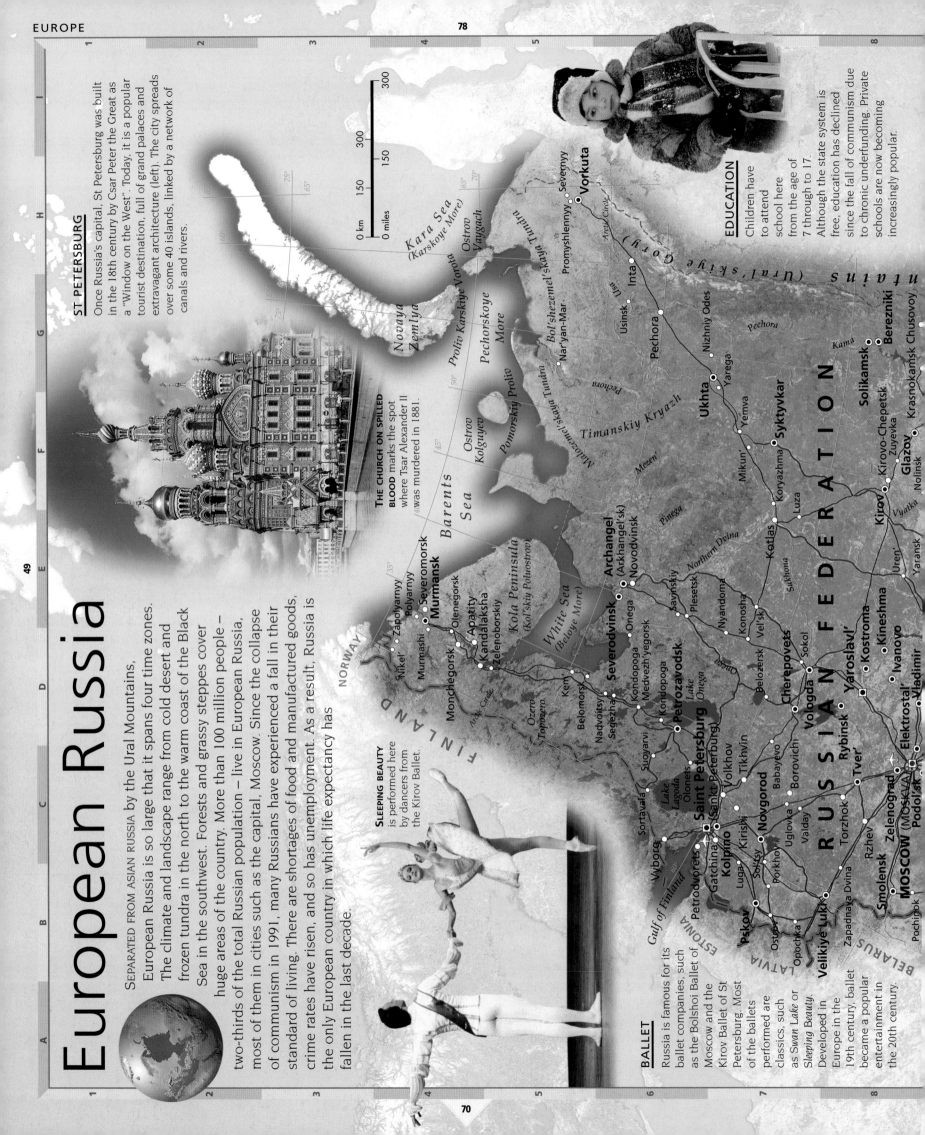

Scale: 300, 300, 150, 150, 0 km, 0 miles

Kara Sea (Karskoye More)

Novaya Zemlya

Proliv Karskiye Vorota

Ostrov Vaygach

Pechorskoye More

Pomorskiy Proliv

Ostrov Kolguyev

Barents Sea

Severnyy

Vorkuta

Promyshlennyy

Inta

Usinsk Usa

Nar'yan-Mar

Pechora

Nizhniy Odes

Yarega

Pechora

Bol'shezemel'skaya Tundra

Malozemel'skaya Tundra

Kola Peninsula (Kol'skiy Poluostrov)

White Sea (Beloye More)

Timanskiy Kryazh

Ural'skiye
Mountains

Mezen'

Ukhta

Yemva

Mikun'

Koryazhma

Syktyvkar

Luza

Vychegda

Kama

Solikamsk

Berezniki

Kirovo-Chepetsk

Zuyevka

Kirov

Glazov

Krasnokamsk Chusovoy

Nolinsk

Vyatka

Zapolyarnyy

Polyarnyy

Severomorsk

Murmansk

Nikel'

Murmashi

Olenegorsk

Monchegorsk

Apatity

Kandalaksha

Zelenoborskiy

Belomorsk

Kem'

Nadvoitsy

Segezha

Kondopoga

Medvezh'yegorsk

Archangel (Arkhangel'sk)

Novodvinsk

Onega

Kondopoga
Lake Onega

Petrozavodsk

Severodvinsk

Northern Dvina

Plesetsk

Savinskiy

Nyandoma

Konosha

Vel'sk

Kotlas

Sukhona

Belozersk

Sokol

Vologda

Cherepovets

Kostroma

Kineshma

Ivanovo

Elektrostal'

Ozero Topozero

Suoyarvi

Olonets

Volkhov

Tikhvin

Babayevo

Borovichi

Yaroslavl'

Rybinsk

Tver'

Torzhok

Vladimir

Podol'sk

MOSCOW (MOSKVA)

Zelenograd

Rzhev

Sortavala

Lake Ladoga

Saint Petersburg (Sankt-Peterburg)

Kolpino

Luga

Soltsy

Novgorod

Uglovka

Valday

Smolensk

Zapadnaya Dvina

Pochinok

Vyborg

Petrodvorets

Gatchina

Kirishi

Porkhov

Velikiye Luki

Pskov

Ostrov

Opochka

Gulf of Finland

FINLAND

NORWAY

ESTONIA

LATVIA

BELARUS

R U S S I A N   F E D E R A T I O N

Arctic Circle

Pinega

Onega

Vaga

Uren'

Yaransk

Nolinsk

RURAL LIFE

Rural life has become extremely tough since the economic collapse of large-scale farms in the 1990s, with many people living in poverty. Smaller co-operatives and farms (above) have sprung up, and the agricultural industry is going through a painful period of reform. Because of the harsh climate, only 10 per cent of the land is suitable for agriculture.

RUSSIAN icons show religious scenes painted on wood.

THE RUSSIAN CHURCH

The main religion in Russia is the Russian Orthodox Church. Under communism, all religion was banned. The new freedom means that many Russians now attend church services on a regular basis. New churches are being built, old ones restored, and seminaries reopened to train new priests.

THE TARTARS

Russia's largest ethnic minority, the Tartars (below), are an Islamic people descended from the Mongols. They live in the Tatarstan Republic, midway between Moscow and the Urals.

MOSCOW METRO

Not many underground railways can claim to be tourist attractions, but Moscow's metro can. Built in the 1930s, many of its stations are decorated with beautiful chandeliers, mosaics, paintings, and sculptures. One of the busiest, most efficient metros in the world, it is used by over seven million people daily.

POLLUTION

The communists invested heavily in industry, but their outdated methods of production have affected the environment. Rivers such as the Volga are badly polluted, and many cities are covered in a permanent and poisonous smog. Chest infections and other diseases related to air pollution are common.

INDUSTRIAL SMOG casts a haze over Moscow.

Did you know?

- Ice cream is popular in Russia, even in winter. It can be bought from places marked *morozhenoe*.

- The title csar, or tzar, once used for Russian rulers, is a word meaning "emperor".

- During the 20th century, St Petersburg went through three revolutions as well as a 900-day siege.

Map labels

Ural Mountains

Kungur
Chaykovskiy
Neftekamsk
Birsk
Izhevsk
Yoshkar-Ola
Novocheboksarsk
Naberezhnyye Chelny
Al'met'yevsk
Ufa
Sterlitamak
Salavat
Oktyabr'skiy
Kumertau
Baymak
Sibay
Saraktash
Sol'-Iletsk
Orenburg
Orsk
Novotroitsk
Beloretsk
Kazan'
Nizhnekamsk
Kanash
Kuybyshevskoye Vodokhranilishche
Buguruslan
Buzuluk
Saransk
Ulyanovsk
Dimitrovgrad
Tol'yatti
Samara
Syzran'
Chapayevsk
Kuznetsk
Balakovo
Penza
Tambov
Michurinsk
Balashov
Vol'sk
Krasnyy Kut
Saratov
Rtishchevo
Nizhniy Novgorod
Murom
Kolomna
Ryazan'
Novomoskovsk
Tula
Aleksin
Sasovo
Shchëkino
Yefremov
Tovarkovskiy
Gryazi
Lipetsk
Orël
Yelets
Kursk
Staryy Oskol
Gubkin
Shebekino
Belgorod
Liski
Borisoglebsk
Voronezh
Rossosh'
Millerovo
Kantemirovka
Kamensk-Shakhtinskiy
Volgodonsk
Zimovniki
Sal'sk
Tikhoretsk
Kropotkin
Starominskaya
Novorossiysk
Tuapse
Sochi
Maykop
Krasnodar
Stavropol'
Svetlograd
Cherkessk
Nevinnomyssk
Kislovodsk
Pyatigorsk
Prokhladnyy
Nal'chik
Vladikavkaz
Groznyy
Khasavyurt
Makhachkala
Buynaksk
Kaspiysk
Derbent
Elista
Ilovlya
Mikhaylovka
Krasnoarmeysk
Kamyshin
Volzhskiy
Volgograd
Akhtubinsk
Astrakhan'

Don
Donets
Volga
Ural
Kuma

Sea of Azov
Black Sea
Caspian Sea
Caspian Depression

UKRAINE
KAZAKHSTAN
GEORGIA
AZERB.
Caucasus

ASIA

ASIA IS THE BIGGEST CONTINENT in the world. From east to west it stretches

almost half way around the globe, from north

to south it spreads from the frozen Arctic to the

sweltering, tropical heat of Southeast Asia. All 17 of the world's

 mountains over 8,000 m (26,246 ft) can be found in

Asia, as well as the largest and deepest lakes – the

Caspian Sea and Lake Baikal. The world's first civilizations started here,

many of the most important inventions were made here, and all the

world's major religions began here. Much of Asia is uninhabited, yet

its 48 countries are home to 3,672,342,000 people –

more than half the world's population. The discovery

 of oil in countries such as Saudi Arabia has made

some people very rich, while many of those who live

on the Indian subcontinent live in rural areas and are extremely poor.

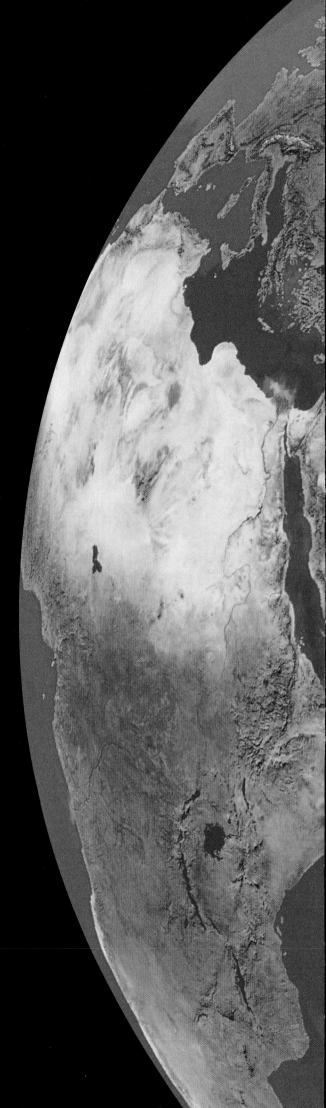

Turkey and the Caucasus

TURKEY LIES IN BOTH ASIA and Europe – separated by the Bosporus – and was once part of the powerful Ottoman Empire. Although the Turks are 99 per cent Muslim, modern Turkey is a country with no official religion. Western Turkey is relatively industrialized, with a tourist industry along the Mediterranean coast that brings in considerable income. Many farmers and herders in the centre and east, however, struggle to make a living in the harsh environment. To the northeast lie the Caucasus countries of Georgia, Azerbaijan, and Armenia. Once part of the USSR, they are now independent.

ISTANBUL

The different faces of Turkey can be seen in its former capital, Istanbul, which lies on both sides of the Bosporus waterway. Churches, mosques, and ancient buildings in both European and Islamic styles sit side by side with modern shops and offices. Bridges link the two parts of the city. In 1923, Ankara became the new capital.

TURKISH FOOD

Turkey is self-sufficient in food, and grows specialized crops such as aubergines, peppers, figs, and dates. A typical Turkish meal might consist of spiced lamb, often grilled on a skewer with onion and tomato to make a *shish kebab*. This would be served with rice or cracked wheat.

EPHESUS

Tourism is one of Turkey's major industries. As well as beach resorts, the country has many ancient sites. One of these is the old Greek city of Ephesus, which lies 56 km (35 miles) south of modern-day Izmir on the Aegean coast. The city was famous for its Temple of Artemis, which was considered one of the seven wonders of the world.

VISITORS to Ephesus admire the remains of the Library of Celsus.

FATHER OF THE TURKS

Mustafa Kemal Atatürk (1881–1939), founder of the modern Turkish state, became its first president in 1923. He introduced many reforms, including more equality for women and better education for all. He also declared that Islam was no longer to be the official religion.

TURKISH REPUBLIC OF NORTHERN CYPRUS
(recognized only by Turkey)

CYPRUS

OIL FROM AZERBAIJAN

Many years ago, caravans of camels carried vessels loaded with oil from Baku to nearby countries. By the end of the 19th century, the city was known as the "black gold" capital of the world. Today, the total amount of oil that could be produced is 1 billion tonnes, which does not include undeveloped areas off the coast.

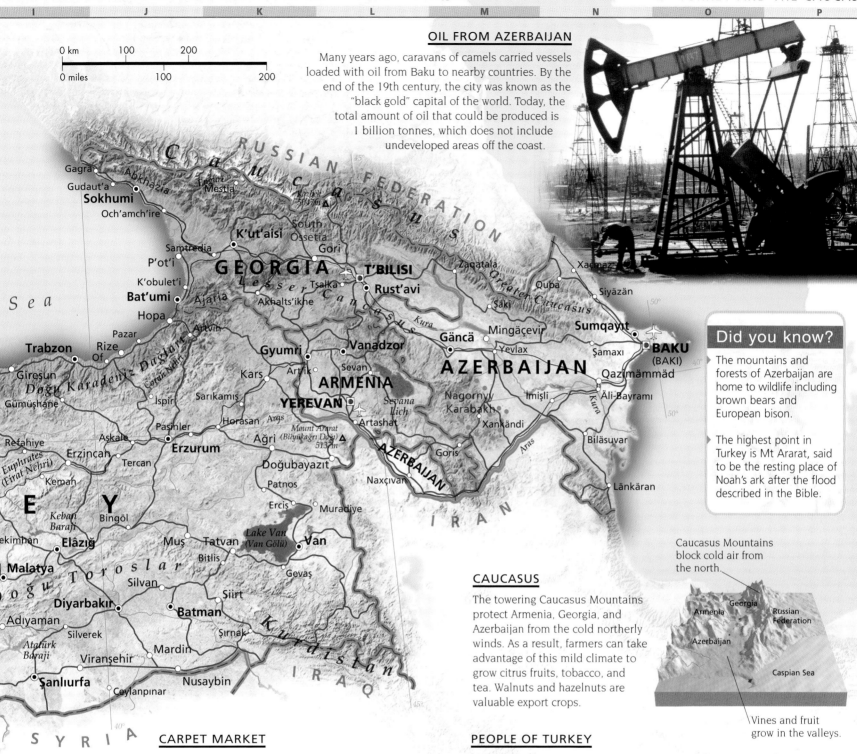

Did you know?

▶ The mountains and forests of Azerbaijan are home to wildlife including brown bears and European bison.

▶ The highest point in Turkey is Mt Ararat, said to be the resting place of Noah's ark after the flood described in the Bible.

CAUCASUS

The towering Caucasus Mountains protect Armenia, Georgia, and Azerbaijan from the cold northerly winds. As a result, farmers can take advantage of this mild climate to grow citrus fruits, tobacco, and tea. Walnuts and hazelnuts are valuable export crops.

Caucasus Mountains block cold air from the north.

Vines and fruit grow in the valleys.

CARPET MARKET

Turkey is world-famous for its knotted-pile carpets, known as kilims, woven by skilled craftworkers. Each region of Turkey produces carpets with different designs and colours. Every worker incorporates into the designs symbols that tell the maker's own family history or origins.

CARPETS are made in centres such as Malatya and Kayseri.

PEOPLE OF TURKEY

The Turks, who make up 70 per cent of the population of 66 million, are a diverse group with a shared sense of national identity. The largest minority in Turkey – about 25 million people – are the Kurds (below), who speak their own language but have no homeland. They live in eastern Turkey, as well as in neighbouring Iraq and Iran.

Russia and Kazakhstan

THE RUSSIAN FEDERATION is the biggest country in the world, almost twice as big as either the USA or China. It extends halfway around the world, crosses two continents, and spans 11 time zones. The vast region of Siberia alone is larger than Canada. Kazakhstan lies to its south and is a large but sparsely populated country. From 1917 to 1991, both countries were part of the Union of Soviet Socialist Republics (USSR), the world's first communist state. When the USSR collapsed, Russia, Kazakhstan, and the 13 other member republics gained independence. Since then, Russia and Kazakhstan have begun to transform themselves from communist states into democratic nations. Both countries have a lot of fertile land, huge mineral deposits, and many other natural resources. However, Russia still has the lowest life expectancy rate of all the industrialized countries.

Did you know?

▶ The Chukchi people of Siberia get their name from the Chukchi word *Chauchu*, meaning "rich in reindeer".

▶ Lake Baikal is up to 1,940 m (6,367 ft) deep. It is the world's largest freshwater lake, containing more than 20 per cent of the world's supply of fresh water.

▶ The traditional home of the Kazakh is called the *yurt*. This is made of felt stretched over a collapsible framework.

▶ The native populations of Siberia are bilingual. They speak their own native languages as well as Russian.

A KAZAKH man hunts with a trained golden eagle.

KAZAKH CULTURE

The majority of people in Kazakhstan are Kazakh Muslims. They were once a nomadic people who travelled around on horseback, herding their sheep. Now the Kazakhs mainly live in the rural areas of the country, retaining a strong loyalty to their clan and family.

COAL MINERS IN SIBERIA

NATURAL WEALTH

Siberia contains one-third of the world's natural gas reserves and has vast deposits of oil, as well as abundant minerals such as coal, and precious metals, including gold. However, many of these resources are inaccessible or in remote places, and the extreme winters make it difficult to extract them.

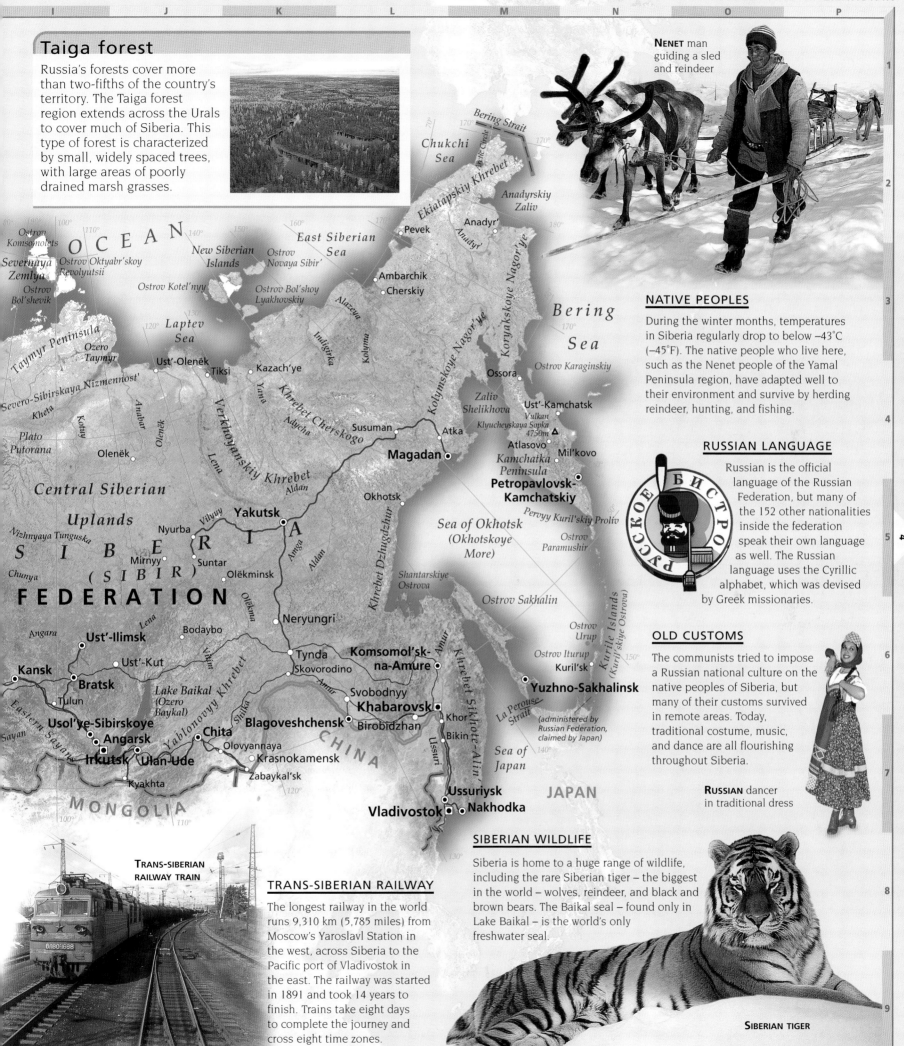

Taiga forest

Russia's forests cover more than two-fifths of the country's territory. The Taiga forest region extends across the Urals to cover much of Siberia. This type of forest is characterized by small, widely spaced trees, with large areas of poorly drained marsh grasses.

NENET man guiding a sled and reindeer

NATIVE PEOPLES

During the winter months, temperatures in Siberia regularly drop to below −43°C (−45°F). The native people who live here, such as the Nenet people of the Yamal Peninsula region, have adapted well to their environment and survive by herding reindeer, hunting, and fishing.

RUSSIAN LANGUAGE

Russian is the official language of the Russian Federation, but many of the 152 other nationalities inside the federation speak their own language as well. The Russian language uses the Cyrillic alphabet, which was devised by Greek missionaries.

OLD CUSTOMS

The communists tried to impose a Russian national culture on the native peoples of Siberia, but many of their customs survived in remote areas. Today, traditional costume, music, and dance are all flourishing throughout Siberia.

RUSSIAN dancer in traditional dress

SIBERIAN WILDLIFE

Siberia is home to a huge range of wildlife, including the rare Siberian tiger – the biggest in the world – wolves, reindeer, and black and brown bears. The Baikal seal – found only in Lake Baikal – is the world's only freshwater seal.

SIBERIAN TIGER

TRANS-SIBERIAN RAILWAY TRAIN

TRANS-SIBERIAN RAILWAY

The longest railway in the world runs 9,310 km (5,785 miles) from Moscow's Yaroslavl Station in the west, across Siberia to the Pacific port of Vladivostok in the east. The railway was started in 1891 and took 14 years to finish. Trains take eight days to complete the journey and cross eight time zones.

The Near East

ISRAEL, JORDAN, SYRIA, AND LEBANON are the countries collectively known as the Near East. This is a land that is dominated by desert but also has fertile coastal plains. Lack of water is a constant problem here, although Israel has introduced computerized irrigation systems to extend the land suitable for agriculture. The creation of the Jewish state of Israel in 1948, in what was previously Arab-dominated Palestine, has led to almost continuous conflict in the region. Arabs and Israelis have fought four major wars, which have cost many lives. The Mediterranean island of Cyprus has also suffered a violent recent history.

LEBANON REBUILT

Beirut, the capital of Lebanon, was once the commercial and banking centre of the Arab world, but was devastated by the civil war that ravaged the country from 1975 to 1989. Today, the country is largely at peace and Beirut is regaining much of its former glory. Lebanon remains dominated, however, by its two powerful neighbours – Syria and Israel.

CYPRUS

Cyprus became independent from Britain in 1960. However, conflict between Greeks and Turks caused Turkey to invade the island in 1974. Since then, Cyprus has been split between a Turkish Cypriot north and a Greek Cypriot south. Most Cypriots make a living from farming grapes, citrus fruit, and olives. Women often sell hand-made lace items to tourists.

SYRIAN MARKET

Damascus is one of the oldest inhabited cities in the world. At its centre is a massive souk (bazaar) where the streets are full of stalls and small shops selling everything from carpets, textiles, and jewellery to household goods and fresh produce.

DAILY LIFE

Even in a war-torn country such as Israel, people continue to live as normal a life as possible. Children listen to pop music and watch their favourite sports stars, either live or on TV. In a peaceful break, these Palestinian boys play soccer in a Jerusalem street.

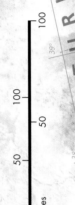

Did you know?

- Cyprus means "Island of Copper", which is why the map on their flag is copper-coloured.
- On *Rosh Hashanah* (Jewish New Year), some people go to a river or the sea to say prayers.
- Lake Assad in Syria was created by a dam across the River Euphrates.

Map labels:

IRAQ

TURKEY

SYRIA

LEBANON

CYPRUS

TURKISH REPUBLIC OF NORTHERN CYPRUS (recognized only by Turkey)

Mediterranean Sea

Al Mālikīyah
Al Qāmishlī
Al Ḥasakah
Al Jazīrah
Ash Shaddādah
Aş Şuwār
Al Manāşif
Subaykhān
Abū Ḥardān
Abū Kamāl
Ra's al 'Ayn
Jabal 'Azīz 'Abd al 'Azīz
Euphrates
Al Mayādīn
Al 'Asharah
Jabal aţ Ţarf 772m
At Tall al Abyaḍ
Nahr Balīkh
Ar Raqqah
Aş Şabkhah
At Tibnī
Dayr az Zawr
Jabal Bishrī
As Sukhnah
Madīnat ath Thawrah
Lake Assad (Buḥayrat al Asad)
Tudmur (Palmyra)
Ar Rāmī
Al Bāridah
Sab' Ābār
Jarābulus
Euphrates
Manbij
Sabkhat al Jabbūl
Salamīyah
Afrin
A'zāz
Al Bāb
Aleppo (Halab)
Abū aḑ Ḑuhūr
Idlib
Ḥārim
Ma'arrat an Nu'mān
Ḥamāh
Arīḩā
Orantes
Jibāl as Sāḩilīyah
Mazyaf
Tall Kalakh
Ḥimṣ
Al Quşayr
Baalbek
Al Lādhiqīyah
Jablah
Bāniyās
Ṭarṭūs
Qoubaïyāt
El Mina
Tripoli
Batroûn
LEBANON
Lebanon

Tigris

Agialoúsa (Yenierenköy)
Keryneia (Girne)
Kythréa (Degirmenlik)
Lápithos (Lapta)
Mórfou (Güzelyurt)
Pólis
Ttyllíria
Páfos
Akrotírion
NICOSIA
Dériyiá
Ammóchostos (Gazimagusa) (Famagusta)
Lárnaka
Límassol (Lemesós)
CYPRUS
Sovereign Base Area (to UK)
Sovereign Base Area (to UK)

Scale bar:
100
100
50
0 km
50
0 miles

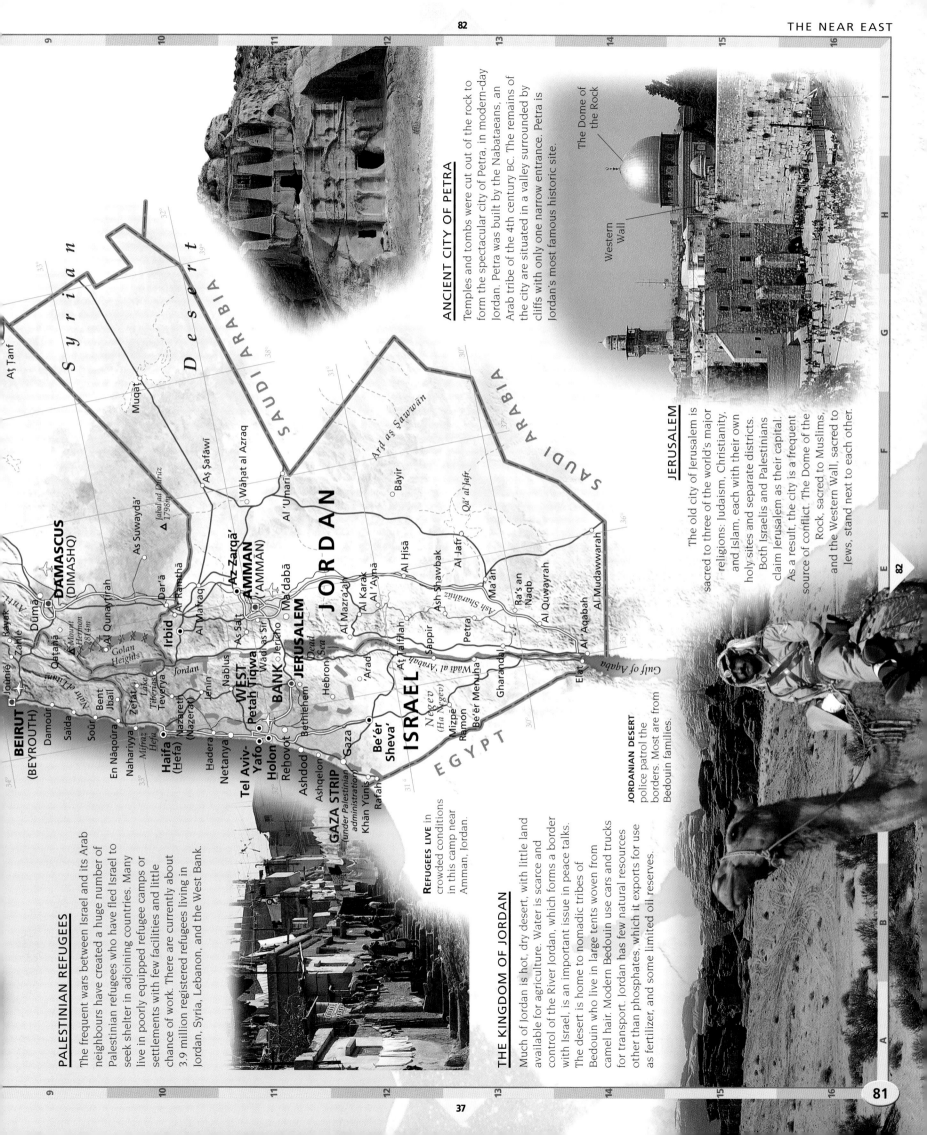

ANCIENT CITY OF PETRA

Temples and tombs were cut out of the rock to form the spectacular city of Petra, in modern-day Jordan. Petra was built by the Nabataeans, an Arab tribe of the 4th century BC. The remains of the city are situated in a valley surrounded by cliffs with only one narrow entrance. Petra is Jordan's most famous historic site.

The Dome of the Rock

Western Wall

JERUSALEM

The old city of Jerusalem is sacred to three of the world's major religions: Judaism, Christianity, and Islam, each with their own holy sites and separate districts. Both Israelis and Palestinians claim Jerusalem as their capital. As a result, the city is a frequent source of conflict. The Dome of the Rock, sacred to Muslims, and the Western Wall, sacred to Jews, stand next to each other.

JORDANIAN DESERT police patrol the borders. Most are from Bedouin families.

PALESTINIAN REFUGEES

The frequent wars between Israel and its Arab neighbours have created a huge number of Palestinian refugees who have fled Israel to seek shelter in adjoining countries. Many live in poorly equipped refugee camps or settlements with few facilities and little chance of work. There are currently about 3.9 million registered refugees living in Jordan, Syria, Lebanon, and the West Bank.

REFUGEES LIVE in crowded conditions in this camp near Amman, Jordan.

THE KINGDOM OF JORDAN

Much of Jordan is hot, dry desert, with little land available for agriculture. Water is scarce and control of the River Jordan, which forms a border with Israel, is an important issue in peace talks. The desert is home to nomadic tribes of Bedouin who live in large tents woven from camel hair. Modern Bedouin use cars and trucks for transport. Jordan has few natural resources other than phosphates, which it exports for use as fertilizer, and some limited oil reserves.

76

The Middle East

THE MIDDLE EAST IS HOME to the world's oldest civilizations, which grew up in the Tigris and Euphrates river valleys of present-day Iraq more than 6,000 years ago. The world's first towns and cities were built here. Since then, many powerful empires have dominated the region, all leaving a wealth of buildings and monuments behind them. Today, the Middle East is at the centre of the Islamic world. The population of every country is Arab and speaks Arabic, except Iran, where half the population are Farsi-speaking Persians.

DESERT WARS

Most international boundaries in the Middle East are just lines drawn in the sand by the former European colonial powers, and have often caused conflict. Iraq and Iran fought a bitter eight-year war along their common border from 1980. Since then, further conflicts between Iraq and international forces have caused much suffering.

OIL PRODUCTION

The Middle East is the world's major oil producer – Saudi Arabia alone produces 10 per cent of the world's supply. Oil has brought great wealth to the region, in particular to Saudi Arabia and the Gulf States.

THE IRANIANS

About half the total population of Iran are Persians, who live in the centre and north of the country. Large numbers of Azeris live in the northwest, while Kurds live in the west and Baluchis in the southeast. The official language of Iran is Farsi, but many other languages are also spoken.

The Persian language is written in Arabic script.

ROLE OF WOMEN

Family life is important throughout the Muslim world. The role of women varies from country to country – traditionally, women stay at home and look after the family, but some now work. In public, many cover their head, or whole body with a burqa.

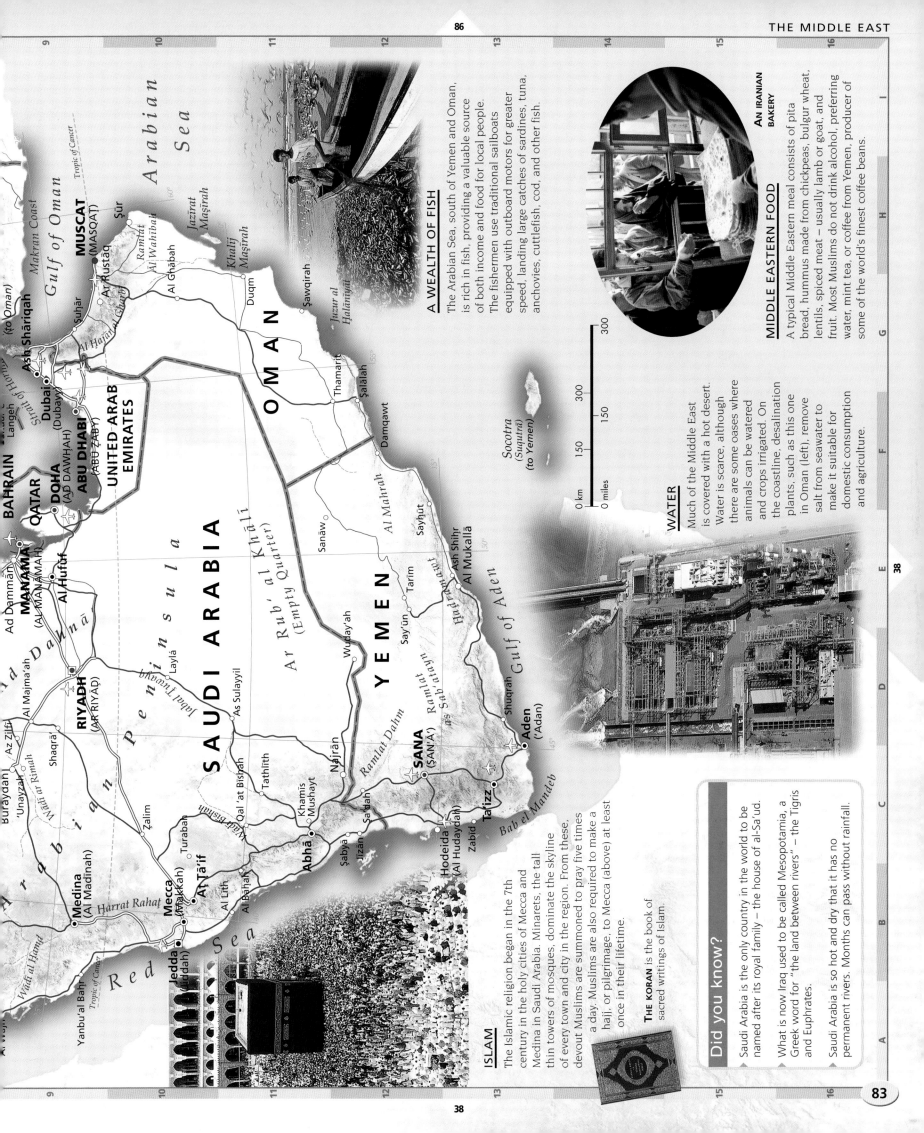

A WEALTH OF FISH

The Arabian Sea, south of Yemen and Oman, is rich in fish, providing a valuable source of both income and food for local people. The fishermen use traditional sailboats equipped with outboard motors for greater speed, landing large catches of sardines, tuna, anchovies, cuttlefish, cod, and other fish.

AN IRANIAN BAKERY

MIDDLE EASTERN FOOD

A typical Middle Eastern meal consists of pita bread, hummus made from chickpeas, bulgur wheat, lentils, spiced meat – usually lamb or goat, and fruit. Most Muslims do not drink alcohol, preferring water, mint tea, or coffee from Yemen, producer of some of the world's finest coffee beans.

WATER

Much of the Middle East is covered with a hot desert. Water is scarce, although there are some oases where animals can be watered and crops irrigated. On the coastline, desalination plants, such as this one in Oman (left), remove salt from seawater to make it suitable for domestic consumption and agriculture.

0 km   150   150   300

0 miles   150   300

ISLAM

The Islamic religion began in the 7th century in the holy cities of Mecca and Medina in Saudi Arabia. Minarets, the tall thin towers of mosques, dominate the skyline of every town and city in the region. From these, devout Muslims are summoned to pray five times a day. Muslims are also required to make a hajj, or pilgrimage, to Mecca (above) at least once in their lifetime.

THE KORAN is the book of sacred writings of Islam.

Did you know?

▶ Saudi Arabia is the only country in the world to be named after its royal family – the house of al-Sa'ud.

▶ What is now Iraq used to be called Mesopotamia, a Greek word for "the land between rivers" – the Tigris and Euphrates.

▶ Saudi Arabia is so hot and dry that it has no permanent rivers. Months can pass without rainfall.

Map labels

Arabian Sea

Gulf of Oman

Makran Coast

Tropic of Cancer

MUSCAT (MASQAT)

Al Rustāq

Suhār

Ash Shāriqah

Dubai (Dubayy)

Al Ḩajar al Gharbī

Strait of Hormuz

Langeh

(to Oman)

BAHRAIN

QATAR

DOHA (AD DAWHAH)

ABU DHABI (ABU ZABY)

UNITED ARAB EMIRATES

Al Ghābah

Ramlat Al Wahībah

Jazīrat Maṣīrah

Khalīj Maṣīrah

Al Ghābah

Duqm

Ṣawqirah

Juzur al Ḩalāniyāt

Thamarīt

Ṣalālah

Damqawt

Socotra (Suquṭrā) (to Yemen)

OMAN

Ad Dammām

MANAMA (AL MANAMAH)

Al Hufūf

SAUDI ARABIA

Ad Dahnā

Az Zilfi

Al Majma'ah

RIYADH (AR RIYĀḌ)

Ar Rub' al Khālī (Empty Quarter)

Jabal Ṭuwayq

Shaqrā'

Laylā

As Sulayyil

Sanāw

Al Mahrah

Tarīm

Ṣay'ūn

Sayḩūt

Ash Shiḩr

Al Mukallā

Ḩaḑramawt

Wuday'ah

Ramlat as Sab'atayn

Ramlat Dahm

Najrān

SANA (ṢAN'Ā')

YEMEN

Gulf of Aden

Aden ('Adan)

Shuqrah

Bab el Mandeb

Buraydan

Wādī ar Rimah

'Unayzah

Wādī al Baṭn

Ḩarrat Rahaṭ

Arabian Peninsula

Turaban

Ẓalim

Qal 'at Bīshah

Tathlīth

Khamis Mushayt

Najrān

Ṣa'dah

Abhā

Ta'izz

Hodeida (Al Ḩudaydah)

Zabid

Sa'dah

Sabyā

Jizān

Wādī Bīshah

Al Birk

Al Qunfudhah

At Ṭā'if

Mecca (Makkah)

Medina (Al Madīnah)

Jedda (Jiddah)

Yanbu'al Baḩr

Red Sea

Wādī al Ḩamḑ

Tropic of Cancer

38

38

Central Asia

THE FIVE CENTRAL ASIAN NATIONS rise up from hot deserts in the west and south to cold, high mountain ranges in the east. The area has oil, gas, and mineral reserves, as well as other natural resources, but water is often scarce and agriculture is limited. The four northern nations were once part of the Soviet Union, and are now independent nations. Afghanistan is a landlocked country with three-quarters of its land being inaccessible terrain. It was invaded by the Soviet Union in 1979, prompting a civil war that has lasted for more than 20 years. In 2002, American and other western forces overthrew a fundamentalist Islamic regime in Afghanistan because of its support for international terrorism. The country, however, has been wrecked by these years of continuous warfare, making it one of the poorest and most deprived nations on Earth.

Did you know?

▶ Almost 90 per cent of Turkmenistan consists of the Garagumy Desert, meaning "black sands" in Turkic.

▶ Tashkent in Uzbekistan is known as the "city of fountains" because it has so many water features.

▶ About 10 million land mines are buried in Afghanistan, making it one of the most heavily mined countries in the world. More than 90 people are maimed or killed every month.

▶ The world's largest gold mine is at Murantau in the Kyzyl Kum desert in Uzbekistan.

CHILDREN IN KABUL, Afghanistan, who have been made homeless by war.

FESTIVALS IN AFGHANISTAN

Despite the horrors of recent years, the Afghans still celebrate important Islamic festivals, notably Eid ul-Fitr, which marks the end of the holy month of Ramadan. People visit friends and family and eat a festive meal together. The art of storytelling still flourishes in Afghanistan, as does the *attan*, the national dance.

AN AFGHAN REFUGEE carries bread with which to break the Ramadan fast.

LIFE EXPECTANCY

As a result of war, drought, and poverty, people in Afghanistan can expect to live an average of only 46 years, one of the lowest life expectancy rates in the world. Infant mortality is extremely high. Health services have almost completely collapsed and few trained doctors and nurses are available to help the sick. Sadly, there are not enough orphanages to cope with the increasing number of children made homeless by war.

Ustyurt Plateau
Aral Sea
KAZAKHSTAN
Müynoq
Chimboy
Takhtaküpir
Sarykamyshkoye Ozero
Nukus
Këneurgench
Takhiatosh
Gubadag
Uchquduq
Il'yaly
Dashkhovuz
Urganch
Türtkül
UZBEKISTAN
Khiwa
Zarafshon
Turkmenbashi
Gaz-Achak
Lebap
Krasnovodskiy Zaliv
Zaunguzskiye
Gazli
Nebitdag
Darvaza
Ghijduwon
Cheleken
Garagumy
Bukhoro
Gazandzhyk
Seydi
Kogon
Gyzylarbat
Kara Kum
Deynau
Kopetdag Gershi
(Garagumy)
Chardzhev
Kara-Kala
Bakharden
Sayat
Caspian Sea
Geok-Tepe
Byuzmeyin
Kelifskiy
Gora Chapan
ASHGABAT
Amu-Dar'ya
2889m
Kara Kum Canal
Kerki
Kaakhka
Tedzhen
Mary
Bayramaly
Uzboy
Murgab
Serakhs
Andkhvoy
Vozvyshennost'
Karabil'
Meymaneh
Bālā Morghāb
Torkestan
Gushgy
Towraghoudī
Ghūrīān
Herāt
Harirū
AFGHAN
Shīndand
Farāh Rūd
Farāh
Delārām
Gereshk
Dasht-e Khāsh
Lashkar Gāh
Hāmūn-e Şāberī
Chakhānsūr
Kandahār
Zaranj
Küchnay Darweyshān
Dasht-e Mārgow
Deh Shū
Rīgestān
Daryā-ye Helmand
Chāgai Hills
PAKISTAN

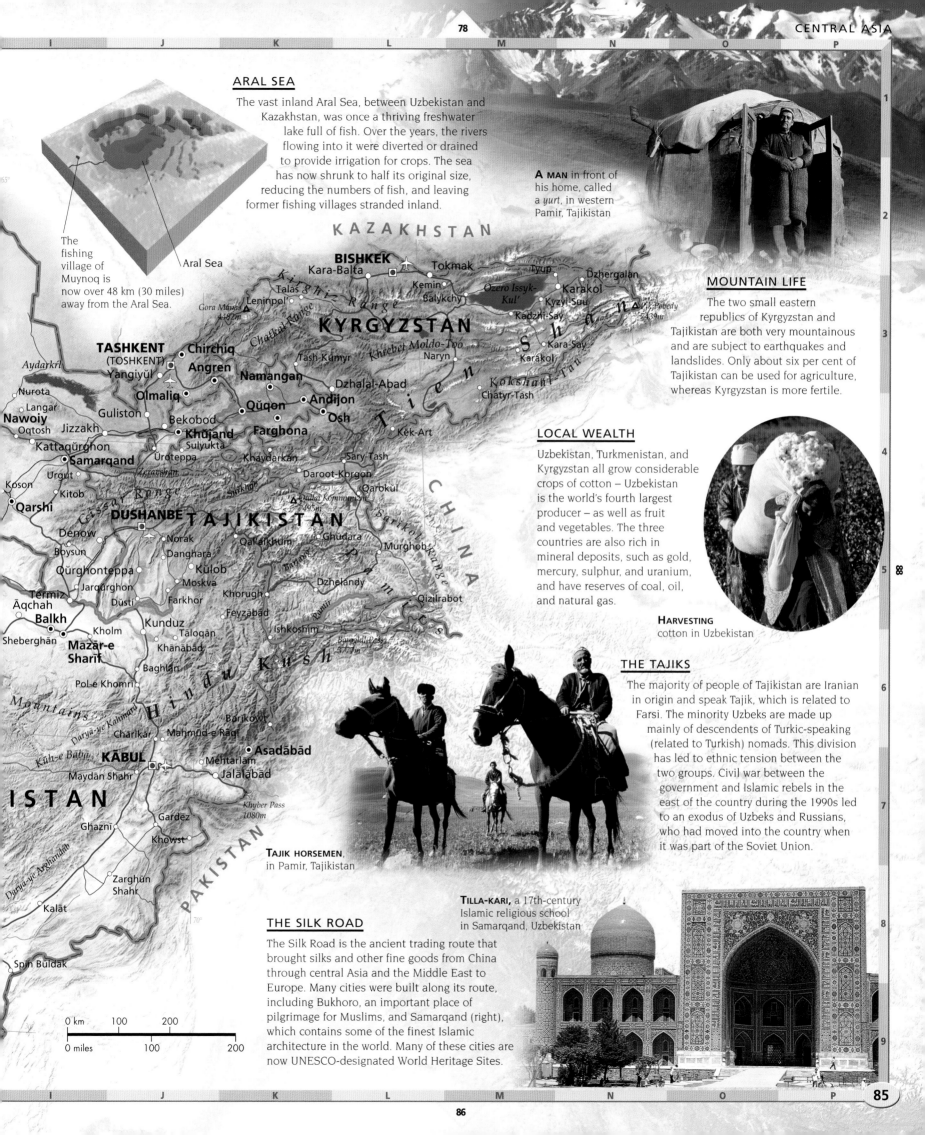

ARAL SEA

The vast inland Aral Sea, between Uzbekistan and Kazakhstan, was once a thriving freshwater lake full of fish. Over the years, the rivers flowing into it were diverted or drained to provide irrigation for crops. The sea has now shrunk to half its original size, reducing the numbers of fish, and leaving former fishing villages stranded inland.

The fishing village of Muynoq is now over 48 km (30 miles) away from the Aral Sea.

Aral Sea

A MAN in front of his home, called a *yurt*, in western Pamir, Tajikistan

MOUNTAIN LIFE

The two small eastern republics of Kyrgyzstan and Tajikistan are both very mountainous and are subject to earthquakes and landslides. Only about six per cent of Tajikistan can be used for agriculture, whereas Kyrgyzstan is more fertile.

LOCAL WEALTH

Uzbekistan, Turkmenistan, and Kyrgyzstan all grow considerable crops of cotton – Uzbekistan is the world's fourth largest producer – as well as fruit and vegetables. The three countries are also rich in mineral deposits, such as gold, mercury, sulphur, and uranium, and have reserves of coal, oil, and natural gas.

HARVESTING cotton in Uzbekistan

THE TAJIKS

The majority of people of Tajikistan are Iranian in origin and speak Tajik, which is related to Farsi. The minority Uzbeks are made up mainly of descendents of Turkic-speaking (related to Turkish) nomads. This division has led to ethnic tension between the two groups. Civil war between the government and Islamic rebels in the east of the country during the 1990s led to an exodus of Uzbeks and Russians, who had moved into the country when it was part of the Soviet Union.

TAJIK HORSEMEN, in Pamir, Tajikistan

TILLA-KARI, a 17th-century Islamic religious school in Samarqand, Uzbekistan

THE SILK ROAD

The Silk Road is the ancient trading route that brought silks and other fine goods from China through central Asia and the Middle East to Europe. Many cities were built along its route, including Bukhoro, an important place of pilgrimage for Muslims, and Samarqand (right), which contains some of the finest Islamic architecture in the world. Many of these cities are now UNESCO-designated World Heritage Sites.

0 km   100   200

0 miles   100   200

Indian Subcontinent

SEPARATED FROM THE rest of Asia by the Himalayas, the Indian subcontinent is home to more than one-fifth of the world's population – a staggering one billion people. They have a long and complex history, form many different ethnic groups, speak a wide variety of languages, and worship many different gods. Some of these countries are relatively wealthy, but many people live in poverty. Tensions between and within countries in this region have sometimes erupted in warfare. The Indian subcontinent is often affected by natural disasters, notably cyclones in the Bay of Bengal, and earthquakes. However, India, the most heavily populated state and once prone to famine, is now more than self-sufficient in food. All but Nepal and Bhutan were once ruled by the British, whose legacy can be seen in the common language of English, in the architecture, the vast railway system, and in sport – most notably cricket.

Monsoon

From May/June to September, warm, moist southerly winds sweep up from the Indian Ocean and the Bay of Bengal across the subcontinent. Once these winds meet dry land, moisture falls as monsoon rainfall. Although this irrigates the land and replenishes the water supply, it can also cause severe flooding.

FAMILY LIFE IN PAKISTAN

Pakistanis have strong ties to their extended families, and often many generations live and work together in family-run businesses. Smaller family units, however, are becoming more common in urban areas. Although some women hold prominent positions in public and commercial life – Benazir Bhutto has twice been prime minister – most women do not work outside the home.

SRI LANKA

In 1983, civil war erupted in Sri Lanka between the Buddhist majority Sinhalese, who dominate the government, and the Hindu minority Tamils, who want to establish their own independent state in the north of the island. The civil war has cost many lives and disrupted the island's economy, yet Sri Lanka still has one of the highest literacy rates in the world and high levels of health care.

SCHOOLCHILD
in Sri Lanka

Map labels

(claimed by India)

Himalaya Hindu Kush Karakoram Range 8611m

AFGHANISTAN

Khyber Pass 1080m
Mingãora
Mardãn
Peshãwar   Wãh   ISLÃMÃBÃD
Jhelum   Rãwalpindi
Potwar Plateau   Jammu
Sargodha Gujrãt   Gujrãnwãla
Chaman   Toba Kãkar Range   Lahore   Amritsar
Faisalãbãd   Ludhiãna
Quetta   Dera Ghãzi Khãn   Multãn Okãra   Chandiga
Chãgai Hills   Bathinda   Haryãna
Kãlat   Sibi   Bahãwalpur   Karnãl
PAKISTAN   Delhi
Baluchistãn   Jacobãbãd   Rahïmyãr   NEW DELHI
Shikãrpur   Khãn   Bïkãner
Central Makrãn Range   Lãrkãna   Sukkur   Alwar
Turbat   Khairpur   Thar Desert   Jaipur
Jaisalmer   Jodhpur   Rajasthãn
Gwãdar   Pasni   Nawãbshãh   Pãli   Beãwar
Hyderãbãd   Mïrpur Khãs   Shivpur
Karãchi   Sind   Kota
Sujãwal   Udaipur
Mouths of the Indus   Rann of Kachchh   Pãlanpur
Tropic of Cancer   Gãndhïdhãm   Gujarãt   Ratlãm
Gulf of Kachchh   Ahmadãbãd   Vindhya Range   Bhopa
Jãmnagar   Godhra   Indore   IN
Rãjkot   Vadodara
Porbandar   Bhãvnagar   Sãtpura Range
Gulf of Khambhãt   Sũrat   Bhusãwal
Dãmãn   Manmãd
Nãshik   Aurangãbãd
Kalyãn   Godãvari
Mumbai   Pune   Nãnded
(Bombay)   Mahãrãshtra   D
Arabian   Bãrãmati
Sea   Solãpur
Gulbarga
Kolhãpur   Rãichu
Karnãtaka
Belgaum   Gadag
Panaji   Hubli
Dãvanger
Shimoga
Udupi
Mangalore   Bangalore
Kãsargod   Mysore
Cannanore   Erode
Calicut
Coimbatore   Tam
Ernãkula
Cochin
Quilon
Trivandrum
Nãgercoil

0 km   150   300
0 miles   150   300

(A "line of control" was agreed between India and Pakistan in 1972)

AKSAI CHIN (administered by China, claimed by India)

Jammu and Kashmir

DEMCHOK/ DÊMQOG (administered by China, claimed by India)

THE HIMALAYAS

The highest chain of mountains in the world, the Himalayas have eight peaks that are more than 8,000 m (26,247 ft) high. Everest, the world's highest mountain at 8,850 m (29,035 ft), is on the border of Nepal and Tibet. Mountaineers come from far and wide to scale these massive peaks.

BHUTANESE PEOPLE

ARUNACHAI PRADESH (claimed by China)

BHUTAN

Hidden away in the Himalayas, the people of Bhutan are devoutly Buddhist and have little contact with the outside world. A minority of the population are Nepalese Hindus who came to the country in the first half of the last century. Most Bhutanese live in the fertile river valleys of the centre and south of the country. Traditional dress – the *kira* for women and the *gho* for men – is widely worn.

Map labels

Meerut
Bareilly
NEPAL
Ganges
CHINA
Salyan
Annapurna △ 8091m
Mount Everest △ 8850m
Kula Kangri △ 7755m
Dibrugarh
Pokhara
KATHMANDU
Bhaktapur
Lalitpur
THIMPHU BHUTAN
Brahmaputra
Agra
Lucknow
Uttar Pradesh
Faizābad
Biratnagar
Darjiling
Bongaigaon
Jorhāt
Assam
Kohima
Gwalior
Kānpur
Gorakhpur
Shiliguri
Guwāhāti
Jhānsi
Allahābād
Chhapra
Dinajpur
Rangpur
Imphāl
MYANMAR (BURMA)
Patna
Jamālpur
Sylhet
Silchar
Sāgar
Varānasi
Gāya
Ganges
Rajshahi
BANGLADESH
Pabna
Murwāra
Dhanbād
Madhya Pradesh
Bihār
Āsānsol
DHAKA
Comilla
Jabalpur
Rānchi
Jessore
Khulna
Tropic of Cancer
Jamshedpur
Chota Nāgpur
West Bengal
Barisal
Chittagong
D I A
Bilāspur
Rāulakela
Kharagpur
Calcutta (Kolkatta)
Korba
Nāgpur
Gondia
Raipur
Sambalpur
Bāleshwar
Mouths of the Ganges
Mahānadi
Bay of Bengal
Chandrapur
Orissa
Cuttack
Bhubaneshwar
Puri
Jagdalpur
Brahmapur
Nizāmābād
Karīmnagar
Andhra Pradesh
Vizianagaram
Warangal
Visākhapatnam
Hyderābād
Rājahmundry
Godāvari
Eastern Ghats
Krishna
Vijayawāda
Chīrala
Kurnool
Ongole
Tādpatri
Kāvali
Cuddapah
Nellore
Chennai (Madras)
Vellore
Kānchīpuram
Salem
Pondicherry
Nādu
Tiruchchirāppalli
Madurai
Jaffna
Palk Strait
Mannar
SRI LANKA
Tuticorin
Trincomalee
Gulf of Mannar
Puttalam
Batticaloa
Negombo
Kandy
COLOMBO
INDIAN OCEAN
Kalutara
Galle
Matara

Did you know?

▸ The name Bhutan means "Land of the Thunder Dragon" in Dzongkha, the country's official language.

▸ India has the second largest population in the world after China, officially passing the one billion mark (1,000 million) in the year 2000.

RELIGION

Two of the world's great religions – Hinduism and Buddhism – began in India more than 2,500 years ago. Most Pakistanis and Bangladeshis are Muslim, most Indians and Nepalese are Hindu, and most Sri Lankans and Bhutanese are Buddhist.

HINDUS BATHE in the River Ganges, considered sacred.

North Andaman
Middle Andaman
Port Blair
Andaman Islands (to India)
South Andaman
Little Andaman
Nicobar Islands (to India)
Car Nicobar
Andaman Sea
Katchall Island
Little Nicobar
Great Nicobar
Indira Point

TEA IN SRI LANKA

Sri Lanka is the world's largest exporter of tea. The plantations are located mainly in the centre of the island, and employ women to pick the delicate, green shoots of the bushes.

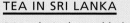

BOLLYWOOD

More films are produced in Mumbai (Bombay) – more than 800 a year – than in the whole USA, turning "Bollywood", as it is known; into a major cultural centre. Bollywood films generally have historical, religious, or social themes, and are famous for their song and dance routines and glamorous stars. These films are an important export to central Asia, the Middle East, and Africa.

Western China and Mongolia

CHINA IS A LAND of great geographical diversity and amazing landscapes. More than 90 per cent of the population is Han Chinese – descendants of people who settled here more than 5,000 years ago. This region includes Western China, Mongolia, and Tibet. Mongolia gained its independence from China in 1911, and is now an independent democracy. Tibet is currently governed by China. Compared with Eastern China, this region is sparsely populated and characterized by vast deserts, remote mountains, and extreme temperatures.

DESERT LANDS

The cold, rocky Gobi Desert (right) stretches for more than 1,000,000 sq km (400,000 sq miles) through Mongolia and northeast China. Many dinosaur bones and eggs have been found here, making it one of the richest dinosaur fossil regions in the world.

THE MONGOLIANS

Most of the people living in Mongolia are Khalkh Mongols. About half of these people now live in urban areas, but some still lead traditional lives as nomadic herders. They live in large felt tents, called yurts. Smoke from the central iron stove escapes through a chimney in the roof.

Did you know?

▶ In traditional Mongolian *khoomi* singing, male singers produce harmonic overtones deep in their throats. They are able to sing several notes at once.

▶ Prayer flags are a Tibetan tradition symbolizing the Buddhist faith. Before the Chinese occupation, they flew from every home as a symbol of good luck.

CHINESE WRITING

The Chinese alphabet is not made up of letters. Instead, separate symbols stand for individual words or parts of words. There are more than 40,000 characters in the Chinese language. The same symbols are used everywhere in China, and no matter what Chinese language or dialect people speak, they can all read the same script.

兒童百科全書

THE STROKES in each symbol have to be written in a certain order.

MONASTERIES IN MONGOLIA

Under communism, Mongolians were forbidden to practise their traditional Buddhist faith, which was viewed as superstitious and unscientific. Since the democratic government was set up in 1990, about 100 monasteries have reopened. Most people, however, no longer follow any religion.

Map labels

KAZAKHSTAN
Altai Mountains
Hangayn Nuruu
Hövsgöl Nuur
Uvs Nuur
Ulaangom
Ölgiy
Altay
Charus Nuur
Hyargas Nuur
Har Nuur
Hovd
Halban
Möron
Tsetserl
Ulungur Hu
Karamay
MON
Altay
Bayanhongo
Gurbantünggüt Shamo
Bogdo Shan
Kuytun
Shihezi
Fukang
Jimsar
Aj Bogd Uul 3802m
Yining
Ürümqi
Qitai
Turpan
Atas Bogd 2702m
G
Tien Shan
Pik Pobedy 7439m
Turpan Pendi
Hami
Bosten Hu
Xingxingxia
Korla
Kuruktag
GANSU
KYRGYZSTAN
Tarim He
Tarim Basin
Yumen
Kashi
XINJIANG
Qilian Shan
Yengisar
Danghe Nanshan
TAJIKISTAN
Shache
Yecheng
Ruoqiang
Altun Shan
CHIN
AFGH
Pishan
Takla Makan Desert
Qaidam Pendi
Qingh
Moyu
Hotan
Qira
Qilian
Golmud
Dulan
K2 8611m
Kunlun Shan
Burhan Budai Shan
Karakoram Range
AKSAI CHIN
AKSAI CHIN (administered by China, claimed by India)
QINGHAI
PAKISTAN
Plateau of Tibet (Qingzang Gaoyuan)
Bayan Har Shan
Tongtian He
INDIA
Indus
Rutog
TIBET
Yushu
DEMCHOK/DÊMQOG (administered by China, claimed by India)
Tanggula Shan
Mekong
Gar
Zanda
Nyima
Siling Co
Amdo
Himalayas
Tangra Yumco
Gyaring Co
Nagqu
Qamdo
Brahmaputra
Ngangzê Co
Nam Co
Damxung
Salween
Nyainqêntanglha Shan
Lhazê
Xigazê
Maizhokunggar
ARUNACHAL PRADESH (claimed by China)
NEPAL
Mount Everest 8850m
Gonggar
Lhasa
Gyangzê
MYANMAR (BURMA)
BHUTAN
INDIA

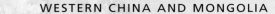

0 km   200   400
0 miles   200   400

RUSS. FED.

RUSSIAN FEDERATION

Mohe
Tahe

Ergun Zuoqi
Jagdaqi

Manzhouli
Yakeshi
Hailar

Sühbaatar

Hulun Nur

Fuyuan

Yichun

Bei'an
Nancha

Hegang

HEILONGJIANG
Jiamusi

Qiqihar
Tonghe
Jixi

Selenga

Darhan
Onon Gol
Choybalsan

Erdenet
Menengiyn Tal

Harbin
Shangzhi
Lake Khanka

ULAN BATOR
(ULAANBAATAR)

Öndörhaan

Bulgan
Kerulen
Baruun-Urt

Dzuunmod

Mudanjiang

Songyuan
Changchun
Jilin

GOLIA

Xi Ujimqin Qi
Tongliao
Siping
JILIN

Yanji

Saynshand

Xilinhot
Liaoyuan

Gobi Desert
Erenhot

Sea of Japan

Baishan

Dalandzadgad

Govĭ Altayn Nuruu

Ejin Qi

INNER MONGOLIA
(Nei Mongol Zizhiqu)

LIAONING
Chifeng
Liao He

NORTH KOREA

o b i

Lang Shan

Jining
HEBEI

Yabrai Shan

Hohhot

Wuhai

Yellow River
(Huang He)
Baotou

SHANXI

Mu Us Shamo

Tengger Shamo

Yinchuan

NINGXIA
Great Wall of China

A

Tongxin

Xining

SHAANXI

Lanzhou
Pingliang

GANSU

Henan

Luqu
Tianshui

Zhuguu

SICHUAN
Wenxian

FESTIVAL OF NADAAM

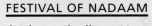

Each July, people all over Mongolia celebrate the sports festival of Naadam. Three sports – wrestling (above), archery, and horse-riding – are the focus of the festivities. The skills needed to take part in these activities are those that would have helped people survive the traditional nomadic lifestyle.

PEOPLE OF TIBET

Most Tibetans live in the valleys of the Tibetan plateau, high in the Himalayas and surrounded by the world's tallest mountains. They have their own language and culture. Recently, many Han Chinese have moved to this region looking for a better life.

TIBETAN VILLAGE CHILDREN

GREAT WALL OF CHINA

About 2,200 years ago, approximately 300,000 slaves began to build China's enormous Great Wall. Originally built to protect China's northern borders, it is the longest human-made structure ever built, and stretches from central Asia to the Yellow Sea, a distance of 6,400 km (3,980 miles).

TRADITIONAL MEDICINE

As well as modern medicine, many Chinese still use alternative remedies. Traditional medicine is based on the belief that health is achieved by balancing a person's mind and body – their yin and yang. Any imbalance is treated with medicines made from dried plant materials (left). Some animals, including Asiatic bears, are now endangered due to the demand for parts used in traditional medicine

BUDDHIST PRAYER FLAGS

BUDDHIST TIBET

Many Tibetans are devout Buddhists. Their religious leader, the Dalai Lama, used to live in Lhasa. In 1951, however, Tibet became part of China and the government restricted the people's religious freedom and lifestyle. This resulted in tension between the Tibetans and the Chinese government. The Dalai Lama now lives in exile in India.

Eastern China and Korea

CHINA HAS A LARGE population of 1.3 billion, with two-thirds living in Eastern China. For thousands of years, powerful emperors ruled China. During this period, Chinese civilization was very advanced, but much of the population lived in poverty. In 1949, after a communist revolution, the People's Republic of China was established. Food, education, and healthcare became available to more people, but there was also a loss of freedom. Today, Chinese people have more freedom, but the government still has tight control over their lives. The Korean peninsula is divided politically into north and south, and attempts are being made to restore peace between the two governments. Since 1949, Taiwan has been in dispute with China over who governs this mountainous island.

NEW YEAR CELEBRATIONS

Chinese New Year, also known as the Spring Festival, is the country's most important festival. It is usually held in January or February. Good-luck messages decorate buildings and there are feasts, fireworks, fairs, and processions. People wear red clothes for good luck and give gifts of coins to symbolize wealth.

CHINESE NEW YEAR PARADE

HONG KONG

For 100 years, Hong Kong was a British colony. Then, in 1997, it was returned to China. These small islands are some of the most densely populated parts of the world. Most people live and work in high-rise buildings. Hong Kong has a prosperous economy and the people have one of the world's highest life expectancies.

THE SKYLINE OF HONG KONG with a Chinese junk in the foreground

ONE-CHILD FAMILIES

Many Chinese children do not have brothers or sisters. This is due to policies brought in by the Chinese goverment in 1979. To try and control the rising population, the government offers special benefits to couples with only one child. Although this has slowed down the rate of growth, China's population still grows by millions each year.

PADDY FIELDS

Rice forms the basis of most Chinese meals. It grows in paddy fields in the southeast of the country. During the growing season, fields are flooded so farmers can grow more rice more quickly. In the drier regions, wheat is grown and used to make noodles, buns, and dumplings. Rice or wheat is combined with local vegetables, meats, and spices to create regional dishes.

0 km   150   300

0 miles   150   300

NORTH KOREA

North Korea is an independent communist country, but since the breakup of the Soviet Union it has lost many of its trading partners and is now very poor. However, the country has a good education system and a high literacy rate. Schooling is free and compulsory for all children for 10 years.

SOUTH KOREA

South Korea is a democratic nation with a thriving electronics and machinery industry. A quarter of the population lives in or near the capital city, Seoul. The Internet has developed quickly in South Korea and plays an important role in work and leisure. The children below are using computers at an internet cafe in the central city of Taejon.

Did you know?

▶ Many of the world's inventions and technological advances originally came from China, including paper, money, compasses, fireworks, and silk.

▶ North Korean students are required to work for the government during part of their summer holidays as payment for their free education.

▶ The majority of the Chinese population lives in just 15 per cent of the total land area.

MODERN SHANGHAI

China's largest city is Shanghai. More than eight million people live in this wealthy east coast port. International trade has recently transformed Shanghai's skyline, which is now crowded with high-rise buildings and modern shopping malls. The centre of town still has some old western-style buildings that have survived from the days before the revolution.

BEAUTY OF TAIWAN

Taiwan's mountainous countryside is famous for its natural beauty, scenic lakes, and many ornate Buddhist temples. This peaceful environment contrasts sharply with Taiwan's capital city, Taipei, which is one of the fastest growing cities in Asia.

CHINESE INDUSTRY

After the revolutionary leader Mao Zedong died in 1976, China's economy opened up. New industry is now encouraged, and many people are moving from the country to cities where there are relatively well-paid jobs.

BICYCLE FACTORY

Map labels

INNER MONGOLIA

JILIN

Sea of Japan

Najin
Ch'ŏngjin
Hyesan
Kimch'aek

Shenyang
Fuxin
Fushun
Kanggye
Chaoyang
LIAONING
Anshan
Jinzhou
Haicheng
Chengde
Fengcheng
Sinŭiju
NORTH KOREA
Zhangjiakou
Qinhuangdao
Dandong
Huailai
Chŏngju
Hamhŭng
Datong
BEIJING (PEKING)
Tangshan
P'YŎNGYANG
East Korea Bay
Shouzhou
Langfang
Tianjin
Dalian
Wŏnsan
Rengiu
TIANJIN SHI
Bo Hai
Sariwŏn
Ch'unch'ŏn
Shijiazhuang
Korea Bay
Haeju
Taiyuan
HEBEI
Botou
Cangzhou
Yantai
Inch'ŏn
SEOUL (SŎUL)
SOUTH KOREA
Yuci
Dezhou
Binzhou
Taejŏn
Taegu
SHANXI
Zibo
Weifang
Chŏnju
Ulsan
Handan
Jinan
Chŏnju
Pusan
Changzhi
SHANDONG
Qingdao
Kwangju
Chinju
Anyang
Mokp'o
Yŏsu
Xinxiang
Jining
Rizhao
Sanmenxia
Kaifeng
Zaozhuang
Yellow Sea
Cheju Strait
Korea Strait
Luoyang
Zhengzhou
Xuzhou
Lianyungang
Cheju-do
Pingdingshan
JIANGSU
HENAN
Suzhou
Bengbu
Nanyang
Xiangfang
Huainan
Xinyang
Nanjing
Yangzhou
Hefei
Wuxi
Suzhou
HUBEI
ANHUI
Wuhu
Shanghai
Yichang
Wuhan
Anqing
Jiaxing
CHINA
Jingzhou
Huangshi
Hangzhou
Yueyang
Jiujiang
Ningbo
Changde
Jingdezhen
Quzhou
Jinhua
Changsha
Nanchang
ZHEJIANG
Wenzhou
Loudi
Linchuan
Shangrao
Xiangtan
HUNAN
JIANGXI
FUJIAN
Fu'an
Hengyang
Nanfeng
Nanping
Hongjiang
Sanming
Lengshuitan
Ganzhou
Yong'an
Fuzhou
Chilung
Quanzhou
Longyan
Quanzhou
TAIPEI
Chenzhou
Guilin
Shaoguan
Zhangzhou
T'aichung
Hexian
Xiamen
Chiai
Hualien
Lipu
GUANGDONG
Chaozhou
TAIWAN
Guangzhou
Shantou
T'ainan
Zhaoqing
Dongguan
Kaohsiung
Jiangmen
Hong Kong (Xianggang)
Macao (Aomen)
Maoming
Suixi
Zhanjiang
Xuwen
Haikou
Hainan Dao

Yellow River (Huang He)

Yangtze

East China Sea

South China Sea

Taiwan Strait

Tropic of Cancer

(North and South Korea have been divided by a ceasefire agreement since 1953)

(China and Taiwan claim all of each other's territory)

92

Japan

JAPAN IS SITUATED in the north Pacific Ocean off the coast of the Asian continent. It is made up of four main islands and more than 3,000 smaller ones. The Japanese people have a distinctive culture based on traditions built up over thousands of years. They have their own language and script. Schoolchildren all learn to read and write both in the traditional script and using letters. Social rules in Japan are strict, and respect and politeness are considered very important. Most people bow when greeting one another, for example. Japan is a very modern country, however, with one of the world's most technologically advanced societies. Its economy is based on the development and production of cutting-edge electronics and vehicles, and most families have the latest consumer goods.

RELIGIONS OF JAPAN

Many Japanese people follow a mix of the Shinto and Buddhist religions, attending wedding blessings in Shinto shrines and funerals in Buddhist temples. Buddhism originated in India, and arrived in Japan in the 6th century, whereas the Shinto faith is native to Japan. Respect for nature is especially important in the Shinto religion. Many natural locations, such as Mount Fuji, are considered sacred.

MOUNT FUJI is a dormant volcano.

JAPANESE TEMPLE

Earthquakes

The islands of Japan are situated in an area where four of the Earth's tectonic plates meet. This causes frequent earthquakes. Japanese schoolchildren are taught how to keep safe during an earthquake by sheltering in a doorway or under a table.

OVERCROWDING

Most of the country's 126 million people live in cities in the flatter, coastal areas. Tokyo and Osaka are very crowded, and homes here are usually very small and are designed to make the most of the limited space.

FASHION IN JAPAN

On ordinary days, Japanese people usually wear western-style clothes. Most children have a school uniform. On festival days, such as Children's Day, many people prefer to wear the traditional kimono. Women's kimonos are often made of colourful silk, decorated with beautiful designs.

Traditional and modern dress side-by-side

Map labels

Kuril'sk
Ostrov Iturup
Kurile Islands
Ostrov Shikotan
Ostrov Kunashir
(Kurile Islands administered by Russian Federation, claimed by Japan)

Sea of Okhotsk

Nemuro
Akkeshi
Kushiro
Shari
Bekkai
Kitami
Abashiri
Shintoku
Obihiro
Hiroo
Meshi-take 2290m
Horoshiri-dake 2052m
Hokkaidō
Monbetsu
Shirataki
Chitose
Tomakomai
Noboribetsu
Muroran
Mutsu
Miyako
Nakagawa
Ebetsu
Uchiura-wan
Fudi
Kuji
Nayoro
Asahikawa
Mutsu-wan
Towada
Kesennuma
Shibetsu
Takikawa
Hakodate
Hachinohe
Shizugawa
Iwate
Ishinomaki
Otaru
Sapporo
Fukushima
Aomori
Morioka
Sendai-wan
Wakkanai
Iwanai
Tsugaru-kaikyō
Kuroishi
Hanamaki
Sendai
Rebun-tō
Ishikari-wan
Esashi
Goshogawara
Hirosaki
Ōdate
Yokote
Rishiri-tō
Setana
Akita
Shinjo
Noshiro
Gojōme
Yuzawa
Tsuruoka
Okushiri-tō
Honjo
Sakata
Furukawa
Atsumi

La Perouse Strait

Scale bar

200
200
100
100
0 km
0 miles

MODERN TECHNOLOGY

Japan's economy is based on high-tech research, development, and production. The country has built up a reputation for providing the latest technology in vehicles and electronic goods, such as televisions, computers, and stereo systems. Their products are usually of a high quality but are still affordable.

A PROTOTYPE of a Mazda car produced in Hiroshima.

MARTIAL ARTS

Kendo is a popular martial art in Japan. It was developed (in its modern form) about 200 years ago, and teaches the art of Japanese Samurai swordsmanship. Children train using bamboo swords (above).

BASEBALL

Baseball, known as *yakyu*, is fast becoming Japan's most popular sport. As well as two professional leagues, the game is played at universities and high schools. It was introduced to Japan in the late 1800s.

A HEALTHY DIET

Rice is the major crop grown on the small amount of flat land in Japan. Along with rice, fish is an important part of most meals, and Japan has one of the world's largest fishing fleets. This healthy diet may be part of the reason why Japanese people have the world's longest life expectancy.

A DISH of raw fish and rice, known as sushi

BULLET TRAIN

One of the fastest ways to travel around Japan is on their high-speed train system, known as the bullet trains, or Shinkansen. This network connects Tokyo with most of the country's other major cities, such as Sapporo and Nagasaki. The trains reach speeds of over 300 kmh (186 mph). Japan ran the world's first high-speed train in 1964.

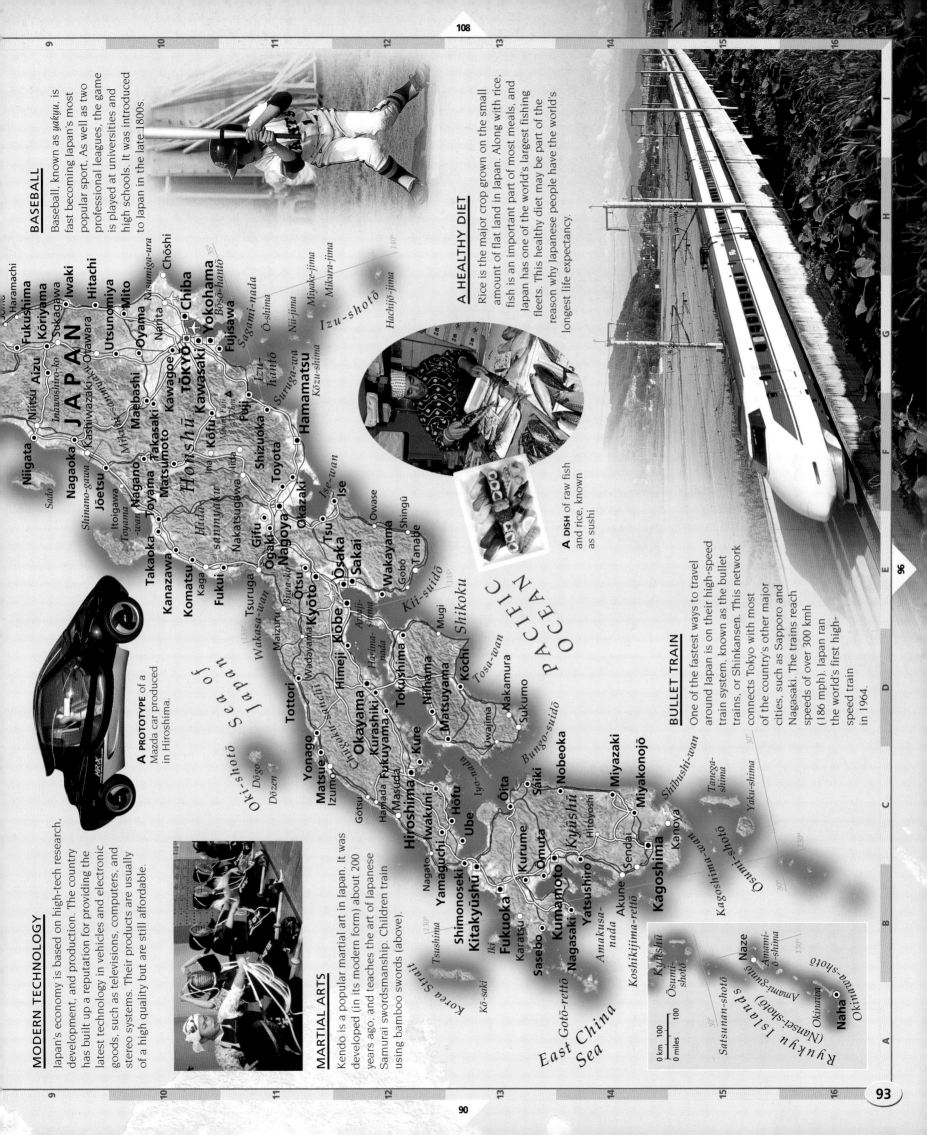

Map labels

Haramachi, Fukushima, Kōriyama, Iwaki, Hitachi, Aizu, Niitsu, Sukagawa, Utsunomiya, Mito, Chōshi

JAPAN, Niigata, Nagaoka, Jōetsu, Takasaki, Maebashi, Oyama, Narita, Chiba, Yokohama, TOKYO, Kawasaki, Fujisawa

Kashiwazaki, Kawagoe, Nagano, Matsumoto, Takaoka, Toyama, Kōfu, Fuji, Mount Fuji 3776m

Kanazawa, Komatsu, Fukui, Gifu, Ogaki, Nagoya, Okazaki, Toyota, Shizuoka, Hamamatsu

Honshū, Tsuruga, Otsu, Kyōto, Kōbe, Ōsaka, Sakai, Tsu, Ise, Owase, Shingū

Tottori, Himeji, Wakayama, Gobō, Tanabe, Mugi

Yonago, Matsue, Okayama, Kurashiki, Fukuyama, Kure, Tokushima, Kōchi, Nakamura, Sukumo

Hiroshima, Iwakuni, Nihama, Matsuyama, Uwajima

Shimonoseki, Kitakyūshū, Yamaguchi, Ube, Hōfu, Ōita, Saiki, Nobeoka, Miyazaki, Miyakonojō

Fukuoka, Karatsu, Kurume, Ōmuta, Kumamoto, Yatsushiro, Sendai, Kanoya, Kagoshima

Sasebo, Nagasaki, Akune, Kyūshū

Tsushima, Iki, Kō-saki

Korea Strait, East China Sea

PACIFIC OCEAN, Sea of Japan, Oki-shotō, Dōgo, Dōzen

Izu-shotō, Ō-shima, Nii-jima, Miyake-jima, Mikura-jima, Hachijō-jima

Kii-suidō, Shikoku, Tosa-wan, Bungo-suidō, Iyo-nada

Kagoshima-wan, Ōsumi-shotō, Tanega-shima, Yaku-shima, Shibushi-wan

Inset map

Ryūkyū Islands (Nansei-shotō), Kyūshū, Ōsumi-shotō, Satsunan-shotō, Satsunan-shotō, Amami-shotō, Naze, Amami-ō-shima, Okinawa, Okinawa-shotō, Naha

0 km 100
0 miles 100

Mainland SE Asia

THE PENINSULA of Southeast Asia lies directly below India and China, between the Pacific and Indian oceans. It is made up of Myanmar (Burma), Thailand, Vietnam, Cambodia, and Laos. Over thousands of years, the influence of people from nearby Indian, Chinese, and Arabian cultures has helped to give this region a diverse mix of cultures and religions. Much of the land here is mountainous, with half the region covered in forest. Most people live in coastal or lowland regions, where they can grow crops such as rice, raise cattle, and catch fish. In recent years, the electronics industry has also become an important part of Southeast Asian economies, especially in Thailand.

ORPHANS IN CAMBODIA

Cambodia has the highest percentage of widows and orphans of any country in the world. Many men were killed in civil wars in recent decades.

CAMBODIAN ORPHANAGE

GROWING RICE

Rice is the most important crop in Southeast Asia. It grows well in wet lowland areas, such as the Mekong River delta in Vietnam, where the plants can be grown in paddy fields. Most rice is planted and harvested by women.

RURAL LIVING

Most people in Southeast Asia live in rural areas rather than cities, and farming is the most common occupation. The steep mountainous regions are often unsuitable for growing crops or raising cattle, however, and many farming communities are based in the fertile river valleys and deltas. There are over 200 villages on and around this lake (right) in Myanmar.

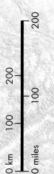

PADAUNG women, who are part of the Karen tribe, wear distinctive gold neck rings.

KAREN TRIBE

There are 600,000 tribespeople living in the northeastern hills of Thailand. The Karen are the largest hill tribe. They originated from Myanmar, but moved into Thailand to escape political unrest.

Scale bar:
200
200
100
100
0 km
0 miles

Map labels

CHINA

INDIA

MYANMAR (BURMA)

LAOS

VIETNAM

CAMBODIA

BANGLADESH

Gulf of Tongking

Bay of Bengal

Hengduan Shan

Kumon Range

Hkakabo Razi 5885m

Naga Hills

Shan Plateau

Chin Hills

Arakan Yoma

Korat Plateau

Tropic of Cancer

Black River

Hoang Lien Son

Mekong

Salween

Irrawaddy

Sittang

Chindwin

Nam Ou

Nam Qu

Nam U

Ang Nam Ngum

Sirikit Reservoir

Mae Nam Nan

Mae Nam Yom

Chaîne Annamitique

Mae Nam Ping

Ramree Island

Cheduba Island

Cities and towns:
Myitkyina, Lashio, Mogaung, Bhamo, Katha, Banmauk, Maingkwan, Palam, Tamu, Monywa, Shwebo, Sagaing, Mandalay, Maymyo, Amarapura, Kyaukse, Myingyan, Meiktila, Pakokku, Chauk, Yenangyaung, Minbu, Magwe, Taungdwingyi, Pyinmana, Pawn, Taunggyi, Loi-Kaw, Toungoo, Allanmyo, Prome, Paungde, Pyu, Nyaunglebin, Pyuntaza, Thayetmyo, Myanaung, Henzada, Letpadan, Pegu, Thaton, Kyaikto, Kayan, Pa-an, RANGOON (YANGON), Bassein, Pyechin, Sittwe, Sandoway

Lao Cai, Ha Giang, Cao Bằng, Lang Son, Bắc Giang, Thai Nguyen, Việt Tri, Bắc Ninh, HA NOI, Hoa Binh, Nam Định, Thanh Hoa, Tuong Duong, Vinh, Đông Hoi, Đông Ha, Hai Phong, Hòng Gai, Cẩm Pha, Thai Binh

Lai Châu, Điện Biên, Sop Hao, Xam Nua, Phongsali, Muong Namo, Muang Sing, Louangnamtha, Viangphoukha, Houayxay, Luang phabang, Muong Xiang Ngeun, Pek, Xaignabouri, Ban Hin Heup, VIENTIANE (VIANGCHAN), Pakxan, Thakhek, Sakon Nakhon, Nong Khai, Udon Thani, Loei, Phitsanulok, Tak, Phrae, Lampang, Phayao, Chiang Rai, Fang, Chiang Mai, Keng Tung

ANGKOR WAT

The impressive temple complex of Angkor Wat in Cambodia attracts visitors interested in its history and architecture. This combination of temples and palaces was built in AD 1113 by the Khmer king Suryavarman II. The buildings are made of stone and brick and are decorated with relief sculptures showing mythical scenes of Hindu gods and great royal processions. The complex was uncovered in 1861 by French naturalist Henri Mouhot, following stories of a "lost city" in the jungle.

TEMPLE AT ANGKOR WAT

MONASTIC LIFE

The main religion in mainland Southeast Asia is Buddhism. Nearly all Thai villages have their own temple, or *wat*, which is the centre of village life. Most young men spend some time in a monastery, where they have few possessions and spend much of their time in meditation.

FLOATING MARKET

The capital of Thailand, Bangkok, is a busy, crowded city with about six million inhabitants. The city was built on an island in the river, and has many canals. Boats, known as *sampans*, (above) act as floating markets from which traders sell fresh fruit and vegetables.

Did you know?

► A traditional greeting in Thailand is the "wai". The hands are placed together in prayer position and slightly raised, as the head is bowed.

► A large, previously unknown mammal, the vu quang ox, was only recently discovered in the forests of northern Vietnam.

THAI BEACHES

Tourism is now a major industry for Thailand. Popular destinations include the country's lively capital, Bangkok, and the beautiful island beach resorts (below). Phuket, Thailand's largest island, is often referred to as the "Pearl of the South".

Map labels

Moulmein
Kanbe Martaban
Kyaiklat
Kalasin
Bogale Kyaikkami
Mudon
Myaungmya
Labutta
Mouths of the Irrawaddy
Great Coco Island
Little Coco Island

T H A I L A N D
Lom Sak
Khon Kaen
Khanthabouli Muang Phalan
Khon Kaen
RoiEt
Nakhon Sawan
Ratchasima
Nakhon
Lop Buri
Ubon Ratchathani
Buriram
Surin
Sara Buri
Ayutthaya
BANGKOK (KRUNG THEP)
Samut Prakan
Chon Buri
Pattaya
Rayong
Ratchaburi
Nakhon Pathom
Phetchaburi
Ao Krung Thep
Ban Hua Hin
Srinagarind Reservoir
Range
Bilauktaung Range
Isthmus of Kra
Gulf of Thailand
Ko Chang
Chumphon
Ranong
Lang Suan
Ko Phangan
Ko Samui
Surat Thani
Sichon
Nakhon Si Thammarat
Pak Phanang
Phatthalung
Thale Luang
Songkhla
Pattani
Narathiwat
Yala
Hat Yai
Trang
Thung Song
Ko Ta Ru Tao
Ko Lanta
Pulau Langkawi
MALAYSIA
Phuket
Ko Phuket
Phang-Nga
Ko Phra Thong
Andaman Sea
Zadetkyi Kyun
Mali Kyun
Kadan Kyun
Mergui
Daung Kyun
Letsôk-aw Kyun
Lanbi Kyun
Tenasserim
Mergui Archipelago
Tavoy
Ye
Mudon

Salavan
Muang Khôngxédôn
Muang Không
Pakxé
Champasak
Khong
Stœng Sên
Xieng Sên
Tônlé Kông
Tônlé Srêpôk
Virôchey
Sên Monôrôm
Tônlé Srêpôk
CAMBODIA
PHNOM PENH (PHNUM PENH)
Phumi Kâmpóng Trâbêk
Trâpeăng Vêng
Kâmpóng Cham
Kâmpóng Chhnăng
Krâchéh
Stœng Trêng
Kâmpóng Thum
Kâmpóng Saôm
Kâmpôt
Chuor Phnum Krâvanh
Châu Dôc
Bătdâmbâng
Reăng Kesei
Môung Roessei
Chamthaburi
Pouthisăt
Phumi Sâmraông
Angkor Wat
Krâlănh
Tônlé Sap
Suông
Vinh Rach Gia
Rach Gia
Ca Mau
Bac Liêu
Soc Trăng
Tra Vinh
Cân Thơ
Long Xuyên
My Tho
Vung Tau
Hô Chi Minh
Biên Hoa
Da Lat
Di Linh
Phan Thiêt
Phan Rang-Thap Cham
Cam Ranh
Nha Trang
Tuy Hoa
Quy Nhon
Plây Cu
Kon Tum
Quang Ngai
Tam Ky
Hôi An
Đà Nang
V I E T N A M
Con Dao
Mouths of the Mekong
Mekong
South China Sea

Maritime SE Asia

To the south of the Asian mainland lies maritime Southeast Asia. It includes Malaysia, Indonesia, East Timor, Singapore, and the Philippines. Part of Malaysia is connected to the mainland, but the rest of the region is made up of more than 20,000 islands that stretch across the Pacific and Indian Oceans. Lying near the Equator, the climate is mostly hot, wet, and humid. Most of the larger islands are mountainous and covered in dense forest, and many people live in villages near rivers or on the coast. Like the rest of Southeast Asia, the population is made up of people from many different cultural backgrounds and hundreds of different languages are spoken. The most common religion is Islam, except in the Philippines, where most people are Roman Catholic.

GREAT APES

The orangutans are great apes that only live in Borneo and the northern corner of Sumatra. They spend most of their time in the trees, even building treetop nests in which to sleep. Sadly, the orangutan is endangered because of deforestation.

PEOPLE OF MALAYSIA

Ethnic Malaysians make up 59 per cent of the population, and are known as *bumiputera*, meaning "sons of the soil". Most Malaysians are Muslim. Ethnic Chinese form 26 per cent of the population.

UBADIAH MOSQUE, MALAYSIA

SINGAPORE

As the financial and industrial centre of Southeast Asia, Singapore is one of the wealthiest countries in this region. It has a thriving high-tech industry and a high standard of living. There are strictly enforced laws forbidding littering and other small crimes. The death penalty is imposed for drug smuggling. The government also controls the press and restricts the Internet.

SULTAN OF BRUNEI

THE SULTAN OF BRUNEI

Brunei is ruled by a sultan who lives in the world's largest palace. The sultan is one of the wealthiest men in the world.

Map labels:

Andaman Sea
THAILAND
South China Sea
Bandaaceh
Sigli
Meulaboh
Langsa
Pulau Pinang
George Town
Butterworth
Kota Bharu
Taiping
Ipoh
Kuala Terengganu
Dungun
Cukai
Kuala Lipis
Medan
Tebingtinggi
Klang
KUALA LUMPUR
Kuantan
Pematangsiantar
Seremban
Melaka
Keluang
Danau Toba
Muar
Batu Pahat
Johor Bahru
M A L A Y S I A
Kepulauan Banyak
Sibolga
Pulau Simeulue
Strait of Malacca
Selat Serasan
Kuching
Sibu
Batang Rajang
Sungai Kayan
Sarawak
Sri Aman
Banjaran Tamabo
Balabac
Gunung Kinabalu 4101m
Kota Kinabalu
BANDAR SERI BEGAWAN
BRUNEI
Miri
Sabah
Kepulauan Natuna
Pulau Nias
Panyabungan
Pekanbaru
SINGAPORE
Singkawang
Pontianak
Sungai Kapuas
Sidas
Pegunungan Muller
Sungai Mahakam
Borneo
Equator
Solok
Rengat
Kepulauan Lingga
Kualatungkal
Selat Karimata
Balikpapan
Padang
Pulau Siberut
Batang Hari
Jambi
Pangkalpinang
Bangka
Kalimantan
INDONESIA (INDO)
Kepulauan Mentawai
Sungaipenuh
Sumatra (Sumatera)
Palembang
Lahat
Sampit
Kandangan
Sungai Barito
Amuntai
Banjarmasin
Pulau Laut
Bengkulu
Pulau Belitung
Kotabumi
Java Sea
Bandarlampung
Cirebon
JAKARTA
Serang
Tegal
Pekalongan
Semarang
Pulau Madura
Selat Sunda
Bogor
Sukabumi
Kudus
Surabaya
Bandung
Java (Jawa)
Probolinggo
Jember
Tasikmalaya
Malang
Bali
Mataram
Cilacap
Kediri
Denpasar
Magelang
Madiun
Pulau Lombok
Yogyakarta
Surakarta
INDIAN OCEAN
Peshunun Barisan

SKYSCRAPERS

in Singapore's financial district

KITE-FLYING

After the harvest, the people of Malaysia celebrate with the Wau-flying (kite-flying) Festival. Here, skilled people demonstrate the traditional Malaysian sport.

Babuyan Island

Babuyan Channel

Laoag · Tuguegarao
· Ilagan
Baguio ·
Dagupan ·
Angeles · Cabanatuan
Mt. Pinatubo 1485m △
MANILA
PHILIPPINES
Lucena ·
Batangas · · Naga
· Legaspi
Mindoro Strait · Mindoro
Sibuyan Sea · Calbayog
Roxas City · *Samar*
Panay Island · Cadiz · Tacloban
Iloilo · *Leyte*
Bacolod City · **Cebu**
Palawan Passage
Puerto Princesa · *Negros* · Butuan
Bohol Sea · Cagayan de Oro
Sulu Sea · Iligan · · Bislig
Mindanao
Zamboanga · Digos · **Davao**
Basilan · *Moro Gulf* · Lebak
Sandakan · *Davao Gulf*
General Santos
Sulu Archipelago
Tawau ·

Did you know?

▶ Indonesia is the world's biggest island chain. It has more than 17,000 islands and covers three time zones.

▶ In Malay, orangutan means "man of the jungle".

STORMS AND VOLCANOES

The islands of the Philippines are on a fault line and form part of the "Pacific Ring of Fire" – an area prone to volcanic activity and earthquakes. When Mount Pinatubo, on the island of Luzon, erupted in 1991, it destroyed more than 40,000 homes.

THE PHILIPPINES

The people of the Philippines are called Filipinos, and are mostly of Malay descent. It is estimated that about 40 per cent of the population live in poverty. As income is higher in the cities, many people move there in the hope of escaping poverty. However, lack of adequate housing means that many poorer families have to live in crowded slums.

THESE CHILDREN live and work in an area of Manila known as "Smokey Mountain".

MOUNT PINATUBO ERUPTING IN 1991

Machine replants rice seedlings.

Celebes Sea

Samarinda ·
Palu ·
Makassar Strait
Tolitoli · · Manado · Bitung
Gorontalo · · Ternate
Gulf of Tomini *Molucca Sea*
Poso ·
Celebes (Sulawesi)
Wotu · *Danau Towuti*
Parepare · *Teluk Bone*
Singkang · Kendari
Watampone · Kolaka
Ujungpandang · *Pulau Buton*
Bulukumba ·

I N D O N E S I A

Kepulauan Talaud
Kepulauan Sangir
Pulau Morotai
Pulau Halmahera
Pulau Waigeo   Equator
Halmahera Sea   Sorong
Selat Dampier   Jazirah Doberai
Ceram Sea   Wahai
Waflia · Tifu · *Pulau Seram*
Pulau Buru   **Ambon**
Kepulauan Sula
Banda Sea
Kepulauan Kai
Kepulauan Aru
Kepulauan Tanimbar
Pulau Yamdena

Molucca Sea (Maluku)

Flores Sea
Lesser Sunda Islands (Nusa Tenggara)
Kepulauan Alor
Flores ·
Selat Sumba
Savu Sea
Endeh ·
Pulau Sumba
Kupang ·
Pulau Wetar   · Tutuala
DILI
EAST TIMOR
Timor
Nikiniki ·
Timor Sea

Pulau Biak
Manokwari · *Pulau Yapen*
Teluk Cenderawasih   Maniwori
Teluk Berau   *Pulau Misool*   Obome ·
Pegunungan Maoke
Amamapare ·   Puncak Jaya △ 5030m
Papua (Irian Jaya)   *Sungai Mamberamo*
New Guinea   Jayapura ·
Sungai Digul
Alotip ·
Arafura Sea

PAPUA NEW GUINEA

RICE RESEARCH

Rice is the primary food source for half the world's population. Near Manila, in the Philippines, scientists are now experimenting with ways of creating rice plants that produce greater yields. New varieties are also being developed to grow faster, allowing farmers to harvest and replant several times during one growing season.

OIL RICHES

Oil was first discovered in Brunei in 1929. Since then, oil has also been drilled offshore (right). Brunei's most important natural resource has made the country very wealthy. Its people enjoy free healthcare and education, and pay no taxes.

0 km   200   400
0 miles   200   400

Indian Ocean

THE THIRD LARGEST ocean in the world, the Indian Ocean is bounded by Africa, Asia, Australasia, and Antarctica. The ocean contains some 5,000 islands. Madagascar and Sri Lanka are large, but most of the islands are small and ringed by coral reefs. The people of the Maldives have very mixed origins, incorporating Indian, Sinhalese, Arab, and African heritage, while two-thirds of those living on Mauritius are Indian immigrants and their descendants. Altogether, about one-fifth of the world's population live on this ocean's warm shores. Those along the northern coasts are often threatened by monsoon rain and tropical storms, which can cause severe flooding.

THE MALDIVES

The Maldives is a low-lying archipelago of 1,300 small, coral islands, of which 202 are inhabited. The main industries are fishing – still carried out by traditional pole and line methods (above) to conserve stocks – and tourism. Holiday resorts are on separate islands to those inhabited by the locals, so as not to disturb the Maldive peoples' traditional Muslim lifestyles.

Coral islands

Coral is a living organism formed in warm water by tiny sea creatures known as polyps. These creatures build limestone skeletons around themselves, which accumulate over thousands of years. As sea levels change, this coral can be exposed as low-lying islands or submerged as reefs.

THE SEYCHELLES

The Seychelles consists of 115 islands – some of which are coral islands while others are mountainous and made of granite. Most Seychellois people are Creoles – people of mixed African, Asian, and European ancestry. There are also small Chinese and Indian communities.

MARKET in the Seychelles capital, Mahé

ENVIRONMENT

Beautiful shells are for sale on this beach in South Africa. If the trader only collects empty shells, no harm is done, but in many parts of the world, dealers hunt live shellfish, sea turtles, and rare species of starfish and sea urchins. Nations such as the Maldives take great care to protect their environment.

LIMITED TOURISM

The tropical climate, sandy beaches, beautiful coral reefs, and abundant marine life make both the Seychelles and the Maldives ideal tourist destinations. These same features also make them extremely attractive to scuba divers. However, the fragile environment of both island nations means that they have deliberately tried to make them exclusive, attracting only limited numbers of wealthy visitors, instead of pursuing mass tourism.

Black Sea

Mediterranean Sea

Arabian Peninsula

Red Sea

Gulf of Aden

Ethiopian Highlands

Horn of Africa

Andrew Tablemount △

AFRICA

Somali Basin

COMOROS

MAYOTTE (to France)

Mozambique Channel

MADAGASCAR

Davie Ridge

Natal Basin

Mozambique Plateau

Africana Seamount △

Agulhas Plateau

Agulhas Plateau Basin

Agulhas Basin

Prince Edward Islands (to South Africa)

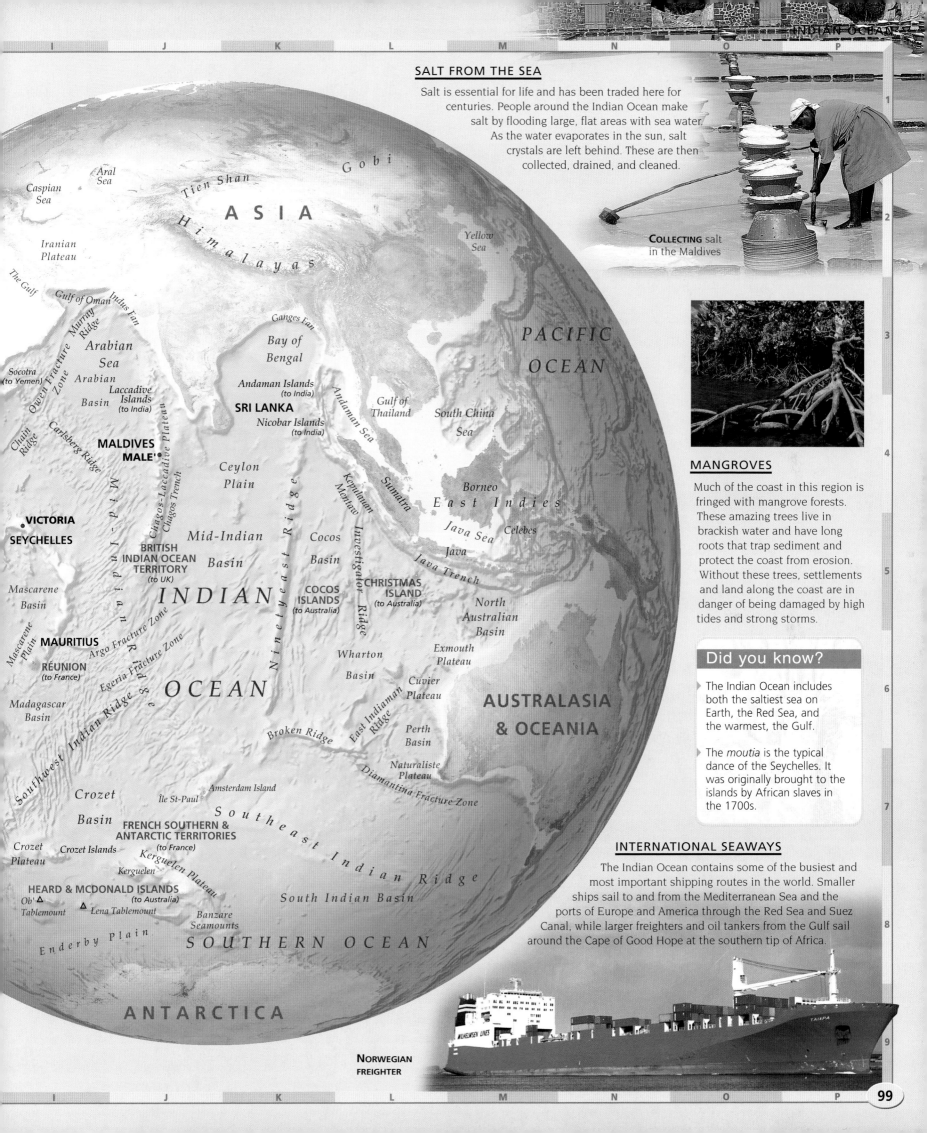

SALT FROM THE SEA

Salt is essential for life and has been traded here for centuries. People around the Indian Ocean make salt by flooding large, flat areas with sea water. As the water evaporates in the sun, salt crystals are left behind. These are then collected, drained, and cleaned.

COLLECTING salt in the Maldives

MANGROVES

Much of the coast in this region is fringed with mangrove forests. These amazing trees live in brackish water and have long roots that trap sediment and protect the coast from erosion. Without these trees, settlements and land along the coast are in danger of being damaged by high tides and strong storms.

Did you know?

▸ The Indian Ocean includes both the saltiest sea on Earth, the Red Sea, and the warmest, the Gulf.

▸ The *moutia* is the typical dance of the Seychelles. It was originally brought to the islands by African slaves in the 1700s.

INTERNATIONAL SEAWAYS

The Indian Ocean contains some of the busiest and most important shipping routes in the world. Smaller ships sail to and from the Mediterranean Sea and the ports of Europe and America through the Red Sea and Suez Canal, while larger freighters and oil tankers from the Gulf sail around the Cape of Good Hope at the southern tip of Africa.

NORWEGIAN FREIGHTER

Map labels

Caspian Sea
Aral Sea
Tien Shan
Gobi
ASIA
Himalayas
Yellow Sea
Iranian Plateau
The Gulf
Gulf of Oman
Murray Ridge
Indus Fan
Ganges Fan
Bay of Bengal
PACIFIC OCEAN
Owen Fracture Zone
Arabian Sea
Arabian Basin
Socotra (to Yemen)
Laccadive Islands (to India)
Andaman Islands (to India)
SRI LANKA
Gulf of Thailand
South China Sea
Chain Ridge
Carlsberg Ridge
MALDIVES
MALE'
Chagos-Laccadive Plateau
Chagos Trench
Ceylon Plain
Nicobar Islands (to India)
Andaman Sea
Kepulauan Mentao
Sumatra
Borneo
East Indies
Java Sea
Celebes
VICTORIA
SEYCHELLES
Mid-Indian Ridge
BRITISH INDIAN OCEAN TERRITORY (to UK)
Mid-Indian Basin
Cocos Basin
Investigator Ridge
Ninetyeast Ridge
Java
Java Trench
Mascarene Basin
INDIAN
COCOS ISLANDS (to Australia)
CHRISTMAS ISLAND (to Australia)
North Australian Basin
Argo Fracture Zone
MAURITIUS
OCEAN
Wharton Basin
Exmouth Plateau
AUSTRALASIA & OCEANIA
Mascarene Plain
RÉUNION (to France)
Egeria Fracture Zone
Cuvier Plateau
Madagascar Basin
Southwest Indian Ridge
East Indiaman Ridge
Perth Basin
Broken Ridge
Naturaliste Plateau
Crozet
Amsterdam Island
Île St-Paul
Southeast Indian Ridge
Diamantina Fracture Zone
Basin
FRENCH SOUTHERN & ANTARCTIC TERRITORIES (to France)
Crozet Plateau
Crozet Islands
Kerguelen Plateau
Kerguelen
South Indian Basin
HEARD & MCDONALD ISLANDS (to Australia)
Ob' △ Tablemount
△ Lena Tablemount
Banzare Seamounts
Enderby Plain
SOUTHERN OCEAN
ANTARCTICA

AUSTRALASIA & OCEANIA

THE CONTINENT OF AUSTRALIA – the smallest of the

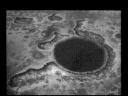

world's seven continents – lies between the Indian

and Pacific oceans. It forms part of a much larger region known

as Oceania that includes numerous small islands

and stretches across the southern half of the Pacific,

the world's deepest and biggest ocean. Australia is by far the biggest

island in Oceania. Nine out of every ten Australians live next

to the coast, as the interior is hot, inhospitable

desert. New Zealand is mountainous and temperate

in climate, while Papua New Guinea is largely

rainforest. The rest of Oceania consists of thousands

of small coral atolls and island outcrops of solid rock. In all, the region

comprises 14 countries with a population of almost 31 million people.

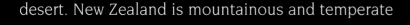

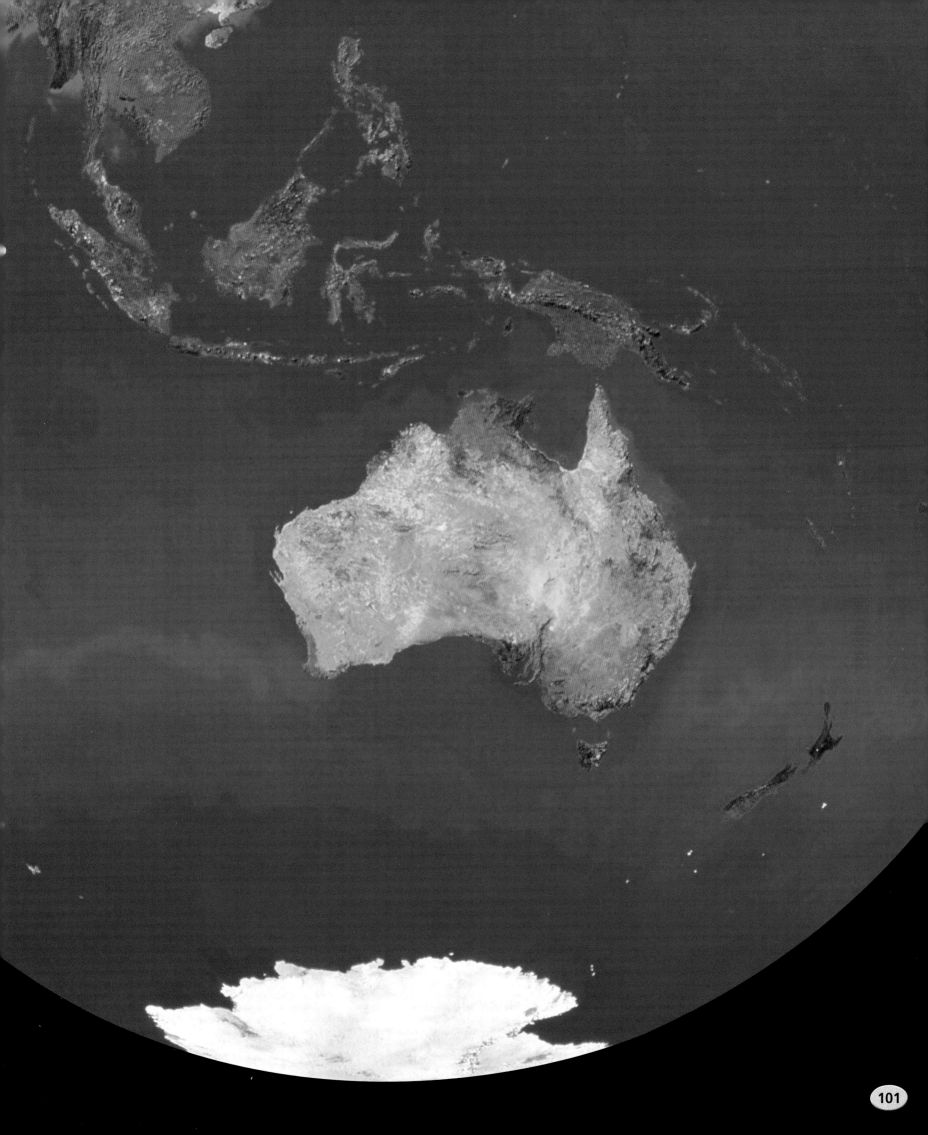

SW Pacific

THE ISLANDS OF THE southwest Pacific are home to people of many different cultures and languages. The islands are divided into three general groups based on their location and the similarities between their peoples. The Polynesian islands to the east include Tonga, Samoa, the Cook Islands, and Tahiti. Melanesia includes Fiji, the Solomon Islands, and Vanuatu. The smallest group, Micronesia, includes the Marshall, Kiribati, and Caroline Islands. The first Europeans came to the southwest Pacific in the 1600s, several thousand years after Melanesians, Micronesians, and Polynesians first settled there.

ISLAND HOLIDAYS

White sandy beaches and warm water makes this region ideal for tourists.

MEN from Papua New Guinea wearing traditional make-up

LAND OF MANY LANGUAGES

Historically, the mountainous landscape of Papua New Guinea made contact between the villages difficult. As a result of many years of isolation, some villages developed their own individual languages. Nationwide, about 750 different languages evolved.

Beads, shells, and feathers form part of the decoration.

A MIX OF RELIGIONS

Christianity is the dominant religion on most southwest Pacific islands, however Islam and Hinduism are also practised. Many people also retain beliefs from traditional religions that existed before the islands were colonized by people from Europe and Asia.

Did you know?

On some Melanesian Islands, people have overcome the problems caused by having so many languages by learning an additional language – Pidgin English. This language is a mixture of English and some common words from island languages.

VANUATU tribespeople dance at a religious ceremony.

NORTHERN MARIANA ISLANDS (to US)

Tinian
Saipan
Rota

GUAM ✈ HAGÅTÑA (to US)

Yap

Babeldaob
OREOR ✈

PALAU

MICRONESIA

Chuuk Islands

PALIKIR ✈
Pohnpei

Caroline Islands

Kosrae

Enewetak Atoll
Bikini Atoll
Rongelap Atoll

MARSHALL

Ujelang Atoll
Kwajalein Atoll
Namu Atoll

Ailinglaplap Atoll

Jaluit Atoll

Ebon Atoll

Ratak Chain
Ralik Chain

NAURU
Banaba

INDONESIA

Admiralty Islands
St.Matthias Group

Bismarck Archipelago
Bismarck Sea
New Ireland

PAPUA NEW GUINEA

Madang
Central Range
△ Mount Wilhelm 4509m
Lae
New Guinea
Owen Stanley Range

Gulf of Papua

PORT MORESBY ✈

Solomon Sea

New Britain

Bougainville Island

Choiseul

Santa Isabel

New Georgia Islands
Malaita

HONIARA ✈

SOLOMON ISLANDS

Guadalcanal
San Cristobal
Rennell

Santa Cruz Islands

D'Entrecasteaux Islands

Louisiade Archipelago

Coral Sea

CORAL SEA ISLANDS (to Australia)

VANUATU

Espiritu Santo

PORT-VILA ✈

NEW CALEDONIA (to France)

Banks Islands

Maéwo
Pentecost
Ambrym
Epi

Malekula

Erromango
Tanna
Aneityum

Ouvéa
Lifou
Maré

New Caledonia

Iles Loyauté

NOUMÉA

Tropic of Capricorn

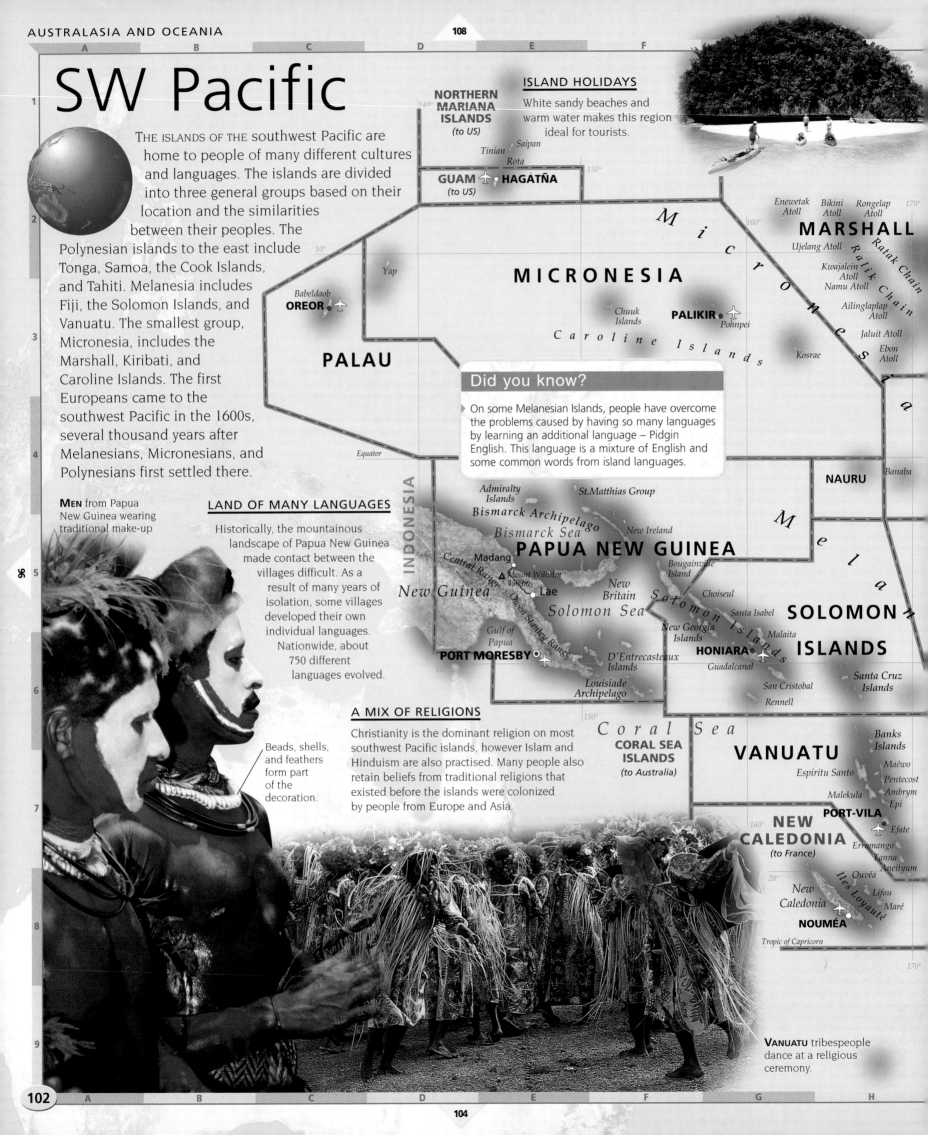

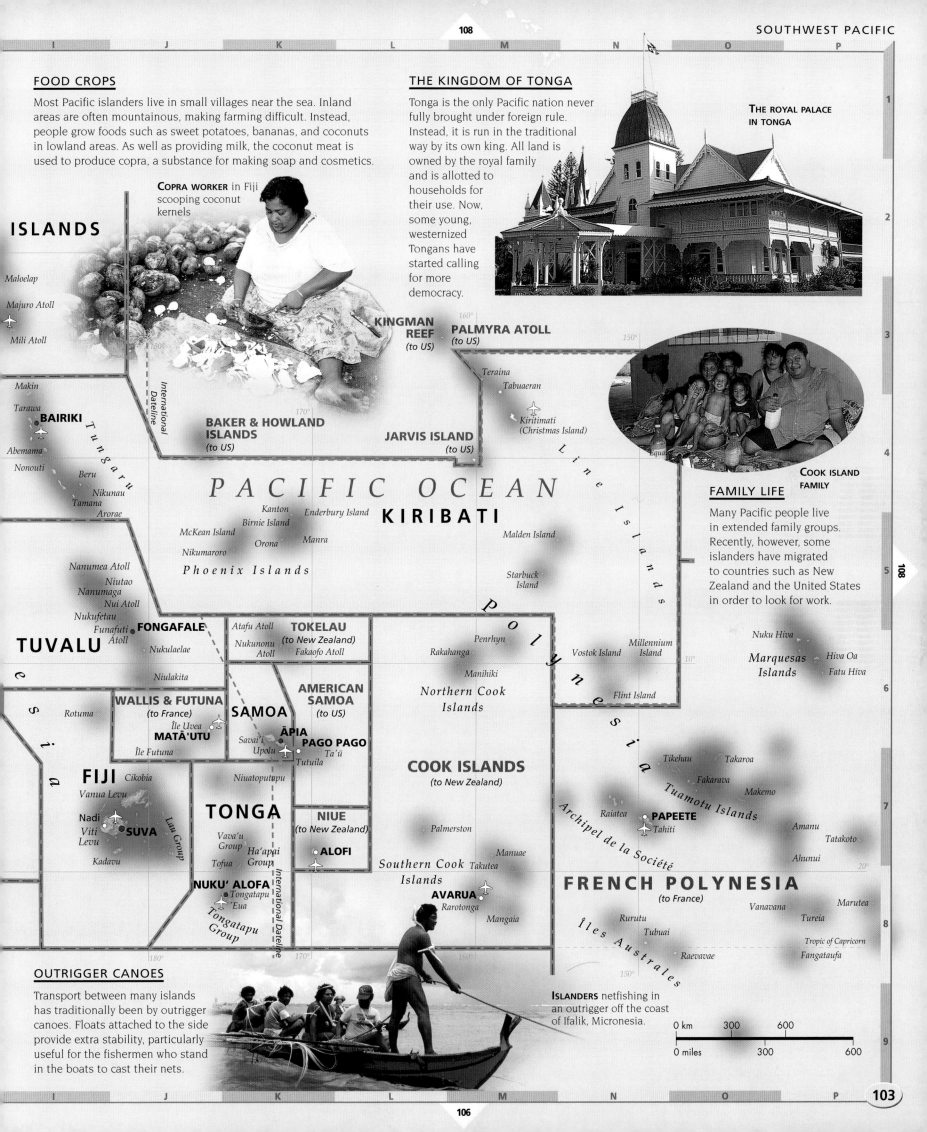

FOOD CROPS

Most Pacific islanders live in small villages near the sea. Inland areas are often mountainous, making farming difficult. Instead, people grow foods such as sweet potatoes, bananas, and coconuts in lowland areas. As well as providing milk, the coconut meat is used to produce copra, a substance for making soap and cosmetics.

COPRA WORKER in Fiji scooping coconut kernels

ISLANDS

THE KINGDOM OF TONGA

Tonga is the only Pacific nation never fully brought under foreign rule. Instead, it is run in the traditional way by its own king. All land is owned by the royal family and is allotted to households for their use. Now, some young, westernized Tongans have started calling for more democracy.

THE ROYAL PALACE IN TONGA

FAMILY LIFE

Many Pacific people live in extended family groups. Recently, however, some islanders have migrated to countries such as New Zealand and the United States in order to look for work.

COOK ISLAND FAMILY

PACIFIC OCEAN

KIRIBATI

OUTRIGGER CANOES

Transport between many islands has traditionally been by outrigger canoes. Floats attached to the side provide extra stability, particularly useful for the fishermen who stand in the boats to cast their nets.

ISLANDERS netfishing in an outrigger off the coast of Ifalik, Micronesia.

Australia

A HUGE, GENERALLY FLAT COUNTRY, Australia has relatively few inhabitants. This is mainly because most of the land is hot, semi-arid desert – known as the outback – unsuitable for towns or farms. In places where there is some vegetation, or the land has been irrigated, sheep and cattle are grazed. Wheat is grown in the fertile south. The first people to live here were the Aboriginals, who arrived from Asia at least 50,000 years ago. Today, most Australians are descendants of European immigrants, with a more recent addition of Asians.

FLYING DOCTOR

For anyone living in the remote Australian outback, the nearest doctor can be many hours away. When emergency help is needed, the Royal Flying Doctor Services can get to the scene to treat a patient or fly them to hospital.

AUSTRALIAN ABORIGINALS

The original inhabitants of Australia had an intimate understanding of their environment. This connection to the land, and its plants and animals, affects every aspect of their culture. When Europeans started arriving in the late 18th century, only the Aboriginals in remote areas escaped contact with the diseases they brought. Today, Aboriginals rarely live off the land, but work in factories or farms.

MINING

Australia has one of the world's most important mining industries, with resources including gold (left), coal, natural gas, iron ore, copper, and opals. However, damage to the environment, and Aboriginal claims over land used for mining, still need to be faced.

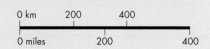

0 km	200	400
0 miles	200	400

AUSTRALIAN FOOTBALL

A popular sport here is Australian Rules Football. One of the rules is that players can kick or punch the ball but they must not throw it. Many Australians either play the game themselves or support their favourite team. As the name implies, the game originated in Australia, but it now has leagues in other countries, such as Great Britain and the USA.

OUTDOOR SPORTS

A warm climate, with easy access to beaches and wilderness areas, has made outdoor activities an important part of modern Australian life. Water sports, such as swimming, sailing, and surfing, are especially popular. Because of the danger of exposure to strong sunlight, people are told to cover up and always use sunscreen.

Melville Island
Bathurst Island
Van Diemen Gulf
Darwin
Pine Creek
Cape Londonderry
Joseph Bonaparte Gulf
Bonaparte Bigge Island Archipelago
Heywood Islands
Wyndham
Kununurra
Top Springs Roadhouse
Kimberley Plateau
King Sound
Broome
Fitzroy Crossing
Halls Creek
Fitzroy River
Tanami Desert
INDIAN OCEAN
Eighty Mile Beach
Great Sandy Desert
N O
Barrow Island
Dampier
Port Hedland
Marble Bar
Percival Lakes
T E R
Exmouth Gulf
Onslow
Fortescue River
Exmouth
Hamersley Range
Newman
Lake Mackay
Macdo
Tropic of Capricorn
Ashburton River
Barlee Range
Lake Disappointment
W E S T E R N
Lake Amadeus
Uluru (Ayers Rock) △ 867m
Bernier Island
Dorre Island
Shark Bay
Gascoyne River
Carnarvon
Denham
Murchison River
Gibson Desert
A U S T
Dirk Hartog Island
Robinson Ranges
Lake Carnegie
Lake Wells
Musgrave Ranges
Meekatharra
A U S T R A L I A
Kalbarri
Mount Magnet
Great Victoria Desert
Lake Carey
Geraldton
Lake Barlee
Lake Moore
Lake Rebecca
Moora
Kalgoorlie
Zanthus
Reid
Southern Cross
Coolgardie
Nullarbor Plain
Perth
Merredin
Lake Cowan
Eucla
Fremantle
Northam
Brookton
Norseman
Balladonia
Mandurah
Narrogin
Bunbury
Wagin
Collie
Katanning
Esperance
Busselton
Manjimup
Augusta
Great Australian Bight
Albany
Gingin

Arafura Sea

Croker Island
South Goulburn Island
Wessel Islands

Torres Strait
Badu Island Moa Island
Prince of Wales Island Cape York
Endeavour Strait

Gulf of Carpentaria

Arnhem Land

Katherine

Groote Eylandt

Sir Edward Pellew Group

Cape York Peninsula

Princess Charlotte Bay

Daly Waters

Wellesley Islands
Mornington Island

Mitchell River

Burketown

Normanton

Cooktown

Port Douglas

Cairns

Atherton
Innisfail
Tully

Hinchinbrook Island

Tennant Creek

Barkly Tableland

Gilbert River

Gregory Range

Flinders River

Selwyn Range

RTHERN

RITORY

ell Ranges

Alice Springs

RALIA

Mount Isa

Cloncurry

Hughenden

Townsville

Bowen

Charters Towers

Whitsunday Group

Bloomsbury

Mackay

Great Dividing Range

Great Barrier Reef

Coral Sea

QUEENSLAND

Winton

Longreach Barcaldine

Clermont
Emerald

Maryborough
Yeppon

Rockhampton *Tropic of Capricorn*

Curtis Island
Gladstone

Springsure

Blackall

Biloela

Fraser Island

Simpson

Windorah

Bundaberg

S O U T H

Desert

Lake Eyre North

Augathella

Charleville

Mitchell

Roma

Gayndah
Murgon
Miles

Maryborough
Gympie

Dalby

Caloundra

Grey Range

Cunnamulla

St. George

Moonie

Toowoomba

Brisbane

A U S T R A L I A

Coober Pedy

Lake Eyre South

Lake Blanche

Bollon

Goondiwindi

Warwick
Ipswich

Surfers Paradise
Murwillumbah

Stanthorpe

Moree

Lismore

Tarcoola

Marree

Lake Callabonna

Warrego River

Barwon River

Grafton

Walgett

Narrabri
Armidale

Coffs Harbour

Lake Torrens

Lake Frome

Bourke

N E W   S O U T H

Cobar

Nyngan

Tamworth

Gunnedah

Port Macquarie

Penong

Lake Everard

Flinders Ranges

Wilcannia

Barrier Range

Broken Hill

Darling River

Ivanhoe

Lachlan River Parkes

Dubbo

Orange

Taree

Muswellbrook

Newcastle

Ceduna

Lake Gairdner

Port Augusta

Whyalla

Peterborough

Crystal Brook

Murray River

Mildura

Hay

Bathurst

Parramatta
Sydney

Gosford

Elliston

Eyre Peninsula

Port Pirie

W A L E S

Cootamundra

Wollongong

Spencer Gulf

Elizabeth
Gawler

Adelaide

Tailem Bend

Ouyen

Murrumbidgee River

Wagga Wagga

Deniliquin

Goulburn

CANBERRA
AUSTRALIAN CAPITAL TERRITORY

Port Lincoln

Investigator Strait

Keith

Shepparton

Albury *Mount Kosciusko 2228m*

Murray River

Wodonga
Wangaratta

Cooma

Bega

Tasman Sea

Kangaroo Island

Naracoorte

Mount Gambier

Bendigo

Sunbury

VICTORIA

Horsham

Ballarat

Melbourne

Moe

Australian Alps

Portland
Warrnambool

Geelong

Sale
Traralgon

South East Point

King Island

Bass Strait

Flinders Island

Hunter Island
Marrawah

Banks Strait
Cape Barren Island

Burnie

Devonport Launceston

TASMANIA

Hobart

Maria Island

UNIQUE WILDLIFE

Animal parks and refuges allow "townies" and tourists to get close to Australia's unique wildlife. They can see marsupials, such as koalas and wallabies (left), as well as crocodiles, snakes, and the world's only egg-laying mammals – the platypus and the echidna.

Did you know?

▶ Voting in government elections in Australia is compulsory. Citizens who fail to vote can be fined.

▶ July and August are the coldest months, when some Australians like to go skiing.

▶ The deadly blue-ringed octopus lives in the waters off the Australian coast.

TOURIST ATTRACTIONS

Tourism is important to Australia's economy, and there is plenty to attract visitors. Popular destinations include the tropical waters around the Great Barrier Reef (above), the modern cities of Sydney and Melbourne, and the impressive sight of Uluru (Ayers Rock), a mountainous rock sacred to the Aboriginals.

VINEYARDS

Australia boasts an impressive range of high-quality wine-growing regions, specializing in different grapes. Wines are exported to more than 90 countries.

LIFE IN THE CITIES

Most Australians live in the coastal towns and cities of southeastern Australia where the climate is cooler. Although Canberra is the capital, Sydney is the largest and oldest city, and is beautifully situated around Sydney Harbour. One of the world's most famous landmarks is the Sydney Opera House (below) which has five separate halls for concerts, operas, and plays. The design echoes the sails of a ship.

New Zealand

MADE UP OF TWO MAIN ISLANDS and several smaller islands, New Zealand is one of the most isolated countries in the world. Located in the southern Pacific, the country has a mild climate, with warm summers and cool, wet winters. Both islands have mountains, short, swift-flowing rivers, forests, and fertile farmland. Until the Europeans arrived, most of the landscape was covered in dense forest, known as native bush. Today, although forests remain, much has been cleared for farming. Most New Zealanders live on North Island, which is warmer and less mountainous. Although New Zealanders are of mainly British descent, the Maoris – a people of Polynesian origin – were the first to arrive about 1,000 years ago. Today, non-Maori Polynesians and Asians are adding to the ethnic mix. The country has a liberal, clean, green image and a high standard of living.

AUCKLAND

With its safe harbour and nearby scenic islands, Auckland is known as the City of Sails. It boasts more pleasure boats per person than anywhere else in the world. The water that separates the bigger islands is home to dolphins, families of blue penguins, and the occasional whale.

MAORI CULTURE

Maoris make up almost 16 per cent of the population, with most living on North Island. Before the coming of the *Pakeha* (white man) Maori history was passed on orally to succeeding generations. This included many legends and *waiata* (song). Their carvings in wood (left) and stone (right) were another way they recorded and remembered events. In recent years, interest in Maori culture has increased, and school children are now taught the Maori language.

GREENSTONE (jade) carving is an example of Maori art.

Did you know?

- The Maori name for New Zealand is Aotearoa, meaning "land of the long white cloud".
- In 1893, New Zealand was the first country to grant women the vote.
- There is only one poisonous animal here, the katipo spider.

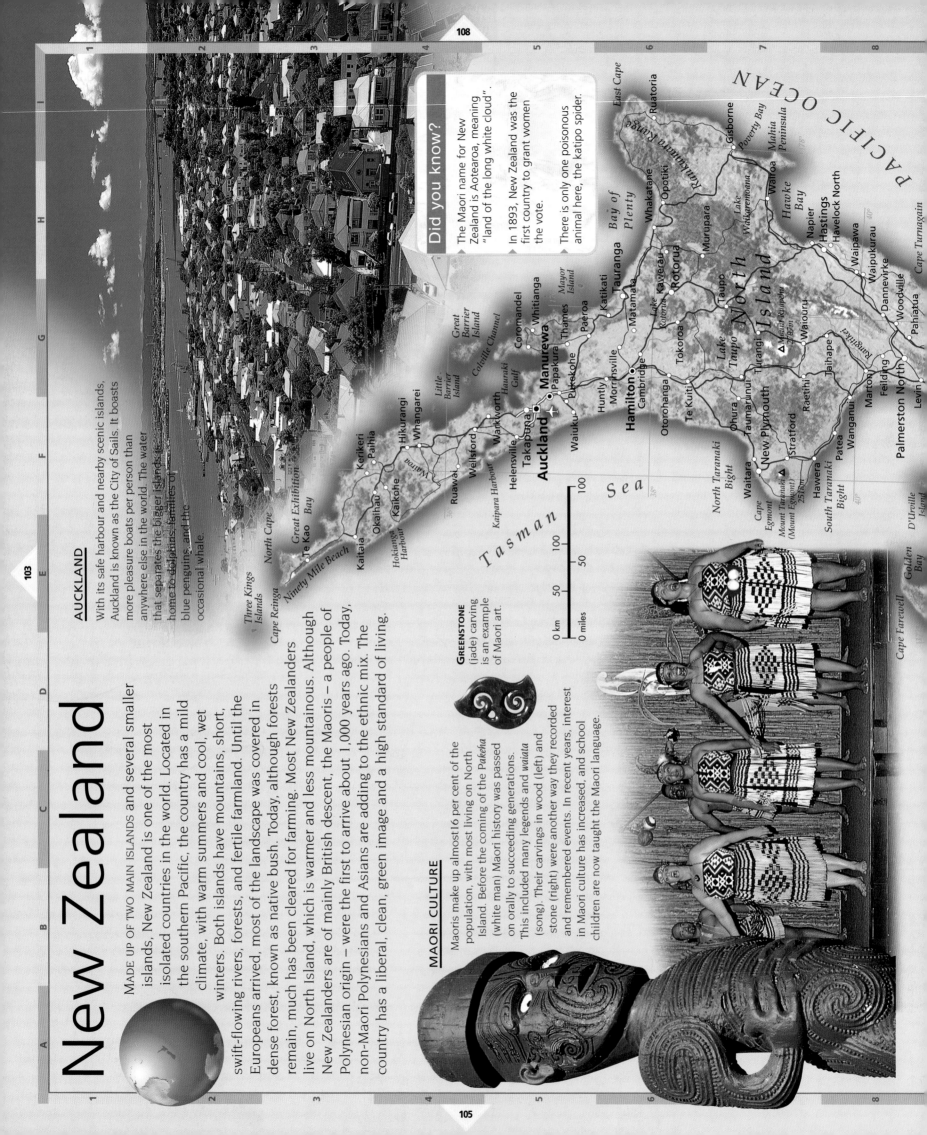

Map labels:

PACIFIC OCEAN

Tasman Sea

North Island

Bay of Plenty

Three Kings Islands
Cape Reinga
North Cape
Ninety Mile Beach
Te Kao
Kaitaia
Okaihau
Kaikohe
Kerikeri
Paihia
Hokianga Harbour
Hikurangi
Whangarei
Wairoa
Kaipara Harbour
Ruawai
Wellsford
Warkworth
Helensville
Takapuna
Auckland
Waiuku
Waiku
Manurewa
Papakura
Pukekohe
Huntly
Morrinsville
Hamilton
Cambridge
Te Kuiti
Otorohanga
Ohura
Taumarunui
Great Barrier Island
Little Barrier Island
Hauraki Gulf
Coromandel
Colville Channel
Whitianga
Mayor Island
Thames
Paeroa
Katikati
Matamata
Tauranga
Whakatane
Opotiki
Lake Rotorua
Kawerau
Rotorua
Murupara
Tokoroa
Lake Taupo
Taupo
Turangi
Raurimu
Mount Ruapehu 2797m
Taihape
Raetihi
Ruahine Range
Rangitikei
North Taranaki Bight
Waitara
New Plymouth
Stratford
Hawera
Cape Egmont
Mount Taranaki (Mount Egmont) 2518m
South Taranaki Bight
Patea
Wanganui
Marton
Feilding
Levin
Palmerston North
Dannevirke
Woodville
Pahiatua
Waipukurau
Waipawa
Havelock North
Hastings
Napier
Hawke Bay
Wairoa
Lake Waikaremoana
Ruatoria
Gisborne
Poverty Bay
Mahia Peninsula
East Cape
Raukumara Range
Cape Turnagain
D'Urville Island
Golden Bay
Cape Farewell

0 km 50 100
0 miles 50 100

NEW ZEALAND

AN AGRICULTURAL NATION

Agriculture is of prime importance, and accounts for more than half of national export earnings. Orchards produce a vast range of fruit from apples (above) to kiwi fruit (below). Cereal and other crops, such as sunflowers, add colour and variety to the landscape. Traditional sheep and cattle farming has expanded to include deer, goats, and even ostriches.

VOLCANIC ACTIVITY

A fault line runs through New Zealand where two major tectonic plates meet. It has caused devastating earthquakes, but has also helped create breathtaking scenery. This includes South Island's Southern Alps, and many smaller volcanic mountains, hot springs, and geysers in North Island.

LADY KNOX geyser, North Island

FLIGHTLESS KIWI BIRD

UNIQUE WILDLIFE

New Zealand has many unique and endangered animal species, especially birds. Because there were no mammal predators before humans introduced them, many species have few means of defence, and some birds, such as the kiwi (above) cannot fly. Conservation schemes are now in place to protect endangered species.

GREEN ENERGY

Most of the country's electricity comes from hydro-electric power. It is generated by river water gushing through turbines inside dams at power stations (left). New Zealand also has geothermal energy using heat from inside the Earth.

FILM INDUSTRY

New Zealand has a well-established film industry. Today, thanks to the acclaimed Tolkien trilogy, *Lord of the Rings* (above), the country has become increasingly popular with international studios for location work. The country offers an unusually wide range of scenery as well as technical experts.

ADVENTURE SPORTS PARADISE

New Zealand offers a huge range of adventure sports and outdoor activities, from whitewater rafting (below) to bungy jumping. The latter originated in Queenstown in South Island. The town is billed as the country's top adventure tourism destination because its surrounding lakes, mountains, and rivers, and its mostly dry climate, are ideal for outdoor pursuits.

WELLINGTON

Masterton
Cape Palliser
Lower Hutt
Porirua
Paraparaumu
Otaki
Cook Strait
Cape Campbell
Cape Campbell
Blenheim
Seddon
Picton
Nelson
Wairau
Richmond
Richmond Range
Clarence
Kaikoura
Tasman Bay
Motueka
Mount Owen 1875m
Hammer Springs
Springs Junction
Waipara
Pegasus Bay
Rangiora
Christchurch
Lyttelton
Banks Peninsula
Kaiapoi
Oxford
Lake Ellesmere
Canterbury Bight
Darfield
Ashburton
Canterbury Plains
Hinds
Mayfield
Geraldine
Temuka
Timaru
Studholme
Waimate
Oamaru
Arthur's Pass 920m
Otira
Lake Brunner
Reefton
Seddonville
Karamea Bight
Westport
Cape Foulwind
Runanga
Greymouth
Hokitika
Ross
Whataroa
Fox Glacier
Abut Head
Haast
Mt Cook 3744m
Mount Cook
Lake Pukaki
Lake Hawea
Lake Wanaka
Wanaka
Lake Wakatipu
Queenstown
Cromwell
Alexandra
Clutha
L Taieri
Mosgiel
Milton
Balclutha
Dunedin
Otago Peninsula
Hampden
Waitaki
Fairlie
Gore
Mataura
Lumsden
Invercargill
Tokanui
Toetoes Bay
Ruapuke Island
Foveaux Strait
Stewart Island
Halfmoon Bay
Codfish Island
Te Anau
Lake Manapouri
Lake Te Anau
Milford Sound
George Sound
Caswell Sound
Resolution Island
West Cape
South West Cape
Muttonbird Islands
Livingstone Mts
Eyre Mts
Te Waewae Bay
Lake Hauroko
Winton
Riverton
Waiau
Mataura
Southern Alps
South Island
Fiordland
NEW ZEALAND

Pacific Ocean

THE LARGEST OCEAN ON EARTH, the Pacific covers one-third of the Earth's surface. The island nations of Japan, Indonesia, Australia, New Zealand, and many others are completely surrounded by this enormous ocean, which stretches from the Arctic in the north to the Antarctic in the south. The Pacific is also the world's deepest ocean – its greatest known depth is in the Mariana Trench, off Guam, which plunges steeply for 11,033 m (36,198 ft). Within the Pacific, there are many smaller seas that lie near land. These include the Tasman Sea, the South China Sea, and the Bering Sea. There are more than 30,000 islands in the Pacific. Most are too small or barren to be inhabited, but others are home to people of many different cultures and religions. The native island peoples fall into three main groups – Polynesians, Melanesians, and Micronesians. Although the word pacific means peaceful, strong currents, tropical storms, and tsunamis can all make this ocean far from peaceful.

HAWAII

This chain of eight volcanic islands and 124 islets forms the 50th state of the United States of America and was admitted to the union in 1959. The dramatic landscape and palm-fringed beaches make Hawaii a popular destination for tourists. Today, native Hawaiians are a minority in their own land.

HAWAIIAN conch shells were once blown to sound a warning.

MARINE iguana on the black volcanic rocks of the Galápagos Islands

Tsunami

Earthquakes beneath the sea may cause giant waves called tsunamis. These can travel great distances across the ocean, building into a huge wall of water as they approach the coast. They can leave immense damage in their wake.

GALÁPAGOS ISLANDS

When British naturalist Charles Darwin (1809–82) went to the Galápagos Islands, he found many unusual animals. He also noticed differences between animals of the same species living elsewhere. This led him to believe that, over time, animals adapt, or evolve, to suit their habitats.

SURFING

The Hawaiian sport of surfing ranks as the oldest sport in the USA. It was first practised by the nobility as a form of religious ceremony until the 1820s when missionaries, who thought it immoral, tried to ban it. Today, surfing is one of the most popular watersports and can be seen from Australia and New Zealand to Mexico.

Black smoker chimneys

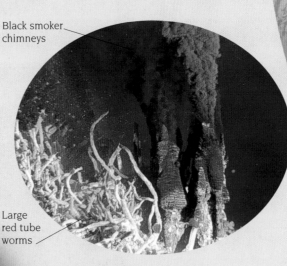

Large red tube worms

DEEP-SEA VENTS

Underwater exploration has revealed some amazing places deep in the Pacific. Large vents, formed by solidified minerals, act as chimneys for superhot steam and gas that stream up from the seabed. These are known as black smokers. Scientists have found a host of new creatures living in this hostile environment.

Map labels

ASIA

Sea of Japan
Yellow Sea
Japan
Japan Trench
East China Sea
Ryukyu Trench
Shikoku Basin
Emperor Seamounts
Taiwan
Philippine Sea
Philippine Basin
NORTHERN MARIANA ISLANDS (to US)
Mariana Trench
South China Basin
Philippines
GUAM (to US)
▽ Challenger Deep 11,034m
PALAU
Caroline Islands
MICRON
South China Sea
Celebes Sea
Borneo
Celebes
Mel
East Indies
Java Sea
Banda Sea
New Guinea
Java
Timor
Timor Sea
Arafura Sea
Torres Strait
Coral Sea
Great Barrier Reef

INDIAN OCEAN

AUSTRALASIA & OCEANIA

Great Australian Bight
South Australian Basin
Bass Strait
Tasmania

Did you know?

➤ The Pacific is larger than Earth's entire land surface.

➤ The Pacific is surrounded by a zone of violent volcanic and earthquake activity, known as the Pacific Ring of Fire.

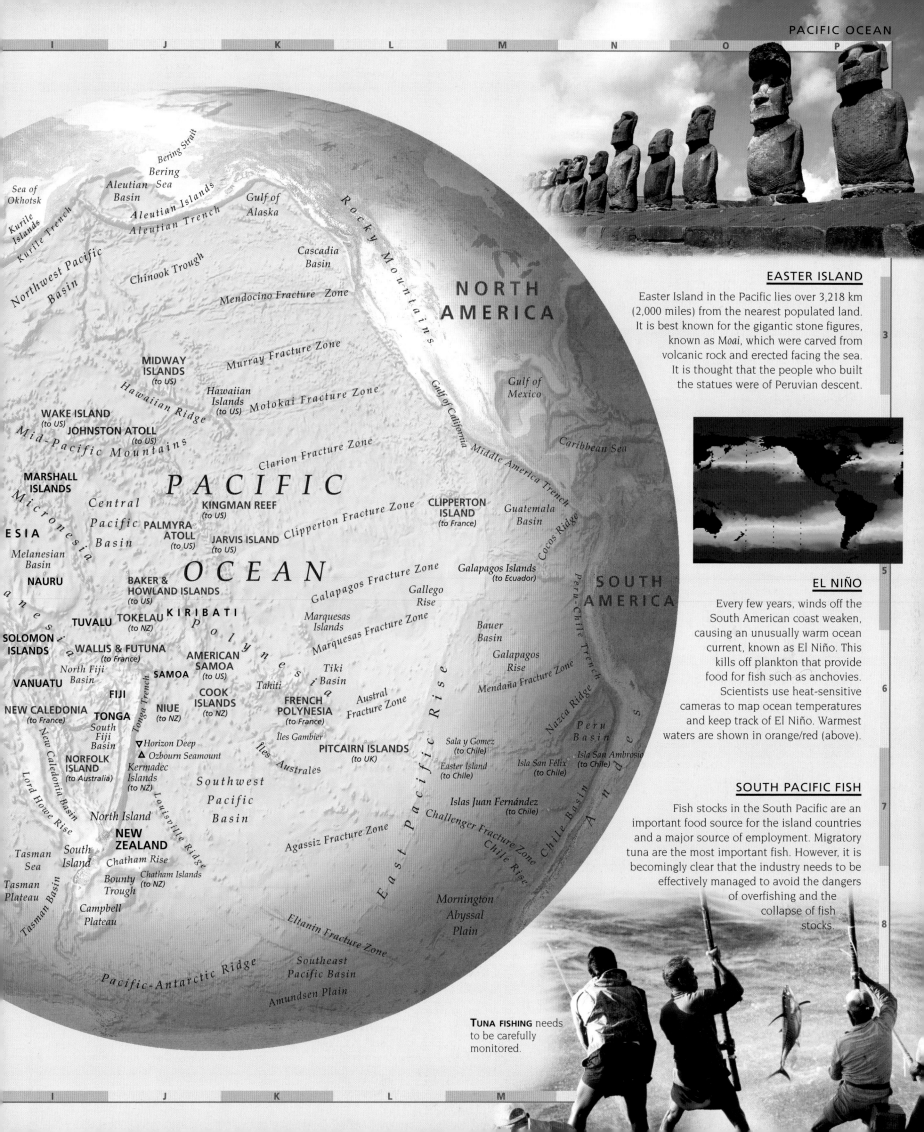

Sea of
Okhotsk

Kurile
Islands

Kurile Trench

Bering Strait

Bering
Sea

Aleutian
Basin

Aleutian Islands

Aleutian Trench

Gulf of
Alaska

Rocky Mountains

Northwest Pacific
Basin

Chinook Trough

Cascadia
Basin

Mendocino Fracture Zone

NORTH
AMERICA

MIDWAY
ISLANDS
(to US)

Murray Fracture Zone

Hawaiian Ridge

Hawaiian
Islands
(to US)

Molokai Fracture Zone

Gulf of
Mexico

WAKE ISLAND
(to US)

JOHNSTON ATOLL
(to US)

Mid-Pacific Mountains

Clarion Fracture Zone

Gulf of California

Middle America Trench

Caribbean Sea

MARSHALL
ISLANDS

PACIFIC

Central
Pacific
Basin

KINGMAN REEF
(to US)

Clipperton Fracture Zone

CLIPPERTON
ISLAND
(to France)

Guatemala
Basin

Micronesia

PALMYRA
ATOLL
(to US)

JARVIS ISLAND
(to US)

Cocos Ridge

ESIA

Melanesian
Basin

OCEAN

Galapagos Fracture Zone

Galapagos Islands
(to Ecuador)

SOUTH
AMERICA

NAURU

BAKER &
HOWLAND ISLANDS
(to US)

Gallego
Rise

nesia

TUVALU

TOKELAU
(to NZ)

KIRIBATI

Marquesas
Islands

Marquesas Fracture Zone

Bauer
Basin

Peru-Chile Trench

SOLOMON
ISLANDS

WALLIS & FUTUNA
(to France)

AMERICAN
SAMOA
(to US)

Polynesia

Galapagos
Rise

Nazca Ridge

North Fiji
Basin

SAMOA

Tiki
Basin

Mendaña Fracture Zone

VANUATU

FIJI

Tahiti

Peru
Basin

Tonga Trench

COOK
ISLANDS
(to NZ)

FRENCH
POLYNESIA
(to France)

Austral
Fracture Zone

NEW CALEDONIA
(to France)

TONGA

NIUE
(to NZ)

Andes

South
Fiji
Basin

Îles Gambier

Sala y Gomez
(to Chile)

New Caledonia Basin

▽ Horizon Deep
△ Ozbourn Seamount

Îles Australes

PITCAIRN ISLANDS
(to UK)

Easter Island
(to Chile)

Isla San Félix
(to Chile)

Isla San Ambrosio
(to Chile)

NORFOLK
ISLAND
(to Australia)

Kermadec
Islands
(to NZ)

Southwest
Pacific
Basin

East Pacific Rise

Chile Basin

Lord Howe Rise

Louisville Ridge

North Island

Islas Juan Fernández
(to Chile)

Chile Rise

NEW
ZEALAND

Chatham Rise

Agassiz Fracture Zone

Challenger Fracture Zone

Tasman
Sea

South
Island

Bounty
Trough

Chatham Islands
(to NZ)

Tasman
Plateau

Campbell
Plateau

Mornington
Abyssal
Plain

Tasman Basin

Eltanin Fracture Zone

Pacific-Antarctic Ridge

Southeast
Pacific Basin

Amundsen Plain

TUNA FISHING needs
to be carefully
monitored.

EASTER ISLAND

Easter Island in the Pacific lies over 3,218 km
(2,000 miles) from the nearest populated land.
It is best known for the gigantic stone figures,
known as *Moai*, which were carved from
volcanic rock and erected facing the sea.
It is thought that the people who built
the statues were of Peruvian descent.

EL NIÑO

Every few years, winds off the
South American coast weaken,
causing an unusually warm ocean
current, known as El Niño. This
kills off plankton that provide
food for fish such as anchovies.
Scientists use heat-sensitive
cameras to map ocean temperatures
and keep track of El Niño. Warmest
waters are shown in orange/red (above).

SOUTH PACIFIC FISH

Fish stocks in the South Pacific are an
important food source for the island countries
and a major source of employment. Migratory
tuna are the most important fish. However, it is
becomingly clear that the industry needs to be
effectively managed to avoid the dangers
of overfishing and the
collapse of fish
stocks.

Antarctica

THE FROZEN CONTINENT OF ANTARCTICA is covered by a vast icecap, many thousands of years old, and surrounded by the freezing seas of the Southern Ocean. It is the only continent with no permanent inhabitants – the only people who come here are scientists or tourists. Although the land is rich in oil and minerals, mining is prohibited under the laws of the Antarctic Treaty. This Treaty, agreed by 45 countries, made Antarctica a "continent for science" to be used for peaceful purposes only.

DAY TRIPPERS

Tourists visit Antarctica in summer. There are no resorts, so visitors generally stay on small cruise ships. When they come ashore, people have to wear insulated clothing and goggles to protect their eyes from glare off the ice.

LONG DAYS

Seasons at the poles are extreme. Polar summers are short but there can be sunshine 24 hours a "day". This is because Earth rotates at an angle to the Sun.

RESEARCH

The only people who stay in Antactica are scientists. They come to study the climate, weather, and geology. By taking ice samples, for example, they can learn about changes in the world's climate over the years.

SCIENTISTS check an ice core.

FLOATING ICE

Icebergs are giant chunks of floating ice that break away, or calve, from ice sheets or glaciers. Most of their mass lies hidden below sea level.

KRILL

Tiny, shrimp-like creatures, krill are the primary food source for a great number of Antarctic animals. These include whales, seals, penguins, squid, and fish.

EMPEROR PENGUINS huddle for warmth.

PENGUINS

Penguins walk awkwardly on land, but can swim swiftly to catch fish. Waterproof feathers and a thick layer of fat help keep them warm.

Did you know?

► Antarctica is actually a desert – a barren region, incapable of supporting people or vegetation.

Map labels:

Orcadas (Argentina)
South Orkney Islands
Signy (UK)
South Shetland Islands
Esperanza (Argentina)
Capitán Arturo Prat (Chile)
Palmer (US)
Rothera (UK)
San Martín (Argentina)
Drake Passage
Antarctic Peninsula
Graham Land
Palmer Land
Bellingshausen Sea
PETER I ISLAND (to Norway)
Ellsworth Land
Lesser Antarctica
Marie Byrd Land
Amundsen Sea
Mount Siple 3100m
Mount Sidley 4181m
Vinson Massif 4897m
Weddell Sea
Ronne Ice Shelf
Berkner Island
Belgrano II (Argentina)
Halley (UK)
Coats Land
Sanae (South Africa)
Georg von Neumayer (Germany)
Novolazarevskaya (Russian Federation)
Dronning Maud Land
Lützow Holmbukta
Syowa (Japan)
Molodezhnaya (Russian Federation)
Enderby Land
Mawson (Australia)
Cape Darnley
Mackenzie Bay
Prydz Bay
Princess Elizabeth Land
Davis (Australia)
Greater Antarctica
Mirny (Russ. Fed.)
Shackleton Ice Shelf
Casey (Australia)
Cape Poinsett
Wilkes Land
Vostok (Russian Federation)
Amundsen-Scott (US) South Pole
Transantarctic Mountains
Mount Kirkpatrick 4528m
Mount Markham 4351m
Ross Ice Shelf
Roosevelt Island
Scott Base (NZ)
McMurdo Base (US)
Mount Erebus 3794m
Ross Sea
SOUTHERN OCEAN
Victoria Land
Terre Adélie
Dumont d'Urville (France)
South Geomagnetic Pole
George V Land
Cape Adare
Leningradskaya (Russian Federation)
Balleny Islands
Antarctic Circle

ANTARCTICA

SOUTHERN OCEAN

0 km   500
0 miles   500

Arctic Ocean

THE SMALLEST OF THE world's oceans, the Arctic is almost entirely surrounded by the northern edges of North America, Europe, and Asia. For most of the year, its waters are covered by a thick sheet of ice, although warmer currents from the Pacific and Atlantic melt the ice along the continental coasts for a short time in summer. Despite the harsh conditions, the region is home to a range of wildlife, such as reindeer, musk ox, foxes, and wolves. Some people, including the Inuit of Canada and the Sami of northern Scandinavia, have also adapted to this tough environment.

OZONE HOLE

High in the atmosphere, ozone (a gas) forms a natural shield that protects us from the Sun's ultraviolet rays. Scientists (right) at both poles have found holes in the ozone layer, caused by chemicals known as CFCs, once used in aerosols, fridges, and plastic packaging.

SATELLITE image shows a hole over the Arctic.

ALASKAN OIL

Reserves of oil and gas in the Beaufort Sea, off the coast of Alaska, have attracted interest However, the introduction of ships and oil platforms brings problems. In a bid to protect the area, several environmental organizations are actively working to prevent drilling for more oil in this area.

Did you know?

▶ The main Arctic icepack is not stationary – strong winds cause it to rotate very slowly clockwise

▶ The Sami are an indigenous people who form an ethnic minority in Norway, Sweden, Finland, and Russia.

▶ Walruses breed off the Arctic coasts.

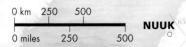

0 km   250   500
0 miles   250   500

ARCTIC SURVIVORS

Polar bears live along the Arctic coasts of Canada, Greenland, and Russia. They hunt seals and fish at points where the sea ice melts. The bears have an insulating layer of fat, called blubber, which helps them survive the cold. Their white fur also provides essential camouflage on the ice.

NORTHERN LIGHTS

In midwinter, the north polar skies are sometimes lit up by dramatic curtains of red and green light. Known as the Northern Lights, these special effects are caused by disturbances in the upper atmosphere. The same happens near Antarctica, where the effect is called the Southern Lights.

Map labels

Bering Strait
Arctic Circle
180°
170°
170°
160°
150°
140°
130°
120°
110°
Chukchi Sea
Ostrov Vrangelya
East Siberian Sea
Beaufort Sea
Amundsen Gulf
Banks Island
Victoria Island
Melville Island
CANADA
Queen Elizabeth Islands
North Geomagnetic Pole
ARCTIC
OCEAN
North Pole
Novosibirskiye Ostrova
Laptev Sea
RUSSIAN FEDERATION
Severnaya Zemlya
Kara Sea
Lancaster Sound
Ellesmere Island
Nares Strait
Knud Rasmussen Land
Lincoln Sea
Franz Josef Land
Kap Morris Jesup
Baffin Bay
Wandel Sea
SVALBARD (to Norway)
Spitsbergen
LONGYEARBYEN
Kong Frederik VIII Land
GREENLAND (to Denmark)
Greenland Sea
Bjørnøya (to Norway)
Barents Sea
NUUK
Kong Christian IX Land
JAN MAYEN (to Norway)
Norwegian Sea
Denmark Strait
ICELAND
REYKJAVÍK

Gazetteer

HOW TO USE THE GAZETTEER

This gazetteer is a selection of the names in *Children's World Atlas*, and can be used to help you find places on the maps. For example, to find the city of Lisbon in Portugal, look up its name in the gazetteer. The entry reads:

Lisbon *Capital* Portugal 58 E6

The first number, 58, tells you that Lisbon appears on the map on page 58. The second number, E6, shows that it is in square E6. Turn to page 58. Trace down from the letter E along the top of the grid (or up from the letter E on the bottom of the grid), and then across from the number 6 on the side of the grid. You will find Lisbon in the area where the letter and number meet.

A

Aachen *Town* Germany 56 B7
Aalborg *Town* Denmark 49 B11
Aalen *Town* Germany 57 E9
Aalst *Town* Belgium 53 D11
Aalter *Town* Belgium 53 C10
Äänekoski *Town* Finland 48 G8
Aba *Town* Nigeria 41 L8
Aba *Town* Democratic Republic of Congo 42 I8
Ābādān *Town* Iran 82 E7
Abakan *Town* Russian Federation 78 H7
Abbeville *Town* France 54 E5
Abéché *Town* Chad 42 F6
Abengourou *Town* Côte d'Ivoire 41 I8
Aberdeen *Town* South Dakota, USA 12 G4
Aberdeen *Town* Maryland, USA 9 H8
Aberdeen *Town* Scotland, UK 50 F5
Aberystwyth *Town* Wales, UK 51 E10
Abhā *Town* Saudi Arabia 83 C11
Abidjan *Town* Côte d'Ivoire 40 H8
Abilene *Town* Texas, USA 17 K5
Åbo *see* Turku
Abomey *Town* Benin 41 J7
Abrantes *Town* Portugal 58 F6
Abu Dhabi *Capital* United Arab Emirates 83 F9
Abu Hamed *Town* Sudan 38 E6
Abuja *Capital* Nigeria 41 L7
Abū Kamāl *Town* Syria 80 I7
Abū Ẓaby *see* Abu Dhabi
Acapulco *Town* Mexico 19 J9
Acarigua *Town* Venezuela 26 D5
Accra *Capital* Ghana 41 I8
Aconcagua, Cerro *Mountain* Argentina 30 D7
A Coruña *Town* Spain 58 E2
Açu *Town* Brazil 29 M3
Adamawa Highlands *Mountain range* Cameroon 42 D8
'Adan *see* Aden
Adana *Town* Turkey 76 G6
Adapazari *Town* Turkey 76 E4
Ad Dahnā' *Desert* Saudi Arabia 83 E9
Ad Dakhla *Town* Western Sahara 36 C7
Ad Dammām *Town* Saudi Arabia 83 E9
Ad Dawḩah *see* Doha
Addis Ababa *Capital* Ethiopia 39 F9
Adelaide *Town* South Australia, Australia 105 J7
Aden *Town* Yemen 83 D13

Aden, Gulf of Indian Ocean 83 E13
Adirondack Mountains New York, USA 8 H4
Ādīs Ābeba *see* Addis Ababa
Adiyaman *Town* Turkey 76 H6
Adrar *Town* Algeria 36 G6
Adrar *Town* Morocco 36 E5
Aegean Sea Greece 67 F9
Afghanistan *Country* 84 H7
Afmadow *Town* Somalia 39 G11
Afyon *Town* Turkey 76 E5
Agadez *Town* Niger 41 L4
Agadir *Town* Morocco 36 E5
Agen *Town* France 55 D10
Agialoúsa *Town* Cyprus 80 B7
Āgra *Town* India 87 I3
Ağri *Town* Turkey 77 K4
Agrigento *Town* Sicily, Italy 61 E13
Agropoli *Town* Italy 61 F10
Aguachica *Town* Colombia 26 C5
Agua Prieta *Town* Mexico 18 F3
Aguascalientes *Town* Mexico 19 I7
Aguaytía *Town* Peru 27 B10
Aguilas *Town* Spain 59 J8
Aguililla *Town* Mexico 19 I8
Ahaggar *Mountain range* Algeria 37 I7
Ahlen *Town* Germany 56 C7
Ahmadābād *Town* India 86 G4
Ahuachapán *Town* El Salvador 22 E5
Ahvāz *Town* Iran 82 E7
Aiken *Town* South Carolina, USA 11 J4
Ailigandí *Town* Panama 23 N7
'Aïn Ben Tili *Town* Mauritania 40 G2
Aiquile *Town* Bolivia 27 E12
Aïr, Massif de l' *Mountain range* Niger 41 L4
Aix-en-Provence *Town* France 55 G11
Aizu *Town* Japan 93 G9
Ajaccio *Town* France 55 I13
Ajo *Town* Arizona, USA 16 E5
Akchâr *Desert* Mauritania 40 E3
Akhalts'ikhe *Town* Georgia 77 K3
Akhisar *Town* Turkey 76 C5
Akhtubinsk *Town* Russian Federation 73 D11
Akita *Town* Japan 92 F8
Akjoujt *Town* Mauritania 40 E3
Akkeshi *Town* Japan 92 H5
Akron *Town* Ohio, USA 13 M6
Akrotírion *Town* Cyprus 80 A8
Aksai Chin *Administrative region* China 88 D6
Aksaray *Town* Turkey 76 F5
Akşehir *Town* Turkey 76 E5
Aktau *Town* Kazakhstan 78 D6
Aktobe *Town* Kazakhstan 78 E6
Aktsyabrski *Town* Belarus 71 F11
Akula *Town* Democratic Republic of Congo 43 F9
Akune *Town* Japan 93 B14
Alabama *State* USA 10 G5
Alabama River Alabama, USA 10 G6
Al 'Amārah *Town* Iraq 82 D7
Alamo *Town* Nevada, USA 14 H7
Alamogordo *Town* New Mexico, USA 16 H5
Åland *Island group* Finland 49 F9
Alanya *Town* Turkey 76 E7
Al 'Aqabah *Town* Jordan 81 D14
Alaşehir *Town* Turkey 76 D5
Alaska *Province* Canada 4 E5
Alaska, Gulf of Alaska, USA 4 E6
Alaska Range *Mountain Range* Alaska, USA 4 E5
Albacete *Town* Spain 59 J6
Alba Iulia *Town* Romania 68 E6
Albania *Country* 65 F12
Albany *River* Ontario, Canada 6 F5
Albany *Town* Western Australia, Australia 104 E7
Albany *Town* Georgia, USA 10 H6
Albany *Town* New York, USA 9 I5
Al Bāridah *Town* Syria 80 F8
Al Baṣrah *Town* Iraq 82 D7
Alberta *Province* Canada 4 H7
Albert, Lake Democratic Republic of Congo 43 I9
Albuquerque *Town* New Mexico, USA 16 H4
Alcañiz *Town* Spain 59 K5
Alcoy *Town* Spain 59 K7
Alderney *Island* Channel Islands, UK 51 G13
Aleksin *Town* Russian Federation 73 C9
Alençon *Town* France 54 D7
Alenquer *Town* Brazil 29 I2

Aleppo *Town* Syria 80 E6
Alessandria *Town* Italy 60 C5
Aleutian Islands *Island Group* Alaska, USA 4 B5
Alexander Archipelago *Island* British Colombia, Canada 4 E7
Alexandria *Town* Louisiana, USA 10 E6
Alexandria *Town* Egypt 38 D4
Alexandria *Town* Romania 68 F7
Alexandroúpoli *Town* Greece 66 G8
Alga *Town* Kazakhstan 78 E6
Algarve *Region* Spain 58 E8
Algeciras *Town* Spain 58 G9
Alger *see* Algiers
Algeria *Country* 36 H5
Algiers *Capital* Algeria 36 H3
Algona *Town* Iowa, USA 12 H5
Al Ḩasakah *Town* Syria 80 H5
Al Ḩillah *Town* Iraq 82 D7
Al Hudaydah *see* Hodeida
Al Hufūf *Town* Saudi Arabia 83 E9
Aliartos *Town* Greece 67 E11
Alicante *Town* Spain 59 L7
Alice Springs *Town* Northern Territory, Australia 105 I4
Aliquippa *Town* Pennsylvania, USA 8 E7
Al Jafr *Town* Jordan 81 E13
Al Jaghbūb *Town* Libya 37 N5
Al Jahrā' *Town* Kuwait 82 D8
Al Jawf *Town* Saudi Arabia 82 B8
Al Jazīrah *Physical region* Syria/Iraq 80 I5
Al Karak *Town* Jordan 81 E12
Al Khufrah *Town* Libya 37 N7
Al Khums *Town* Libya 37 K4
Alkmaar *Town* Netherlands 52 E7
Al Kūt *Town* Iraq 82 D7
Al Kuwayt *see* Kuwait
Al Lādhiqīyah *Town* Syria 80 D7
Allahābād *Town* India 87 I4
Allegheny Plateau Pennsylvania/New York, USA 8 F6
Allentown *Town* Pennsylvania, USA 9 H7
Al Līth *Town* Saudi Arabia 83 B11
Alma-Ata *see* Almaty
Al Madīnah *see* Medina
Al Mafraq *Town* Jordan 81 E10
Al Majma'ah *Town* Saudi Arabia 83 D9
Al Mālikīyah *Town* Syria 80 I4
Al Manāmah *see* Manama
Almansa *Town* Spain 59 K7
Al Marj *Town* Libya 37 M4
Almaty *Town* Kazakhstan 78 G8
Al Mawṣil *Town* Iraq 82 C6
Al Mayādīn *Town* Syria 80 H6
Almelo *Town* Netherlands 52 G8
Almere *Town* Netherlands 52 F8
Almería *Town* Spain 59 J8
Al'met'yevsk *Town* Russian Federation 73 F9
Almirante *Town* Panama 23 K8
Al Mukallā *Town* Yemen 83 E13
Alofi *Capital* Niue 103 K7
Alotip *Town* Indonesia 97 N8
Alpena *Town* Michigan, USA 13 L4
Alpine *Town* Texas, USA 17 I7
Alps *Mountain range* Central Europe 57 D12
Al Qāmishlī *Town* Syria 80 I4
Al Qunayṭirah *Town* Syria 81 D9
Altai Mountains *Mountain range* Mongolia/Russian Federation 88 F4
Altamaha River Georgia, USA 11 I5
Altamira *Town* Brazil 29 J2
Altamura *Town* Italy 61 H10
Altar, Desierto de *Desert* Mexico 18 D2
Altay *Town* China 88 F3
Altay *Town* Mongolia 88 H3
Altin Köprü *Town* Iraq 82 C6
Altiplano *Physical region* Bolivia 27 E13
Altoona *Town* Pennsylvania, USA 9 F7
Altun Ha *Ancient site* Belize 22 F2
Altun Shan *Mountain range* China 88 G5
Al 'Umarī *Town* Jordan 81 F11
Al 'Uwaynāt *Town* Libya 37 J6
Alupka *Town* Ukraine 69 K7
Alva *Town* Oklahoma, USA 17 L3

Al Wajh *Town* Saudi Arabia 83 A9
Alwar *Town* India 86 H3
Al Wari'ah *Town* Saudi Arabia 82 D8
Alytus *Town* Lithuania 70 D8
Amamapare *Town* Indonesia 97 N7
Amantea *Town* Italy 61 G12
Amarapura *Town* Myanmar 94 B6
Amarillo *Town* Texas, USA 17 J4
Amazon *River* Brazil 29 J2
Amazon Basin Brazil 28 G3
Ambanja *Town* Madagascar 45 M4
Ambarchik *Town* Russian Federation 78 L3
Ambato *Town* Ecuador 26 A8
Amboasary *Town* Madagascar 45 L6
Ambon *Town* Indonesia 97 K7
American Samoa *Dependent territory* USA, Pacific Ocean 103 K6
Amersfoort *Town* Netherlands 52 F8
Amfilochía *Town* Greece 67 C10
Amherst *Town* Nova Scotia, Canada 7 K7
Amiens *Town* France 54 E6
Amman *Capital* Jordan 81 E11
'Ammān *see* Amman
Ammóchostos *Town* Cyprus 80 B8
Āmol *Town* Iran 82 F5
Amos *Town* Quebec, Canada 6 H6
Amritsar *Town* India 86 H2
Amstelveen *Town* Netherlands 52 F8
Amsterdam *Capital* Netherlands 52 E8
Am Timan *Town* Chad 42 F6
Amu Darya *River* Uzbekistan 84 G4
Amundsen Gulf Canada 4 H4
Amundsen-Scott *Research station* Antarctica 110 E6
Amundsen Sea Southern Ocean 110 B7
Amuntai *Town* Indonesia 96 H7
Amur *River* China 89 L2
Anadyr' *Town* Russian Federation 78 M2
Anamur *Town* Turkey 76 F7
Anápolis *Town* Brazil 29 K5
Anatolia *Plateau* Turkey 76 E6
Anchorage *Town* Alaska, Canada 4 E5
Ancona *Town* Italy 60 F7
Andalucía *Region* Spain 58 H8
Andaman Islands *Island group* India 87 M8
Andaman Sea Indian Ocean 87 M8
Anderson *Town* Indiana, USA 13 K6
Andes *Mountain range* South America 26–27, 30–31
Andijon *Town* Uzbekistan 85 K4
Andkhvoy *Town* Afghanistan 84 H5
Andorra *Country* 55 D12
Andorra la Vella *Capital* Andorra 55 D12
Andreanof Islands *Island Group* Alaska, USA 4 A4
Andrews *Town* Texas, USA 17 J5
Andria *Town* Italy 61 H10
Andros Island Bahamas 24 F2
Andros Town Bahamas 24 F2
Angarsk *Town* Russian Federation 79 I7
Angeles *Town* Philippines 97 I2
Angel Falls *Waterfall* Venezuela 26 F6
Ångermanälven *River* Sweden 48 E7
Angers *Town* France 54 C7
Angkor Wat *Ancient site* Cambodia 95 F10
Anglesey *Island* Wales, UK 51 E9
Angola *Country* 44 E3
Angola Basin *Undersea feature* Atlantic Ocean 33 M6
Angoulême *Town* France 55 D9
Angren *Town* Uzbekistan 85 J3
Anguilla *Dependent territory* UK, Atlantic Ocean 25 N5
Anhui *Administrative region* China 91 J5
Ankara *Capital* Turkey 76 F4
Annaba *Town* Algeria 37 I3
An Nafūd *Desert* Saudi Arabia 82 B8
'Annah *Town* Iraq 82 C6
An Najaf *Town* Iraq 82 C7
Annamitique, Chaîne *Mountain range* Laos 94 F8
Annapolis *Town* Maryland, USA 8 G8
Ann Arbor *Town* Michigan, USA 13 L5
An Nāṣirīyah *Town* Iraq 82 D7
Annecy *Town* France 55 G9

Anniston *Town* Alabama, USA 10 H4
Anqing *Town* China 91 J6
Anshan *Town* China 91 L2
Anshun *Town* China 90 G7
Antakya *Town* Turkey 76 H7
Antalya *Town* Turkey 76 E6
Antananarivo *Capital* Madagascar 45 M5
Antarctica 110
Antarctic Peninsula Antarctica 110 B4
Antibes *Town* France 55 H11
Anticosti, Île d' *Island* Quebec, Canada 7 K5
Antigua *Island* Antigua & Barbuda 25 N6
Antigua & Barbuda *Country* 25 N5
Anti-Lebanon *Mountain range* Syria 81 E9
Antofagasta *Town* Chile 30 D5
Antony *Town* France 54 E7
Antsiranana *Town* Madagascar 45 M3
Antwerp *Town* Belgium 53 E10
Antwerpen *see* Antwerp
Anyang *Town* China 91 J4
Anzio *Town* Italy 61 E9
Aomen *see* Macao
Aomori *Town* Japan 92 F7
Aosta *Town* Italy 60 B4
Aozou *Town* Chad 42 E3
Apatity *Town* Russian Federation 72 D5
Apeldoorn *Town* Netherlands 52 F8
Apennines *Mountain range* Italy 60 C8
Appingedam *Town* Netherlands 52 G6
Appleton *Town* Wisconsin, USA 13 J4
Apuseni, Munpii *Mountain range* Romania 68 E5
Āqchah *Town* Afghanisatan 85 I5
Aquidauana *Town* Brazil 29 I6
Arabian Peninsula Saudi Arabia 82 B8
Arabian Sea Indian Ocean 83 H10
Aracaju *Town* Brazil 29 N4
Araçuai *Town* Brazil 29 L6
'Arad *Town* Israel 81 D12
Arad *Town* Romania 68 D6
Arafura Sea Australia 105 I1
Araguaia, Rio *River* Brazil 29 J5
Araguaína *Town* Brazil 29 K3
Araguari *Town* Brazil 29 K6
Arāk *Town* Iran 82 E6
Arakan Yoma *Mountain range* Myanmar 94 B7
Aral Sea Uzbekistan/Kazakhstan 84 G1
Aral'sk *Town* Kazakhstan 78 E7
Aranda de Duero *Town* Spain 59 I4
'Ar'ar *Town* Saudi Arabia 82 C7
Ararat, Mount Turkey 77 L4
Arbīl *Town* Iraq 82 D6
Archangel *Town* Russian Federation 72 E6
Arco *Town* Italy 60 D5
Arctic Ocean 111 M5
Ardabīl *Town* Iran 82 E5
Ardakān *Town* Iran 82 F7
Ardennes *Physical region* Belgium 53 F13
Arequipa *Town* Peru 27 D12
Arezzo *Town* Italy 60 E7
Argalastí *Town* Greece 67 E10
Argenteuil *Town* France 54 E6
Argentina *Country* 31 E9
Argentine Basin *Undersea feature* Atlantic Ocean 33 J8
Argo *Town* Sudan 38 D6
Århus *Town* Denmark 49 C12
Arica *Town* Chile 30 C3
Arizona *State* USA 16 E4
Arkansas *State* USA 10 E3
Arkansas City *Town* Kansas, USA 12 G8
Arkhangel'sk *see* Archangel
Arklow *Town* Ireland 51 D9
Arles *Town* France 55 F11
Arlington *Town* Texas, USA 17 M5
Arlington *Town* Virginia, USA 11 K2
Arlon *Town* Belgium 53 F13
Armenia *Country* 77 L4
Armenia *Town* Colombia 26 B6
Armstrong *Town* Ontario, Canada 6 E5
Arnaía *Town* Greece 67 E9
Arnhem *Town* Netherlands 53 F9

Arnhem Land *Region* Australia 105 I2
Ar Ramādī *Town* Iraq 82 C6
Arran, Isle of *Island* Scotland, UK 50 E7
Ar Raqqah *Town* Syria 80 G6
Arras *Town* France 54 F5
Ar Rawḍatayn *Town* Kuwait 82 D8
Arriaga *Town* Mexico 19 M9
Ar Riyāḍ *see* Riyadh
Ar Rub' al Khālī *Desert* Saudi Arabia 83 E11
Ar Rustāq *Town* Oman 83 G9
Ar Ruṭbah *Town* Iraq 82 B6
Artashat *Town* Armenia 77 L4
Artemisa *Town* Cuba 24 D3
Artvin *Town* Turkey 77 J3
Arua *Town* Uganda 39 E10
Aruba *Dependent territory* Netherlands, Atlantic Ocean 25 J8
Arusha *Town* Tanzania 39 F12
Arvidsjaur *Town* Sweden 48 E6
Arys' *Town* Kazakhstan 78 F7
Asadābād *Town* Afghanisatan 85 K7
Asahikawa *Town* Japan 92 G5
Asamankese *Town* Ghana 41 I8
Āsānsol *Town* India 87 K4
Ascension Island *Dependent territory* St Helena, Atlantic Ocean 33 K5
Ascoli Piceno *Town* Italy 60 F8
Aseb *Town* Eritrea 38 G8
Ashdod *Town* Israel 81 C11
Asheville *Town* North Carolina, USA 11 I4
Ashgabat *Capital* Turkmenistan 84 F5
Ashmyany *Town* Belarus 70 E8
Ashqelon *Town* Israel 81 C11
Ash Shadādah *Town* Syria 80 H5
Ash Shāriqah *Town* United Arab Emirates 83 G9
Ash Shihr *Town* Yemen 83 E13
Asipovichy *Town* Belarus 71 F10
Asmara *Capital* Eritrea 38 F7
As Sabkhah *Town* Syria 80 G6
Assad, Lake Syria 80 F6
Aş Şafāwī *Town* J
As Salv *Town* Jordan 81 D11
Assam *Region* India 87 L3
Assamakka *Town* Niger 41 K4
As Samāwah *Town* Iraq 82 D7
Assen *Town* Netherlands 52 G6
As Sukhnah *Town* Syria 80 G7
As Sulaymānīyah *Town* Iran 82 D6
As Sulayyil *Town* Saudi Arabia 83 D11
Aş Şuwār *Town* Syria 80 H6
As Suwaydā' *Town* Syria 81 E10
Astana *Capital* Kazakhstan 78 F6
Asti *Town* Italy 60 C5
Astrakhan' *Town* Russian Federation 73 D12
Asunción *Capital* Paraguay 30 G4
Aswân *Town* Egypt 38 E5
Asyût *Town* Egypt 38 E5
Atacama Desert Chile 30 D6
Atbara *Town* Sudan 38 E7
Atbasar *Town* Kazakhstan 78 F6
Ath *Town* Belgium 53 D11
Athabasca, Lake Saskatchewan, Canada 5 I7
Athens *Capital* Greece 67 E11
Athens *Town* Georgia, USA 11 I4
Athína *see* Athens
Athlone *Town* Ireland 51 C9
Ati *Town* Chad 42 E6
Atka *Town* Russian Federation 78 L4
Atka *Town* Alaska, USA 4 B5
Atlanta *Town* Georgia, USA 10 H4
Atlantic City *Town* New Jersey, USA 9 I8
Atlantic Ocean 32–33
Atlas Mountains *Mountain range* Morocco/Algeria 36 F4
Atsumi *Town* Japan 92 F8
Aṭ Ṭā'if *Town* Saudi Arabia 83 B10
Aṭ Ṭalfīlah *Town* Jordan 81 E12
At Tall al Abyaḍ *Town* Syria 80 F5
Aṭ Ṭanf *Town* Syria 81 G4
Attawapiskat *Town* Ontario, Canada 6 G5
Atyrau *Town* Kazakhstan 78 E6
Auch *Town* France 55 D11
Auckland *Town* New Zealand 106 F5
Augsburg *Town* Germany 57 E10

Augusta *Town* Georgia, USA 11 I5
Augusta *Town* Maine, USA 9 K3
Aurangābād *Town* India 86 H5
Aurillac *Town* France 55 E10
Aurora *Town* Colorado, USA 15 L6
Aurora *Town* Illinois, USA 13 J6
Austin *Town* Texas, USA 17 L7
Australes, Îles *Island chain* French Polynesia 103 N8
Australia *Country* 105 L5
Australian Capital Territory *Territory* Australia 105 L8
Austria *Country* 57 G11
Ausuituq *see* Grise Fiord
Auxerre *Town* France 54 F7
Avarua *Capital* Cook Islands 103 M8
Aveiro *Town* Portugal 58 E5
Avellino *Town* Italy 61 F10
Avezzano *Town* Italy 61 F9
Aviemore *Town* Scotland, UK 50 E5
Avignon *Town* France 55 F11
Ávila *Town* Spain 58 H5
Avilés *Town* Spain 58 G2
Avon *Town* New York, USA 8 F5
Āwash *Town* Ethiopia 39 G9
Awbārī *Town* Libya 37 K6
Axel Heiberg Island Nunavut, Canada 5 I2
Ayacucho *Town* Peru 27 C11
Ayaguz *Town* Kazakhstan 78 G7
Ayaviri *Town* Peru 27 D11
Aydin *Town* Turkey 76 C6
Ayers Rock *see* Uluru
Ayorou *Town* Niger 41 J5
Ayutthaya *Town* Thailand 95 D10
Ayvalik *Town* Turkey 76 C5
Azaouâd *Desert* Mali 41 I4
A'zāz *Town* Syria 80 E5
Azerbaijan *Country* 77 M4
Azores *Island group* Portugal 32 H5
Azov, Sea of Black Sea 69 L6
Azuaga *Town* Spain 58 G7
Azul *Town* Argentina 31 G9
Az Zarqā' *Town* Jordan 81 E11
Az Zāwiyah *Town* Libya 37 K4

B

Baalbek *Town* Lebanon 80 E8
Baardheere *Town* Somalia 39 G11
Baarn *Town* Netherlands 52 E8
Babayevo *Town* Russian Federation 72 C7
Babruysk *Town* Belarus 71 F10
Babuyan Channel *Strait* Philippines 97 J1
Bacabal *Town* Brazil 29 L3
Bacău *Town* Romania 68 G6
Bačka Palanka *Town* Serbia & Montenegro 64 G7
Bac Liêu *Town* Vietnam 95 G12
Bacolod City *Town* Philippines 97 J3
Badajoz *Town* Spain 58 F6
Baden-Baden *Town* Germany 57 C9
Bad Hersfeld *Town* Germany 56 D7
Badlands *Region* North Dakota, USA 12 E3
Bafatá *Town* Guinea-Bissau 40 E6
Baffin Bay Nunavut, Canada 5 K3
Baffin Island Nunavut, Canada 5 K4
Bafoussam *Town* Cameroon 42 C8
Bafra *Town* Turkey 76 G3
Bagé *Town* Brazil 29 J9
Baghdad *Capital* Iraq 82 D6
Baghlān *Town* Afghanistan 85 J6
Bagrationovsk *Town* Kaliningrad 70 B7
Baguio *Town* Philippines 97 I2
Bahamas *Country* 24 G3
Bahāwalpur *Town* Pakistan 86 G3
Bahía Blanca *Town* Argentina 31 F9
Bahir Dar *Town* Ethiopia 38 F8
Bahrain *Country* 83 F9
Bahushewsk *Town* Belarus 71 G9
Baia Mare *Town* Romania 68 E5
Baikal, Lake Russian Federation 79 J6
Bailén *Town* Spain 59 I7

Ba Illi *Town* Chad 42 E6
Bairiki *Capital* Kiribati 103 I4
Baishan *Town* China 89 M4
Baja *Town* Hungary 63 E12
Baja California *Peninsula* Mexico 18 D4
Bajram Curri *Town* Albania 65 F10
Baker *Town* Oregon, USA 14 H3
Baker & Howland Islands *Dependent territory* USA, Pacific Ocean 103 J4
Baker Lake *Town* Nunavut, Canada 5 J6
Bakersfield *Town* California, USA 14 G7
Bakharden *Town* Turkmenistan 84 F4
Bākhtarān *Town* Iran 82 D6
Baki *see* Baku
Baku *Capital* Azerbaijan 77 N3
Balakovo *Town* Russian Federation 73 E10
Balashov *Town* Russian Federation 73 D10
Balaton *Lake* Hungary 63 D12
Balclutha *Town* New Zealand 107 C13
Baleares, Islas *see* Balearic Islands
Balearic Islands *Island group* Spain 59 M5
Bāleshwar *Town* India 87 K5
Bali *Island* Indonesia 96 H8
Balikesir *Town* Turkey 76 C4
Balikpapan *Town* Indonesia 96 H6
Balkan Mountains *Mountain range* Bulgaria 66 D6
Balkh *Town* Afghanisatan 85 I6
Balkhash *Town* Kazakhstan 78 G7
Balkhash, Lake Kazakhstan 78 G7
Ballarat *Town* Victoria, Australia 105 K8
Balsas *Town* Brazil 29 L3
Balsas, Río *River* Mexico 19 J8
Bălpi *Town* Moldova 68 H5
Baltic Sea Northern Europe 49 D12
Baltimore *Town* Maryland, USA 9 G8
Balykchy *Town* Kyrgyzstan 85 M3
Bam *Town* Iran 82 G8
Bamako *Capital* Mali 40 G6
Bambari *Town* Central African Republic 42 F8
Bamberg *Town* Germany 56 E8
Bamenda *Town* Cameroon 42 C8
Bandaaceh *Town* Indonesia 96 C4
Bandarbeyla *Town* Somalia 39 I9
Bandar-e 'Abbās *Town* Iran 82 G8
Bandar-e Būshehr *Town* Iran 82 E8
Bandar-e Khamīr *Town* Iran 82 G8
Bandarlampung *Town* Indonesia 96 E7
Bandar Seri Begawan *Capital* Brunei 96 H5
Banda Sea Indonesia 97 K7
Bandirma *Town* Turkey 76 C4
Bandundu *Town* Democratic Republic of Congo 43 E11
Bandung *Town* Indonesia 96 F8
Bangalore *Town* India 86 H7
Banghāzī *see* Benghazi
Bangkok *Capital* Thailand 95 D10
Bangladesh *Country* 87 K4
Bangor *Town* Maine, USA 9 L3
Bangor *Town* Wales, UK 51 E9
Bangui *Capital* Central African Republic 42 E8
Ban Hua Hin *Town* Thailand 95 D10
Bāniyās *Town* Syria 80 D7
Banja Luka *Town* Bosnia & Herzegovina 64 D7
Banjarmasin *Town* Indonesia 96 H7
Banjul *Capital* Gambia 40 E5
Banks Peninsula New Zealand 107 E11
Banská Bystrica *Town* Slovakia 63 E10
Bantry *Town* Ireland 51 B11
Baoji *Town* China 90 H5
Baoshan *Town* China 90 E7
Baotou *Town* China 89 J5
Ba'qūbah *Town* Iraq 82 D6
Bar *Town* Serbia & Montenegro 65 E11
Bārāmati *Town* India 86 H6
Baranavichy *Town* Belarus 71 D10
Barbados *Country* 25 P7
Barbuda *Island* Antigua & Barbuda 25 N5
Barcelona *Town* Venezuela 26 E5
Barcelona *Town* Spain 59 M4
Bareilly *Town* India 87 I3
Barents Sea Arctic Ocean 111 N8
Bar Harbor *Town* Maine, USA 9 L3
Bari *Town* Italy 61 H10

Brazil *Country* 28 G4
Brazzaville *Capital* Congo 43 D11
Brecon Beacons *Hills* Wales, UK 51 F10
Breda *Town* Netherlands 53 E9
Bregovo *Town* Bulgaria 66 D5
Bremen *Town* Germany 56 D5
Bremerhaven *Town* Germany 56 D5
Brenner Pass *Italy/Austria* 60 E4
Brescia *Town* Italy 60 D5
Brest *Town* Belarus 71 B10
Brest *Town* France 54 A6
Brezovo *Town* Bulgaria 66 F6
Bria *Town* Central African Republic 42 F8
Briançon *Town* France 55 G10
Bridgeport *Town* Connecticut, USA 9 I6
Bridgetown *Capital* Barbados 25 P7
Bridlington *Town* England, UK 50 H8
Brig *Town* Switzerland 57 C12
Brighton *Town* England, UK 51 H11
Brindisi *Town* Italy 61 I10
Brisbane *Town* Queensland, Australia 105 M6
Bristol *Town* England, UK 51 F11
Bristol Channel *Wales/England, UK* 51 E11
British Columbia *Province* Canada 4 G7
British Indian Ocean Territory
    Dependent territory UK, Indian Ocean 99 J5
British Virgin Islands *Dependent territory*
    UK, Atlantic Ocean 25 M5
Brittany *Region* France 54 B6
Brive-la-Gaillarde *Town* France 55 D10
Brno *Town* Czech Republic 63 D9
Broken Arrow *Town* Okahoma, USA 17 M3
Brookhaven *Town* Mississippi, USA 10 F6
Brooks Range *Mountain range* Alaska, USA 4 F4
Broome *Town* Western Australia, Australia 104 F3
Brownfield *Town* Texas, USA 17 J5
Brownwood *Town* Texas, USA 17 L6
Brownsville *Town* Texas, USA 17 M9
Bruges *Town* Belgium 53 C10
Brugge *see* Bruges
Brunei *Country* 96 H5
Brussel *see* Brussels
Brussels *Capital* Belgium 53 D11
Bruxelles *see* Brussels
Bryan *Town* Texas, USA 17 M6
Bryansk *Town* Russian Federation 73 B9
Bucaramanga *Town* Colombia 26 C5
Bucharest *Capital* Romania 68 F7
Bucureşti *see* Bucharest
Budapest *Capital* Hungary 63 E11
Buenaventura *Town* Colombia 26 B6
Buena Vista *Town* Bolivia 27 E12
Buenos Aires *Capital* Argentina 30 G8
Buffalo *Town* New York, USA 8 F5
Buffalo *Town* South Dakota, USA 12 E3
Bug *River* Poland 62 G6
Buguruslan *Town* Russian Federation 73 F10
Buḩayrat al Asad *see* Lake Assad
Bujanovac *Town* Serbia & Montenegro 65 G10
Bujumbura *Capital* Burundi 39 D12
Bukavu *Town* Democratic Republic of Congo
    43 H10
Bukhoro *Town* Uzbekistan 84 H4
Bukoba *Town* Tanzania 39 E11
Bulawayo *Town* Zimbabwe 44 H5
Bulgaria *Country* 66 F6
Bumba *Town* Democratic Republic of Congo
    43 G9
Bungo-suidō *Strait* Japan 93 D13
Bünyan *Town* Turkey 76 G5
Buraydah *Town* Saudi Arabia 83 C9
Burdur *Town* Turkey 76 D6
Burgas *Town* Bulgaria 66 H6
Burgos *Town* Spain 59 I3
Burgundy *Region* France 54 F8
Buriram *Town* Thailand 95 E9
Burketown *Town* Queensland, Australia 105 J3
Burkina Faso *Country* 41 I6
Burlington *Town* New York, USA 9 I4
Burma *see* Myanmar
Burns *Town* Oregon, USA 14 G4
Burnsville *Town* Minnesota, USA 12 H4
Bursa *Town* Turkey 76 D4
Burundi *Country* 39 D12

Buta *Town* Democratic Republic of Congo 43 G9
Butterworth *Town* Malaysia 96 D4
Butuan *Town* Philippines 97 K4
Buynaksk *Town* Russian Federation 73 D14
Büyükağri Daği *see* Ararat, Mount
Buzău *Town* Romania 68 G7
Buzuluk *Town* Russian Federation 73 F10
Byahoml' *Town* Belarus 71 F9
Byalynichy *Town* Belarus 71 G10
Bydgoszcz *Town* Poland 62 E6
Byelaruskaya Hrada *Ridge* Belarus 71 D9
Bytom *Town* Poland 62 E8
Bytča *Town* Slovakia 63 E9

C

Cabanatuan *Town* Philippines 97 J2
Cabimas *Town* Venezuela 26 D5
Cabinda *Town* Angola 44 D1
Cabinda *Province* Angola 44 D1
Caborca *Town* Mexico 18 E3
Cabot Strait *Canada* 7 L6
Cáceres *Town* Spain 58 G6
Cachimbo *Town* Brazil 29 I4
Cachimbo, Serra do *Mountain range* Brazil 29 I4
Cadiz *Town* Philippines 97 J3
Cádiz *Town* Spain 58 G9
Cadiz, Gulf of *Spain* 58 F8
Caen *Town* France 54 D6
Cagayan de Oro *Town* Philippines 97 K4
Cagliari *Town* Sardinia, Italy 61 B11
Caguas *Town* Puerto Rico 25 L5
Caicos Passage *Strait* Bahamas 25 I3
Cairns *Town* Queensland, Australia 105 L3
Cairo *Capital* Egypt 38 E4
Cajamarca *Town* Peru 27 B9
Čakovec *Town* Croatia 64 D5
Calabar *Town* Nigeria 41 L8
Calafat *Town* Romania 68 E7
Calais *Town* France 54 E5
Calais *Town* Maine, USA 9 L2
Calama *Town* Chile 30 D4
Călăraşi *Town* Romania 68 G7
Calatayud *Town* Spain 59 J4
Calbayog *Town* Philippines 97 J3
Calcutta *Town* India 87 K4
Calgary *Town* Alberta, Canada 4 H8
Cali *Town* Colombia 26 B6
Calicut *Town* India 86 H8
California *State* USA 14 H7
California, Gulf of *Mexico* 18 E4
Callao *Town* Peru 27 B11
Caltanissetta *Town* Sicily, Italy 61 E13
Caluula *Town* Somalia 38 I8
Camacupa *Town* Angola 44 E3
Camagüey *Town* Cuba 24 F4
Camaná *Town* Peru 27 C12
Ca Mau *Town* Vietnam 95 F12
Cambodia *Country* 95 F10
Cambrai *Town* France 54 F5
Cambrian Mountains *Wales, UK* 51 F10
Cambridge *Town* England, UK 51 H10
Cambridge *Town* Maryland, USA 8 H9
Cambridge *Town* Ohio, USA 13 M6
Cambridge Bay *Town* Nunavut, Canada 5 I5
Camden *Town* Maine, USA 9 K4
Cameroon *Country* 42 C8
Camopi *Town* French Guiana 26 I7
Campeche *Town* Mexico 19 N7
Campeche, Bay of *Mexico* 19 M7
Câm Pha *Town* Vietnam 94 G6
Câmpina *Town* Romania 68 F7
Campina Grande *Town* Brazil 29 N4
Campinas *Town* Brazil 29 K7
Campobasso *Town* Italy 61 F9
Campo Grande *Town* Brazil 29 I6
Campos *Town* Brazil 29 L7
Câmpulung *Town* Romania 68 E6
Cam Ranh *Town* Vietnam 95 H11
Çanakkale *Town* Turkey 76 C4
Çanakkale Boğazi *see* Dardanelles
Canada *Country* 4 G8

Canary Islands *Island group*
    Spain, Atlantic Ocean 33 K3
Canaveral, Cape *Coastal feature* Florida,
    USA 11 J7
Canavieiras *Town* Brazil 29 M5
Canberra *Capital* Australia 105 L8
Cancún *Town* Mexico 19 P6
Cangzhou *Town* China 91 J3
Caniapiscau, Réservoir de *Reservoir*
    Quebec, Canada 7 I4
Çankiri *Town* Turkey 76 F4
Cannanore *Town* India 86 H8
Cannes *Town* France 55 H12
Canoas *Town* Brazil 29 J8
Canon City *Town* Colorado, USA 15 K6
Cantábrica, Cordillera *Mountain range*
    Spain 58 G3
Canterbury *Town* England, UK 51 I11
Cân Tho *Town* Vietnam 95 G12
Canton *Town* Ohio, USA 13 M6
Canyon *Town* Texas, USA 17 J4
Cape Basin *Undersea feature*
    Atlantic Ocean 33 M7
Cape Breton Island *Nova Scotia, Canada* 7 L7
Cape Charles *Town* Virginia, USA 11 L2
Cape Coast *Town* Ghana 41 I8
Cape Horn *Coastal feature* Chile 31 E15
Cape Town *Capital* South Africa 44 F8
Cape Verde *Country* 33 K4
Cape Verde Basin *Undersea feature*
    Atlantic Ocean 33 J4
Cape York Peninsula *Queensland,*
    Australia 105 K2
Cap-Haïtien *Town* Haiti 25 I5
Capitán Arturo Prat *Research station*
    Antarctica 110 B4
Caprivi Strip *Physical region* Namibia 44 G4
Caracaraí *Town* Brazil 28 H1
Caracas *Capital* Venezuela 26 E4
Caravelas *Town* Brazil 29 M6
Carbonia *Town* Sardinia, Italy 61 B11
Cárdenas *Town* Cuba 24 E3
Cardiff *Town* Wales, UK 51 F11
Carei *Town* Romania 68 E5
Caribbean Sea *Atlantic Ocean* 32 H4
Carlisle *Town* England, UK 50 F7
Carlisle *Town* Pennsylvania, USA 8 G7
Carlow *Town* Ireland 51 D9
Carlsbad *Town* New Mexico, USA 17 I5
Carmarthen *Town* Wales, UK 51 E10
Carmelita *Town* Guatemala 22 E2
Carmen *Town* Mexico 19 N7
Carnarvon *Town* Western Australia,
    Australia 104 D5
Carolina *Town* Brazil 29 K3
Caroline Islands *Island group* Micronesia 102 F3
Carpathian Mountains *Mountain range*
    Poland/Slovakia/Romania 68 F5
Carpentaria, Gulf of *Australia* 105 J2
Carpi *Town* Italy 60 D6
Carrara *Town* Italy 60 D6
Carson City *Town* Nevada, USA 14 G6
Cartagena *Town* Colombia 26 B5
Cartagena *Town* Spain 59 K8
Carthage *Ancient site* Tunisia 37 J3
Cartwright *Town* Newfoundland & Labrador,
    Canada 7 L4
Carúpano *Town* Venezuela 26 F4
Caruthersville *Town* Missouri, USA 13 J8
Cary *Town* North Carolina, USA 11 K3
Casablanca *Town* Morocco 36 E4
Cascade Range *Mountain Range*
    Oregon/Washington, USA 14 F4
Caserta *Town* Italy 61 F10
Casey *Research station* Antarctica 110 G7
Casper *Town* Wyoming, USA 15 K4
Caspian Depression *Lowland* Russian Federation
    73 D12
Caspian Sea *Asia* 73 D13
Casteggio *Town* Italy 60 C5
Castelló de la Plana *Town* Spain 59 K5
Castelvetrano *Town* Sicily, Italy 61 D13
Castlebar *Town* Ireland 50 B8
Castricum *Town* Netherlands 52 E7

Castries *Capital* St. Lucia 25 O7
Castrovillari *Town* Italy 61 G11
Catacamas *Town* Honduras 22 H4
Catalonia *Region* Spain 59 L4
Cataluña *see* Catalonia
Catania *Town* Sicily, Italy 61 G13
Catanzaro *Town* Italy 61 H12
Catskill Mountains *New York, USA* 8 H5
Caucasia *Town* Colombia 26 B5
Caucasus *Mountain range* Asia/Europe 77 J2
Caviana de Fora, Ilha *Island* Brazil 29 K2
Cayenne *Capital* French Guiana 26 I6
Cayes *Town* Haiti 24 H5
Cayman Islands *Dependent territory*
    UK, Atlantic Ocean 24 E5
Cebu *Town* Philippines 97 J3
Cecina *Town* Italy 60 D7
Cedar City *Town* Utah, USA 15 I6
Cedar Falls *Town* Iowa, USA 12 H5
Cedar Rapids *Town* Iowa, USA 13 I5
Cefalù *Town* Sicily, Italy 61 E12
Celebes *Island* Indonesia 97 J7
Celebes Sea *Pacific Ocean* 97 I5
Celje *Town* Slovenia 57 H12
Celldömölk *Town* Hungary 63 D11
Celle *Town* Germany 56 E6
Celtic Sea *Atlantic Ocean* 51 C11
Cenderawasih, Teluk *Bay* Indonesia 97 M6
Central African Republic *Country* 42 G8
Central, Cordillera *Mountain range*
    Colombia 26 B7
Central, Cordillera *Mountain range*
    Dominican Republic 25 J5
Central, Cordillera *Mountain range* Panama
    23 K8
Central Pacific Basin *Undersea feature* Pacific
    Ocean 109 J5
Central, Planalto *Physical region* Brazil 29 K5
Central Range *Mountain range* Papua New
    Guinea 102 E5
Central Siberian Uplands *Plateau* Russian
    Federation 79 I5
Central, Sistema *Mountain range* Spain 58 H5
Central Valley *California, USA* 14 G5
Ceram Sea *Pacific Ocean* 97 K7
Cerignola *Town* Italy 61 G10
Cerro de Pasco *Town* Peru 27 B10
Cesena *Town* Italy 60 E6
České Budějovice *Town* Czech Republic 63 B9
Český Krumlov *Town* Czech Republic 63 B10
Ceuta *Town* Spain 58 H9
Cévennes *Mountain range* France 55 F11
Ceyhan *Town* Turkey 76 G6
Ceylanpinar *Town* Turkey 77 J6
Chachapoyas *Town* Peru 27 B9
Chad *Country* 42 E5
Chad, Lake *Chad* 42 D5
Chãgai Hills *Mountain range* Pakistan 86 E2
Chaillu, Massif du *Mountain range* Gabon
    43 C10
Chakhānsūr *Town* Afghanisatan 84 G8
Chalatenango *Town* El Salvador 22 F4
Chalkidikí *Peninsula* Greece 67 E9
Challans *Town* France 54 C8
Challenger Deep *Undersea feature* Pacific Ocean
    108 H4
Châlons-en-Champagne *Town* France 54 G6
Chalon-sur-Saône *Town* France 54 G8
Chaman *Town* Pakistan 86 F2
Chambéry *Town* France 55 G10
Champagne *Region* France 54 F7
Champaign *Town* Illinois, USA 13 J6
Champlain, Lake *New York, USA* 9 I4
Champotón *Town* Mexico 19 N7
Chañaral *Town* Chile 30 C5
Chandīgarh *Town* India 86 H2
Chandrapur *Town* India 87 I5
Changchun *Town* China 89 M3
Changde *Town* China 91 I6
Chang Jiang *see* Yangtze
Changsha *Town* China 91 I6
Changzhi *Town* China 91 I4
Channel Islands *Dependent territory* UK 51 G13
Channel Tunnel *Town* UK/France 51 I11

Giurgiu *Town* Romania 68 F8
Glace Bay *Town* Nova Scotia, Canada 7 L6
Glâma *River* Norway 49 C9
Glasgow *Town* Scotland, UK 51 E6
Glazov *Town* Russian Federation 72 F8
Glendale *Town* Arizona, USA 16 E5
Glens Falls *Town* New York, USA 9 I5
Gliwice *Town* Poland 62 E8
Globe *Town* Arizona, USA 16 F5
Głogów *Town* Poland 62 D7
Gloucester *Town* England, UK 51 F10
Gniezno *Town* Poland 62 D6
Gobi *Desert* Mongolia 89 I4
Godávari *River* India 86 H5
Godhra *Town* India 86 G4
Godoy Cruz *Town* Argentina 30 D8
Goes *Town* Netherlands 53 D10
Goiânia *Town* Brazil 29 K6
Göksun *Town* Turkey 76 H6
Golan Heights *Mountain range* Syria 81 D10
Goldsboro *Town* North Carolina, USA 11 K3
Goleniów *Town* Poland 62 C5
Golmud *Town* China 88 G6
Goma *Town* Democratic Republic of Congo 43 H10
Gombi *Town* Nigeria 41 M6
Gómez Palacio *Town* Mexico 18 H5
Gonaïves *Town* Haiti 25 I5
Gonder *Town* Ethiopia 38 F8
Gondia *Town* India 87 I5
Good Hope, Cape of *Coastal feature* South Africa 44 F9
Goor *Town* Netherlands 52 G8
Göppingen *Town* Germany 57 D9
Gorakhpur *Town* Pakistan 87 J3
Goražde *Town* Bosnia & Herzegovina 65 E9
Gorē *Town* Ethiopia 39 F9
Gorgān *Town* Iran 82 F5
Gori *Town* Georgia 77 L3
Görlitz *Town* Germany 56 G7
Gorontalo *Town* Indonesia 97 J6
Gorzów Wielkopolski *Town* Poland 62 C6
Gosford *Town* New South Wales, Australia 105 M7
Goshogawara *Town* Japan 92 F7
Göteborg *see* Gothenburg
Gotel Mountains Nigeria 41 M7
Gotha *Town* Germany 56 E7
Gothenburg *Town* Sweden 49 C11
Gotland *Island* Sweden 49 E11
Gōtsu *Town* Japan 93 C12
Göttingen *Town* Germany 56 D7
Gouda *Town* Netherlands 53 E9
Governador Valadares *Town* Brazil 29 L6
Gradaús, Serra dos *Mountain range* Brazil 29 J4
Grafton *Town* New South Wales, Australia 105 N6
Grafton *Town* North Dakota, USA 12 G2
Grampian Mountains Scotland, UK 50 E5
Granada *Town* Spain 59 I8
Granada *Town* Nicaragua 22 H6
Gran Chaco *Plain* Paraguay 30 G4
Grand Bahama Island Bahamas 24 F1
Grand Canyon Arizona, USA 16 E3
Grand Cayman *Island* West Indies 24 E5
Grande, Bahía *Bay* Argentina 31 E13
Grand Erg Occidental *Desert* Algeria 36 G5
Grand Erg Oriental *Desert* Algeria 37 I5
Grande, Rio *River* Mexico/USA 16 G5
Grand Forks *Town* North Dakota, USA 12 G2
Grand Rapids *Town* Minnesota, USA 12 H3
Grand Rapids *Town* Michigan, USA 13 K5
Grand-Santi *Town* French Guiana 24 H6
Grants Pass *Town* Oregon, USA 14 F4
Grayling *Town* Alaska, USA 4 D4
Graz *Town* Austria 57 H11
Great Australian Bight *Sea feature* Australia 104 G7
Great Barrier Island New Zealand 106 G4
Great Barrier Reef *Coral reef* Australia 105 L3
Great Basin Nevada, USA 14 H6
Great Bear Lake Northwest Territories, Canada 4 H5

Great Dividing Range *Mountain range* Queensland/New South Wales, Australia 105 L4
Greater Antarctica *Region* Antarctica 110 F5
Greater Antilles *Island group* Caribbean Sea 24 G5
Greater Caucasus *Mountain range* Asia/Europe 77 M3
Great Falls *Town* Montana, USA 15 J2
Great Hungarian Plain Hungary 63 F12
Great Inagua *Island* Bahamas 25 I4
Great Karoo *Plateau* South Africa 44 F8
Great Khingan Range *Mountain range* China 89 L3
Great Rift Valley Africa 39 F12
Great Sand Sea *Desert* Egypt 38 C4
Great Sandy Desert Western Australia, Australia 104 G4
Great Slave Lake Northwest Territories, Canada 4 H6
Great Victoria Desert Western Australia/South Australia, Australia 104 G6
Great Wall of China *Ancient monument* China 89 J5
Great Yarmouth *Town* England, UK 51 I9
Greece *Country* 67 D11
Greeley *Town* Colorado, USA 15 L5
Green Bay *Town* Wisconsin, USA 13 J4
Greenfield *Town* Massachusetts, USA 9 J5
Greeneville *Town* Tennessee, USA 11 I3
Greenland *Dependent territory* Denmark, Atlantic Ocean 111 C8
Greenland Sea Arctic Ocean 111 M7
Green Mountains Vermont, USA 9 I5
Greenock *Town* Scotland, UK 50 E6
Greensboro *Town* North Carolina, USA 11 J3
Greenville *Town* Mississippi, USA 10 F5
Greenville *Town* South Carolina, USA 11 I4
Greifswald *Town* Germany 56 F4
Grenada *Country* 25 O8
Grenadines, The *Island group* St Vincent & The Grenadines 25 O8
Grenoble *Town* France 55 G10
Gresham *Town* Oregon, USA 14 F3
Grevenmacher *Town* Luxembourg 53 G13
Greymouth *Town* New Zealand 107 D10
Grey Range *Mountain range* New South Wales/Queensland, Australia 105 K6
Griffin *Town* Georgia, USA 10 H5
Grimsby *Town* England, UK 51 H9
Grise Fiord *Town* Nunavut, Canada 5 J3
Grójec *Town* Poland 62 F7
Groningen *Town* Netherlands 52 G6
Grootfontein *Town* Namibia 44 F5
Grosseto *Town* Italy 60 D8
Groznyy *Town* Russian Federation 73 D14
Gubkin *Town* Russian Federation 73 C10
Grudziądz *Town* Poland 62 E5
Gryazi *Town* Russian Federation 73 C10
Guadalajara *Town* Spain 59 I5
Guadalajara *Town* Mexico 19 I7
Guadalcanal *Island* Solomon Islands 102 G6
Guadalupe *Town* Mexico 19 I6
Guadeloupe *Dependent territory* France, Atlantic Ocean 25 O6
Guaimaca *Town* Honduras 22 G4
Gualeguaychú *Town* Argentina 30 G8
Guam *Dependent territory* USA, Pacific Ocean 102 D2
Guamúchil *Town* Mexico 18 G5
Guanabacoa *Town* Cuba 24 D3
Guanajuato *Town* Mexico 19 J7
Guanare *Town* Venezuela 26 D5
Guangdong *Administrative region* China 91 J8
Guangxi *Administrative region* China 90 H8
Guangyuan *Town* China 90 H5
Guangzhou *Town* China 91 I8
Guantánamo *Town* Cuba 24 H4
Guantánamo Bay *Territory* USA, Cuba 24 H5
Guasave *Town* Mexico 18 G5
Guatemala *Country* 22 D3
Guatemala City *Capital* Guatemala 22 D4
Guayaquil *Town* Ecuador 26 A8
Guaymas *Town* Mexico 18 E4

Guéret *Town* France 55 E9
Guernsey *Island* Channel Islands, UK 51 F13
Guerrero Negro *Town* Mexico 18 D4
Guiana Highlands *Mountain range* Colombia/Venezuela/Brazil 26 F7
Guider *Town* Cameroon 42 D7
Guildford *Town* England, UK 51 G11
Guilin *Town* China 91 I7
Guinea *Country* 40 F6
Guinea-Bissau *Country* 40 E6
Guinea, Gulf of *Atlantic Ocean* 33 M5
Guiyang *Town* China 90 H7
Guizhou *Administrative region* China 90 G7
Gujrānwāla *Town* Pakistan 86 H2
Gujrāt *Town* Pakistan 86 H2
Gulbarga *Town* India 86 H6
Gulbene *Town* Latvia 70 G6
Gulf, The *Middle East* 82 E6
Guliston *Town* Uzbekistan 85 J4
Gulu *Town* Uganda 39 E10
Gümüşhane *Town* Turkey 76 H4
Güney Doğu Toroslar *Mountain range* Turkey 76 H6
Gusau *Town* Nigeria 41 K6
Gushgy *Town* Turkmenistan 84 G6
Güstrow *Town* Germany 56 F5
Gütersloh *Town* Germany 56 D6
Guwāhāti *Town* India 87 L3
Guyana *Country* 26 G6
Gwādar *Town* Pakistan 86 D3
Gwalior *Town* India 87 I3
Gyomaendrőd *Town* Hungary 63 G11
Gyöngyös *Town* Hungary 63 F11
Győr *Town* Hungary 63 D11
Gyumri *Town* Armenia 77 K

H

Haarlem *Town* Netherlands 52 E8
Haast *Town* New Zealand 107 B11
Hachinohe *Town* Japan 92 G7
Hadera *Town* Israel 81 D10
Ha Đông *Town* Vietnam 94 G7
Haeju *Town* North Korea 91 L3
Hagåtña *Capital* Guam 102 E2
Hagerstown *Town* Maryland, USA 8 F8
Ha Giang *Town* Vietnam 94 G6
Hague, The *Capital* Netherlands 52 D8
Haicheng *Town* China 91 L2
Haifa *Town* Israel 81 D10
Haikou *Town* China 91 I9
Ḥā'il *Town* Saudi Arabia 82 C8
Hailar *Town* China 89 L2
Hainan *Administrative region* China 90 H9
Hainan Dao *Island* China 91 I9
Hai Phong *Town* Vietnam 94 G7
Haiti *Country* 25 I5
Hajdúhadház *Town* Hungary 63 G11
Hakodate *Town* Japan 92 F6
Ḥalab *see* Aleppo
Halifax *Town* Nova Scotia, Canada 7 L7
Halle *Town* Germany 56 F7
Halle *Town* Belgium 53 D11
Halle-Neustadt *Town* Germany 56 F7
Halley *Research station* Antarctica 110 D4
Halmstad *Town* Sweden 49 C11
Hamadān *Town* Iran 82 E6
Ḥamāh *Town* Syria 80 E7
Hamamatsu *Town* Japan 93 F11
Hamar *Town* Norway 49 C9
Hamburg *Town* Germany 56 E5
Hamburg *Town* New York, USA 9 F5
Hamersley Range *Mountain range* Western Australia, Australia 104 F4
Hamhŭng *Town* North Korea 91 M3
Hami *Town* China 88 G4
Hamilton *Town* Scotland, UK 50 E6
Hamilton *Town* New Zealand 106 G6
Hamilton *Town* Ontario, Canada 6 G8
Hamm *Town* Germany 56 C7
Hanamaki *Town* Japan 92 G8
Handan *Town* China 91 J4

Ha Negev *see* Negev
Hangzhou *Town* China 91 K6
Hannover *Town* Germany 56 D6
Ha Nôi *Capital* Vietnam 94 G7
Hantsavichy *Town* Belarus 71 D10
Hanzhong *Town* China 90 H5
Haradok *Town* Belarus 70 H8
Harare *Capital* Zimbabwe 45 I4
Harbel *Town* Liberia 40 F8
Harbin *Town* China 89 M3
Hardangervidda *Plateau* Norway 49 B9
Hardenberg *Town* Netherlands 52 G7
Härer *Town* Ethiopia 39 G9
Hargeysa *Town* Somalia 39 H9
Ḥārim *Town* Syria 80 D6
Harlingen *Town* Texas, USA 17 M9
Harlow *Town* England, UK 51 H10
Harper *Town* Liberia 40 G8
Harrisburg *Town* Pennsylvania, USA 9 G7
Harrogate *Town* England, UK 50 G6
Hârşova *Town* Romania 68 G7
Hartford *Town* Connecticut, USA 9 J6
Hartlepool *Town* England, UK 50 G7
Hasselt *Town* Belgium 53 E11
Hastings *Town* New Zealand 106 H8
Hastings *Town* England, UK 50 H11
Hapeg *Town* Romania 68 E6
Hatteras, Cape *Coastal feature* North Carolina, USA 11 L3
Hat Yai *Town* Thailand 95 D13
Haugesund *Town* Norway 49 A10
Havana *Capital* Cuba 24 D3
Havant *Town* England, UK 51 G11
Havelock *Town* North Carolina, USA 11 L4
Hawaiian Ridge *Undersea feature* Pacific Ocean 109 J4
Hawera *Town* New Zealand 106 F8
Haysyn *Town* Ukraine 68 H4
Heard & McDonald Islands *Dependent territory* Australia, Indian Ocean 99 I8
Hearst *Town* Ontario, Canada 6 F6
Hebei *Administrative region* China 91 J3
Hebron *Town* Israel 81 D11
Heerlen *Town* Netherlands 53 F11
Ḥefa *see* Haifa
Hefei *Town* China 91 J5
Hegang *Town* China 89 M2
Heidelberg *Town* Germany 57 D9
Heidenheim an der Brenz *Town* Germany 57 E10
Heilbronn *Town* Germany 57 D9
Heilong Jiang *see* Amur
Heilongjiang *Administrative region* China 89 M2
Heimdal *Sweden* 48 D7
Hekimhan *Town* Turkey 76 H5
Helena *Town* Montana, USA 15 I3
Helmond *Town* Netherlands 53 F10
Helsingborg *Town* Sweden 49 C12
Helsinki *Capital* Finland 49 G9
Henan *Administrative region* China 91 I5
Henan *Town* Qinghai, China 89 I6
Hengduan Shan *Mountain range* China 90 E7
Hengelo *Town* Netherlands 52 G8
Hengyang *Town* China 91 I7
Henzada *Town* Myanmar 94 B8
Herāt *Town* Afghanisatan 84 G7
Herford *Town* Germany 56 D6
Hermosillo *Town* Mexico 18 E4
Hexian *Town* China 91 I8
Hidalgo del Parral *Town* Mexico 18 H5
Hida-sanmyaku *Mountain range* Japan 93 E10
High Point *Town* North Carolina, USA 11 J3
Hikurangi *Town* New Zealand 106 F4
Hildesheim *Town* Germany 56 D6
Hillsboro *Town* New Hampshire, USA 9 J5
Hilversum *Town* Netherlands 52 E8
Himalayas *Mountain range* Asia 87 I2
Himeji *Town* Japan 93 D12
Ḥimş *Town* Syria 80 E8
Hincești *Town* Moldova 68 H5
Hindu Kush *Mountain range* Afghanisatan/Pakistan 85 J6
Hirosaki *Town* Japan 92 F7
Hiroshima *Town* Japan 93 C12
Hitachi *Town* Japan 93 G9

Jordan *Country* 81 E11
Jordan *River* Jordan 81 D10
Jorhāt *Town* India 87 M3
Jos *Town* Nigeria 41 L6
Joseph Bonaparte Gulf Australia 104 H2
Jos Plateau *Upland* Nigeria 41 L7
Jotunheimen *Mountain range* Norway 48 B8
Joûnié *Town* Lebanon 81 D9
Joure *Town* Netherlands 52 F6
Juazeiro *Town* Brazil 29 M4
Juazeiro do Norte *Town* Brazil 29 M4
Juba *Town* Sudan 39 E10
Juchitán *Town* Mexico 19 M9
Judenburg *Town* Austria 57 G11
Juiz de Fora *Town* Brazil 29 L7
Juliaca *Town* Peru 27 D11
Junction City *Town* Kansas, USA 12 G7
Juneau *Town* Alaska, USA 4 F7
Junín *Town* Argentina 30 F8
Jura *Mountain range* Switzerland 57 C11
Jūrmala *Town* Latvia 70 E5
Juruá, Rio *River* Brazil 28 G3
Jutiapa *Town* Guatemala 22 E4
Juticalpa *Town* Honduras 22 H4
Jutland *Peninsula* Denmark 49 B12
Jwaneng *Town* Botswana 44 G6
Jylland *see* Jutland
Jyväskylä *Town* Finland 48 G8

K

K2 *Mountain* Pakistan/China 86 H1
Kabale *Town* Uganda 39 D11
Kabinda *Town* Democratic Republic of Congo 43 G11
Kabul *Capital* Afghanisatan 85 J7
Kabwe *Town* Zambia 44 H4
Kachchh, Rann of *Salt marsh* India 86 G4
Kadoma *Town* Zimbabwe 44 H4
Kaduna *Town* Nigeria 41 L6
Kadzhi-Say *Town* Kyrgyzstan 85 M3
Kaga *Town* Japan 93 E10
Kagoshima *Town* Japan 93 C14
Kahramanmaraş *Town* Turkey 76 H6
Kaifeng *Town* China 91 J4
Kaikoura *Town* New Zealand 107 F10
Kaili *Town* China 90 H7
Kairouan *Town* Tunisia 37 J3
Kaiserslautern *Town* Germany 57 C9
Kaiyuan *Town* China 90 F8
Kajaani *Town* Finland 48 H7
Kalahari Desert Namibia 44 F6
Kalamariá *Town* Greece 66 E8
Kalámata *Town* Greece 67 D12
Kalamazoo *Town* Michigan, USA 13 K5
Kalasin *Town* Thailand 95 F9
Kalāt *Town* Afghanistan 85 I8
Kālat *Town* Pakistan 86 F2
Kalbarri *Town* Western Australia, Australia 104 D5
Kalemie *Town* Democratic Republic of Congo 43 I11
Kalgoorlie *Town* Western Australia, Australia 104 F6
Kalima *Town* Democratic Republic of Congo 43 H10
Kalimantan *Region* Indonesia 96 G6
Kaliningrad *Administrative region* Russian Federation 70 B7
Kaliningrad *Town* Kaliningrad 70 B6
Kalisz *Town* Poland 62 E7
Kalmar *Town* Sweden 49 E12
Kaluga *Town* Russian Federation 73 C9
Kalyān *Town* India 86 G5
Kamarang *Town* Guyana 26 F6
Kamchatka Peninsula Russian Federation 79 M4
Kamensk-Shakhtinskiy *Town* Russian Federation 73 C11
Kamina *Town* Democratic Republic of Congo 43 G12
Kamloops *Town* British Colombia, Canada 4 G8

Kampala *Capital* Uganda 39 E11
Kâmpóng Cham *Town* Cambodia 95 G11
Kam"yanets'-Podil's'kyy *Town* Ukraine 68 G4
Kamyshin *Town* Russian Federation 73 D11
Kananga *Town* Democratic Republic of Congo 43 F11
Kanash *Town* Russian Federation 73 E9
Kanazawa *Town* Japan 93 E10
Kānchīpuram *Town* India 87 I7
Kandahār *Town* Afghanisatan 84 H8
Kandalaksha *Town* Russian Federation 72 D5
Kandi *Town* Benin 41 J6
Kandy *Town* Sri Lanka 87 I9
Kanggye *Town* North Korea 91 M2
Kanjiža *Town* Serbia & Montenegro 64 G6
Kankan *Town* Guinea 40 G6
Kano *Town* Nigeria 41 L6
Kanoya *Town* Japan 93 C14
Kānpur *Town* India 87 I3
Kansas *State* USA 12 F7
Kansas City *Town* Kansas, USA 12 H7
Kansas River Kansas, USA 12 G7
Kansk *Town* Russian Federation 79 I6
Kaohsiung *Town* Taiwan 91 K8
Kaolack *Town* Senegal 40 E5
Kaoma *Town* Zambia 44 G4
Kaposvár *Town* Hungary 63 E12
Kara-Balta *Town* Kyrgyzstan 85 L3
Karabük *Town* Turkey 76 F3
Karāchi *Town* Pakistan 86 F4
Karaganda *Town* Kazakhstan 78 G7
Karakol *Town* Kyrgyzstan 85 M3
Karakoram Range *Mountain range* Pakistan/India 86 H1
Kara Kum *Desert* Turkmenistan 84 F4
Kara Kum Canal Turkmenistan 84 H5
Karaman *Town* Turkey 76 F6
Karamay *Town* China 88 F4
Kara Sea *Arctic Ocean* 111 O6
Karatau *Town* Kazakhstan 78 F7
Karatsu *Town* Japan 93 B13
Karbalā' *Town* Iraq 82 C7
Kardítsa *Town* Greece 67 D10
Kärdla *Town* Estonia 70 F3
Kargi *Town* Turkey 76 G3
Karibib *Town* Namibia 44 E6
Karigasniemi *Town* Finland 48 G4
Karimata, Selat *Strait* Indonesia 96 F7
Karīmnagar *Town* India 87 I6
Karin *Town* Somalia 38 H8
Karlovac *Town* Croatia 64 C6
Karlovy Vary *Town* Czech Republic 62 B8
Karlskrona *Town* Sweden 49 D12
Karlsruhe *Town* Germany 57 C9
Karlstad *Town* Sweden 49 D10
Karnāl *Town* India 86 H3
Karnobat *Town* Bulgaria 66 H6
Kars *Town* Turkey 77 K4
Kárystos *Town* Greece 67 F11
Kaş *Town* Turkey 76 D7
Kasai *River* Democratic Republic of Congo 43 E11
Kāsargod *Town* India 86 H7
Kāshān *Town* Iran 82 E4
Kashi *Town* China 88 D5
Kashiwazaki *Town* Japan 93 F9
Kasongo *Town* Democratic Republic of Congo 43 H11
Kasongo-Lunda *Town* Democratic Republic of Congo 43 E11
Kaspiysk *Town* Russian Federation 73 D14
Kassala *Town* Sudan 38 F7
Kassel *Town* Germany 56 D7
Kasserine *Town* Tunisia 37 J4
Kastamonu *Town* Turkey 76 F3
Kasulu *Town* Tanzania 39 D12
Katahdin, Mount *Maine*, USA 9 L2
Katha *Town* Myanmar 94 C5
Katherine *Town* Northern Territory, Australia 105 I2
Kathmandu *Capital* Nepal 87 J3
Katikati *Town* New Zealand 106 G6
Katiola *Town* Côte d'Ivoire 40 H7
Katowice *Town* Poland 62 E8

Katsina *Town* Nigeria 41 L6
Kattaqŭrghon *Town* Uzbekistan 85 I4
Kattegat *Sea* Denmark/Sweden 49 C12
Kaunas *Town* Lithuania 70 D7
Kavála *Town* Greece 66 F8
Kāvali *Town* India 87 I7
Kavarna *Town* Bulgaria 66 I5
Kawagoe *Town* Japan 93 G10
Kawasaki *Town* Japan 93 G10
Kayan *Town* Myanmar 94 C8
Kayseri *Town* Turkey 76 G5
Kazach'ye *Town* Russian Federation 78 K4
Kazakhstan *Country* 78 F6
Kazakh Uplands Kazakhstan 78 F7
Kazan' *Town* Russian Federation 73 E9
Kazanlŭk *Town* Bulgaria 66 F6
Kāzerūn *Town* Iran 82 F8
Kecskemét *Town* Hungary 63 F11
Kediri *Town* Indonesia 96 G8
Kędzierzyn Koźle *Town* Poland 62 E8
Keith *Town* South Australia, Australia 105 J8
Kёk-Art *Town* Kyrgyzstan 85 L4
Kelowna *Town* British Colombia, Canada 4 G9
Kelso *Town* Washington, USA 14 F3
Keluang *Town* Malaysia 96 E5
Kemah *Town* Turkey 76 H5
Kemerovo *Town* Russian Federation 78 H6
Kemi *Town* Finland 48 G6
Kemijärvi *Town* Finland 48 G5
Kempten *Town* Germany 57 E10
Kendal *Town* England, UK 50 F8
Keng Tung *Town* Myanmar 94 D6
Kénitra *Town* Morocco 36 F4
Kenora *Town* Ontario, Canada 6 D5
Kenosha *Town* Wisconsin, USA 13 J5
Kentau *Town* Kazakhstan 78 F7
Kentucky *State* USA 10 G3
Kenya *Country* 39 F11
Kerch *Town* Ukraine 69 L7
Kerkrade *Town* Netherlands 53 F11
Kérkyra *see* Corfu
Kermadec Islands *Island group* New Zealand 109 J7
Kermān *Town* Iran 82 G7
Kesennuma *Town* Japan 92 G8
Kettering *Town* Ohio, USA 13 L7
Key Largo *Town* Florida, USA 11 J9
Key West *Town* Florida, USA 11 J9
Khabarovsk *Town* Russian Federation 78 D4
Khairpur *Town* Pakistan 86 G3
Khanthabouli *Town* Laos 95 F9
Khanty-Mansiysk *Town* Russian Federation 78 G5
Khān Yūnis *Town* Israel 81 C12
Kharagpur *Town* India 87 K4
Kharkiv *Town* Ukraine 69 L3
Khartoum *Capital* Sudan 38 E7
Khasavyurt *Town* Russian Federation 73 D14
Khaskovo *Town* Bulgaria 66 F7
Khaydarkan *Town* Kyrgyzstan 85 K4
Kherson *Town* Ukraine 69 J6
Khmel'nyts'kyy *Town* Ukraine 68 G3
Khon Kaen *Town* Thailand 95 E9
Khouribga *Town* Morocco 36 E4
Khowst *Town* Afghanistan 85 J7
Khŭjand *Town* Tajikistan 85 J4
Khulna *Town* Bangladesh 87 L4
Khust *Town* Ukraine 68 E4
Khvoy *Town* Iran 82 D5
Khyber Pass Afghanistan/Pakistan 86 G1
Kidderminster *Town* England, UK 51 F10
Kiel *Town* Germany 56 E4
Kielce *Town* Poland 62 F8
Kiev *Capital* Ukraine 69 I3
Kigali *Capital* Rwanda 39 D12
Kigoma *Town* Tanzania 39 D12
Kii-suidō *Bay* Japan 93 E12
Kikinda *Town* Serbia & Montenegro 64 G6
Kikwit *Town* Democratic Republic of Congo 43 E11
Kilis *Town* Turkey 76 H7
Killarney *Town* Ireland 51 B10
Killeen *Town* Texas, USA 17 L6
Kilmarnock *Town* Scotland, UK 50 E6

Kimberley *Town* South Africa 44 G7
Kimberley Plateau Western Australia, Australia 104 G3
Kimch'aek *Town* North Korea 91 M2
Kindia *Town* Guinea 40 F6
Kineshma *Town* Russian Federation 72 D8
Kingman Reef *Dependent territory* USA, Pacific Ocean 103 L3
Kingston *Capital* Jamaica 24 G6
Kingston *Town* Ontario, Canada 6 H8
Kingston upon Hull *Town* England, UK 50 H6
Kingstown *Capital* St Vincent & The Grenadines 25 O8
Kinshasa *Capital* Democratic Republic of Congo 43 D11
Kipushi *Town* Democratic Republic of Congo 43 H13
Kirghiz Range *Mountain range* Kyrgyzstan 85 K3
Kiribati *Country* 103 L5
Kirikhan *Town* Turkey 76 H7
Kirikkale *Town* Turkey 76 F4
Kirishi *Town* Russian Federation 72 C7
Kirkenes *Town* Norway 48 H3
Kirkland Lake *Town* Ontario, Canada 6 G6
Kirklareli *Town* Turkey 76 C3
Kirkūk *Town* Iraq 82 D6
Kirkwall *Town* Scotland, UK 50 F3
Kirov *Town* Russian Federation 72 F8
Kirovo-Chepetsk *Town* Russian Federation 72 F8
Kirovohrad *Town* Ukraine 69 J4
Kiruna *Town* Sweden 48 F5
Kisangani *Town* Democratic Republic of Congo 43 H9
Kislovodsk *Town* Russian Federation 73 C11
Kismaayo *Town* Somalia 39 G11
Kissidougou *Town* Guinea 40 G7
Kissimmee, Lake Florida, USA 11 J7
Kisumu *Town* Kenya 39 E11
Kitakyūshū *Town* Japan 93 B13
Kitami *Town* Japan 92 G4
Kitchener *Town* Ontario, Canada 6 G8
Kitwe *Town* Zambia 44 H3
Kivalo *Ridge* Finland 48 G6
Kivertsi *Town* Ukraine 68 G2
Kivu, Lake Democratic Republic of Congo 43 H10
Kladno *Town* Czech Republic 62 B8
Klagenfurt *Town* Austria 57 G11
Klaipėda *Town* Lithuania 70 C6
Klamath Falls *Town* Oregon, USA 14 F4
Klang *Town* Malaysia 96 D5
Klarälven *River* Sweden 49 D9
Klerksdorp *Town* South Africa 44 H7
Klintsy *Town* Russian Federation 73 B9
Ključ *Town* Bosnia & Herzegovina 64 D7
Klosters *Town* Switzerland 57 D11
Kluczbork *Town* Poland 62 E8
Knin *Town* Croatia 64 C8
Knoxville *Town* Tennessee, USA 11 I3
Kōbe *Town* Japan 93 E12
København *see* Copenhagen
Koblenz *Town* Germany 56 C8
Kočani *Town* Macedonia 65 H11
Kočevje *Town* Slovenia 57 H12
Kōchi *Town* Japan 93 D13
Kodiak *Town* Alaska, USA 4 D6
Kōfu *Town* Japan 93 F10
Kohīma *Town* India 87 M3
Kohtla-Järve *Town* Estonia 70 H4
Koko *Town* Nigeria 41 K6
Kokshetau *Town* Kazakhstan 78 F6
Kola Peninsula Russian Federation 72 E5
Kolari *Town* Finland 48 F5
Kolda *Town* Senegal 40 E5
Kolhāpur *Town* India 86 G6
Kolkatta *see* Calcutta
Köln *see* Cologne
Kołobrzeg *Town* Poland 62 C5
Kolomna *Town* Russian Federation 73 C9
Kolpino *Town* Russian Federation 72 C7
Kol'skiy Poluostrov *see* Kola Peninsula
Kolwezi *Town* Democratic Republic of Congo 43 G13
Komatsu *Town* Japan 93 E10
Kommunizm, Qullai *Mountain* Tajikistan 85 K4

Martinique Passage *Strait* Dominica 25 O7
Mary *Town* Turkmenistan 84 G5
Maryborough *Town* Queensland, Australia 105 N5
Maryland *State* USA 8 G8
Maryville *Town* Missouri, USA 12 H6
Masai Steppe *Grassland* Tanzania 39 F12
Masaka *Town* Uganda 39 E11
Masaya *Town* Nicaragua 22 H6
Mascarene Islands *Island group* Indian Ocean 45 O6
Maseru *Capital* Lesotho 44 H7
Mashhad *Town* Iran 82 G5
Masindi *Town* Uganda 39 E11
Masqaṭ *see* Muscat
Massa *Town* Italy 60 D6
Massachusetts *State* USA 9 J5
Massawa *Town* Eritrea 38 G7
Massif Central *Upland* France 55 E10
Masuda *Town* Japan 93 C12
Matadi *Town* Democratic Republic of Congo 43 D11
Matamoros *Town* Mexico 19 I5
Matamoros *Town* Mexico 19 K5
Matanzas *Town* Cuba 24 E3
Matara *Town* Sri Lanka 87 I9
Mataram *Town* Indonesia 96 H8
Mataró *Town* Spain 59 M4
Matā 'Utu *Capital* Wallis & Futuna 103 F6
Matera *Town* Italy 61 H10
Matosinhos *Town* Portugal 58 E4
Matsue *Town* Japan 93 C11
Matsumoto *Town* Japan 93 F10
Matsuyama *Town* Japan 93 D12
Matterhorn *Mountain* Switzerland/Italy 57 C12
Matthews Ridge *Town* Guyana 26 G5
Matthew Town *Town* Bahamas 24 H4
Maturín *Town* Venezuela 26 F5
Maun *Town* Botswana 44 G5
Mauritania *Country* 40 F4
Mauritius *Country* 45 O6
Mawson *Research station* Antarctica 110 G4
Mayagüez *Town* Puerto Rico 25 L5
Mayamey *Town* Iran 82 G5
Maya Mountains *Mountain range* Belize 22 F3
Maych'ew *Town* Ethiopia 38 F8
Maykop *Town* Russian Federation 73 B12
Maymyo *Town* Myanmar 94 C6
Mayotte *Dependent territory* France, Indian Ocean 45 L3
Mazabuka *Town* Zambia 44 H4
Mazār-e Sharīf *Town* Afghanisatan 85 I6
Mazatlán *Town* Mexico 18 G6
Mazury *Physical region* Poland 62 G5
Mazyr *Town* Belarus 71 F12
Mbabane *Capital* Swaziland 45 I7
Mbaké *Town* Senegal 40 E5
Mbale *Town* Uganda 39 E11
Mbandaka *Town* Democratic Republic of Congo 43 E10
Mbarara *Town* Uganda 39 D11
Mbeya *Town* Tanzania 39 E13
Mbuji-Mayi *Town* Democratic Republic of Congo 43 F11
McAlester *Town* Okahoma, USA 17 M4
McAllen *Town* Texas, USA 17 L9
McKinley, Mount *Mountain* Alaska, USA 4 E5
McMurdo Base *Research station* Antarctica 110 E7
Mdantsane *Town* South Africa 44 H8
Meadville *Town* Pennsylvania, USA 8 E6
Mecca *Town* Saudi Arabia 83 B10
Mechelen *Town* Belgium 53 D11
Medan *Town* Indonesia 96 D5
Medellín *Town* Colombia 26 B6
Médenine *Town* Tunisia 37 J4
Mediaş *Town* Romania 68 F6
Medicine Hat *Town* Alberta, Canada 5 I9
Medina *Town* Saudi Arabia 83 B9
Medinaceli *Town* Spain 59 J4
Mediterranean Sea *Africa/Asia/Europe* 67 D14
Meerut *Town* India 87 I3
Mehtarlām *Town* Afghanistan 85 J7
Meiktila *Town* Myanmar 94 B7
Mékhé *Town* Senegal 40 E5

Mekong *River* Asia 95 F11
Mekong, Mouths of the *Coastal feature* Vietnam 95 G12
Melaka *Town* Malaysia 96 E5
Melanesia *Region* Pacific Ocean 102 H7
Melbourne *Town* Victoria, Australia 105 K8
Melilla *Town* Spain 36 G3
Melilla *Town* Spain 36 G3
Melitopol' *Town* Ukraine 69 K6
Mellerud *Town* Sweden 49 C10
Melo *Town* Uruguay 30 H8
Melville Island *Northern Canada* 5 I3
Memmingen *Town* Germany 57 E10
Memphis *Town* Tennessee, USA 10 F4
Mende *Town* France 55 F10
Mendoza *Town* Argentina 30 D8
Menongue *Town* Angola 44 F4
Menorca *see* Minorca
Meppel *Town* Netherlands 52 F7
Merano *Town* Italy 60 E4
Mercer *Town* Pennsylvania, USA 8 E7
Mergui Archipelago *Island chain* Myanmar 95 C11
Mérida *Town* Venezuela 26 D5
Mérida *Town* Spain 58 G6
Mérida *Town* Mexico 19 O6
Mérignac *Town* France 55 C10
Mersin *Town* Turkey 76 G6
Meru *Town* Kenya 39 F11
Mesa *Town* Arizona, USA 16 E5
Messina *Town* Sicily, Italy 61 G12
Messina, Strait of *Italy* 61 G13
Mestia *Town* Georgia 77 K2
Mestre *Town* Italy 60 E5
Metairie *Town* Louisiana, USA 10 F6
Metan *Town* Argentina 30 E5
Metapán *Town* El Salvador 22 E4
Meta, Río *River* Colombia 26 D6
Metz *Town* France 54 H6
Meulaboh *Town* Indonesia 96 C5
Mexicali *Town* Mexico 18 D2
Mexico *Country* 19 I5
Mexico City *Capital* Mexico 19 K8
Mexico, Gulf of *Atlantic Ocean/Caribbean Sea* 32 G3
Miami *Town* Florida, USA 11 J9
Miami Beach *Town* Florida, USA 11 J8
Mīāneh *Town* Iran 82 D5
Mianyang *Town* China 90 H5
Michalovce *Town* Slovakia 63 G10
Michigan *State* USA 13 K4
Michigan, Lake *Central USA,* 13 K4
Michurinsk *Town* Russian Federation 73 D9
Micronesia *Country* 102 E2
Micronesia *Region* Pacific Ocean 102 F2
Mid-Atlantic Ridge *Undersea feature* Atlantic Ocean 33 I4
Middlesbrough *Town* England, UK 50 G8
Middletown *Town* New Jersey, USA 9 I7
Mid-Indian Basin *Undersea feature* Indian Ocean 99 K5
Midland *Town* Texas, USA 17 J6
Midland *Town* Ontario, Canada 6 G8
Mid-Pacific Mountains *Undersea feature* Pacific Ocean 109 I4
Midway Islands *Dependent territory* USA, Pacific Ocean 109 J3
Międzyrzec Podlaski *Town* Poland 62 G7
Mielec *Town* Poland 62 G8
Miercurea-Ciuc *Town* Romania 68 F6
Mieres de Camino *Town* Spain 58 G3
Miguel Asua *Town* Mexico 19 I6
Mikashevichy *Town* Belarus 71 E11
Mikhaylovka *Town* Russian Federation 73 D11
Milagro *Town* Ecuador 26 A8
Milan *Town* Italy 60 C5
Milano *see* Milan
Milas *Town* Turkey 76 C6
Miles City *Town* Montana, USA 15 K3
Milford *Town* Pennsylvania, USA 8 H6
Milford Haven *Town* Wales, UK 51 E11
Milford Sound *Town* New Zealand 107 B12
Milford Sound *Inlet* New Zealand 107 A12
Mil'kovo *Town* Russian Federation 78 N4

Millbridge *Town* Maine, USA 9 L3
Millennium Island *Island* Kiribati 103 N6
Milo *Town* Maine, USA 9 K3
Milton *Town* Pennsylvania, USA 8 G7
Milton Keynes *Town* England, UK 51 G10
Milwaukee *Town* Wisconsin, USA 13 J5
Minatitlán *Town* Mexico 19 M8
Minbu *Town* Myanmar 94 B7
Mindanao *Island* Philippines 97 J4
Minden *Town* Germany 56 D6
Mindoro Strait *South China Sea* 97 I3
Mineral Wells *Town* Texas, USA 17 L5
Mingäçevir *Town* Azerbaijan 77 M3
Mingãora *Town* Pakistan 86 G1
Minna *Town* Nigeria 41 K7
Minneapolis *Town* Minnesota, USA 12 H4
Minnesota *State* USA 12 H4
Minorca *Island* Balearic Islands, Spain 59 N5
Minot *Town* North Dakota, USA 12 F2
Minsk *Capital* Belarus 71 E9
Miraflores *Town* Mexico 18 F6
Miranda de Ebro *Town* Spain 59 I3
Miri *Town* Malaysia 96 H5
Mirim Lagoon *Brazil* 29 J9
Mirny *Research station* Antarctica 110 G6
Mirnyy *Town* Russian Federation 78 J5
Mīrpur Khās *Town* Pakistan 86 F3
Miskolc *Town* Hungary 63 F10
Miṣrātah *Town* Libya 37 K4
Mississippi *State* USA 10 F5
Mississippi River *Central USA,* 13 I5
Mississippi River Delta *Coastal feature* Louisiana, USA 10 F7
Missouri *State* USA 13 I7
Missouri River *Central USA,* 12 G6
Mistelbach an der Zaya *Town* Austria 57 H9
Mitchell *Town* South Dakota, USA 12 G5
Mitchell *Town* South Dakota, USA 12 G5
Mito *Town* Japan 93 G10
Mitú *Town* Colombia 26 D7
Mitumba Range *Mountain range* Democratic Republic of Congo 43 H12
Miyako *Town* Japan 92 G7
Miyakonojō *Town* Japan 93 C14
Miyazaki *Town* Japan 93 C14
Mizpé Ramon *Town* Israel 81 D12
Mladenovac *Town* Serbia & Montenegro 64 G8
Moab *Town* Utah, USA 15 J6
Mobile *Town* Alabama, USA 10 G6
Mocímboa da Praia *Town* Mozambique 45 K3
Modena *Town* Italy 60 D6
Modesto *Town* California, USA 14 F6
Modica *Town* Sicily, Italy 61 F14
Moe *Town* Victoria, Australia 105 K8
Mogadishu *Capital* Somalia 39 H11
Mogilno *Town* Poland 62 E6
Mohammedia *Town* Morocco 36 E4
Mohawk River *New York, USA* 8 H5
Mohe *Town* China 89 L1
Mohyliv-Podil's'kyy *Town* Ukraine 68 H4
Mo i Rana *Town* Norway 48 D6
Mojave Desert *California, USA* 14 H8
Mokp'o *Town* South Korea 91 M4
Molde *Town* Norway 48 B8
Moldova *Country* 68 H5
Molfetta *Town* Italy 61 H10
Mölndal *Town* Sweden 49 C11
Molodezhnaya *Research station* Antarctica 110 F4
Moluccas *Island group* Indonesia 97 L7
Molucca Sea *Pacific Ocean* 97 K6
Mombasa *Town* Kenya 39 G12
Monaco *Country* 55 H11
Monaco *Capital* Monaco 55 H11
Monahans *Town* Texas, USA 17 J6
Mona, Isla *Island* Puerto Rico 25 K5
Mona Passage *Strait* Dominican Republic 25 K5
Moncalieri *Town* Italy 60 B5
Monchegorsk *Town* Russian Federation 72 D4
Monclova *Town* Mexico 19 I4
Moncton *Town* New Brunswick, Canada 7 K7
Mondovi *Town* Italy 60 B6
Monfalcone *Town* Italy 60 F5
Mongolia *Country* 88 H3
Monroe *Town* Louisiana, USA 10 E5

Monrovia *Capital* Liberia 40 F8
Mons *Town* Belgium 53 D12
Monselice *Town* Italy 60 E5
Montagua, Río *River* Guatemala 22 E4
Montana *State* USA 15 J2
Montana *Town* Bulgaria 66 E5
Montauban *Town* France 55 D11
Mont Blanc *Mountain* France 55 H9
Mont-de-Marsan *Town* France 55 C11
Monteagudo *Town* Bolivia 27 E13
Monte Alban *Ancient site* Mexico 19 L9
Monte Caseros *Town* Argentina 30 G7
Monte Cristi *Town* Dominican Republic 25 I5
Montego Bay *Town* Jamaica 24 F5
Montélimar *Town* France 55 F10
Montemorelos *Town* Mexico 19 J5
Montenegro *Administrative region* Serbia & Montenegro 65 F10
Monterey *Town* California, USA 14 F7
Montería *Town* Colombia 26 B5
Montero *Town* Bolivia 27 F12
Monterrey *Town* Mexico 19 J5
Montes Claros *Town* Brazil 29 L6
Montevideo *Capital* Uruguay 30 H8
Montgomery *Town* Alabama, USA 10 G5
Montluçon *Town* France 55 E9
Montpellier *Town* France 55 F11
Montréal *Town* Quebec, Canada 7 I7
Montserrat *Dependent territory* UK, Atlantic Ocean 25 N6
Monywa *Town* Myanmar 94 B6
Monza *Town* Italy 60 C5
Moorhead *Town* Minnesota, USA 12 G3
Mopti *Town* Mali 40 H5
Moravia *Region* Czech Republic 63 D9
Moree *Town* New South Wales, Australia 105 M6
Morelia *Town* Mexico 19 J8
Morena, Sierra *Mountain range* Spain 58 G7
Morioka *Town* Japan 92 G7
Morocco *Country* 36 E5
Morogoro *Town* Tanzania 39 F13
Morón *Town* Cuba 24 F3
Mörön *Town* Mongolia 88 H3
Morondava *Town* Madagascar 45 L5
Moroni *Capital* Comoros 45 L3
Moscow *Capital* Russian Federation 72 C8
Moshi *Town* Tanzania 39 F12
Moskva *see* Moscow
Mosquito Coast *Coastal feature* Nicaragua 23 J5
Mosselbaai *Town* South Africa 44 G8
Mossendjo *Town* Congo 43 D10
Mossoró *Town* Brazil 29 M3
Most *Town* Czech Republic 62 B8
Mostaganem *Town* Algeria 36 G3
Mostar *Town* Bosnia & Herzegovina 65 D9
Mosul *see* Al Mawṣil
Motueka *Town* New Zealand 107 E9
Mould Bay *Town* Northwest Territories, Canada 4 H3
Moulins *Town* France 54 F8
Moulmein *Town* Myanmar 95 C9
Moundou *Town* Chad 42 E7
Mount Cook *Town* New Zealand 107 C11
Mount Isa *Town* Queensland, Australia 105 J4
Mount Magnet *Town* Western Australia, Australia 104 E6
Mouscron *Town* Belgium 53 C11
Mozambique *Country* 45 J4
Mozambique Channel *Indian Ocean* 45 K5
Mpika *Town* Zambia 45 I3
Muang Không *Town* Laos 95 G10
Muang Namo *Town* Laos 94 E7
Muang Phalan *Town* Laos 95 G9
Muar *Town* Malaysia 96 E5
Mudanjiang *Town* China 89 N3
Mufulira *Town* Zambia 44 H3
Mugi *Town* Japan 93 E12
Mukacheve *Town* Ukraine 68 E4
Mulhouse *Town* France 54 H8
Mull, Isle of *Island* Scotland, UK 50 D6
Mulongo *Town* Democratic Republic of Congo 43 H12
Multān *Town* Pakistan 86 G2
Mumbai *Town* India 86 G6

Münchberg *Town* Germany 56 F8
München *see* Munich
Muncie *Town* Indiana, USA 13 K6
Munich *Town* Germany 57 F10
Munster *Cultural region* Ireland 51 B10
Münster *Town* Germany 56 C6
Muonioälv *River* Sweden 48 F4
Muqāv *Town* Jordan 81 G10
Muqdisho *see* Mogadishu
Murcia *Town* Spain 59 K7
Murmansk *Town* Russian Federation 72 E4
Murom *Town* Russian Federation 73 D9
Muroran *Town* Japan 92 F6
Murray River *New South Wales/Victoria/South Australia*, Australia 105 K8
Murska Sobota *Town* Slovenia 57 H11
Murwāra *Town* India 87 I4
Murzuq, Idhán *Desert* Libya 37 K7
Muş *Town* Turkey 77 J5
Muscat *Capital* Oman 83 H9
Musgrave Ranges *Mountain range* South Australia, Australia 104 H5
Musoma *Town* Tanzania 39 E11
Mutare *Town* Zimbabwe 45 I5
Mutsu *Town* Japan 92 G6
Muttonbird Islands *Island group* New Zealand 107 B14
Mŭynoq *Town* Uzbekistan 84 F2
Mwanza *Town* Tanzania 39 E12
Mwene-Ditu *Town* Democratic Republic of Congo 43 F12
Mweru, Lake *Democratic Republic of Congo* 43 H12
Myanmar *Country* 94 B5
Myanaung *Town* Myanmar 94 B8
Myaungmya *Town* Myanmar 95 B9
Myingyan *Town* Myanmar 94 B6
Myitkyina *Town* Myanmar 94 C5
Mykolayiv *Town* Ukraine 69 J5
Myrhorod *Town* Ukraine 69 K3
Mýrina *Town* Greece 67 F9
Myrtle Beach *Town* South Carolina, USA 11 K4
Mysore *Town* India 86 H8
My Tho *Town* Vietnam 95 G11
Mzuzu *Town* Malawi 45 J3

N

Naberezhnyye Chelny *Town* Russian Federation 73 F9
Nablus *Town* Israel 81 D11
Nacala *Town* Mozambique 45 K4
Nadi *Town* Fiji 103 I7
Nadvirna *Town* Ukraine 68 F4
Nadym *Town* Russian Federation 78 G5
Naga *Town* Philippines 97 J2
Nagano *Town* Japan 93 F10
Nagaoka *Town* Japan 93 F9
Nagasaki *Town* Japan 93 B14
Nagato *Town* Japan 93 C12
Nāgercoil *Town* India 86 H9
Nagornyy Karabakh *Region* Azerbaijan 77 M4
Nagoya *Town* Japan 93 F11
Nāgpur *Town* India 87 I5
Nagqu *Town* China 88 G7
Nagykanizsa *Town* Hungary 63 D12
Nagykőrös *Town* Hungary 63 F11
Naha *Town* Ryukyu Islands 93 A16
Nā'īn *Town* Iran 82 F7
Nain *Town* Newfoundland & Labrador, Canada 7 K3
Nairobi *Capital* Kenya 39 F11
Najin *Town* North Korea 91 M2
Najrān *Town* Saudi Arabia 83 C12
Nakagawa *Town* Japan 92 F4
Nakamura *Town* Japan 93 D13
Nakatsugawa *Town* Japan 93 F11
Nakhodka *Town* Russian Federation 79 M7
Nakhon Ratchasima *Town* Thailand 95 E9
Nakhon Sawan *Town* Thailand 95 D9
Nakhon Si Thammarat *Town* Thailand 95 D12
Nakuru *Town* Kenya 39 F11

Nal'chik *Town* Russian Federation 73 C13
Nālūt *Town* Libya 37 J5
Namangan *Town* Uzbekistan 85 K3
Nam Đinh *Town* Vietnam 94 G7
Namib Desert *Namibia* 44 E5
Namibe *Town* Angola 44 D4
Namibia *Country* 44 E5
Nampa *Town* Idaho, USA 14 H4
Nampula *Town* Mozambique 45 K4
Namur *Town* Belgium 53 E12
Nanaimo *Town* British Colombia, Canada 4 G9
Nancha *Town* China 89 M2
Nanchang *Town* China 91 J6
Nanchong *Town* China 90 H6
Nancy *Town* France 54 H7
Nānded *Town* India 86 H6
Nanfeng *Town* China 91 J7
Nanjing *Town* China 91 K5
Nanning *Town* China 90 H8
Nanping *Town* China 91 K7
Nanterre *Town* France 54 E6
Nantes *Town* France 54 C8
Nantucket *Town* Massachusetts, USA 9 K6
Nantucket Island *Massachusetts*, USA 9 K6
Nanyang *Town* China 91 I5
Napa *Town* California, USA 14 F6
Napier *Town* New Zealand 106 H7
Naples *Town* Italy 61 F10
Napoli *see* Naples
Napo, Rio *River* Peru 26 C8
Narathiwat *Town* Thailand 95 E13
Narita *Town* Japan 93 G10
Närpes *Town* Finland 48 F8
Närpiö *see* Närpes
Narva *Town* Estonia 70 H4
Narvik *Town* Norway 48 E4
Năsăud *Town* Romania 68 F5
Nāshik *Town* India 86 G5
Nashua *Town* New Hampshire, USA 9 J5
Nashville *Town* Tennessee, USA 10 G3
Nassau *Capital* Bahamas 24 G2
Nasser *Lake* Egypt 38 E6
Nata *Town* Botswana 44 H5
Natal *Town* Brazil 29 N3
Natitingou *Town* Benin 41 J6
Nauru *Country* 102 H4
Nauta *Town* Peru 27 C9
Navapolatsk *Town* Belarus 70 G8
Navassa Island *Dependent territory* USA, Atlantic Ocean 24 H5
Navojoa *Town* Mexico 18 F5
Nawābshāh *Town* Pakistan 86 F3
Nawoiy *Town* Uzbekistan 85 I4
Nayoro *Town* Japan 92 F4
Nazareth *Town* Israel 81 D10
Nazca *Town* Peru 27 C11
Nazerat *see* Nazareth
Nazilli *Town* Turkey 76 D6
Nazrēt *Town* Ethiopia 39 G9
N'Dalatando *Town* Angola 44 E2
Ndélé *Town* Central African Republic 42 F7
Ndjamena *Capital* Chad 42 D6
Ndola *Town* Zambia 44 H3
Neagh, Lough *Lake* Northern Ireland, UK 50 D8
Neápoli *Town* Greece 67 G14
Neápoli *Town* Greece 67 C9
Near Islands *Island Group* Alaska, USA 4 A3
Nebitdag *Town* Turkmenistan 84 D4
Nebraska *State* USA 12 F5
Necochea *Town* Argentina 31 G10
Neftekamsk *Town* Russian Federation 73 F9
Negēlē *Town* Ethiopia 39 G10
Negev *Desert* Israel 81 D12
Negombo *Town* Sri Lanka 87 I9
Negotin *Town* Serbia & Montenegro 64 H8
Negro, Rio *River* Brazil 28 G2
Neijiang *Town* China 90 G6
Nei Mongol Zizhiqu *see* Inner Mongolia
Neiva *Town* Colombia 26 B7
Nellore *Town* India 87 I7
Nelson *Town* New Zealand 107 E9
Nemuro *Town* Japan 92 H4
Nepal *Country* 87 J3
Neringa *Town* Lithuania 70 C6

Neryungri *Town* Russian Federation 79 K6
Netanya *Town* Israel 81 D11
Netherlands *Country* 52 E7
Netherlands Antilles *Dependent territory* Netherlands, Atlantic Ocean 25 K8
Neubrandenburg *Town* Germany 56 F5
Neuchâtel *Town* Switzerland 57 C11
Neufchâteau *Town* Belgium 53 F13
Neumünster *Town* Germany 56 D4
Neunkirchen *Town* Germany 57 C9
Neuquén *Town* Argentina 31 D10
Neustadt an der Weinstrasse *Town* Germany 57 C9
Neu-Ulm *Town* Germany 57 E10
Neuwied *Town* Germany 56 C8
Nevada *State* USA 14 H6
Nevinnomyssk *Town* Russian Federation 73 C11
Nevşehir *Town* Turkey 76 G5
New Amsterdam *Town* Guyana 26 G6
Newark *Town* New Jersey, USA 9 I7
Newark *Town* New York, USA 8 G5
New Bedford *Town* Massachusetts, USA 9 K6
Newberg *Town* Oregon, USA 14 F3
New Britain *Island* Papua New Guinea 102 F5
New Caledonia *Island* New Caledonia 102 G8
New Caledonia *Dependent territory* France, Pacific Ocean 102 G7
Newcastle *Town* New South Wales, Australia 105 M7
Newcastle upon Tyne *Town* England, UK 50 F7
New Delhi *Capital* India 86 H3
Newfoundland *Island* Ontario, Canada 7 M5
Newfoundland Basin *Undersea feature* Atlantic Ocean 33 J2
New Glasgow *Town* Nova Scotia, Canada 7 L7
New Guinea *Island* Indonesia/Papua New Guinea 102 F5
New Hampshire *State* USA 9 J4
New Haven *Town* Connecticut, USA 8 I6
New Iberia *Town* Louisiana, USA 10 E6
New Jersey *State* USA 9 I7
Newman *Town* Western Australia, Australia 104 E4
New Mexico *State* USA 17 I4
New Orleans *Town* Louisiana, USA 10 F6
New Plymouth *Town* New Zealand 106 F7
Newport *Town* Vermont, USA 9 I3
Newport *Town* Wales, UK 51 F11
Newport News *Town* Virginia, USA 11 L3
New Providence *Island* Bahamas 24 G2
Newquay *Town* England, UK 51 E12
Newry *Town* Northern Ireland, UK 50 D8
New Siberian Islands *Island group* Russian Federation 79 K3
New South Wales *State* Australia 105 L7
Newtownabbey *Town* Northern Ireland, UK 50 D7
New York *State* USA 8 G5
New York *Town* New York, USA 9 I7
New Zealand *Country* 107 E9
Ngaoundéré *Town* Cameroon 42 D7
Ngo *Town* Congo 43 D10
Nguigmi *Town* Niger 41 M5
Nha Trang *Town* Vietnam 95 H10
Niagara Falls *Town* Ontario, Canada 6 G8
Niagara Falls *Town* New York, USA 8 E5
Niagara Falls *Waterfall* Canada/USA 8 E6
Niamey *Capital* Niger 41 J5
Nia-Nia *Town* Democratic Republic of Congo 43 H9
Nicaragua *Country* 22 H5
Nicaragua, Lago de *Lake* Nicaragua 23 I6
Nice *Town* France 55 H11
Nicholls Town *Town* Bahamas 24 F2
Nicobar Islands *Island group* India 87 M8
Nicosia *Capital* Cyprus 80 B8
Nicoya *Town* Costa Rica 22 H7
Nicoya, Golfo de *Gulf* Costa Rica 23 I7
Nieuw-Bergen *Town* Netherlands 53 F9
Niğde *Town* Turkey 76 G6
Niger *Country* 41 K5
Niger *River* Niger/Nigeria 41 J6
Nigeria *Country* 41 M7

Niger, Mouths of the *Coastal feature* Nigeria 41 K8
Niigata *Town* Japan 93 F9
Niihama *Town* Japan 93 D12
Niitsu *Town* Japan 93 F9
Nijmegen *Town* Netherlands 53 F9
Nikiniki *Town* Indonesia 97 J8
Nikopol' *Town* Ukraine 69 K5
Nikšić *Town* Serbia & Montenegro 65 E10
Nile *River* East Africa 38 E5
Nile Delta *Egypt* 38 E4
Nîmes *Town* France 55 F11
Ninetyeast Ridge *Undersea feature* Indian Ocean 99 K4
Ninety Mile Beach *Coastal feature* New Zealand 106 E3
Ningbo *Town* China 91 L6
Ningxia *Administrative region* China 89 J6
Niort *Town* France 54 D8
Nipigon, Lake *Quebec, Canada* 6 E6
Niš *Town* Serbia & Montenegro 65 H9
Nişab *Town* Saudi Arabia 82 D8
Nitra *Town* Slovakia 63 E10
Niue *Dependent territory* New Zealand, Pacific Ocean 103 K7
Nizāmābād *Town* India 87 I6
Nizhnekamsk *Town* Russian Federation 73 F9
Nizhnevartovsk *Town* Russian Federation 78 G5
Nizhniy Novgorod *Town* Russian Federation 73 E9
Nizhniy Odes *Town* Russian Federation 72 G7
Nizhyn *Town* Ukraine 69 J2
Nkayi *Town* Congo 43 D11
Nkongsamba *Town* Cameroon 42 C8
Nobeoka *Town* Japan 93 C14
Noboribetsu *Town* Japan 92 F6
Nogales *Town* Arizona, USA 16 F6
Nogales *Town* Mexico 18 E3
Nogales *Town* Arizona, USA 16 F6
Nogales *Town* Mexico 18 E3
Nokia *Town* Finland 48 G8
Nokou *Town* Chad 42 D5
Nong Khai *Town* Thailand 94 E8
Noordwijk aan Zee *Town* Netherlands 52 D8
Norak *Town* Tajikistan 85 J5
Norderstedt *Town* Germany 56 E5
Nordhorn *Town* Germany 56 C6
Nordkapp *see* North Cape
Norfolk *Town* Nebraska, USA 12 G5
Norfolk *Town* Virginia, USA 11 L3
Norfolk Island *Dependent territory* Australia, Pacific Ocean 109 I7
Noril'sk *Town* Russian Federation 78 H4
Norman *Town* Oklahoma, USA 17 L4
Normandy *Region* France 54 D6
Norrköping *Town* Sweden 49 E10
Norrtälje *Town* Sweden 49 E10
North Albanian Alps *Mountain range* Serbia & Montenegro 65 F10
Northampton *Town* England, UK 51 G10
North Bay *Town* Ontario, Canada 6 G7
North Cape *Coastal feature* New Zealand 106 E3
North Cape *Coastal feature* Norway 48 G2
North Carolina *State* USA 11 K4
North Charleston *Town* South Carolina, USA 11 J5
North Dakota *State* USA 12 F3
Northern Cook Islands *Island group* Cook Islands 103 M6
Northern Dvina *River* Russian Federation 72 E7
Northern Ireland *Political region* UK 50 D7
Northern Mariana Islands *Dependent territory* USA, Pacific Ocean 102 D1
Northern Sporades *Island group* Greece 67 E10
Northern Territory *State* Australia 104 H4
North Island *New Zealand* 106 G7
North Korea *Country* 91 M3
North Little Rock *Town* Arkansas, USA 10 E4
North Sea *Europe* 50 G4
North West Highlands *Mountain range* Scotland, UK 50 E4
Northwest Pacific Basin *Undersea feature* Pacific Ocean 109 I3
Northwest Territories *Province* Canada 4 H6
Norway *Country* 48 B8

PATNA – QUARTU SANT' ELENA

Patna *Town* India 87 J4
Patnos *Town* Turkey 77 K5
Pátra *Town* Greece 67 C11
Pau *Town* France 55 C11
Paulatuk *Town* Northwest Territories, Canada 4 H5
Pavia *Town* Italy 60 C5
Pāvilosta *Town* Latvia 70 D5
Pavlodar *Town* Kazakhstan 78 G7
Pavlohrad *Town* Ukraine 69 L4
Pawtucket *Town* Rhode Island, USA 8 J6
Paysandú *Town* Uruguay 30 H7
Pazar *Town* Turkey 77 J3
Pazardzhik *Town* Bulgaria 66 F7
Pearl River Mississippi, USA 10 F5
Peć *Town* Serbia & Montenegro 65 F10
Pechora *River* Russian Federation 72 G6
Pechora *Town* Russian Federation 72 G6
Pécs *Town* Hungary 63 E12
Pedro Juan Caballero *Town* Paraguay 30 H4
Pegu *Town* Myanmar 94 B8
Peiraías *see* Piraeus
Pekalongan *Town* Indonesia 96 G7
Pekanbaru *Town* Indonesia 96 D6
Peking *see* Beijing
Peloponnese *Peninsula* Greece 67 D12
Pelopónnisos *see* Peloponnese
Pematangsiantar *Town* Indonesia 96 D5
Pemba *Town* Mozambique 45 K3
Pennines *Hills* England, UK 50 F8
Pennsylvania *State* USA 8 F7
Penonomé *Town* Panama 23 L8
Penrith *Town* England,UK 50 F7
Pensacola *Town* Florida, USA 10 G6
Penza *Town* Russian Federation 73 D10
Penzance *Town* England, UK 51 D12
Peoria *Town* Illinois, USA 13 J6
Perchtoldsdorf *Town* Austria 57 H10
Pereira *Town* Colombia 26 B6
Pergamino *Town* Argentina 30 F8
Perm' *Town* Russian Federation 73 G9
Pernik *Town* Bulgaria 66 D6
Perote *Town* Mexico 19 K7
Perpignan *Town* France 55 E12
Persian Gulf *see* Gulf, The
Perth *Town* Western Australia, Australia 104 E7
Perth *Town* Scotland,UK 50 F6
Peru *Country* 27 C10
Perugia *Town* Italy 60 E8
Pervomays'k *Town* Ukraine 69 I5
Pesaro *Town* Italy 60 F7
Pescara *Town* Italy 60 F8
Peshāwar *Town* Pakistan 86 G1
Pessac *Town* France 55 C10
Petah Tiqwa *Town* Israel 81 D11
Peterborough *Town* South Australia, Australia 105 J7
Peterborough *Town* Ontario, Canada 6 H8
Peterborough *Town* England, UK 51 H10
Peterborough *Town* South Australia, Australia 105 J7
Peterhead *Town* Scotland, UK 50 F5
Peter I Island *Dependent Territory* Norway, Southern Ocean 110 B6
Petersburg *Town* Virginia, USA 11 K2
Peters Mine *Town* Guyana 26 G6
Petra *Town* Jordan 81 E13
Petrinja *Town* Croatia 64 C6
Petrodvorets *Town* Russian Federation 72 C6
Petropavlovsk *Town* Kazakhstan 78 G6
Petropavlovsk-Kamchatskiy *Town* Russian Federation 79 M5
Petrozavodsk *Town* Russian Federation 72 D6
Pevek *Town* Russian Federation 78 L2
Pforzheim *Town* Germany 57 D9
Phan Thiêt *Town* Vietnam 95 H11
Phetchaburi *Town* Thailand 95 D10
Philadelphia *Town* Pennsylvania, USA 8 H7
Philippines *Country* 97 J2
Phitsanulok *Town* Thailand 94 D8
Phnom Penh *Capital* Cambodia 95 F11
Phoenix *Town* Arizona, USA 16 E5
Phoenix Islands *Island group* Kiribati 103 J5
Phuket *Town* Thailand 95 C13
Phuket, Ko *Island* Thailand 95 C12
Piacenza *Town* Italy 60 D5
Piatra-Neamp *Town* Romania 68 G5
Picos *Town* Brazil 29 L3
Picton *Town* New Zealand 107 F9
Piedras Negras *Town* Mexico 19 J4
Pielinen *Lake* Finland 48 H7
Pierre *Town* South Dakota, USA 12 F4
Pietermaritzburg *Town* South Africa 45 I7
Pietersburg *see* Polokwane
Pikeville *Town* Kentucky, USA 11 I2
Piła *Town* Poland 62 D6
Pinar del Río *Town* Cuba 24 D3
Píndos *see* Pindus Mountains
Pindus Mountains *Mountain range* Greece 67 C10
Pine Bluff *Town* Arkansas, USA 10 E4
Pingdingshan *Town* China 91 I5
Pinsk *Town* Belarus 71 D11
Piotrków Trybunalski *Town* Poland 62 F7
Piraeus *Town* Greece 67 E11
Pirot *Town* Serbia & Montenegro 65 H10
Pisa *Town* Italy 60 D7
Pisco *Town* Peru 27 B11
Pisek *Town* Czech Republic 63 B9
Pistoia *Town* Italy 60 D6
Pitcairn Islands *Dependent Territory* UK, Pacific Ocean 109 L6
Pitești *Town* Romania 68 F7
Pittsburgh *Town* Pennsylvania, USA 8 E7
Pittsfield *Town* Massachusetts, USA 8 J5
Piura *Town* Peru 27 A9
Placetas *Town* Cuba 24 E3
Plano *Town* Texas, USA 17 M5
Plata, Río de la *River* Argentina 31 H9
Platinum *Town* Alaska, USA 4 D5
Platte River Nebraska, USA 12 G6
Plattsburgh *Town* New York, USA 9 I3
Plauen *Town* Germany 56 F8
Plenty, Bay of New Zealand 106 H6
Plesetsk *Town* Russian Federation 72 E7
Pleven *Town* Bulgaria 66 F5
Płock *Town* Poland 62 F6
Ploiești *Town* Romania 68 F7
Plovdiv *Town* Bulgaria 66 F7
Plungė *Town* Lithuania 70 C6
Plymouth *Capital* Montserrat 25 N6
Plymouth *Town* England, UK 51 E12
Plzeň *Town* Czech Republic 63 B9
Po *River* Italy 60 E6
Pobedy, Pik *Mountain* China 88 E4
Pocahontas *Town* Arkansas, USA 10 F3
Podgorica *Town* Serbia & Montenegro 65 E10
Podil's'ka Vysochyna *Mountain range* Ukraine 68 H4
Podol'sk *Town* Russian Federation 72 C8
Pointe-à-Pitre *Town* Guadeloupe 25 O6
Pointe-Noire *Town* Congo 43 C11
Poitiers *Town* France 54 D8
Pokhara *Town* Nepal 87 J3
Poland *Country* 62 E7
Polatli *Town* Turkey 76 F5
Polatsk *Town* Belarus 70 G8
Pólis *Town* Cyprus 80 A8
Polokwane *Town* South Africa 45 H7
Poltava *Town* Ukraine 69 K3
Polýkastro *Town* Greece 66 D8
Polynesia *Region* Pacific Ocean 103 N6
Pomeranian Bay Poland 62 C5
Pompano Beach *Town* Florida, USA 11 J8
Ponce *Town* Puerto Rico 25 L5
Pondicherry *Town* India 87 I8
Ponferrada *Town* Spain 58 G3
Ponta Grossa *Town* Brazil 29 J7
Pontevedra *Town* Spain 58 E3
Pontiac *Town* Michigan, USA 13 L5
Pontianak *Town* Indonesia 96 F6
Poole *Town* England, UK 51 G12
Popayán *Town* Colombia 26 B7
Popocatépetl *Mountain* Mexico 19 K8
Porbandar *Town* India 86 F5
Pordenone *Town* Italy 60 F5
Poreč *Town* Croatia 64 A6
Pori *Town* Finland 49 F9
Porirua *Town* New Zealand 107 F9
Póros *Town* Greece 67 E12
Port Alfred *Town* South Africa 44 H8
Port Arthur *Town* Texas, USA 17 N7
Port Augusta *Town* South Australia, Australia 105 J7
Port-au-Prince *Capital* Haiti 25 J5
Port Blair *Town* India 87 M7
Port Elizabeth *Town* South Africa 44 H8
Port-Gentil *Town* Gabon 43 B10
Port Harcourt *Town* Nigeria 41 L8
Portland *Town* Oregon, USA 14 F3
Portland *Town* Maine, USA 8 K4
Portland *Town* Victoria, Australia 105 J8
Port Laoise *Town* Ireland 51 C9
Port Louis *Capital* Mauritius 45 O6
Port Macquarie *Town* New South Wales, Australia 105 N7
Port Moresby *Capital* Papua New Guinea 102 E6
Porto *see* Oporto
Porto Alegre *Town* Brazil 29 J9
Portobelo *Town* Panama 23 M7
Port-of-Spain *Capital* Trinidad & Tobago 25 O9
Porto-Novo *Capital* Benin 41 J7
Porto Torres *Town* Sardinia, Italy 61 B9
Porto Velho *Town* Brazil 28 G4
Portoviejo *Town* Ecuador 26 A8
Port Said *Town* Egypt 38 E4
Portsmouth *Town* England, UK 51 G12
Portsmouth *Town* New Hampshire, USA 9 K5
Portsmouth *Town* Virginia, USA 11 L3
Port Sudan *Town* Sudan 38 F6
Portugal *Country* 58 F5
Port-Vila *Capital* Vanuatu 102 H7
Porvoo *Town* Finland 49 G9
Posadas *Town* Argentina 30 H6
Poso *Town* Indonesia 97 J6
Potenza *Town* Italy 61 G10
P'ot'i *Town* Georgia 77 J3
Potiskum *Town* Nigeria 41 M6
Potomac River Virginia, USA 11 K2
Potosí *Town* Bolivia 27 E13
Potsdam *Town* Germany 56 F6
Po Valley Italy 60 D5
Poza Rica *Town* Mexico 19 K7
Požega *Town* Serbia & Montenegro 65 F9
Poznań *Town* Poland 62 D6
Pozzallo *Town* Sicily, Italy 61 F14
Prague *Capital* Czech Republic 62 B8
Praha *see* Prague
Praia *Capital* Cape Verde 33 K4
Prato *Town* Italy 60 D7
Prenzlau *Town* Germany 56 G5
Přerov *Town* Czech Republic 63 D9
Presidente Epitácio *Town* Brazil 29 J7
Prešov *Town* Slovakia 63 G9
Prespa, Lake Macedonia 65 G12
Presque Isle *Town* Maine, USA 9 L1
Preston *Town* England, UK 50 F8
Prestwick *Town* Scotland, UK 50 E7
Pretoria *Capital* South Africa 44 H6
Préveza *Town* Greece 67 C10
Price *Town* Utah, USA 15 J6
Prichard *Town* Alabama, USA 10 G6
Prienai *Town* Lithuania 70 D8
Prieska *Town* South Africa 44 G7
Prilep *Town* Macedonia 65 G12
Primorsk *Town* Kaliningrad 70 B6
Primorsko *Town* Bulgaria 66 H7
Prince Edward Islands *Island group* South Africa 98 H7
Prince George *Town* British Colombia, Canada 4 G8
Prinzapolka *Town* Nicaragua 23 J5
Pripet *River* Belarus 71 E11
Pripet Marshes *Wetland* Belarus/Ukraine 71 D11
Priština *Town* Serbia & Montenegro 65 G10
Prizren *Town* Serbia & Montenegro 65 G10
Probolinggo *Town* Indonesia 96 H8
Progreso *Town* Mexico 19 O6
Prokhladnyy *Town* Russian Federation 73 C13
Prokuplje *Town* Serbia & Montenegro 65 G9
Prome *Town* Myanmar 94 B8
Prostějov *Town* Czech Republic 63 D9
Providence *Town* Rhode Island, USA 8 J6
Provincetown *Town* Massachusetts, USA 9 K5
Provo *Town* Utah, USA 15 J5
Prudhoe Bay *Town* Alaska, USA 4 F4
Pruszków *Town* Poland 62 F7
Pryluky *Town* Ukraine 69 J3
Przemyśl *Town* Poland 63 G9
Pskov *Town* Russian Federation 72 B7
Pucallpa *Town* Peru 27 C10
Pudasjärvi *Town* Finland 48 G6
Puebla *Town* Mexico 19 K8
Pueblo *Town* Colorado, USA 15 L6
Puerto Angel *Town* Mexico 19 L9
Puerto Ayacucho *Town* Venezuela 26 E6
Puerto Barrios *Town* Guatemala 22 F3
Puerto Cortés *Town* Honduras 22 F3
Puerto Deseado *Town* Argentina 31 E12
Puerto Escondido *Town* Mexico 19 L9
Puerto La Cruz *Town* Venezuela 26 E5
Puerto Lempira *Town* Honduras 23 I3
Puertollano *Town* Spain 58 H7
Puerto López *Town* Colombia 26 D4
Puerto Maldonado *Town* Peru 27 D11
Puerto Montt *Town* Chile 31 C10
Puerto Plata *Town* Dominican Republic 25 J5
Puerto Princesa *Town* Philippines 97 I4
Puerto Rico *Dependent territory* USA, Atlantic Ocean 25 L6
Puerto Suárez *Town* Bolivia 27 G12
Puerto Vallarta *Town* Mexico 18 H7
Puerto Varas *Town* Chile 31 C10
Puget Sound *Bay* Washington, USA 14 F2
Pula *Town* Croatia 64 A6
Puławy *Town* Poland 62 G7
Pune *Town* India 86 G6
Punjab *Region* Pakistan/India 86 H2
Puno *Town* Peru 27 D12
Punta Alta *Town* Argentina 31 F10
Punta Arenas *Town* Chile 31 D14
Puntarenas *Town* Costa Rica 23 I7
Puri *Town* India 87 K5
Purmerend *Town* Netherlands 52 E8
Purus, Rio *River* Brazil 28 F4
Pusan *Town* South Korea 91 M4
Putumayo, Río *River* Colombia 26 C8
Puurmani *Town* Estonia 70 G5
Pyatigorsk *Town* Russian Federation 73 C11
Pyechin *Town* Myanmar 94 A7
Pýlos *Town* Greece 67 C12
P'yŏngyang *Capital* North Korea 91 L3
Pyrenees *Mountain range* France/Spain 55 C12
Pyryatyn *Town* Ukraine 69 J3

Q

Qaidam Pendi *Basin* China 88 H6
Qal 'at Bīshah *Town* Saudi Arabia 83 C11
Qamdo *Town* China 88 H7
Qarokŭl *Town* Tajikistan 85 L4
Qarshi *Town* Uzbekistan 85 I5
Qasr Farâfra *Town* Egypt 38 D5
Qavanā *Town* Syria 81 D9
Qatar *Country* 83 F9
Qattara Depression *Desert basin* Egypt 38 D4
Qazimämmäd *Town* Azerbaijan 77 N4
Qazvīn *Town* Iran 82 E6
Qena *Town* Egypt 38 E5
Qilian Shan *Mountain range* China 88 H5
Qingdao *Town* China 91 K4
Qinghai *Administrative region* China 88 H6
Qingzang Gaoyuan *see* Tibet, Plateau of
Qinhuangdao *Town* China 91 K3
Qinzhou *Town* China 90 H8
Qiqihar *Town* China 89 L2
Qira *Town* China 88 D6
Qitai *Town* China 88 F4
Qizilrabot *Town* Tajikistan 85 L5
Qom *Town* Iran 82 E6
Qorveh *Town* Iran 82 D6
Quang Ngai *Town* Vietnam 95 H9
Quanzhou *Town* China 91 K7
Quartu Sant' Elena *Town* Sardinia, Italy 61 B11

Quba *Town* Azerbaijan 77 N3
Québec *Town* Quebec, Canada 7 I7
Queen Elizabeth Islands *Island Group*
   Northern Canada 5 I3
Queensland *State* Australia 105 K4
Queenstown *Town* New Zealand 107 B12
Quelimane *Town* Mozambique 45 J4
Querétaro *Town* Mexico 19 J7
Quesada *Town* Costa Rica 23 I7
Quetta *Town* Pakistan 86 F2
Quezaltenango *Town* Guatemala 22 D4
Quibdó *Town* Colombia 26 B6
Quillabamba *Town* Peru 27 D11
Quilon *Town* India 86 H9
Quimper *Town* France 54 B7
Quincy *Town* Missouri, USA 13 I7
Quito *Capital* Ecuador 26 B7
Qŭqon *Town* Uzbekistan 85 K4
Qŭrghonteppa *Town* Tajikistan 85 J5
Quy Nhon *Town* Vietnam 95 H10
Quzhou *Town* China 91 K6

R

Rabat *Capital* Morocco 36 E4
Rabinal *Town* Guatemala 22 E4
Rabyānah, Ramlat *Desert* Libya 37 M6
Race, Cape *Coastal feature* Newfoundland &
   Labrador, Canada 7 N6
Rach Gia *Town* Vietnam 95 F12
Racine *Town* Wisconsin, USA 13 J5
Radom *Town* Poland 62 G7
Rafaela *Town* Argentina 30 F7
Rafah *Town* Israel 81 C12
Ragusa *Town* Sicily, Italy 61 F14
Rahīmyār Khān *Town* Pakistan 86 G3
Rāichūr *Town* India 86 H6
Raipur *Town* India 87 J5
Rājahmundry *Town* India 87 J6
Rājkot *Town* India 86 G4
Rajshahi *Town* Bangladesh 87 K4
Raleigh *Town* North Carolina, USA 11 K3
Ralik Chain *Island chain* Marshall Islands 102 H2
Râmnicu Vâlcea *Town* Romania 68 E7
Rancagua *Town* Chile 30 D8
Rānchi *Town* India 87 J4
Randers *Town* Denmark 49 B12
Rangoon *Capital* Myanmar 94 B8
Rangpur *Town* Pakistan 87 L3
Rankin Inlet *Town* Nunavut, Canada 5 J6
Rapid City *Town* South Dakota, USA 12 E4
Ra's al 'Ayn *Town* Syria 80 G4
Rasht *Town* Iran 82 E5
Ratak Chain *Island chain* Marshall Islands 102 H2
Rathkeale *Town* Ireland 51 B10
Rat Islands *Island Group* Alaska, USA 4 A4
Ratlām *Town* India 86 H4
Raton *Town* New Mexico, USA 17 I3
Rättvik *Town* Sweden 49 D9
Raukumara Range *Mountain range*
   New Zealand 106 I7
Rāulakela *Town* India 87 J5
Rauma *Town* Finland 49 F9
Ravenna *Town* Italy 60 E6
Rāwalpindi *Town* Pakistan 86 G1
Rawicz *Town* Poland 62 D7
Rawlins *Town* Wyoming, USA 15 K5
Rawson *Town* Argentina 31 F11
Razgrad *Town* Bulgaria 66 G5
Reading *Town* Pennsylvania, USA 9 H7
Reading *Town* England, UK 51 G11
Realicó *Town* Argentina 30 E8
Rechytsa *Town* Belarus 71 F11
Recife *Town* Brazil 29 N4
Recklinghausen *Town* Germany 56 C7
Recogne *Town* Belgium 53 E13
Reconquista *Town* Argentina 30 G6
Red Deer *Town* Alberta, Canada 4 H8
Redding *Town* California, USA 14 F5
Red River *USA* 17 K4
Red Sea *Africa/Asia* 83 B9
Reefton *Town* New Zealand 107 D10

Regensburg *Town* Germany 57 F9
Reggane *Town* Algeria 36 G6
Reggio di Calabria *Town* Italy 61 G13
Reggio nell' Emilia *Town* Italy 60 D6
Regina *Town* Saskatchewan, Canada 5 I9
Reḥovot *Town* Israel 81 D11
Reims *Town* France 54 F6
Rengat *Town* Indonesia 96 E6
Rennes *Town* France 54 C7
Reno *Town* Nevada, USA 14 G5
Renqiu *Town* Hebei, China 91 J3
Republika Srpska *Administrative region*
   Bosnia & Herzegovina 64 D7
Repulse Bay *Town* Nunavut, Canada 5 K5
Resistencia *Town* Argentina 30 G6
Reşipa *Town* Romania 68 D6
Resolute *Town* Nunavut, Canada 5 J3
Réunion *Dependent territory* France,
   Indian Ocean 45 O6
Reus *Town* Spain 59 L4
Reutlingen *Town* Germany 57 D10
Reyes *Town* Bolivia 27 E11
Reykjavík *Capital* Iceland 111 D9
Reynosa *Town* Mexico 19 K5
Rēzekne *Town* Latvia 70 G7
Rheine *Town* Germany 56 C6
Rhine *River* Europe 56 C8
Rho *Town* Italy 60 C5
Rhode Island *State* USA 9 J6
Rhodes *Town* Greece 67 I13
Rhodope Mountains *Mountain range*
   Bulgaria 66 G7
Rhône *River* France 55 F11
Ribeirão Preto *Town* Brazil 29 K7
Rîbnipa *Town* Moldova 68 H5
Richmond *Town* Kentucky, USA 10 H2
Richmond *Town* Virginia, USA 11 K2
Ried im Innkreis *Town* Austria 57 G10
Rīga *Capital* Latvia 70 E5
Riga, Gulf of *Latvia* 70 E5
Rijeka *Town* Croatia 64 B6
Rimini *Town* Italy 60 E7
Rimouski *Town* Quebec, Canada 7 J6
Riobamba *Town* Ecuador 26 A8
Río Bravo *Town* Mexico 19 K5
Río Cuarto *Town* Argentina 30 E8
Rio de Janeiro *Town* Brazil 29 L7
Rio Gallegos *Town* Argentina 31 E14
Rio Grande *Town* Brazil 29 J9
Riohacha *Town* Colombia 26 C4
Rio Lagartos *Town* Mexico 19 O6
Río Verde *Town* Mexico 19 J7
Rivera *Town* Uruguay 30 H7
River Falls *Town* Wisconsin, USA 13 I4
Riverside *Town* California, USA 14 G8
Riverton *Town* Wyoming, USA 15 K4
Rivne *Town* Ukraine 68 G2
Rivoli *Town* Italy 60 B5
Riyadh *Capital* Saudi Arabia 83 D9
Road Town *Capital* British Virgin Islands 25 M5
Rize *Town* Turkey 77 J3
Roanoke *Town* Virginia, USA 11 J3
Roatán *Town* Honduras 22 G3
Robinson Ranges *Mountain range*
   Western Australia, Australia 104 F5
Robstown *Town* Texas, USA 17 L8
Rochefort *Town* Belgium 53 E12
Rochefort *Town* France 55 D9
Rochester *Town* New York, USA 8 F5
Rochester *Town* Minnesota, USA 13 I4
Rockford *Town* Illinois, USA 13 J5
Rockhampton *Town* Queensland,
   Australia 105 M4
Rock Hill *Town* South Carolina, USA 11 J4
Rock Sound *Town* Bahamas 24 G2
Rocky Mountains *Canada/USA* 4, 14
Ródos *see* Rhodes
Roeselare *Town* Belgium 53 C11
Rogatica *Town* Bosnia & Herzegovina 64 E8
Rogers *Town* Arkansas, USA 10 D3
Roi Et *Town* Thailand 95 F9
Rokycany *Town* Czech Republic 63 B9
Roma *Town* Queensland, Australia 105 M5
Roma *see* Rome

Roman *Town* Romania 68 G5
Romania *Country* 68 E6
Rome *Capital* Italy 61 E9
Romny *Town* Ukraine 69 J2
Rondónopolis *Town* Brazil 29 I6
Ronne Ice Shelf *Ice feature* Antarctica 110 C5
Roosendaal *Town* Netherlands 53 D10
Røros *Town* Norway 48 C8
Rosario *Town* Argentina 30 F8
Rosario *Town* Paraguay 30 H5
Rosarito *Town* Mexico 18 C2
Roseau *Capital* Dominica 25 O6
Rosenheim *Town* Germany 57 F10
Roslavl' *Town* Russian Federation 73 B9
Ross *Town* New Zealand 107 D10
Ross Ice Shelf *Ice feature* Antarctica 110 D7
Rosso *Town* Mauritania 40 E4
Rossosh' *Town* Russian Federation 73 C10
Ross Sea *Antarctica* 110 D7
Rostock *Town* Germany 56 F4
Rostov-na-Donu *Town* Russian Federation 73 C11
Roswell *Town* New Mexico, USA 17 I5
Rothera *Research station* Antarctica 110 B5
Rotorua *Town* New Zealand 106 G6
Rotorua, Lake *New Zealand* 106 G6
Rotterdam *Town* Netherlands 53 E9
Roubaix *Town* France 54 F5
Rouen *Town* France 54 E6
Round Rock *Town* Texas, USA 17 L6
Rovigo *Town* Italy 60 E6
Roxas City *Town* Philippines 97 J3
Rozdol'ne *Town* Ukraine 69 J6
Rožňava *Town* Slovakia 63 F10
Ruatoria *Town* New Zealand 106 I6
Rubizhne *Town* Ukraine 69 M4
Rudnik *Town* Bulgaria 66 H6
Rudnyy *Town* Kazakhstan 78 E6
Rudzyensk *Town* Belarus 71 E10
Rufino *Town* Argentina 30 F8
Rukwa, Lake *Tanzania* 39 E13
Ruoqiang *Town* China 88 F5
Ruse *Town* Bulgaria 66 G5
Rushmore, Mount *Mountain* South Dakota,
   USA 12 E4
Russellville *Town* Arkansas, USA 10 E3
Russian Federation *Country* 78 G6
Rust'avi *Town* Georgia 77 L3
Ruston *Town* Louisiana, USA 10 E5
Rutland *Town* Vermont, USA 9 I4
Rwanda *Country* 39 D12
Ryazan' *Town* Russian Federation 73 D9
Rybinsk *Town* Russian Federation 72 D8
Rybnik *Town* Poland 62 E8
Ryki *Town* Poland 62 G7
Ryukyu Islands *Island chain* Japan 93 A16
Rzeszów *Town* Poland 63 G9
Rzhev *Town* Russian Federation 72 C8

S

Saalfeld *Town* Germany 56 E8
Saarbrücken *Town* Germany 57 C9
Sab' Ābār *Town* Syria 80 F8
Šabac *Town* Serbia & Montenegro 64 F7
Sabadell *Town* Spain 59 M4
Sabah *Cultural region* Malaysia 96 H5
Sabaya *Town* Bolivia 27 D12
Sabhā *Town* Libya 37 K6
Sabinas *Town* Mexico 19 J4
Sabinas Hidalgo *Town* Mexico 19 J4
Sable Island *Quebec, Canada* 7 M7
Sabzevār *Town* Iran 82 G5
Sacramento *Town* California, USA 14 F6
Sacramento Mountains *New Mexico/Texas,*
   USA 16 H5
Sacramento Valley *California, USA* 14 F5
Şa'dah *Town* Yemen 83 C12
Safi *Town* Morocco 36 E4
Sagaing *Town* Myanmar 94 B6
Sāgar *Town* India 87 I4
Saginaw *Town* Michigan, USA 13 L5

Sagua la Grande *Town* Cuba 24 E3
Sagunto *Town* Spain 59 K6
Sahara *Desert* North Africa 36–37, 40–41
Sahel *Desert* North Africa 41 K5
Saïda *Town* Lebanon 81 D9
Saiki *Town* Japan 93 C13
Saimaa *Lake* Finland 48 H8
St Albans *Town* England, UK 51 H10
Saint Albans *Town* West Virginia, USA 11 I2
St Andrews *Town* Scotland,UK 50 F6
St. Anthony *Town* Newfoundland & Labrador,
   Canada 7 M4
Saint Augustine *Town* Florida, USA 11 J6
St-Brieuc *Town* France 54 B6
St. Catharines *Town* Ontario, Canada 6 G8
St-Chamond *Town* France 55 F10
St-Claude *Town* France 55 G9
St Croix *Island* Virgin Islands 25 M5
St-Denis *Capital* Réunion 45 O6
St-Étienne *Town* France 55 F10
St-Gaudens *Town* France 55 D11
St-Georges *Town* French Guiana 26 I6
St. George's *Capital* Grenada 25 O8
St George's Channel *Europe* 51 D10
St Helena *Dependent Territory* UK,
   Atlantic Ocean 33 L6
St Helier *Capital* Jersey, Channel Islands 51 G13
St-Jean, Lac *Lac* Canada 7 I6
Saint John *Town* New Brunswick, Canada 7 K7
St John's *Capital* Antigua & Barbuda 25 N5
St. John's *Town* Newfoundland & Labrador,
   Canada 7 N5
Saint Joseph *Town* Missouri, USA 12 H7
Saint Kitts & Nevis *Country* 25 N6
St-Laurent-du-Maroni *Town* French Guiana
   26 H6
St. Lawrence *River* Canada/USA 7 J6
St. Lawrence, Gulf of *Canada* 7 L6
Saint Lawrence Island *Alaska, USA* 4 D4
Saint Louis *Town* Senegal 40 E5
Saint Louis *Town* Illinois, USA 13 J7
St. Lucia *Country* 25 O7
St Lucia Channel *Martinique* 25 O7
St-Malo *Town* France 54 C6
St. Moritz *Town* Switzerland 57 D12
St-Nazaire *Town* France 54 B8
St-Omer *Town* France 54 E5
Saint Paul *Town* Minnesota, USA 13 I4
St Peter Port *Capital* Guernsey, Channel Islands
   51 F13
Saint Petersburg *Town* Russian Federation 72 C7
Saint Petersburg *Town* Florida, USA 11 I8
St Pierre & Miquelon *Dependent Territory*
   France, Atlantic Ocean 7 M6
St-Quentin *Town* France 54 F6
Saint Vincent *Island* St Vincent and the
   Grenadines 25 O7
Saint Vincent & The Grenadines
   Country 25 O7
Saint Vincent Passage *Strait* St. Lucia 25 O7
Sakai *Town* Japan 93 E12
Sakata *Town* Japan 92 F8
Sakhalin, Ostrov *Island* Russian Federation
   79 M6
Şäki *Town* Azerbaijan 77 M3
Salado, Río *River* Argentina 30 F6
Salamanca *Town* Chile 30 C7
Salamanca *Town* Spain 58 G5
Salamīyah *Town* Syria 80 F7
Salavat *Town* Russian Federation 73 G10
Saldus *Town* Latvia 70 D5
Salé *Town* Morocco 36 F4
Salem *Town* Nepal 87 I8
Salem *Town* Oregon, USA 14 F3
Salerno *Town* Italy 61 F10
Salihorsk *Town* Belarus 71 E10
Salima *Town* Malawi 45 J3
Salina *Town* Kansas, USA 12 G7
Salina Cruz *Town* Mexico 19 M9
Salinas *Town* California, USA 14 F7
Salisbury *Town* Maryland, USA 9 H9
Salonica *Town* Greece 66 E8
Salonta *Town* Romania 68 D5
Sal'sk *Town* Russian Federation 73 C11

Salta *Town* Argentina 30 E5
Saltillo *Town* Mexico 19 J5
Salt Lake City *Town* Utah, USA 15 I5
Salto *Town* Uruguay 30 G7
Salvador *Town* Brazil 29 M5
Salween *River* Myanmar 94 C7
Salyan *Town* Nepal 87 J3
Salzburg *Town* Austria 57 F10
Salzgitter *Town* Germany 56 E6
Samalayuca *Town* Mexico 18 G3
Samar *Island* Philippines 97 K3
Samara *Town* Russian Federation 73 E10
Samarinda *Town* Indonesia 97 I6
Samarqand *Town* Uzbekistan 85 I4
Şamaxı *Town* Azerbaijan 77 N3
Sambalpur *Town* India 87 J5
Samoa *Country* 103 K6
Sampit *Town* Indonesia 96 G7
Samsun *Town* Turkey 76 H3
Samtredia *Town* Georgia 77 K3
Samui, Ko *Island* Thailand 95 D12
Samut Prakan *Town* Thailand 95 E10
San *Town* Mali 40 H6
Şan'ā' *see* Sana
Sana *Capital* Yemen 83 C12
Sanae *Research station* Antarctica 110 D3
Sanandaj *Town* Iran 82 D6
San Andrés Tuxtla *Town* Mexico 19 L8
San Angelo *Town* Texas, USA 17 K6
San Antonio *Town* Chile 30 C8
San Antonio *Town* Texas, USA 17 L7
San Antonio Oeste *Town* Argentina 31 E10
Sanāw *Town* Yemen 83 E11
San Bernardino *Town* California, USA 14 G8
San Carlos de Bariloche *Town* Argentina 31 D10
San Cristóbal *Town* Venezuela 26 C5
San Cristóbal *Town* Venezuela 26 C5
San Cristóbal de Las Casas *Town* Mexico 19 N8
Sancti Spíritus *Town* Cuba 24 F3
Sandakan *Town* Malaysia 97 I4
Sand Hills *Mountain range* Nebraska, USA 12 E5
San Diego *Town* California, USA 14 G9
Sandoway *Town* Myanmar 94 B8
Sandpoint *Town* Idaho, USA 14 H2
Sandvika *Norway* 49 B9
Sandy City *Town* Utah, USA 15 I5
San Fernando *Town* Venezuela 26 E5
San Fernando *Town* Spain 58 G9
San Fernando *Town* Trinidad & Tobago 25 O9
San Fernando del Valle de Catamarca *Town* Argentina 30 E6
San Francisco *Town* California, USA 14 F6
San Francisco del Oro *Town* Mexico 18 H5
San Francisco de Macorís *Town* Dominican Republic 25 J5
San Ignacio *Town* Guatemala 22 E2
San Ignacio *Town* Mexico 18 E5
San Joaquin Valley *California*, USA 14 F7
San Jorge, Golfo *Gulf* Argentina 31 E12
San José *Town* Bolivia 27 F12
San José *Capital* Costa Rica 23 J7
San José *Town* Guatemala 22 D5
San Jose *Town* California, USA 14 F6
San Juan *Capital* Puerto Rico 25 L5
San Juan *Town* Argentina 30 D7
San Juan del Norte *Town* Nicaragua 23 J6
San Juan Mountains *New Mexico/Colorado*, USA 16 H3
Sankt Gallen *Town* Switzerland 57 E11
Sankt-Peterburg *see* Saint Petersburg
Sankt Pölten *Town* Austria 57 H10
Sankuru *River* Democratic Republic of Congo 43 G11
Şanlıurfa *Town* Turkey 77 I6
San Luis *Town* Guatemala 22 E3
San Luis *Town* Argentina 30 E8
San Luis *Town* Mexico 18 D2
San Luis Potosí *Town* Mexico 19 J6
San Marcos *Town* Guatemala 22 D4
San Marino *Country* 60 E7
San Marino *Capital* San Marino 60 E7
San Martín *Research station* Antarctica 110 B5
San Matías *Town* Bolivia 27 G12
San Matías, Golfo *Gulf* Argentina 31 F10

Sanmenxia *Town* China 91 I4
San Miguel *Town* El Salvador 22 F5
San Miguel *Town* Mexico 19 I4
San Miguel de Tucumán *Town* Argentina 30 E6
San Miguelito *Town* Panama 23 M8
Sanming *Town* China 91 K7
San Pedro *Town* Belize 22 F2
San Pedro de la Cueva *Town* Mexico 18 F4
San Pedro de Lloc *Town* Peru 27 A9
San Pedro Mártir, Sierra *Mountain range* Mexico 18 D3
San Pedro Sula *Town* Honduras 22 F3
San Rafael *Town* Argentina 30 D8
San Remo *Town* Italy 60 B6
San Salvador *Capital* El Salvador 22 F5
San Salvador de Jujuy *Town* Argentina 30 E5
Sansanné-Mango *Town* Togo 41 J6
Sansepolcro *Town* Italy 60 E7
San Severo *Town* Italy 61 G9
Santa Ana *Town* California, USA 14 G8
Santa Ana *Town* El Salvador 22 E4
Santa Barbara *Town* California, USA 14 G8
Santa Clara *Town* Cuba 24 E3
Santa Cruz *Town* Bolivia 27 F12
Santa Fe *Town* New Mexico, USA 16 H3
Santa Fe *Town* Argentina 30 F7
Santa Maria *Town* Brazil 29 J8
Santa Marta *Town* Colombia 26 C4
Santander *Town* Spain 59 I2
Santarém *Town* Brazil 29 I2
Santa Rosa *Town* Argentina 31 E9
Santa Rosa *Town* California, USA 14 F6
Santa Rosa de Copán *Town* Honduras 22 F4
Santiago *Capital* Chile 30 D8
Santiago *Town* Dominican Republic 25 J5
Santiago *Town* Spain 58 F3
Santiago de Cuba *Town* Cuba 24 G5
Santiago del Estero *Town* Argentina 30 E6
Santo Domingo *Capital* Dominican Republic 25 J5
Santo Domingo de los Colorados *Town* Ecuador 26 A7
Santos *Town* Brazil 29 K7
Santo Tomé *Town* Argentina 30 H6
San Vicente *Town* El Salvador 22 F5
São Fransisco, Rio *River* Brazil 29 L4
Sao Hill *Town* Tanzania 39 F13
São José do Rio Preto *Town* Brazil 29 K6
São Luís *Town* Brazil 29 L2
São Paulo *Town* Brazil 29 K7
São Roque, Cabo de *Coastal feature* Brazil 29 N3
São Tomé *Capital* São Tomé & Príncipe 43 B10
Sao Tome & Principe *Country* 43 B9
Sapele *Town* Nigeria 41 K8
Sapporo *Town* Japan 92 F5
Saqqez *Town* Iran 82 D6
Sarajevo *Capital* Bosnia & Herzegovina 64 E8
Sarakhs *Town* Iran 82 H5
Saraktash *Town* Russian Federation 73 G11
Saran' *Town* Kazakhstan 78 F7
Saransk *Town* Russian Federation 73 E9
Saratov *Town* Russian Federation 73 D10
Sarawak *Cultural region* Malaysia 96 G6
Sardegna *see* Sardinia
Sardinia *Island* Italy 61 A9
Sargasso Sea *Atlantic Ocean* 33 I3
Sargodha *Town* Pakistan 86 G2
Sarh *Town* Chad 42 E7
Sārī *Town* Iran 82 F5
Sariwŏn *Town* North Korea 91 L3
Sark *Island* Channel Islands, UK 51 G13
Sarmiento *Town* Argentina 31 D12
Sarnia *Town* Ontario, Canada 6 F8
Sarny *Town* Ukraine 68 G2
Sasebo *Town* Japan 93 B13
Saskatchewan *River* Saskatchewan, Canada 5 I8
Saskatchewan *Province* Canada 5 I8
Saskatoon *Town* Saskatchewan, Canada 5 I8
Sasovo *Town* Russian Federation 73 D9
Sassari *Town* Sardinia, Italy 61 B9
Sātpura Range *Mountain range* India 86 H5
Sattanen *Town* Finland 48 G5
Satu Mare *Town* Romania 68 E4
Saudi Arabia *Country* 83 D10
Sault Ste. Marie *Town* Ontario, Canada 6 F7

Sava *River* Serbia & Montenegro 64 F8
Savá *Town* Honduras 22 H3
Savannah *Town* Georgia, USA 11 J5
Savannah River *Georgia/South Carolina*, USA 11 I5
Saverne *Town* France 54 H7
Savona *Town* Italy 60 C6
Savu Sea *Indonesia* 97 J8
Saxony *Region* Germany 56 G7
Sayat *Town* Turkmenistan 84 H4
Sayḩūt *Town* Yemen 83 F12
Saynshand *Town* Mongolia 89 J4
Say'ūn *Town* Yemen 83 E12
Scarborough *Town* England, UK 50 H8
Schaerbeek *Town* Belgium 53 D11
Schagen *Town* Netherlands 52 E7
Schefferville *Town* Newfoundland & Labrador, Canada 7 J3
Scheldt *River* Belgium 53 D10
Schenectady *Town* New York, USA 8 I5
Schwandorf *Town* Germany 57 F9
Schwaz *Town* Austria 57 F11
Schweinfurt *Town* Germany 56 E8
Schwerin *Town* Germany 56 E5
Schwyz *Town* Switzerland 57 D11
Scilly, Isles of *Island group* England, UK 51 D13
Scotland *Political region* UK 50 E5
Scott Base *Research station* Antarctica 110 E7
Scottsbluff *Town* Nebraska, USA 12 E5
Scottsdale *Town* Arizona, USA 16 E5
Scranton *Town* Pennsylvania, USA 8 H6
Seattle *Town* Washington, USA 14 G2
Sébaco *Town* Nicaragua 22 H5
Sedan *Town* France 54 G6
Sedona *Town* Arizona, USA 16 E4
Seesen *Town* Germany 56 E6
Segezha *Town* Russian Federation 72 D6
Ségou *Town* Mali 40 H5
Segovia *Town* Spain 58 H5
Séguédine *Town* Niger 41 M3
Seine *River* France 54 E6
Sekondi-Takoradi *Town* Ghana 41 I8
Selby *Town* South Dakota, USA 12 F4
Selwyn Range *Mountain range* Queensland, Australia 105 K4
Semarang *Town* Indonesia 96 G8
Semipalatinsk *Town* Kazakhstan 78 G7
Semnān *Town* Iran 82 F6
Sendai *Town* Japan 93 B14
Sendai *Town* Japan 92 G8
Sendai-wan *Bay* Japan 92 G8
Senegal *Country* 40 E5
Senegal *River* Senegal 40 E4
Senj *Town* Croatia 64 B6
Senlis *Town* France 54 E6
Sennar *Town* Sudan 38 E8
Sens *Town* France 54 F7
Seoul *Capital* South Korea 91 M3
Sept-Îles *Town* Quebec, Canada 7 J5
Seraing *Town* Belgium 53 F11
Serang *Town* Indonesia 96 F7
Serbia *Administrative region* Serbia & Montenegro 64 F8
Serbia & Montenegro *Country* 64 G8
Seremban *Town* Malaysia 96 E5
Serov *Town* Russian Federation 78 F5
Serpukhov *Town* Russian Federation 73 C9
Sérres *Town* Greece 66 E8
Sesto San Giovanni *Town* Italy 60 C5
Setana *Town* Japan 92 F6
Sète *Town* France 55 F11
Sétif *Town* Algeria 37 I3
Setté Cama *Town* Gabon 43 C10
Setúbal *Town* Portugal 58 E7
Sevan *Town* Armenia 77 L4
Sevastopol' *Town* Ukraine 69 J7
Severn *River* England, UK 51 F11
Severnaya Zemlya *Island group* Russian Federation 79 I3
Severnyy *Town* Russian Federation 72 H5
Severodvinsk *Town* Russian Federation 72 E6
Severomorsk *Town* Russian Federation 72 E4
Sevilla *see* Seville
Seville *Town* Spain 58 G8

Sevlievo *Town* Bulgaria 66 F6
Seychelles *Country* 99 I5
Sfákia *Town* Greece 67 E14
Sfântu Gheorghe *Town* Romania 68 F6
Sfax *Town* Tunisia 37 J4
's-Gravenhage *see* Hague, The
Shaanxi *Administrative region* China 90 H5
Shanxi *Administrative region* China 91 I4
Shackleton Ice Shelf *Ice feature* Antarctica 110 G6
Shāhrūd *Town* Iran 82 F5
Shandong *Administrative region* China 91 J4
Shanghai *Town* China 91 L5
Shangrao *Town* China 91 K6
Shannon *River* Ireland 51 C9
Shan Plateau *Myanmar* 94 C6
Shantou *Town* China 91 J8
Shaoguan *Town* China 91 J7
Shar *Town* Kazakhstan 78 G7
Shari *Town* Japan 92 H4
Shchuchinsk *Town* Kazakhstan 78 F6
Sheberghān *Town* Afghanistan 85 I6
Sheboygan *Town* Wisconsin, USA 13 J5
Shebshi Mountains *Mountain range* Nigeria 41 M7
Sheffield *Town* England, UK 51 G9
Shelby *Town* Montana, USA 15 I2
Shenyang *Town* China 91 L2
Shepparton *Town* Victoria, Australia 105 K8
Sherbrooke *Town* Quebec, Canada 7 I7
's-Hertogenbosch *Town* Netherlands 53 F9
Shetland Islands *Island group* Scotland, UK 50 F2
Shihezi *Town* China 88 F4
Shijiazhuang *Town* China 91 J3
Shikārpur *Town* Pakistan 86 F3
Shikoku *Island* Japan 93 E13
Shiliguri *Town* India 87 K3
Shimoga *Town* India 86 H7
Shimonoseki *Town* Japan 93 B13
Shīndand *Town* Afghanistan 84 G7
Shingū *Town* Japan 93 E12
Shintoku *Town* Japan 92 G5
Shinyanga *Town* Tanzania 39 E12
Shiprock *Town* New Mexico, USA 16 G3
Shirataki *Town* Japan 92 G4
Shīrāz *Town* Iran 82 F8
Shivpuri *Town* India 86 H4
Shizugawa *Town* Japan 92 G8
Shizuoka *Town* Japan 93 F11
Shkodër *Town* Albania 65 E11
Shouzhou *Town* China 91 I3
Shreveport *Town* Louisiana, USA 10 D5
Shrewsbury *Town* England, UK 51 F9
Shu *Town* Kazakhstan 78 F8
Shumen *Town* Bulgaria 66 H5
Shuqrah *Town* Yemen 83 D13
Shwebo *Town* Myanmar 94 B6
Shymkent *Town* Kazakhstan 78 F8
Šiauliai *Town* Lithuania 70 D6
Šibenik *Town* Croatia 64 C8
Siberia *Region* Russian Federation 79 J5
Sibi *Town* Pakistan 86 F2
Sibir *see* Siberia
Sibiu *Town* Romania 68 F6
Sibolga *Town* Indonesia 96 D5
Sibut *Town* Central African Republic 42 E8
Sibuyan Sea *Philippines* 97 J3
Sichuan *Administrative region* China 90 F5
Sichuan Pendi *Depression* China 90 G6
Sicilia *see* Sicily
Sicily *Island* Italy 61 E13
Sicily, Strait of *Mediterranean Sea* 61 E14
Sidas *Town* Indonesia 96 F6
Sîdi Barrâni *Town* Egypt 38 C4
Sidi Bel Abbès *Town* Algeria 36 G4
Sidney *Town* Nebraska, USA 12 E6
Sidney *Town* Montana, USA 15 L2
Siedlce *Town* Poland 62 G2
Siegen *Town* Germany 56 C7
Siena *Town* Italy 60 D7
Sieradz *Town* Poland 62 E7
Sierra Leone *Country* 40 F7
Sierra Madre *Mountain range* Guatemala 22 D4

SIERRA MADRE OCCIDENTAL – TAMBACOUNDA

Sierra Madre Occidental *Mountain range* Mexico 18 G5
Sierra Madre Oriental *Mountain range* Mexico 19 J6
Sierra Nevada *Mountain range* Spain 59 I8
Sierra Nevada *Mountain Range* California, USA 14 G6
Sierra Vieja *Mountain Range* Texas, USA 17 I7
Sigli *Town* Indonesia 96 C4
Signy *Research station* Antarctica 110 B3
Siguiri *Town* Guinea 40 G6
Siirt *Town* Turkey 77 K6
Sikhote-Alin', Khrebet *Mountain range* Russian Federation 79 M6
Silchar *Town* India 87 L4
Silesia *Region* Poland 62 C7
Silifke *Town* Turkey 76 F7
Silistra *Town* Bulgaria 66 H5
Sillamäe *Town* Estonia 70 H4
Silvan *Town* Turkey 77 J5
Silverek *Town* Turkey 76 H6
Simferopol' *Town* Ukraine 69 K7
Simpson Desert Northern Territory/ Queensland/South Australia, Australia 105 J5
Sinai *Desert* Egypt 38 E4
Sincelejo *Town* Colombia 26 B5
Singapore *Country* 96 E6
Singida *Town* Tanzania 39 E12
Singkang *Town* Indonesia 97 I7
Singkawang *Town* Indonesia 96 F6
Siniscola *Town* Sardinia, Italy 61 C9
Sinnamary *Town* French Guiana 26 I6
Sinsheim *Town* Germany 57 D9
Sint Maarten *Island* Caribbean Sea 25 N5
Sint-Niklaas *Town* Belgium 53 D10
Sinŭiju *Town* North Korea 91 L3
Sioux City *Town* Iowa, USA 12 G5
Sioux Falls *Town* South Dakota, USA 12 G5
Siping *Town* China 89 M3
Siquirres *Town* Costa Rica 23 J7
Siracusa *Town* Sicily, Italy 61 F13
Sīrjan *Town* Iran 82 G8
Şirnak *Town* Turkey 77 K6
Sirte, Gulf of Libya 37 L4
Sittang *River* Myanmar 94 C8
Sittwe *Town* Myanmar 94 A7
Siuna *Town* Nicaragua 23 I4
Sivas *Town* Turkey 76 H4
Sjælland *Island* Denmark 49 C12
Skagerrak *Sea* Norway 49 B11
Skaudvilė *Town* Lithuania 70 D6
Skegness *Town* England, UK 51 H9
Skellefteå *Town* Sweden 48 F7
Skopje *Capital* Macedonia 65 G11
Skovorodino *Town* Russian Federation 78 K6
Slagelse *Town* Denmark 49 C12
Slatina *Town* Romania 68 E7
Slavonski Brod *Town* Croatia 64 E7
Sligo *Town* Ireland 50 B8
Sliven *Town* Bulgaria 66 G6
Slonim *Town* Belarus 71 D9
Slovakia *Country* 63 E10
Slovenia *Country* 57 G12
Slov"yans'k *Town* Ukraine 69 M4
Słupsk *Town* Poland 62 D5
Slutsk *Town* Belarus 71 E10
Smallwood Reservoir Nova Scotia, Canada 7 K4
Smara *Town* Western Sahara 36 D6
Smederevo *Town* Serbia & Montenegro 64 G8
Smolensk *Town* Russian Federation 72 B8
Snake River Idaho/Oregon, USA 14 H3
Snowdonia *Physical region* Wales, UK 51 F9
Sochi *Town* Russian Federation 73 B12
Société, Archipel de la *Island chain* French Polynesia 103 N7
Socotra *Island* Yemen 83 F13
Soc Trăng *Town* Vietnam 95 G12
Söderhamn *Town* Sweden 49 E9
Södertälje *Town* Sweden 49 E10
Sofia *Capital* Bulgaria 66 E6
Sofiya *see* Sofia
Sogamoso *Town* Colombia 26 C6
Sohâg *Town* Egypt 38 E5
Sokal' *Town* Ukraine 68 F2
Sokhumi *Town* Georgia 77 J2
Sokodé *Town* Togo 41 J7
Sokone *Town* Senegal 40 E5
Sokoto *Town* Nigeria 41 K6
Solāpur *Town* Pakistan 86 H6
Sol, Costa del *Coastal region* Spain 58 H9
Soledad *Town* Colombia 26 B4
Solikamsk *Town* Russian Federation 72 G8
Solingen *Town* Germany 56 C7
Sollentuna *Town* Sweden 49 E10
Solok *Town* Indonesia 96 D6
Solomon Islands *Country* 102 H5
Solomon Islands *Island group* Papua New Guinea/Solomon Islands 102 F5
Solomon Sea Pacific Ocean 102 F5
Solwezi *Town* Zambia 44 H3
Sōma *Town* Japan 93 G9
Somalia *Country* 39 H9
Somerset *Town* Kentucky, USA 10 H3
Somme *River* France 54 E5
Somotillo *Town* Nicaragua 22 G5
Somoto *Town* Nicaragua 22 H5
Songea *Town* Tanzania 39 F14
Songkhla *Town* Thailand 95 D13
Sonoran Desert Arizona, USA 16 D5
Sonsonate *Town* El Salvador 22 E5
Sop Hao *Town* Laos 94 F7
Sopron *Town* Hungary 63 D11
Sorgun *Town* Turkey 76 G4
Soria *Town* Spain 59 J4
Sorong *Town* Indonesia 97 L6
Sortavala *Town* Russian Federation 72 C6
Sŏul *see* Seoul
Sousse *Town* Tunisia 37 J3
South Africa *Country* 44 G7
Southampton *Town* England, UK 51 F12
Southampton Island Nunavut, Canada 5 K5
South Australia *State* Australia 105 J6
South Bend *Town* Indiana, USA 13 K6
South Carolina *State* USA 11 J4
South China Sea Pacific Ocean 91 L8
South Dakota *State* USA 12 F4
Southeast Indian Ridge *Undersea feature* Indian Ocean 99 K7
Southend-on-Sea *Town* England, UK 51 H11
Southern Alps *Mountain range* New Zealand 107 C11
Southern Cook Islands *Island group* Cook Islands 103 L8
Southern Cross *Town* Western Australia, Australia 104 E6
Southern Ocean 110 G3
Southern Uplands *Mountain range* Scotland, UK 50 E7
South Georgia & The Sandwich Islands *Dependent Territory* UK, Atlantic Ocean 33 J8
South Island New Zealand 107 D11
South Korea *Country* 91 M4
South Orkney Islands *Island group* Antarctica 110 B3
South Shetland Islands *Island group* Antarctica 110 B4
South Shields *Town* England, UK 50 G7
Southwest Indian Ridge *Undersea feature* Indian Ocean 99 I6
Southwest Pacific Basin *Undersea feature* Pacific Ocean 109 K7
Soweto *Town* South Africa 44 H6
Spain *Country* 58 H5
Spanish Town *Town* Jamaica 24 G5
Spartanburg *Town* South Carolina, USA 11 I4
Spijkenisse *Town* Netherlands 53 D9
Spīn Būldak *Town* Afghanistan 85 I8
Spitsbergen *Island* Arctic Ocean 111 M7
Split *Town* Croatia 64 C8
Spokane *Town* Washington, USA 14 H2
Springfield *Town* Massachusetts, USA 8 J6
Springfield *Town* Illinois, USA 13 J7
Springfield *Town* Ohio, USA 13 L6
Springfield *Town* Missouri, USA 12 H8
Spring Hill *Town* Florida, USA 11 I7
Srbobran *Town* Serbia & Montenegro 64 F7
Srebrenica *Town* Bosnia & Herzegovina 64 F8
Sri Lanka *Country* 87 J9
Stafford *Town* England, UK 51 F9
Stakhanov *Town* Ukraine 69 M4
Stalowa Wola *Town* Poland 62 G8
Stamford *Town* Connecticut, USA 8 I6
Starachowice *Town* Poland 62 F8
Stara Zagora *Town* Bulgaria 66 G6
Stargard Szczeciński *Town* Poland 62 C5
Starobil's'k *Town* Ukraine 69 M4
Staryy Oskol *Town* Russian Federation 73 C10
State College *Town* Pennsylvania, USA 8 F7
Statesboro *Town* Georgia, USA 11 I5
Staunton *Town* Virginia, USA 11 K2
Stavanger *Town* Norway 49 A10
Stavropol' *Town* Russian Federation 73 C11
Steamboat Springs *Town* Colorado, USA 15 K5
Steinkjer *Town* Norway 48 C7
Sterling *Town* Illinois, USA 13 J6
Sterlitamak *Town* Russian Federation 73 G10
Stevenage *Town* England, UK 51 H10
Stevens Point *Town* Wisconsin, USA 13 J4
Stewart Island New Zealand 107 B14
Stillwater *Town* Okahoma, USA 17 L3
Stockholm *Capital* Sweden 49 E10
Stockton *Town* California, USA 14 F6
Stockton Plateau Texas, USA 17 J7
Stœng Trĕng *Town* Cambodia 95 G10
Stoke-on-Trent *Town* England, UK 51 F9
Stonehenge *Ancient site* England, UK 51 G11
Stornoway *Town* Scotland,UK 50 D4
Storuman *Town* Sweden 48 E6
Stralsund *Town* Germany 56 F4
Strasbourg *Town* France 54 H7
Strelka *Town* Russian Federation 78 H6
Strumica *Town* Macedonia 65 H12
Stryy *Town* Ukraine 68 F3
Stuttgart *Town* Germany 57 D9
Subotica *Town* Serbia & Montenegro 64 F6
Suceava *Town* Romania 68 G5
Sucre *Capital* Bolivia 27 E12
Sudan *Country* 38 D8
Sudbury *Town* Ontario, Canada 6 G7
Sudd *Region* Sudan 39 D9
Sudeten *Region* Poland 62 C8
Suez *Town* Egypt 38 E4
Suez, Gulf of Egypt 38 E4
Sühbaatar *Town* Mongolia 89 I2
Suhl *Town* Germany 56 E8
Sujāwal *Town* Pakistan 86 F4
Sukabumi *Town* Indonesia 96 F8
Sukagawa *Town* Japan 93 G9
Sukkur *Town* Pakistan 86 F3
Sukumo *Town* Japan 93 D13
Sulawesi *see* Celebes
Sullana *Town* Peru 27 A9
Sulu Archipelago *Island chain* Philippines 97 I5
Sulu Sea Pacific Ocean 97 J4
Sumatera *see* Sumatra
Sumatra *Island* Indonesia 96 E7
Sumbawanga *Town* Tanzania 39 E13
Sumbe *Town* Angola 44 D3
Sumqayit *Town* Azerbaijan 77 N3
Sumy *Town* Ukraine 69 K2
Sunderland *Town* England, UK 50 F7
Sundsvall *Town* Sweden 48 E8
Sungaipenuh *Town* Indonesia 96 D7
Sunnyvale *Town* California, USA 14 F6
Suŏng *Town* Cambodia 95 G11
Superior *Town* Wisconsin, USA 13 I3
Superior, Lake Canada/USA, 13 I3
Suqutrā *see* Socotra
Şūr *Town* Oman 83 H10
Surabaya *Town* Indonesia 96 G8
Surakarta *Town* Indonesia 96 G8
Sūrat *Town* India 86 G5
Surat Thani *Town* Thailand 95 D12
Surdulica *Town* Serbia & Montenegro 65 H10
Surfers Paradise *Town* Queensland, Australia 105 N6
Surgut *Town* Russian Federation 78 G5
Suriname *Country* 26 G6
Surt *Town* Libya 37 L5
Surt, Khalīj *see* Sirte, Gulf of
Susa *Town* Italy 60 B5
Susteren *Town* Netherlands 53 F10
Susuman *Town* Russian Federation 78 L4
Suva *Capital* Fiji 103 J7
Suwałki *Town* Poland 62 G5
Suzhou *Town* China 91 K5
Svalbard *Dependent Territory* Norway, Arctic Ocean 111 F7
Svartisen *Glacier* Norway 48 D5
Svenstavik *Town* Sweden 48 D8
Svilengrad *Town* Bulgaria 66 G7
Svobodnyy *Town* Russian Federation 79 L6
Svyetlahorsk *Town* Belarus 71 F11
Swansea *Town* Wales, UK 51 E11
Swaziland *Country* 45 I7
Sweden *Country* 48 D7
Świdnica *Town* Poland 62 D8
Świebodzin *Town* Poland 62 C7
Swindon *Town* England, UK 51 G11
Świnoujście *Town* Poland 62 B5
Switzerland *Country* 57 C11
Sydney *Town* New South Wales, Australia 105 M7
Syeverodonets'k *Town* Ukraine 69 M4
Syktyvkar *Town* Russian Federation 72 F7
Sylhet *Town* Bangladesh 87 L4
Syowa *Research station* Antarctica 110 F4
Syracuse *Town* New York, USA 8 G5
Syria *Country* 80 F7
Syrian Desert Jordan 81 G10
Syzran' *Town* Russian Federation 73 E10
Szczecin *Town* Poland 62 C5
Szeged *Town* Hungary 63 F12
Székesfehérvár *Town* Hungary 63 E11
Szolnok *Town* Hungary 63 F11
Szombathely *Town* Hungary 63 D11

T

Tabora *Town* Tanzania 39 E12
Tabrīz *Town* Iran 82 D5
Tabūk *Town* Saudi Arabia 82 A8
Täby *Town* Sweden 49 E10
Tacloban *Town* Philippines 97 K3
Tacoma *Town* Washington, USA 14 F2
Tacuarembó *Town* Uruguay 30 H7
Tademaït, Plateau du Algeria 36 H6
Tādpatri *Town* Bhutan 87 I7
Taegu *Town* South Korea 91 M4
Taejŏn *Town* South Korea 91 M4
Taganrog *Town* Russian Federation 73 B11
Taguatinga *Town* Brazil 29 K5
Tagus *River* Spain/Portugal 58 F6
Tahoua *Town* Niger 41 K5
T'aichung *Town* Taiwan 91 L8
T'ainan *Town* Taiwan 91 K8
Taipei *Capital* Taiwan 91 L7
Taiping *Town* Malaysia 96 D5
Taiwan *Country* 91 L8
Taiwan Strait China/Taiwan 91 L8
Taiyuan *Town* China 91 I4
Ta'izz *Town* Yemen 83 C13
Tajikistan *Country* 85 K5
Takaoka *Town* Japan 93 E10
Takapuna *Town* New Zealand 106 F5
Takasaki *Town* Japan 93 F10
Takhiatosh *Town* Uzbekistan 84 F2
Takikawa *Town* Japan 92 F5
Takla Makan Desert China 88 E5
Talamanca, Cordillera de *Mountain range* Costa Rica 23 J8
Talas *Town* Kyrgyzstan 85 K3
Talavera de la Reina *Town* Spain 58 H5
Talca *Town* Chile 30 C8
Talcahuano *Town* Chile 31 C9
Taldykorgan *Town* Kazakhstan 78 G8
Tallahassee *Town* Florida, USA 10 H6
Tallinn *Capital* Estonia 70 G3
Talnakh *Town* Russian Federation 78 H4
Talsi *Town* Latvia 70 E5
Talvik *Town* Norway 48 F3
Tamale *Town* Ghana 41 I7
Tamanrasset *Town* Algeria 37 I7
Tamazunchale *Town* Mexico 19 K7
Tambacounda *Town* Senegal 40 E5

Tambov *Town* Russian Federation 73 D10
Tampa *Town* Florida, USA 11 I7
Tampa Bay *Bay* Florida, USA 11 I8
Tampere *Town* Finland 48 G8
Tampico *Town* Mexico 19 K6
Tamworth *Town* New South Wales, Australia 105 M6
Tana *Town* Norway 48 G3
Tanabe *Town* Japan 93 E12
Tanami Desert Northern Territory, Australia 104 H3
Tandil *Town* Argentina 31 G9
Tane Range *Mountain range* Thailand 94 D8
Tanezrouft *Desert* Algeria 36 H7
Tanga *Town* Tanzania 39 G12
Tanganyika, Lake Democratic Republic of Congo 43 I12
Tanggula Shan *Mountain range* China 88 G7
Tangier *Town* Morocco 36 F3
Tangshan *Town* China 91 K3
Tan-Tan *Town* Morocco 36 D5
Tanzania *Country* 39 E12
Taoudenni *Town* Mali 40 H3
Tapa *Town* Estonia 70 G4
Tapachula *Town* Mexico 19 N9
Tapajós, Rio *River* Brazil 29 I3
Ţarābulus *see* Tripoli
Tarancón *Town* Spain 59 I6
Taranto *Town* Italy 61 H10
Taranto, Gulf *Gulf* Italy 61 H11
Tarapoto *Town* Peru 27 B9
Taraz *Town* Kazakhstan 78 F8
Tarbes *Town* France 55 D11
Târgoviște *Town* Romania 68 F7
Târgu Jiu *Town* Romania 68 E7
Târgu Mureş *Town* Romania 68 F5
Tarija *Town* Bolivia 27 E13
Tarim Basin China 88 F5
Tarnobrzeg *Town* Poland 62 G8
Tarnów *Town* Poland 63 F9
Tarragona *Town* Spain 59 L4
Tarsus *Town* Turkey 76 G6
Tartu *Town* Estonia 70 G5
Ţarţūs *Town* Syria 80 D7
Tarvisio *Town* Italy 60 F4
Tashkent *Capital* Uzbekistan 85 J3
Tash-Kumyr *Town* Kyrgyzstan 85 K3
Tasikmalaya *Town* Indonesia 96 F8
Tasmania *State* Australia 105 K9
Tasman Sea Pacific Ocean 105 M8
Tassili-n-Ajjer *Plateau* Algeria 37 I6
Tatabánya *Town* Hungary 63 E11
Tathlīth *Town* Saudi Arabia 83 C11
Tatra Mountains Slovakia 63 F9
Tatvan *Town* Turkey 77 K5
Taungdwingyi *Town* Myanmar 94 B7
Taunggyi *Town* Myanmar 94 C7
Taunton *Town* England, UK 51 F11
Taupo *Town* New Zealand 106 G7
Taupo, Lake New Zealand 106 G7
Tauranga *Town* New Zealand 106 G6
Taurus Mountains *Mountain range* Turkey 76 E6
Tavoy *Town* Myanmar 95 C10
Tawau *Town* Malaysia 97 I5
Taxco *Town* Mexico 19 K8
Taymā' *Town* Saudi Arabia 82 B8
Taymyr Peninsula Russian Federation 79 I3
T'bilisi *Capital* Georgia 77 L3
Tczew *Town* Poland 62 E5
Te Anau *Town* New Zealand 107 B13
Teapa *Town* Mexico 19 N8
Tebingtinggi *Town* Indonesia 96 D5
Tecomán *Town* Mexico 19 I8
Tecpan *Town* Mexico 19 J9
Tecuci *Town* Romania 68 G6
Tedzhen *Town* Turkmenistan 84 F5
Tegal *Town* Indonesia 96 F7
Tegucigalpa *Capital* Honduras 22 G4
Tehrān *Capital* Iran 82 E6
Tehuacán *Town* Mexico 19 L8
Tehuantepec *Town* Mexico 19 M9
Tehuantepec, Gulf of Mexico 19 M9
Tehuantepec, Istmo de *Isthmus* Mexico 19 M8
Te Kao *Town* New Zealand 106 E3

Tekeli *Town* Kazakhstan 78 G8
Tekirdağ *Town* Turkey 76 C3
Tel Aviv-Yafo *Town* Israel 81 C11
Temirtau *Town* Kazakhstan 78 F7
Temple *Town* Texas, USA 17 M6
Temuco *Town* Chile 31 C10
Ténéré *Physical region* Niger 41 M4
Tennessee *State* USA 10 G3
Tennessee River Alabama/Tennessee, USA 10 G4
Tepic *Town* Mexico 18 H7
Teplice *Town* Czech Republic 62 B8
Tequila *Town* Mexico 19 I7
Teramo *Town* Italy 60 F8
Teresina *Town* Brazil 29 M3
Termiz *Town* Uzbekistan 85 I5
Ternate *Town* Indonesia 97 K6
Terni *Town* Italy 60 E8
Ternopil' *Town* Ukraine 68 G3
Terrassa *Town* Spain 59 M4
Terre Haute *Town* Indiana, USA 13 K7
Teruel *Town* Spain 59 K5
Teseney *Town* Eritrea 38 F8
Tessalit *Town* Mali 41 J3
Tete *Town* Mozambique 45 I4
Tetouan *Town* Morocco 36 F3
Tevere *River* Italy 60 E8
Texarkana *Town* Texas, USA 17 N5
Texas *State* USA 17 L6
Teziutlán *Town* Mexico 19 K7
Thai Binh *Town* Vietnam 94 G7
Thailand *Country* 95 D9
Thailand, Gulf of Pacific Ocean 95 E11
Thai Nguyên *Town* Vietnam 94 G6
Thakhèk *Town* Laos 94 F8
Thamarit *Town* Oman 83 G11
Thames *River* England, UK 51 G11
Thanh Hoa *Town* Vietnam 94 F7
Thar Desert Pakistan/India 86 F3
Thaton *Town* Myanmar 94 C8
Thayetmyo *Town* Myanmar 94 B7
The Fens *Physical region* England, UK 51 H9
The Gulf Asia 82 E8
Thessaloníki *see* Salonica
The Valley *Capital* Anguilla 25 N5
Thimphu *Capital* Bhutan 87 L3
Thira *Town* Greece 67 G13
Thracian Sea Greece 66 F8
Thun *Town* Switzerland 57 C11
Thunder Bay *Town* Ontario, Canada 6 E6
Thurso *Town* Scotland,UK 50 E3
Tianjin *Town* China 91 J3
Tianjin Shu *Administrative region* China 91 J3
Tianshui *Town* China 89 J6
Tiberias, Lake Israel 81 D10
Tibesti *Mountain range* Chad 42 E3
Tibet *Administrative region* China 88 F7
Tibet, Plateau of China 88 F6
Tichît *Town* Mauritania/China 40 G4
Ticul *Town* Mexico 19 O6
Tien Shan *Mountain range* Kyrgyzstan 85 L3
Tierra del Fuego *Region* Argentina/Chile 31 D14
Tifu *Town* Indonesia 97 K7
Tighina *Town* Moldova 68 H6
Tigris *River* Iraq 82 C6
Tiguentourine *Town* Algeria 37 J6
Tijuana *Town* Mexico 18 C2
Tikal *Ancient site* Guatemala 22 E2
Tikhoretsk *Town* Russian Federation 73 C12
Tikhvin *Town* Russian Federation 72 C7
Tiksi *Town* Russian Federation 78 J4
Tilburg *Town* Netherlands 53 E10
Timaru *Town* New Zealand 107 D12
Timbedgha *Town* Mauritania 40 G5
Timbuktu *Town* Mali 41 I4
Timişoara *Town* Romania 68 D6
Timor Sea Asia/Australasia 97 J9
Tindouf *Town* Algeria 36 E6
Tirana *Capital* Albania 65 F11
Tiranë *see* Tirana
Tiraspol *Town* Moldova 68 H6
Tirol *Region* Austria 57 F11
Tiruchchiráppalli *Town* India 87 I8
Tisza *River* Hungary 63 F11
Titicaca, Lake *Lake* Peru 27 D12

Tivoli *Town* Italy 61 E9
Tizi Ouzou *Town* Algeria 36 H3
Tiznit *Town* Morocco 36 E5
Tlaquepaque *Town* Mexico 19 I7
Tlaxcala *Town* Mexico 19 K8
Tlemcen *Town* Algeria 36 G4
Toamasina *Town* Madagascar 45 M5
Tobago *Island* Trindad & Tobago 25 O8
Tobol'sk *Town* Russian Federation 78 G5
Tocantins, Rio *River* Brazil 29 K4
Tocopilla *Town* Chile 30 D4
Todi *Town* Italy 60 E8
Togo *Country* 41 J7
Tokar *Town* Sudan 38 F7
Tokat *Town* Turkey 76 H4
Tokelau *Dependent territory* New Zealand, Pacific Ocean 103 K6
Tokmak *Town* Kyrgyzstan 85 L3
Tokmak *Town* Ukraine 69 L5
Tokoroa *Town* New Zealand 106 G6
Tokushima *Town* Japan 93 D12
Tōkyō *Capital* Japan 93 G10
Toledo *Town* Spain 59 I6
Toledo *Town* Ohio, USA 13 L6
Toliara *Town* Madagascar 45 L6
Tolitoli *Town* Indonesia 97 J6
Tolmin *Town* Slovenia 57 G12
Toluca *Town* Mexico 19 J8
Tol'yatti *Town* Russian Federation 73 E10
Tomakomai *Town* Japan 92 F5
Tomaszów Mazowiecki *Town* Poland 62 F7
Tombouctou *see* Timbuktu
Tomini, Gulf of Indonesia 97 J6
Tomsk *Town* Russian Federation 78 H6
Tonga *Country* 103 K7
Tongatapu Group *Island group* Tonga 103 J8
Tongchuan *Town* China 90 H4
Tonghe *Town* China 89 M2
Tongzi *Town* China 90 H6
Tongking, Gulf of South China Sea 90 H9
Tongliao *Town* China 89 L3
Tongxin *Town* China 89 J6
Tongzi *Town* China 90 H6
Tônlé Sap *Lake* Cambodia 95 F10
Tonopah *Town* Nevada, USA 14 H6
Tooele *Town* Utah, USA 15 I5
Toowoomba *Town* Queensland, Australia 105 M6
Topeka *Town* Kansas, USA 12 G7
Torez *Town* Ukraine 69 M5
Torgau *Town* Germany 56 F7
Torino *see* Turin
Torkestan Mountains *Mountain range* Afghanistan 84 H6
Toro *Town* Spain 58 H4
Toronto *Town* Ontario, Canada 6 G8
Toros Dağlari *see* Taurus Mountains
Torquay *Town* England, UK 51 F12
Torre del Greco *Town* Italy 61 F10
Torrejón de Ardoz *Town* Spain 59 I5
Torrelavega *Town* Spain 59 I2
Torrente *Town* Spain 59 K6
Torreón *Town* Mexico 19 I5
Torres Strait Australia/Papua New Guinea 105 K1
Torres Vedras *Town* Portugal 58 E6
Torrington *Town* Wyoming, USA 15 L5
Toruń *Town* Poland 62 E6
Torzhok *Town* Russian Federation 72 C8
Toscana *see* Tuscany
Toscano, Archipelago *Coastal feature* Italy 60 D8
Toshkent *see* Tashkent
Totness *Town* Suriname 26 H6
Tottori *Town* Japan 93 D11
Touggourt *Town* Algeria 37 I4
Toukoto *Town* Mali 40 G5
Toul *Town* France 54 G7
Toulon *Town* France 55 G12
Toulouse *Town* France 55 D11
Tourcoing *Town* France 54 F5
Tournai *Town* Belgium 53 C11
Tours *Town* France 54 D8
Tovarkovskiy *Town* Russian Federation 73 C9
Towada *Town* Japan 92 G7
Townsville *Town* Queensland, Australia 105 L3
Towson *Town* Maryland, USA 8 G8

Toyama *Town* Japan 93 F10
Toyota *Town* Japan 93 F11
Tozeur *Town* Tunisia 37 I4
Trabzon *Town* Turkey 76 H3
Trang *Town* Thailand 95 D13
Transantarctic Mountains *Mountain range* Antarctica 110 D6
Transylvania *Cultural region* Romania 68 E5
Transylvanian Alps *Mountain range* Romania 68 E6
Trapani *Town* Sicily, Italy 61 D12
Trâpeăng Vêng *Town* Cambodia 95 F10
Trasimeno, Lago *Lake* Italy 60 E7
Tra Vinh *Town* Vietnam 95 G12
Tremelo *Town* Belgium 53 E11
Trenčín *Town* Slovakia 63 E10
Trenque Lauquen *Town* Argentina 31 F9
Trent *River* England, UK 51 G9
Trento *Town* Italy 60 E4
Trenton *Town* Pennsylvania, USA 8 G7
Tres Arroyos *Town* Argentina 31 F9
Treviso *Town* Italy 60 E5
Trier *Town* Germany 56 B8
Trieste *Town* Italy 60 F5
Trincomalee *Town* Sri Lanka 87 I9
Trinidad *Island* Trinidad & Tobago 25 O9
Trinidad *Town* Uruguay 30 G8
Trinidad *Town* Bolivia 27 E11
Trinidad & Tobago *Country* 25 O9
Tripoli *Town* Lebanon 80 D8
Tripoli *Capital* Libya 37 K4
Tristan de Cunha *Dependent Territory* St Helena, Atlantic Ocean 33 L7
Trivandrum *Town* India 86 H9
Trnava *Town* Slovakia 63 D10
Trois-Rivières *Town* Quebec, Canada 7 I7
Trollhättan *Town* Sweden 49 C10
Tromsø *Town* Norway 48 E4
Trondheim *Town* Norway 48 C7
Troy *Town* New York, USA 8 I5
Troyes *Town* France 54 F7
Trujillo *Town* Spain 58 G6
Trujillo *Town* Peru 27 A10
Trzcianka *Town* Poland 62 D6
Tshela *Town* Democratic Republic of Congo 43 D11
Tshikapa *Town* Democratic Republic of Congo 43 F12
Tsu *Town* Japan 93 E11
Tsugaru-kaikyō *Strait* Japan 92 F7
Tsuruga *Town* Japan 93 E11
Tsuruoka *Town* Japan 92 F8
Tuamotu Islands *Island group* French Polynesia 103 O7
Tuapse *Town* Russian Federation 73 B12
Tuba City *Town* Arizona, USA 16 E3
Tubmanburg *Town* Liberia 40 F7
Ţubruq *Town* Libya 37 N4
Tucson *Town* Arizona, USA 16 E5
Tucumcari *Town* New Mexico, USA 17 I4
Tudmur *Town* Syria 80 F7
Tuguegarao *Town* Philippines 97 J1
Tukums *Town* Latvia 70 E5
Tula *Town* Russian Federation 73 C9
Tulancingo *Town* Mexico 19 K7
Tulcán *Town* Ecuador 26 B7
Tulcea *Town* Romania 68 H7
Tulsa *Town* Oklahoma, USA 17 M3
Tuluá *Town* Colombia 26 B6
Tumbes *Town* Peru 26 A8
Tumuc Humac Mountains *Mountain range* Brazil 29 I1
Tungaru *Island chain* Kiribati 103 I4
Tungsten *Town* Northwest Territories, Canada 4 G6
Tunis *Capital* Tunisia 37 J3
Tunisia *Country* 37 J4
Tunja *Town* Colombia 26 C6
Tuong Đuong *Town* Vietnam 94 G7
Tupelo *Town* Mississippi, USA 10 G4
Turan Lowland *Plain* Central Asia 84 F2
Ţurayf *Town* Saudi Arabia 82 B7
Turbat *Town* Pakistan 86 E3
Turda *Town* Romania 68 F5

Turin *Town* Italy 60 B5
Turkana, Lake Kenya 39 F10
Turkestan *Town* Kazakhstan 78 F7
Turkey *Country* 76 F5
Turkmenbashi *Town* Turkmenistan 84 D3
Turkmenistan *Country* 84 F4
Turks & Caicos Islands *Dependent Territory*
    UK, Atlantic Ocean 25 I3
Turku *Town* Finland 49 F9
Turnov *Town* Czech Republic 63 C9
Tuscaloosa *Town* Mississippi, USA 10 G5
Tuscany *Region* Italy 60 D7
Tuticorin *Town* India 87 I9
Tutuala *Town* East Timor 97 K8
Tuvalu *Country* 103 I6
Tuxpán *Town* Mexico 19 K7
Tuxpan *Town* Mexico 19 I8
Tuxtepec *Town* Mexico 19 L8
Tuxtla *Town* Mexico 19 N8
Tuy Hoa *Town* Vietnam 95 H10
Tuz Gölü *see* Tuz, Lake
Tuzla *Town* Bosnia & Herzegovina 64 E7
Tuz, Lake Turkey 76 F5
Tver' *Town* Russian Federation 72 C8
Twin Falls *Town* Idaho, USA 15 I4
Tychy *Town* Poland 63 E9
Tyler *Town* Texas, USA 17 M5
Tynda *Town* Russian Federation 79 K6
Tyrrhenian Sea Mediterranean Sea 61 F11
Tyumen' *Town* Russian Federation 78 F5

U

Ubangi *River* Central Africa 42 F8
Ube *Town* Japan 93 C13
Uberaba *Town* Brazil 29 K6
Uberlândia *Town* Brazil 29 K6
Ubon Ratchathani *Town* Thailand 95 F9
Ubrique *Town* Spain 58 G8
Uchiura-wan *Bay* Japan 92 G6
Uchquduq *Town* Uzbekistan 84 H3
Udaipur *Town* India 86 G4
Udine *Town* Italy 60 F5
Udon Thani *Town* Thailand 94 E8
Udupi *Town* India 86 G7
Uele *River* Democratic Republic of Congo 42 H8
Uelzen *Town* Germany 56 E5
Ufa *Town* Russian Federation 73 G10
Uganda *Country* 39 D11
Uitenhage *Town* South Africa 44 G8
Ujungpandang *Town* Indonesia 97 I7
Ukhta *Town* Russian Federation 72 G7
Ukmergė *Town* Lithuania 70 E7
Ukraine *Country* 68 G3
Ulaanbaatar *see* Ulan Bator
Ulaangom *Town* Mongolia 88 G3
Ulan Bator *Capital* Mongolia 89 J3
Ulan-Ude *Town* Russian Federation 79 J7
Ulft *Town* Netherlands 53 G9
Ullapool *Town* Scotland, UK 50 E4
Ulm *Town* Germany 57 D10
Ulsan *Town* South Korea 91 M4
Ulster *Cultural region* Northern Ireland, UK 50 C8
Uluru *Peak* Northern Territory, Australia 104 H5
Ulyanivka *Town* Ukraine 69 I4
Ul'yanovsk *Town* Russian Federation 73 E9
Uman' *Town* Ukraine 69 I4
Umeå *Town* Sweden 48 F7
Umm Ruwaba *Town* Sudan 38 E8
Umtata *Town* South Africa 44 H8
Uncía *Town* Bolivia 27 E12
Ungava Bay Quebec, Canada 7 I2
Ungava Peninsula Quebec, Canada 6 H2
Uniontown *Town* Pennsylvania, USA 8 E8
United Arab Emirates *Country* 83 F10
United Kingdom *Country* 50 E8
United States of America *Country* 8 I7
Ünye *Town* Turkey 76 H3
Upington *Town* South Africa 44 F7
Uppsala *Town* Sweden 49 E10
Ural Mountains *Mountain range*
    Russian Federation 73 H9

Ural'sk *Town* Kazakhstan 78 E5
Ural'skiye Gory *see* Ural Mountains
Uraricoera *Town* Brazil 28 H1
Uren' *Town* Russian Federation 72 E8
Urganch *Town* Uzbekistan 84 G3
Uroševac *Town* Serbia & Montenegro 65 G10
Üroteppa *Town* Tajikistan 85 J4
Uruapan *Town* Mexico 19 J8
Uruguay *Country* 30 G8
Ürümqi *Town* China 88 F4
Uşak *Town* Turkey 76 D5
Ushuaia *Town* Argentina 31 D15
Usinsk *Town* Russian Federation 72 G6
Usol'ye-Sibirskoye *Town* Russian Federation
    79 I7
Ussel *Town* France 55 E9
Ussuriysk *Town* Russian Federation 79 M7
Ust'-Ilimsk *Town* Russian Federation 79 I6
Ústí nad Labem *Town* Czech Republic 62 B8
Ustka *Town* Poland 62 D4
Ust'-Kamchatsk *Town* Russian Federation 79 M4
Ust'-Kamenogorsk *Town* Kazakhstan 78 G7
Ust'-Kut *Town* Russian Federation 79 J6
Ust'-Olenëk *Town* Russian Federation 79 J4
Ustyurt Plateau Uzbekistan 84 F1
Usulután *Town* El Salvador 22 F5
Utah *State* USA 15 I6
Utica *Town* New York, USA 8 H5
Utrecht *Town* Netherlands 52 E8
Utsunomiya *Town* Japan 93 G10
Uulu *Town* Estonia 70 F5
Uvalde *Town* Texas, USA 17 K7
Uvarovichy *Town* Belarus 71 G11
Uwajima *Town* Japan 93 D13
Uxmal *Ancient site* Mexico 19 O6
Uyo *Town* Nigeria 41 L8
Uyuni *Town* Bolivia 27 E13
Uzbekistan *Country* 84 H3
Uzhhorod *Town* Ukraine 68 E4

V

Vaal *River* South Africa 44 H7
Vaasa *Town* Finland 48 F8
Vaassen *Town* Netherlands 52 F8
Vác *Town* Hungary 63 E11
Valdés, Peninsula Argentina 31 F11
Val-d'Or *Town* Quebec, Canada 6 H6
Vadodara *Town* India 86 G5
Vaduz *Capital* Liechtenstein 57 D11
Valday *Town* Russian Federation 72 C7
Valdez *Town* Alaska, USA 4 E5
Valdivia *Town* Chile 31 C10
Valdosta *Town* Georgia, USA 11 I6
Valence *Town* France 55 F10
Valencia *Town* Spain 59 K6
Valencia *Town* Venezuela 26 D5
Valencia, Golfo de *Gulf* Spain 59 L6
Valera *Town* Venezuela 26 D5
Valga *Town* Estonia 70 G5
Valladolid *Town* Mexico 19 O6
Valladolid *Town* Spain 58 H4
Valledupar *Town* Colombia 26 C5
Vallenar *Town* Chile 30 C6
Valletta *Capital* Malta 61 E15
Valley, The *Capital* Anguilla 25 N5
Valls *Town* Spain 59 L4
Valmiera *Town* Latvia 70 F5
Valozhyn *Town* Belarus 71 E9
Valparaíso *Town* Chile 30 C8
Van *Town* Turkey 77 K5
Vanadzor *Town* Armenia 77 L3
Vancouver *Town* British Columbia, Canada 4 G5
Vancouver Island British Columbia,
    Canada 4 F9
Van Diemen Gulf Australia 104 H1
Vänern *Lakes* Sweden 49 D10
Van Gölü *see* Van, Lake
Van, Lake Turkey 77 K5
Vantaa *Town* Finland 49 G9
Vanua Levu *Island* Fiji 103 I7
Vanuatu *Country* 102 G7

Vārānasi *Town* India 87 J4
Varberg *Town* Sweden 49 C11
Vardar *River* Macedonia 65 H12
Varde *Town* Denmark 49 B12
Varese *Town* Italy 60 C4
Varna *Town* Bulgaria 66 H5
Vasa *see* Vaasa
Vaslui *Town* Romania 68 G6
Västerås *Town* Sweden 49 E10
Vatican City *Country* 61 E9
Vättern *Lake* Sweden 49 D10
Vaughn *Town* New Mexico, USA 17 I4
Vawkavysk *Town* Belarus 71 C9
Växjö *Town* Sweden 49 D11
Velebit *Mountain range* Croatia 64 B7
Veles *Town* Macedonia 65 G11
Velikiye Luki *Town* Russian Federation 72 B8
Veliko Tŭrnovo *Town* Bulgaria 66 G6
Vellore *Town* India 87 I7
Velsen-Noord *Town* Netherlands 52 E8
Vel'sk *Town* Russian Federation 72 E7
Vendôme *Town* France 54 D7
Venezia *see* Venice
Venezuela *Country* 26 E5
Venice *Town* Louisiana, USA 10 F7
Venice *Town* Italy 60 E5
Venice, Gulf of Italy 60 F6
Venlo *Town* Netherlands 53 G10
Ventimiglia *Town* Italy 60 B6
Ventspils *Town* Latvia 70 D4
Veracruz *Town* Mexico 19 L7
Vercelli *Town* Italy 60 C5
Verkhoyanskiy Khrebet *Mountain range*
    Russian Federation 79 K4
Vermont *State* USA 9 I4
Verona *Town* Italy 60 D5
Versailles *Town* France 54 E7
Verviers *Town* Belgium 53 F11
Vesterålen *Island group* Norway 48 D4
Vesuvius *Volcano* Italy 61 F10
Veszprém *Town* Hungary 63 E11
Veurne *Town* Belgium 53 B10
Viangchan *see* Vientiane
Viareggio *Town* Italy 60 D6
Vicenza *Town* Italy 60 E5
Vichy *Town* France 55 F9
Victoria *Capital* Seychelles 99 I5
Victoria *Town* British Columbia, Canada 4 G9
Victoria *Town* Texas, USA 17 M7
Victoria *State* Australia 105 K8
Victoria Falls *Waterfall* Zambia 44 G4
Victoria Island Northern Canada 5 I5
Victoria, Lake East Africa 39 E11
Victoria Land *Region* Antarctica 110 E7
Vidin *Town* Bulgaria 66 D5
Vienna *Capital* Austria 57 H10
Vientiane *Capital* Laos 94 E8
Vierzon *Town* France 54 E8
Vietnam *Country* 94 G8
Vieux Fort *Town* St. Lucia 25 O7
Vigo *Town* Spain 58 E3
Vijayawāda *Town* India 87 I6
Vila Nova de Gaia *Town* Portugal 58 E4
Vila Real *Town* Portugal 58 F4
Villa Acuña *Town* Mexico 19 I3
Villach *Town* Austria 57 G11
Villahermosa *Town* Mexico 19 N8
Villa María *Town* Argentina 30 F7
Villa Martín *Town* Bolivia 27 D13
Villa Mercedes *Town* Argentina 30 E8
Villarrica *Town* Paraguay 30 H5
Villavicencio *Town* Colombia 26 C6
Villeurbanne *Town* France 55 G9
Villingen-Schwenningen *Town*
    Germany 57 D10
Vilnius *Capital* Lithuania 70 E8
Viña del Mar *Town* Chile 30 C8
Vinaròs *Town* Spain 59 L5
Vindhya Range *Mountain range* India 86 H4
Vineland *Town* New Jersey, USA 8 H8
Vinh *Town* Vietnam 94 G8
Vinnytsya *Town* Ukraine 68 H4
Vinson Massif *Mountain* Antarctica 110 C5
Viranşehir *Town* Turkey 76 H6

Virginia *State* USA 11 K2
Virginia Beach *Town* Virginia, USA 11 L3
Virgin Islands *Dependent territory*
    USA, Atlantic Ocean 25 M5
Virôchey *Town* Cambodia 95 G10
Virovitica *Town* Croatia 64 D6
Virton *Town* Belgium 53 F14
Virtsu *Town* Estonia 70 F4
Visaginas *Town* Lithuania 70 F7
Visākhapatnam *Town* India 87 J6
Viscount Melville Sound *Bay* Canada 5 I4
Viseu *Town* Portugal 58 F5
Viterbo *Town* Italy 60 E8
Viti Levu *Island* Fiji 103 I7
Vitória *Town* Brazil 29 M6
Vitória da Conquista *Town* Brazil 29 L5
Vitoria-Gasteiz *Town* Spain 59 I3
Vitsyebsk *Town* Belarus 71 H9
Vittoria *Town* Sicily, Italy 61 F13
Vizianagaram *Town* India 87 J6
Vlaardingen *Town* Netherlands 53 D9
Vladikavkaz *Town* Russian Federation 73 C13
Vladimir *Town* Russian Federation 72 D8
Vladivostok *Town* Russian Federation 79 M7
Vlagtwedde *Town* Netherlands 52 G6
Vlijmen *Town* Netherlands 53 E9
Vlissingen *Town* Netherlands 53 C10
Vlorë *Town* Albania 65 E12
Vojvodina *Region* Serbia & Montenegro 64 F6
Volga *River* Russian Federation 73 D11
Volgodonsk *Town* Russian Federation 73 C11
Volgograd *Town* Russian Federation 73 D11
Volkhov *Town* Russian Federation 72 C7
Volnovakha *Town* Ukraine 69 L5
Vologda *Town* Russian Federation 72 D7
Vólos *Town* Greece 67 E10
Vol'sk *Town* Russian Federation 73 E10
Volta *River* Ghana 41 J8
Volta, Lake Ghana 41 I7
Volturno *River* Italy 61 F9
Volzhskiy *Town* Russian Federation 73 D11
Vóreioi Sporádes *see* Northern Sporades
Vorkuta *Town* Russian Federation 72 H5
Voronezh *Town* Russian Federation 73 C10
Vostok *Research station* Antarctica 110 F6
Voznesens'k *Town* Ukraine 69 I5
Vratsa *Town* Bulgaria 66 E6
Vrbas *Town* Serbia & Montenegro 64 F6
Vršac *Town* Serbia & Montenegro 64 G7
Vung Tau *Town* Vietnam 95 G11
Vyborg *Town* Russian Federation 72 C6

W

Waal *River* Netherlands 53 F9
Waco *Town* Texas, USA 17 M6
Wadayama *Town* Japan 93 D11
Waddān *Town* Libya 37 L5
Waddeneilanden *see* West Frisian Islands
Waddenzee *Sea* Netherlands 52 E6
Waddington, Mount *Mountain* British Colombia,
    Canada 4 G8
Wadi Halfa *Town* Sudan 38 E6
Wad Medani *Town* Sudan 38 E8
Wagga Wagga *Town* New South Wales,
    Australia 105 L8
Wāh *Town* Pakistan 86 G1
Wahai *Town* Indonesia 97 L7
Waiouru *Town* New Zealand 106 G7
Wairoa *Town* New Zealand 106 H7
Wakayama *Town* Japan 93 E12
Wake Island *Dependent Territory*
    US, Pacific Ocean 109 I4
Wakkanai *Town* Japan 92 F4
Wałbrzych *Town* Poland 62 D8
Wales *Political Region* UK 51 F10
Wallachia *Cultural region* Romania 68 E7
Wallis & Futuna *Dependent Territory*
    France, Pacific Ocean 103 J6
Walvis Bay *Town* Namibia 44 E6
Wanaka *Town* New Zealand 107 C12

Index

Credits

The publisher would like to thank the following for their kind permission to reproduce their photographs:

Abbreviations key: a=above, c=centre; b=below; l=left; r=right; t=top

Agence France Presse: 59tr; 84c; 91cra.

Alaska Stock: 4clb.

American Museum of Natural History: 12cl.

Art Directors & TRIP: 61car, T. Bognar 87tr, D. Iusupov 73c, P. Mercea 68br, D. Mossienko 69tr, T. Noorits 70tl, N & J Wiseman 69cr.

British Antarctic Survey: R. Mulvaney 110clb.

British Library: 82c.

British Museum: 27br; 37tc.

Cephas Picture Library: Fred R Palmer 6tr.

Bruce Coleman Ltd: Astrophoto iv t.

Corbis: 94cl; 96cl, Theo Allofs 99cra, Jean Pierre Amet/Corbis Sygma 49tl, Tony Arruza 11br; 30br, William A. Bake 7br, Anthony Bannister 44cl, Paul Barton 9cr, Dave Bartruff 49tr; 53bc, Morton Beebe 58bl, Niall Benvie 71cr, Yann Arthus Bertrand 28cr, Georgina Bowater 54cb, Tom Brakefield 96tr, B.S.P.I. i tr; 16br; 20br; 102tr, Dean Conger 15c; 73br; 97br, Keith Dannemiller 18tr, Tim Davis 100cla; 111bc, Carlos Dominguez 32ccr, Terry W. Eggers vii clb; 3cla, Jim Erickson vi bl, Robert Estall vii car, Macduff Everton 19tr, Owen Franken 10cbr; 52br; 53tl; 53tr, Stephen Frink ii crb; 22cl, Arvino Garg 23tcl, Bill Gentile 24cl, Philip Gould 13br, Farrell Grehan 9c, Julie Habel 13tl, John Heseltine 65cb, Ralf-Finn Hestoft/Corbis Saba 9tl, Arne Hodalic 77bl, Robert Holmes 92tl, Dave G. Houser 76br, Robbie Jack 72bc, Ray Juno vii cal; 53br; 57br, Wolfgang Kaehler vii cla; 25bc; 32br; 79bl; 100cbr; 103bc; 109tr, Bob Krist vii cra; 100car; 105cra, Frank Leather/Eye Ubiquitous viii clb, Lester Lefkowitz 15br, Danny Lehman 18br, Charles & Josette Lenars 41bl; 48tcl, George D. Lepp vii tr; 33br, Barry Lewis 69bl, Steve Liss/Corbis Sygma 108tc, Lawrence Manning 76cl, Gunter Marx Photography 4bl, Stephanie Maze 29cra; 49cla; 109br, NASA iv bc, Richard J. Nowitz 7cra, Charles O'Rear 4tcr, Christine Osborne 81crb, Douglas Peebles v br; 90car, Caroline Penn viii tl, Clay Perry 67tl, Ledru Philippe/Corbis Sygma 37bc, Perrin Pierre/Corbis Sygma 55bl, Sergio Pitamitz iii br; 22br; 105br, Richard Ransier 16tr, Steve Rayner ibr; 72tr, Roger Ressmeyer 54tl, Benjamin Rondel 6bl, Bill Ross viii b, Galen Rowell v cla; 110cal, Saba/Shepard Sherbell 111tr, Michael St. Maur Sheil 50br, Kim Sayer 55bc, Alan Schein Photography 3cra; 9br, Gregor Schmid 79crb, Flip Schulke 11c, Attal Serge/Corbis Sygma 71bl, Alex Steedman 51tr, Hans Strand 33tr, Vince Streano 11cla, Keren Su 86br, Torleif Svensson 111cr, TempSport 71tc, Tim Thompson 19tc, David Turnley 77tr; 80cal; 83tr; 85cr, Peter Turnley 25bl; 45bl; 78bc, Penny Tweedie 100clb; 104cla, Pablo Corral Vega 26cl, Francesco Venturi 19cr, Patrick Ward 59br, Nevada Wier 74cla; 85cra; 85tr; 85cb, Nik Wheeler 71tl; 77br, Staffan Widstrand 5tc; 71bc, Peter M. Wilson 3crb; 5bcr, Wildcountry 50tr, Adam Woolfitt 76tc, Michael S. Yamashita 91bc; 93bcl.

Empics Ltd: Tony Marshall 3bl; 6bc; 64bc, Phil Walter104bc.

Getty Images: Samuel Ashfield 47crb, Paul Chesley 92cl, Jim Cummins ii cra; 13cr, Frans Lemmens iii tl, Photodisc/Jeremy Woodhouse 108car, Martin Puddy 86c, Andy Sacks 10cl, Bruce Stoddard 19tl.

Getty Images News Service: Scott Harrison 60cl, Mike Powell 55ca, Matthew Stockman 11tc.

Robert Harding Picture Library: vii crb; 12ccl; 28cl; 31tr; 32tr; 62tc; 66tr; 79br; 83tc; 87tl; 95bl, Max Alexander 10br, Paul Allen 34bl; 45br, Mohamed Amin 83bcl, Bildagentur Schuster GMBH 108bl, Bildagentur Schuster/Gluske 30cl, Jeremy Bright 107c, Martyn F. Chillmaid 45ccr, Neale Clark 105crb, Victor Englebert 31bl, Alain Evrard 95tr, Explorer/D. Riffet 43cra, Warren Finlay/International Stock 109cr, Nigel Francis 8bl, Robert Francis 14tc, Robert Frerck iii cl; 27cr; 31tl; 59bc, Robert Frerck/Odyssey/Chicago 18cl, Lee Frost vii cbr, Kim Hart 48tl, Gavin Hellier 89br; 3ca, D. Jacobs 104tr, Maurice Joseph 70bc, Paolo Koch 88–89; 107tl, J. Lightfoot 40cla, David Lomax 74cca; 84bl, John Miller 25tr, MPH 56bc, Louise Murray vii cbl, Nakamura 23crbl; 38ca; 110br, Mike Newton 58cla, J. Nov. iii cra; 87clb, Photrl1LC.056.XXXX 15tc, Roy Rainford 9tr; 32ca, Geoff Renner 110tr, G. R. Richardson 65tr, R. Richardson 60br, Phil Robinson 65bl, Peter Scholey 66tl, Schuster 30tl; 44bc, Michael Short 81br, Johnny Stockshooter 67cbr, J. C. Thoret 42tr, Doug Traverso 89cr, Hardie Truesdale 12bl, Upperhall Ltd 103cal, Tony Waltham 85br, Nik Wheeler 14bl, T.D. Winter 37tl, Keith Wood/International Stock 17bl; 50tc, Adam Woolfitt 32cl; 52tl.

Hopi Learning Centre: 16bc.

Hutchison Library: 39tr; 43c; 64ca; 78bl; 81bc; 82tc; 91br; 94tl, Jon Burbank 93tl, Sarah Errington 39bc; 42bcr; 45tl; 86bl, Robert Francis 22cb; 23cbl; 104–105bc, Melanie Friend 66cb; 66br; 89bl; 90cbl, Norman Froggatt 95cb, John Fuller 25tc, Bernard Gerard 82bc, Andrew Hill 45tr, John Halt 96br, Nick Haslam 68clb; 93clb; 103cra, J. Henderson 81tr, Jeremy Horner 39bl; 56tc; 87bc; 90bl; 91tl; 97c, Crispin Hughes 41cr; 41bc; 45tc, Mary Jelliffee 27tr; 36bc, Eric Lawrie 27ca, R. Ian Lloyd 96bl, Michael Macintyre 102bc; 103tr, N. Durrell McKenna 104clb, Sarah Murray 88bc, John Nowell 83cr, Trevor Page 43br; 61bc, Stephen Pem 88cla, PERN 89tr, Dr Nigel Smith 28br; 97cr, Liba Taylor 63cb; 69br; 73tl; 73bl, Isabella Tree 98tr; 110bl, David Watson 65br, Philip Wolmoth 51br, Andrey Zvoznikov vi cl; vi cla; vi clb; vi tr; 73tr; 79tl; 79tr.

Impact Photos: Rupert Connant 62tr.

Barnabas Kindersley: 40bcl; 83bcr.

Masterfile UK: Didier Dorval 56tr.

NASA: 17tr.

Natural History Museum: 43ca.

N.H.P.A.: B & C Alexander 32bl, T. Kitchin and V. Hurst 5cbr, Stephen Oliver 15bcl, Andy Rouse 5br.

Panos Pictures: David Constantine 59cr; 62cl, Neil Cooper 38tcr, Clive Shirley 41tl, Teun Voeten 40bcr.

Pictorial Press Ltd: 87crb.

Pictures Colour Library: 8ca; 16tc; 50bc; 51tr; 61cl; 68cla; 79cra; 92tc, © FMGB Guggenheim Bilbao Museoa. Photo by Charles Bowman. All rights reserved. Total or partial reproduction is prohibited. 59tl.

Pitt Rivers Museum: 73tc.

Popperfoto: 51bc, Ho/Reuters 108ccl.

Powell Cotton Museum: 42bcl.

Redferns: 10bc.

Rex Features: Stuart Clarke 82tl, Simon Runting 107bl, Enrica Scalfari 60tr, Sipa Press 12bc; 15bc; 97tr, Tim Rooke 96cr, Wilhemsen 99br.

Floyd Sayers: 39br; 45bcr.

Science Photo Library: George Bernard 15bl, Laboratory for Atmospheres, NASA/ Goddard Space Flight Center 111car, Nasa vi br, Tom Van Sant, Geosphere Project/Planetary Visions 34–35; 46–47; 74–75, 1995 Worldsat International and J. Knighton 2–3; 20–21; 100–101.

South American Pictures: 26tl; 28bl; 31br.

Still Pictures: Julio Etchart 18bl, Roland Seitre 98cb, Annelies Van Brink viii tr; 74crb.

Marie Tharp: v tr.

Topham Picturepoint: Francis Dean/Imageworks 49crb.

V. Tunnicliffe: 108cbr.

World Pictures: i bl; i tl; 4bc; 7tl; 7tr; 20clb; 20crb; 22bl; 23tr; 24bl; 25ca; 26cr; 27bl; 29tr; 29br; 30bc; 31ca; 34car; 36tr; 36cl; 37tr; 38bc; 42tc; 44bl; 47tr; 47cla; 47clb; 48bc; 52bc; 54tc; 55tc; 57tr; 57cr; 61r; 63tc; 63tr; 63br; 64tl; 67tr; 67br; 67bcl; 68bl; 71br; 72cl; 74bl; 76bl; 80cla; 80cb; 80bcr; 81tc; 89c; 90cl; 91cb; 92br; 93tr; 94tc; 94tr; 95br; 98bl; 98ccl; 98ccr; 99tr; 104cal; 106tl; 106crb; 106br; 107tr.

Jacket images

Front: Corbis: Owen Franken cra, Richard Ransier crb, Stephen Frink br, Getty Images: Keren Su ca, Robert Harding Picture Library: Lee Frost bcl, Masterfile UK: Hans Blohm cb.

Front Inside Flap: Corbis: Richard Ransier br, Owen Franken tr, Masterfile UK: Hans Blohm bl, Getty Images: Keren Su tl.

Back: Corbis: Dave Bartruff cb, B.S.P.I. cbr, Stephen Frink br, Alan Schein Photography crb, Tim Davis cbl, Robert Harding Picture Library: Lee Frost bcl, Getty Images: Kevin Morris clb.

Spine: Corbis: Owen Franken t, Richard Ransier b.

All other images © Dorling Kindersley

For further information see: **www.dkimages.com**

Dorling Kindersley would also like to thank:

Clare Shedden, Philip Letsu, Kate Bradshaw, and Neal Cobourne for the jacket design, and Chris Bernstein for the index.

NORTH AMERICA

CANADA
Pages 4–7

UNITED STATES OF AMERICA
Pages 8-17

MEXICO
Pages 18-19

CENTRAL & SOUTH AMERICA

BELIZE
Pages 22-23

COSTA RICA
Pages 22-23

EL SALVADOR
Pages 22-23

GUATEMALA
Pages 22-23

HONDURAS
Pages 22-23

GRENADA
Pages 24-25

HAITI
Pages 24-25

JAMAICA
Pages 24-25

ST KITTS & NEVIS
Pages 24-25

ST LUCIA
Pages 24-25

**ST VINCENT &
THE GRENADINES**
Pages 24-25

TRINIDAD & TOBAGO
Pages 24-25

BOLIVIA
Pages 26-27

AFRICA

CHILE
Pages 30-31

PARAGUAY
Pages 30-31

URUGUAY
Pages 30-31

ALGERIA
Pages 36-37

LIBYA
Pages 36-37

MOROCCO
Pages 36-37

TUNISIA
Pages 36-37

BURUNDI
Pages 38-39

TANZANIA
Pages 38-39

UGANDA
Pages 38-39

BENIN
Pages 40-41

BURKINA FASO
Pages 40-41

CAPE VERDE
Pages 40-41

**CÔTE D'IVOIRE
(IVORY COAST)**
Pages 40-41

GAMBIA
Pages 40-41

GHANA
Pages 40-41

SIERRA LEONE
Pages 40-41

TOGO
Pages 40-41

CAMEROON
Pages 42-43

CENTRAL AFRICAN REPUBLIC
Pages 42-43

CHAD
Pages 42-43

CONGO
Pages 42-43

DEM. REP. CONGO
Pages 42-43

EQUATORIAL GUINEA
Pages 42-43

EUROPE

MAURITIUS
Pages 44-45

MOZAMBIQUE
Pages 44-45

NAMIBIA
Pages 44-45

SOUTH AFRICA
Pages 44-45

SWAZILAND
Pages 44-45

ZAMBIA
Pages 44-45

ZIMBABWE
Pages 44-45

DENMARK
Pages 48-49

NETHERLANDS
Pages 52-53

ANDORRA
Pages 54-55

FRANCE
Pages 54-55

MONACO
Pages 54-55

AUSTRIA
Pages 56-57

GERMANY
Pages 56-57

LIECHTENSTEIN
Pages 56-57

SLOVENIA
Pages 56-57

HUNGARY
Pages 62-63

POLAND
Pages 62-63

SLOVAKIA
Pages 62-63

ALBANIA
Pages 64-65

BOSNIA & HERZEGOVINA
Pages 64-65

CROATIA
Pages 64-65

MACEDONIA
Pages 64-65

**SERBIA & MONTENEGRO
(YUGOSLAVIA)**
Pages 64-65

ASIA

LITHUANIA
Pages 70-71

RUSSIAN FEDERATION
Pages 78-79

CYPRUS
Pages 80-81

ARMENIA
Pages 76-77

AZERBAIJAN
Pages 76-77

GEORGIA
Pages 76-77

TURKEY
Pages 76-77

ISRAEL
Pages 80-81

QATAR
Pages 82-83

SAUDI ARABIA
Pages 82-83

UNITED ARAB EMIRATES
Pages 82-83

YEMEN
Pages 82-83

KAZAKHSTAN
Pages 78-79

AFGHANISTAN
Pages 84-85

KYRGYZSTAN
Pages 84-85

TAJIKISTAN
Pages 84-85

MONGOLIA
Pages 88-89

NORTH KOREA
Pages 90-91

SOUTH KOREA
Pages 90-91

TAIWAN
Pages 90-91

JAPAN
Pages 92-93

CAMBODIA
Pages 94-95

LAOS
Pages 94-95

MYANMAR (BURMA)
Pages 94-95

AUSTRALASIA & OCEANIA

MALDIVES
Pages 98-99

SEYCHELLES
Pages 98-99

FIJI
Pages 102-103

KIRIBATI
Pages 102-103

MARSHALL ISLANDS
Pages 102-103

MICRONESIA
Pages 102-103

NAURU
Pages 102-103

PALAU
Pages 102-103